# Doing News Framing Analysis

D1079633

"*Doing News Framing Analysis* is a treasure trove for almost anything that the graduate student or seasoned scholar would want to know about the burgeoning cross-disciplinary exploration of the framing of news. Offering a readable mixture of theory, experiment, critique and case study, this volume would be extremely useful in any classroom devoted to better understanding how publics, media professionals, and politicians create and see news through different kinds of frames."

David D. Perlmutter, PhD, The University of Iowa

"This book brings together the field's leading authors who provide stimulating and informative perspectives on doing framing research. It is a rich compendium of conceptual and empirical articles, and an essential reference for researchers and scholars in mass communication, media effects and political communication."

Fuyuan Shen, PhD, The Pennsylvania State University

*Doing News Framing Analysis* provides an interpretive guide to news frames—what they are, how they can be observed in news texts, and how framing effects are uncovered and substantiated in cultural, group, and individual sites. Chapters feature framing analysts reflecting on their own empirical work in research, classroom, and public settings to address specific aspects of framing analysis. Taken as a whole, the collection covers the full range of ways in which framing has been theorized and applied—across topics, sources, mechanisms, and effects.

**Paul D'Angelo** (PhD, Temple University) is an assistant professor of mass media and political communication at The College of New Jersey. His research on theories and effects of news framing in political campaign settings has appeared in *American Behavioral Scientist*, *Journal of Communication*, *Harvard International Journal of Press/Politics*, and the *Atlantic Journal of Communication*.

**Jim A. Kuypers** (PhD, Louisiana State University) is an assistant professor of political communication at Virginia Tech. He has authored or co-authored six books, including *Press Bias and Politics: How the Media Frame Controversial Issues*, and *Bush's War: Media Bias and Justifications for War in the Terrorist Age*. His research interests include political communication, meta-criticism, and the moral/poetic use of language.

# Communication Series

Jennings Bryant / Dolf Zillman, General Editors

# Doing News Framing Analysis

## Empirical and Theoretical Perspectives

Edited by

## Paul D'Angelo and Jim A. Kuypers

Routledge
Taylor & Francis Group

NEW YORK AND LONDON

First published 2010
by Routledge
270 Madison Avenue, New York, NY 10016

Simultaneously published in the UK
by Routledge
2 Park Square, Milton Park, Abingdon, Oxon OX14 4RN

*Routledge is an imprint of the Taylor & Francis Group, an informa business*

© 2010 Taylor & Francis

Typeset in Sabon and Gill Sans by EvS Communication Networx, Inc.
Printed and bound in the United States of America on acid-free paper by Edwards
Brothers, Inc.

*Library of Congress Cataloging in Publication Data*
Doing news framing analysis : empirical and theoretical perspectives / edited by Paul
D'Angelo and Jim A. Kuypers.
p. cm. — (Routledge communication series)
1. Journalism—Social aspects. 2. Journalism—Objectivity. I. D'Angelo, Paul. II. Kuypers,
Jim A.
PN4749.D68 2009
302.23—dc22
2009028601

ISBN 10: 0-415-99235-4 (hbk)
ISBN 10: 0-415-99236-2 (pbk)
ISBN 10: 0-203-86446-8 (ebk)

ISBN 13: 978-0-415-99235-0 (hbk)
ISBN 13: 978-0-415-99236-7 (pbk)
ISBN 13: 978-0-203-86446-3 (ebk)

# Contents

# About the Authors

**Cory L. Armstrong** (PhD, University of Wisconsin-Madison) is an assistant professor in the College of Journalism and Communications and a faculty affiliate with the Center for Women's Studies and Gender Research at the University of Florida. She has 8 years of professional journalism experience on newspapers in Ohio, as a copy editor, reporter, and bureau chief. Her recent work focuses on the framing of gender representations in media coverage and the influence of community pluralism on news content. She received the Mary Gardner Award from AEJMC's Commission on the Status of Women and a top research paper award from the Newspaper Division. She has had articles published in *Journal of Broadcasting & Electronic Media*, *Mass Communication & Society*, and *Journalism & Mass Communication Quarterly*.

**Michael P. Boyle** (PhD, University of Wisconsin-Madison) is an Assistant Professor in the Department of Communication Studies at West Chester University. His research explores the relationship between the media and social protest and social conflict. Specifically, this work has focused on three key areas: (1) the nature of news coverage of protests and conflicts; (2) the implications of news treatment of protest events, groups, and conflicts on participation in the political process including participation in protest events; and (3) the role that emotions and values play in willingness to seek information about conflicts. This research has been supported by grants from the Kansas Health Foundation, The Wichita State University LINK fund, and the PASSHE Faculty Professional Development Council.

**Paul R. Brewer** (PhD, University of North Carolina, Chapel Hill) is an associate professor in the Department of Journalism and Mass Communication at the University of Wisconsin-Milwaukee. His research on political communication and public opinion has appeared in such publications as the *American Journal of Political Science*, the *Journal* *of Politics, Political Communication, Political Psychology,* and *Public Opinion Quarterly.*

**Renita Coleman** (PhD, University of Missouri) is an assistant professor in the Department of Communication at the University of Texas, Austin. Her research on visual communication and ethics, the effects of photographs on ethical reasoning, the role of images in agenda setting, and the moral development of journalists and public relations practitioners, has appeared in *Journal of Communication, Journalism & Mass Communication Quarterly, Journal of Broadcasting and Electronic Media, Journal of Mass Media Ethics, Visual Communication Quarterly, Newspaper Research Journal, Journalism,* and *Journalism Studies.* Her coauthored (with Lee Wilkins) book, *The Moral Media: How Journalists Reason About Ethics,* was published in 2005. Before beginning her academic career, Coleman was a journalist at newspapers and magazines for 15 years. She was a reporter, editor, and designer at the Raleigh, NC *News & Observer,* the Sarasota, FL *Herald-Tribune,* and the Orlando, FL *Sentinel* among other news organizations.

**Stephen D. Cooper** (PhD, Rutgers University) is professor of communication studies at Marshall University, where he teaches courses in group communication, business and professional communication, small-group communication, computer-mediated communication, and research foundations. He is the author of *Watching the Watchdog: Bloggers as the Fifth Estate,* a book about the relationship of media criticism blogging and the mainstream press.

**Paul D'Angelo** (PhD, Temple University) is an assistant professor of mass media and political communication at The College of New Jersey. His research on theories and effects of news framing in political campaign settings, both within the United States and in comparative perspectives, has appeared in *American Behavioral Scientist, Journal of Communication, Harvard International Journal of Press/Politics,* and the *Atlantic Journal of Communication.* His work on the disciplinary historiography of political communication has in appeared in *Mass Communication and Society* and *Communication Yearbook.*

**Robert M. Entman** (PhD, Yale) is J. B. and Maurice C. Shapiro Professor of Media and Public Affairs at The George Washington University. His most recent books include *Projections of Power: Framing News, Public Opinion, and U.S. Foreign Policy,* the coedited *Mediated Politics: Communication in the Future of Democracy,* and the coauthored *The Black Image in the White Mind: Media and Race in America,* winner of Harvard's Goldsmith Book Prize and the Lane Award from the

American Political Science Association. For his work on media framing, he won the 2005 Woolbert Research Prize from the National Communication Association. Entman also received the Murray Edelman Distinguished Career Achievement Award in Political Communication at the 2006 Annual Meeting of the American Political Science Association. He edits the book series *Communication, Society and Politics* (with Lance Bennett) for Cambridge University Press. Dr. Entman has been a visiting professor at Harvard and at the University of Rome. He taught previously at Duke, Northwestern, and North Carolina State.

**Kimberly Gross** (PhD, University of Michigan) is an associate professor in the School of Media and Public Affairs at the George Washington University. Her research on public opinion and political communication has appeared in such publications as the *American Journal of Political Science*, *Political Psychology*, the *Journal of Communication*, and the *Harvard International Journal of Press/Politics*.

**Marie Hardin** (PhD, University of Georgia) is an associate professor and associate director of research in the John Curley Center for Sports Journalism at Penn State. She teaches courses in journalism and sports-related issues and a graduate course on feminist media studies. Her work has been published in *Mass Communication & Society*, *Critical Studies in Media Communication*, *Journalism & Mass Communication Quarterly*, and *Sex Roles*.

**Heejo Keum** (PhD, University of Wisconsin-Madison) is an assistant professor in the Department of Journalism and Mass Communication at Sungkyunkwan University in South Korea. Her research interests include media framing, social capital, consumer culture, and communication research methods. Her theoretical orientation focuses on media effects on individual attitudes and behaviors in the context of both political and strategic communication. She employs experimental and survey methods in her empirical research. She has published her research in peer-reviewed journal articles in leading communication journals, including *Political Communication*, *Human Communication Research*, *Mass Communication and Society*, and *Journal of Broadcasting and Electronic Media*. She has also presented about 20 papers in major communication conferences such as ICA, AEJMC, and MAPOR.

**Jim A. Kuypers** (PhD, Louisiana State University) is an assistant professor of political communication at Virginia Polytechnic Institute and State University. He is the author or coauthor of six books, including *Press Bias and Politics: How the Media Frame Controversial Issues*, and *Bush's War: Media Bias and Justifications for War in the Terrorist Age*.

He is a former coeditor for the *American Communication Journal*. He is the recipient of the American Communication Association's Outstanding Contribution to Communication Scholarship Award, the Southern States Communication Association's Early Career Research Award, and Dartmouth College's Distinguished Lecturer Award. His research interests include political communication, meta-criticism, and the moral/poetic use of language.

**Regina G. Lawrence** (PhD, University of Washington) is Kevin P. Reilly, Senior Chair of Political Communication in the Manship School of Communication at Louisiana State University. She is the coauthor (with W. Lance Bennett and Steven Livingston) of *When the Press Fails: Political Power and the News Media from Iraq to Katrina* (University of Chicago Press, 2007) and the author of *The Politics of Force: Media and the Construction of Police Brutality* (University of California Press, 2000). She has authored numerous scholarly articles and reports analyzing news coverage of public policy issues, including welfare reform, school shootings, juvenile substance abuse, children's health, obesity, 9/11, and the anthrax attacks of 2001. Lawrence was a fellow at the Shorenstein Center for the Press, Politics, and Public Policy at Harvard University in 2003.

**Matthew C. Nisbet** (PhD, Cornell University) is assistant professor in the School of Communication at American University. His research tracks scientific and environmental controversies, examining the interactions between experts, journalists, and various publics. Along with numerous peer-reviewed studies, Nisbet has contributed articles to popular outlets such as *Science*, the *Sunday Washington Post*, the *Columbia Journalism Review*, *Foreign Policy,* and *Geotimes* magazines. He tracks current events related to science communication at his blog *Framing Science*, recently named "a top political blog" by the *New York Daily News*. Nisbet is a frequent invited lecturer at conferences and meetings across the United States and Canada and he is often called upon for his expert analysis by major news organizations. He has served as a consultant to the National Academies, the National Science Foundation, the Centers for Disease Control as well as several nongovernment organizations.

**Stephen D. Reese** (PhD, University of Wisconsin-Madison) is the Jesse H. Jones Professor of Journalism and Associate Dean for Academic Affairs, College of Communication, University of Texas at Austin. His research examines a variety of issues concerning media effects and press performance and has been published in numerous book chapters and articles in, among others, *Journalism & Mass Communication Quarterly*, *Communication Research*, *Journal of Communication*, *Journal of Broadcasting & Electronic Media*, *Public Opinion Quarterly*, *Harvard*

*Journal of Press-Politics, Journalism Studies*, and *Critical Studies in mass Communication*. He is coauthor of *Mediating the Message: Theories of Influence on Mass Media Content* and a coeditor of the volume *Framing Public Life: Perspectives on Media and Our Understanding of the Social World*. He was a recipient of the Krieghbaum Under-40 Award for teaching, research, and service from AEJMC. His 1994 article (coauthored with August Grant and Lucig Danielian), "The Structure of News Sources on Television: A Network Analysis of CBS News, Nightline, MacNeil/Lehrer, and This Week with David Brinkley," in the *Journal of Communication* won ICA's Political Communication Division's Distinguished Essay Award. Reese has lectured internationally at universities in Mexico, Spain, Germany, and Finland, and was the Kurt Baschwitz Professor at the University of Amsterdam in 2004.

**Bertram T. Scheufele** (PhD, University of Mainz, Germany) is Professor for Empirical Methods of Communication Science at the University of Jena, Germany. His research focuses on political communication, media and violence, media content and media effects, quantitative and qualitative methods and statistics, and has been funded by a number of grants from the German Research Foundation (DFG).

**Dietram A. Scheufele** (PhD, University of Wisconsin-Madison) is professor in the Department of Life Sciences Communication and the School of Journalism & Mass Communication at the University of Wisconsin-Madison. His current research interests include the societal impacts of new technologies, communication research methods, and the impact of mass and interpersonal communication on various forms of political behavior.

**Mike Schmierbach** (PhD, University of Wisconsin-Madison) is an assistant professor in the College of Communications at Pennsylvania State University. His research focuses on the effects of news texts, with a particular interest in the cognitive influence of framing and on subsequent information-seeking and engagement effects. In addition, he studies video games as a form of mass communication, exploring the effects of play modes on enjoyment and other salient outcomes. He has authored nearly a dozen articles in a variety of prominent communication journals including *Journal of Communication*, *Human Communication Research*, and *Journalism & Mass Communication Quarterly*. He is currently working on an ongoing project investigating how uncertainty and issue understanding affect subsequent use of the news media.

**Dhavan V. Shah** (PhD, University of Minnesota) is Louis A. and Mary E. Maier-Bascom Professor of Journalism and Mass Communication and Political Science at the University of Wisconsin-Madison. His research concerns the social psychology of political communication, with particular attention to the role of mass media in political evaluations, conscientious consumption, and civic participation. His recent work has focused on (1) the interplay of news frames on social judgment and expression, and (2) the role of the Internet in mediating news and campaign effects. To date, he has authored over 50 articles in communication and political science journals and is currently working on two book manuscripts extending these programs of inquiry. This work has been supported by grants from both private foundations and public sector entities, including Public Broadcasting Service, Rockefeller Brothers Fund, Carnegie Corporation, Russell Sage Foundation, and C.I.R.C.L.E. He is the recipient of the Nafziger-White Award for the field's outstanding dissertation, the Krieghbaum Under-40 Award for early career contributions, and the Article of the Year Award in the field of Political Communication.

**Baldwin Van Gorp** (PhD, University of Antwerp, Belgium) is a former journalist and is currently an assistant professor in the Communication Department at the Radboud University, Nijmegen, the Netherlands. His research interests include news, public relations, and political communication. His contributions on framing have been published in international journals, including *European Journal of Communication* and *Journal of Communication*.

**Claes H. de Vreese** (PhD, University of Amsterdam) is Professor and Chair of Political Communication and Scientific Director of the Amsterdam School of Communications Research (ASCoR) in the Department of Communication Science at the University of Amsterdam. His research interests include comparative journalism research, the effects of news, public opinion and European integration, effects of information and campaigning on elections, referendums and direct democracy. He has published more than 35 articles in international peer-reviewed journals, including *Communication Research, Journalism Studies, Political Communication, International Journal of Public Opinion Research, European Journal of Communication, West European Politics, Journalism & Mass Communication Quarterly, Mass Communication & Society,* and *European Journal of Political Research.*

**Erin Whiteside** is a doctoral candidate in mass communication at Penn State University. Her research focuses on the relationship between sports media and culture from a feminist perspective and her work has been published in *Newspaper Research Journal, Media Report to Women,* and *Women in Sport and Physical Activity Journal.*

# Foreword

In his classic book *Frame Analysis*, Erving Goffman commented that "opposing rooters at a football game do not experience the 'same' game" (see Lemert & Branaman, 1997, p. 154). Most of us who have attended a game with a fan of the opposing team can understand this: fans of the winning team attribute the outcome to the skilled play of the victors while supporters of the losers argue poor refereeing led to the result. A similar dynamic of alternative understanding of single issues or events is evident in debates about climate change—some see it as concerning "scientific truth," while others view it as a threat to our very existence. Alternatively, a terrorist attack can be construed as reflecting the relative depravation and desperation of the culprit, or an unjustifiable assault on civilized communities. Analogous, although perhaps less dramatic, examples can be easily generated for virtually any social, political, or economic issue or event. In short, it takes little creativity to invent distinct interpretations of the same phenomenon.

Analysts have come to understand varying portrayals of issues and events as examples of framing. To appreciate the reach of the "framing" concept, consider that it not only can be applied to a nearly unlimited range of topics, but it also involves multiple actors and mechanisms. Indeed, any group wishing to push an agenda—such as a political interest group—frames the relevant issue in a way that advances its cause. The National Rifle Association's constant reference to the "right to bear arms," with little attention to the dangers of guns is just one example. News organizations choose how to package their stories in understandable ways; in so doing, they juggle remaining faithful to the frames used by their sources with simultaneously accounting for news values (e.g., "balanced" coverage), while sometimes injecting their own unique perspectives. Individuals, in daily conversations, constantly frame topics, such as when one person describes a restaurant positively based on the exquisite food and another paints a negative picture focusing on the atrocious service. Frames also appear in various guises including in speech, writing, pictures, and, most recently, novel technologies such as interactive new media.

All these frames from competing actors have notable effects. Not only do they shape what others think of an issue (e.g., a right to bear arms frame may generate opposition to gun control), but also how they understand and discuss the world around them. More fundamentally, frames become attached to particular issues or events (e.g., the "War on Terror" in the case of 9/11), reflecting the power of certain actors and the very basis of the culture in which we live. It is the very pervasiveness of frames that make it such a challenging concept to employ. Reflecting this is the fact that many scholars have endeavored, with varying success, to write integrative reviews that tie together research traditions. The breadth of the framing concept also has led to debate about whether it is underlaid by a coherent self-contained theory or is more of a practical heuristic used to understand a range of topics.

This volume constitutes a transformative point in the framing literature because it does *not* aim to definitively resolve the issue of "what framing is." Instead, it takes a much more productive route by bringing together a group of some of the most influential framing researchers. These scholars either offer cutting-edge applications representative of their larger agendas, or reflect more holistically on their research programs. The value of these chapters lies in that each of the authors has already produced influential work; thus, the individual chapters serve as substantial contributions to distinct scholarly trajectories. Taken together, the chapters constitute a collection that covers the full range of ways in which framing has been theorized and applied—across all of the aforementioned dimensions of topics, sources, mechanisms, and effects. Rarely, in my experience, has an edited volume so successfully incorporated high quality individual chapters while maintaining a consistent central theme, in this case, concerning the multiple uses of framing. The book is necessary reading for anyone interested in the framing concept. In the end, it becomes clear that answering the question of whether a coherent theory of framing should be pursued may miss the point of framing research—which is to show, perhaps ironically, that a single concept can be applied to a wide assortment of phenomena.

## Reference

Lemert, C., & Branaman, A. (Eds.). (1997). *The Goffman reader.* Somerset, NJ: Wiley-Blackwell.

James N. Druckman
*Northwestern University*

# Acknowledgments

We are greatly indebted to the contributors to this volume, each of whom is committed not only to the study of news framing, but also to clarifying and advancing the many ways of studying news framing. Paul D'Angelo would like to thank The College of New Jersey, which has provided both financial and intellectual support for his research on news framing over the years. Jim A. Kuypers would like to thank his family for their unreserved and continued support of his writing. With gratitude, he mentions Virginia Tech, which paid his salary and also funded library services such as interlibrary loan, Ebscohost, and Lexis-Nexis, all absolutely necessary to the completion of this project. The value Virginia Tech places on research allows projects such as this book to be undertaken and completed. He also wishes to thank his Department Head, R. L. Holloway, whose support during difficult times is exceptional. Special thanks go to the publisher, to Linda Bathgate, and to the series editors, Jennings Bryant and Max McCombs, for their steadfast support of our project.

# Chapter 1

# Introduction
## Doing News Framing Analysis

*Paul D'Angelo and Jim A. Kuypers*

Framing is a rapidly growing area of study in communication research. Framing analyses noticeably populate our professional conferences, and hardly an issue of a communication journal is published today without a framing study. Much framing research focuses on ways that politicians, issue advocates, and stakeholders use journalists and other news professionals to communicate their preferred meanings of events and issues. The word *use* is important. Its dual meaning—*use* as a conduit of information and *use* as a manipulated channel for information dissemination—captures the essence of framing: sources frame topics to make information interesting and palatable to journalists, whom they need to communicate information to wider publics, and journalists cannot not frame topics because they need sources' frames to make news, inevitably adding or even superimposing their own frames in the process (see Gamson & Modigliani, 1989; Kuypers, 2006).

Many of the growing number of review and synthesis articles refer to this process as "media framing" (Carragee, & Roefs, 2004; Reese, 2001; B. Scheufele, 2004; D. Scheufele, 1999, 2000; Wicks, 2005). In this volume, however, we call it *news framing* (cf. D'Angelo, 2002). News is easily the most prominent discursive site in which communication researchers strive to understand what framing is and how framing works.

Much research on news framing is situated within the subfields of political communication and mass communication. This work encompasses a wide array of topic areas, including political campaigns, policy formation, legislation, litigation and court decisions, and international affairs. But the purview of news framing research expands well beyond these quintessentially political sites and topics. For example, news framing research is conducted on health campaign coverage and on sports and religion news, to name a few areas that make up the specialized institutional architecture of mass communication.

A review of the field mass communication by Jennings Bryant and Dorina Miron (2004) attests to the ascendancy of framing, finding that it was the most frequently utilized theory in top mass communication journals since the beginning of the 21st century. Their choice of the word *theory* is interesting because it is but one of many different ways that framing has been described. Framing is, no doubt, a concept (e.g., Tewksbury, Jones, Peske, Raymond, & Vig, 2000). But scholars have used many other terms to classify this concept vis-à-vis epistemology and practice. Framing has been called an *approach* (e.g., a framing analysis approach to news discourse; Pan & Kosicki, 1993; see also McLeod & Detenber, 1999), a *theory* (e.g., a theory of media effects; Scheufele, 1999), a *class of media effects* (Price & Tewksbury, 1997), a *perspective*(Kuypers, 2005), an *analytical technique* (Endres, 2004), a *paradigm* (Entman, 1993), and *a multiparadigmatic research program* (D'Angelo, 2002). Some researchers have used more than one term; for example, Reese (2001) called framing an *approach* and a *paradigm.*

This brings us to a crucial concern underlying the works in this volume on news framing. Underlying Bryant and Miron's seemingly simple conclusion about framing's ascendancy are foundational questions about its nature. In our view, the most important set of questions about framing dovetails with a continuing debate about communication's status as a "borrowing" discipline (see Hudson, 1931; Craig, 1999). Namely, is framing a communication theory that lays out unique propositions to guide empirical inquiry? Or, is framing better characterized as an approach to theory integration, one that allows researchers to draw from and build upon established theories within the broader social sciences and humanities in order guide empirical inquiry? The answers to these questions not only will give vital clues to how news framing research is conducted, but also to how communication sees itself as a discipline. In this vein, debate about the nature of framing may very well be a barometer of how communication "thinks" about itself within the academy (D'Angelo, 2002).

Added to these foundational questions is a continuing and unresolved debate about the composition and location of frames and about the mechanisms and processes of frame building and framing effects. Entman (1993) and others (e.g., Nelson & Willey, 2001) have located frames within audience members, news organizations, news sources, news texts, and, more heuristically, within the culture in which news is constructed. This leaves a great deal of leeway for theorizing the mechanisms and processes of news framing. Even still, one conjecture in the literature is that frames are powerful units of discourse (D'Angelo, 2002). With this in mind, it is reasonable to inquire about the discursive characteristics that make frames powerful and, in turn, about the mechanisms through which framing effects occur. For example, on the individual level, we may ask: Do frames shape attitudes of individuals directly by forming or changing opinions? Do frames make certain considerations more salient in the public domain, thereby making them more likely to be used by individuals to interpret an issue or topic? Do frames activate emotional responses that mediate the cognitive mechanisms through which framing effects occur? Are there limits of framing effects; for example, must individuals perceive the source who frames a message, or the journalist or media organization that passes along the frame, as being credible in order for an effect to occur (e.g., Druckman, 2001)? On the group level, we may ask: How do interest groups and advocates take into consideration the framing behaviors of journalists when designing frames they believe will influence the public? In other words, how do these groups react to coverage they receive in order to reshape both internal and external framing behaviors? It is questions such as these that the following chapters attempt to answer.

Interestingly, the news framing literature already contains close to two dozen theoretical and metatheoretical essays (e.g., Carragee & Roefs, 2004; D'Angelo, 2002; de Vreese, 2005; Chong & Druckman, 2007; Entman, 1993; McCombs, 1992; Pan & Kosicki, 1993; B. Scheufele, 2004; D. Scheufele, 1999, 2000; Simon, 2001) that address these foundational questions. Several of these essays were published in a 2007 issue of the *Journal of Communication* (see Kinder, 2007; Reese, 2007; Scheufele & Tewksbury, 2007; Van Gorp, 2007; Weaver, 2007), and before that, in what some consider the bible of news framing analysis, *Framing Public Life*, edited by Stephen Reese, Oscar Gandy, and August Gant (2001). Some of these big picture articles hold that framing research is, in essence, a victim of its own success. They maintain that academic specialization, along with theoretical and methodological pluralism, has led to a fragmented understanding of what framing is and how framing works. Other big picture articles praise the pluralist premises of framing research, arguing that framing research realizes in piecemeal fashion communication's mission to meaningfully integrate theories and methods from across the social sciences and humanities in order to illuminate a complex process.

It is directly into this brew of theoretical concerns that we offer our project. Herein we present original, big picture articles about news framing. Our goal is not to judge which foundational position is correct; that is, framing is fragmented, or framing is necessarily pluralistic. Nor is it our aim to judge which theory or method yields the most important empirical findings or insights. Rather, we acknowledge the integrationist impulses that propel the use of different theoretical and methodological approaches and we aim to provide interpretive guides to the community of news framing scholars and interested readers regarding what news frames are, how they can be observed in news texts, and how framing effects are uncovered and substantiated in cultural, group, and individual sites. In short, we offer here theoretical insights commingled with practical applications.

To achieve these goals, each chapter in this volume features a framing analyst or team of framing analysts who take a reflective, and even at times self-reflexive, look at their own empirical work. We feel that giving talented researchers the opportunity to reflect on their work allows us to then provide interpretive guides about news framing. In turn, these guides will help framing researchers at all levels to better understand news framing and do better news framing research. These chapters offer fresh perspectives from which to begin new research programs, to puzzle through perplexing problems in an existing research program, or to expand an existing research program. The chapters here provide conceptual and methodological guides for future framing research.

## Approach of the Book

The two models we shall draw upon to structure this book are the process models of D. Scheufele (1999) and D'Angelo (2002). Of course, there are other models that we could have used; for example, Price and Tewksbury's (1997) cognitive processing model or B. Scheufele's (2004) model of framing perspectives. But we chose to use the process models by D. Scheufele and D'Angelo for two reasons.

First, both of these models are process models: they comprehensively lay out the subprocesses of news framing, positing that these subprocesses are continuous, not discrete. As D. Scheufele (1999) noted, news framing can be conceptualized as "a continuous process where outcomes of certain [sub] processes serve as inputs for subsequent [sub] processes." (pp. 114–115). Likewise, D'Angelo (2002) held that the various subcomponents of news framing "flow" into each other. Second, both models (D. Scheufele's in particular) have provided the vernacular with which the process and subprocesses of news framing are broadly conceptualized and discussed in theoretical and metatheoretical discourses, as well as within empirical studies. For example, Scheufele discussed two frame building subprocesses; in one, journalists are audiences for the framing behaviors of other social actors; in the other subprocess journalists use those framing elements to construct news stories. D'Angelo (2002) also acknowledged the dual nature of frame building, calling it a "frame construction flow." His model shows that the events and discourses drawn upon by journalists to make news (e.g., sources' comments) are themselves shaped by framing processes internal to news organizations. In turn, framing analysts examine these composite units for evidence of the frames in news stories.

Taken together, these models demonstrate the complexity of news framing and allude to the practical necessity of studying manageable parts of it. These models allude, too, to the tendency for framing analysts to not only draw from core theoretical notions within the direct lineage of framing research—notions like "primary framework" from Goffman (1974), "typification" from Tuchman (1978), "script" from Schank and Abelson (1977) and Minsky (1975)—but also to import theoretical perspectives from various fields in the social sciences and the humanities in order to supplement or complement theoretical propositions that appear to be indigenous to framing research.

Thus, theoretical integration seems to be an ineluctable part of doing news framing analysis, evident in empirical work on each of the subprocesses of news framing. In fact, the framing analysts who have contributed to this volume have demonstrated remarkable creativity regarding theoretical integration. For example, Dhavan Shah and his colleagues have extended our understanding of framing effects by elaborating how the mind works when it processes frames. Specifically, they have extended our understanding of the associative networks that frames influence by developing and integrating notions of cognitive complexity and values-based judgments into framing research (Keum et al, 2005; Shah, Kwak, Schmierbach, & Zubric, 2004). Others have enriched framing analysis by integrating gender and feminist theory (e.g., Hardin, Simpson, Whiteside, & Garris, 2007), by extending our understanding of visual presentation (e.g., Coleman & Wasike, 2004), and by developing theories of journalistic norms and rules that, together, explain why certain frames are prominent in news coverage while others languish (e.g., Bennett, Lawrence, & Livingston, 2006).

In summary, news framing research is burgeoning, a situation which beckons interpretation and critique. And who best to interpret and critique news framing than those who empirically study it. In this book, we provide some of the most talented news framing analysts with a model and the settings from which to reflect upon their work and mull over the state of news framing analysis. That, in essence, is the approach of this book.

## Outline of the Book

*Doing News Framing Analysis* consists of 13 individual chapters divided into three main sections. Part I deals with frame building and defining news frames. Paying homage to his pioneering coedited volume, *Framing Public Life* (Reese et al. 2001), which is on the bookshelf of every framing analyst, the first chapter is by Stephen D. Reese. In "Finding Frames in a Web of Culture," Reese suggests that the concept of framing brings an intuitively appealing and provocative openness. However, he complicates this pastoral view with his own definition that emphasizes the embedded quality of frames across a number of domains: policy, journalistic, and public. Harkening back to his important prologue in *Framing Public Life*, Reese stresses that frames are "organizing principles that are socially shared and persistent over time, that work symbolically to meaningfully structure the social world." This definition underscores both the latent quality of frames and the importance of understanding the routines and values of news work that engender certain frames over others. Rather than focusing on a linear transmission of effects, Reese instead addresses how social actors participate in the crystallization and maintenance of certain frames. Toward this end, he offers a very interesting analysis of frames surrounding the War on Terror. Consistent with his robust sociological perspective, Reese argues that framing analysts should look beyond particular policy options and instead train their eye on macrolevel processes that give meaning and force to the terms in which those policies are articulated.

In "Knowledge Into Action: Framing the Debates Over Climate Change and Poverty," Matthew C. Nisbet discusses his dual roles as an analyst of the frames of advocates and sponsors, particularly those who work in the arena of science and public policy, and as a participant in framing debates that occur within this arena. From a theoretical standpoint, Nisbet argues that identifying and applying a common set of frames within an issue domain should be a common goal of news framing analysis. Ameliorating the tendency to reinvent the wheel with each new framing study will allow for comparisons across studies or national settings, enable predictions relative to the trajectory of the "frame-building" process, and lead to insight into how frames might interact with the predispositions and schema of various publics, journalists, and decision makers. From both an analytical and participant standpoint, Nisbet discusses case studies from the debates over climate change and low wage work.

In "Strategies to Take Subjectivity out of Framing Analysis," Baldwin Van Gorp follows in the footsteps of Gamson and Modigliani's pioneering work (1989) and advocates for the constructionist paradigm in framing research. He briefly discusses the characteristics of this paradigm, and then develops conceptual definitions of framing, frames, and "frame packages." He advances a basic assumption that frames are part of culture, and from this point he discusses research techniques—both quantitative and qualitative—that can help to validate cultural frames empirically and to take subjectivity largely out of the reconstruction of frame packages. He begins his exploration by reconstructing a repertoire of frames inductively on the bases of a literature study, content produced by advocacy groups, and a strategically composed sample of material. A checklist is presented to test the suitability of the reconstructed frames, which can be useful both in classroom and research settings to help independent coders deductively identify in a larger sample of coding material the framing and reasoning devices that tie in with the defined frames. Van Gorp reflects on his experiences with doing framing analysis on a diversity of issues, such as immigration, alcohol consumption, and poverty. Finally, he explores the role of the receivers in processing the news—how their interpretation of news' content can be unexpectedly self-willed and how that aspect can be taken into account during a framing analysis.

Bertram T. Scheufele and Dietram A. Scheufele integrate their influential and comprehensive models of the framing process in "Of Spreading Activation, Applicability, and Schemas: Conceptual Distinctions and Their Operational Implications for Measuring Frames and Framing Effects." They caution all scholars interested in news framing to heed conceptual distinctions between the terms *frame* and *schema,* doing so not to wall off the frame concept from seemingly related constructs, but rather to suggest more meaningful integration among these constructs as they exist within news gathering practices, source articulations of issues, and audience members' cognitions upon reading or watching news. They propose a model for operationalizing and measuring news frames, independent of specific issues or communication contexts—a model that serves as a blueprint for communication researchers developing operational definitions of framing. They demonstrate the model with data from a large-scale content analysis of media coverage of ethnic violence in Germany.

In "The Oppositional Framing of Bloggers," Stephen D. Cooper describes his exploration of media criticism blogging. Bloggers often take issue with the broad interpretations of facts woven into mainstream news reporting of events, which Cooper found amounted to a critique of news story framing. Cooper explains why he feels an inductive, rhetorical approach to framing analysis is appropriate for exploratory research into a new genre of computer-mediated content, and how that approach helped him to develop the typology of blog media criticism described in his book *Watching the Watchdog.* In his chapter he develops a "reasonable person" standard, in many ways similar to that used in tort law, that he believes is overtly the benchmark for a qualitative study of framing. Additionally, he makes the case that this standard implicitly lies behind quantitative studies of framing. Along those lines, Cooper suggests that a holistic approach to framing is often the method best suited to understanding such oppositional work as that of media criticism bloggers. He provides a number of blog posts which illustrate the utility of the reasonable person standard.

Part II of *Doing News Framing Analysis* deals with perspectives on framing effects. Leading off this section, Paul Brewer and Kimberly Gross discuss the important area of issue framing. They hold that when covering political issues, the news media do more than provide just the facts; they also provide frames that tell readers how to understand policy controversies. In "Studying the Effects of Issue Framing on Public

Opinion: Does What We See Depend on How We Look?" Brewer and Gross argue that the media transmit elite debates over how to frame particular issues, and that they serve as conduits for frames developed by politicians and activists who advocate specific issue positions. At the same time, the news media also rely on more general frames in telling stories about issues. Brewer and Gross argue, however, that researchers' decisions regarding how to study issue framing effects may shape their conclusions about the nature and extent of such effects. As a result, these same decisions may also shape researchers' conclusions about the implications of framing effects for theoretical models of framing and normative models of democracy. They explore these points by discussing their research on issue framing effects, and then suggest ways in which future research on issue framing effects could use more diverse methods and draw on broader understandings of what constitutes a framing effect.

In "Framing the Economy: Effects of Journalistic News Frames," Claes De Vreese provides a typology of news frames as he investigates the notion of journalistic news frames. His chapter focuses primarily on one dominant journalistic news frame: economic consequences. Additionally, De Vreese explains and explores the differential effects of positive and negative economic consequences of news framing of a political issue. In his chapter he tests competing hypotheses about the psychological mechanisms mediating framing by manipulating the valence of economic consequences news frame; what he finds suggests that the valence of news frames affected participants' economic expectations. A mediation analysis demonstrated that framing effects occurred both directly and indirectly by endowing certain considerations with more importance in subsequently made evaluations. De Vreese concludes his chapter with a discussion of how journalistic practices are manifest in news framing and how and why they matter for public opinion and preferences.

In "Specificity, Complexity, and Validity: Rescuing Experimental Research on Framing Effects," Dhavan V. Shah and colleagues respond to Donald Kinder's (2007) "curmudgeonly advice" by reiterating the vital role experiments play in both clarifying the discursive nature of particular sets of framing devices and in understanding how (textual) news frames are interpreted and used by individuals in their everyday lives. They argue that framing devices that operate at different levels of textual specificity, particularly differentiating story elements that color the entire press report vs. issue labels that contest a particular term. In a well-constructed experiment typical of Shah's research program, he and his colleagues examine the interaction of frames (i.e., organizing devices used to construct and structure press accounts) with cues (i.e., labels and terms used to identify issue domains and define policy debates). Using a 2×2 experimental design embedded within a probability survey, they examined the influence of these frames and cues on subjects' cognitive responses. Specifically, the study shifted the frame of the issue from the individual to the societal level and alternately used the loss and gain cues of "urban sprawl" and "suburban development" to label the issue. As predicted, based on prospect and attribution theories, the combination of individual frame/sprawl cue and societal frame/development cue generated the most intricate mental models about urban growth. Thus, the much more specific and simple gain–loss cue shift worked almost exactly like the broader and more holistic gain–loss frame shift. This is theoretically meaningful, they argue, because it shows that framing at various levels of language construction and textual specificity works similarly. Back to their response to Kinder, Shah and his colleagues contend that the criticism of experiments is misguided, for it is not the methodology, per se, but the designs of studies that should raise concern.

In "Framing the Pictures in our Heads: Exploring the Framing and Agenda-Setting Effects of Visual Images," Renita Coleman examines some of the noteworthy visual studies that use framing theory as a foundation, noting, too, that framing theory is sometimes an unacknowledged perspective within studies of visuals in news texts. She discusses her program of research that develops the visual side of a theory, agenda-setting, that is often linked to framing analysis. Particularly useful is the chapter's discussion of methodological issues pertaining to observing and coding visual images, a still thorny aspect of news framing analysis.

Part III of *Doing News Framing Analysis* deals with what we consider to be the core of news framing analysis, its openness to various theoretical perspectives from which to understand, and study, frame building and framing effects. Regina G. Lawrence, in "Researching Political News Framing: Established Ground and New Horizons," offers a concise review of the current state of theory and evidence regarding the framing of political news in the United States, particularly news pertaining to the president, Congress, and domestic and foreign policy. Specifically, Lawrence reviews the leading and complementary/competing theories of political news frames. Beginning with Robert Entman's effort over 16 years ago to move "toward clarification of a fractured paradigm," Lawrence relates the contributions of the indexing hypothesis (developed by Lance Bennett) and of "event-driven news" (developed by Lawrence) to a prevailing paradigm of political news frames. She argues that this paradigm has been further refined—and challenged—by Entman and others, and that empirical debates are currently brewing over the particular mechanisms that trigger news frames (e.g., the degree to which lower-level and nongovernmental news sources can influence predominant frames in new or developing news stories) and over the degree of independence that journalists exhibit from top government officials in framing major news stories.

Jim A. Kuypers, in "Framing Analysis from a Rhetorical Perspective," addresses framing analysis from the point of view of a rhetorical critic. Beginning with an overview of the nature of validity and evidence in rhetorical and social scientific studies, he next provides a brief overview of how frames work, discusses the relationship of frames to the news media, and explains how a social scientific framing analysis produces different knowledge than that produced by a rhetorical analysis. As an example of how this works, Kuypers examines reviews of his latest framing work, demonstrating how the point of view of the reviewer—rhetorical or social scientific—changes the reception of that work. Kuypers ends by arguing forcefully that framing analysis allows for both rhetorical and social scientific orientations, and that the products of each must be judged by the standards inherent to each.

In "Framing through a Feminist Lens: A Tool in Support of an Activist Research Agenda," Marie Hardin and Erin Whiteside approach news framing analysis from an activist perspective. They suggest that although many feminist media researchers question the methodology, methods, and assumptions used in research that employs the concept of framing, such skepticism does not negate the value of framing research, especially the use of such research in realizing feminist goals. Hardin and Whiteside argue that framing can be used in feminist scholarship to illuminate the operation of postfeminist ideology in material ways within media texts, and that such research can contribute pragmatically to feminist goals. Their chapter explores issues for feminists in relation to framing, provides examples of effective feminist incorporation of framing, and suggests ways that feminists can powerfully incorporate the concept in their research.

Robert M. Entman proposes integrating the insights generated by framing, priming, and agenda setting research through a systematic effort to conceptualize and understand their larger implications for political power and democracy. In his chapter, "Framing, Media Bias, and Political Power," he builds upon an earlier statement concerning the organizing concept of bias in framing research (Entman, 2007). After showing how agenda setting, framing, and priming fit together as tools of power, Entman connects them to explicit definitions of news slant and the related but distinct phenomenon of bias. In so doing Entman suggests improved measures of slant and bias. Properly defined and measured, slant and bias provide insight into how the media influence the distribution of power: who gets what, when, and how. Delving further into this area, Entman argues that content analysis should be informed by explicit theory linking patterns of framing in the media text to predictable priming and agenda-setting effects on audiences. When unmoored by such underlying theory, measures and conclusions of media bias are suspect.

Taken together, these chapters present a wide ranging and detail-oriented look at the current nature of news framing research. Oriented toward future applications, these chapters offer insights that will allow students and researchers to implement old ideas in new ways, and to incorporate new ideas immediately into their work. Our sincere hope is that this book offers a point of departure for future news framing work, expanding even more greatly the already heady growth of this fascinating research domain.

## References

Bennett, W. L., Lawrence, R. L., & Livingston, S. (2006). None dare call it torture: Indexing and the limits of press independence in the Abu Ghraib scandal. *Journal of Communication, 56*(3), 467–485.

Bryant, J., & Miron, D. (2004). Theory and research in mass communication. *Journal of Communication, 54*(4), 662–704.

Carragee, K. M., & Roefs, W. (2004). The neglect of power in recent framing research. *Journal of Communication, 54*(2), 214–233.

Chong, D., & Druckman, J. N. (2007). Framing theory. *American Review of Political Science, 10*, 103–126.

Coleman, R., & Wasike, B. (2004). Visual elements in public journalism newspapers in an election: A content analysis of the photographs and graphics in Campaign 2000. *Journal of Communication, 54*(3), 456–473.

Cooper, S. D. (2006). *Watching the watchdog: Bloggers as the fifth estate.* Spokane, WA: Marquette Academic.

Craig, R. T. (1999). Communication theory as a field. *Communication Theory, 9*(2), 119–161.

D'Angelo, P. (2002). News framing as a multiparadigmatic research program: A response to Entman. *Journal of Communication, 52*(4), 870–888.

De Vreese, C. H. (2005). News framing: Theory and typology. *Information Design Journal, 13*(1), 51–62.

Druckman, J. (2001). On the limits of framing effects: Who can frame? *Journal of Politics, 63*(4), 1041–1066.

Endres, K. L. (2004). "Help-wanted female": *Editor and Publisher* frames a civil rights issue. *Journalism & Mass Communication Quarterly, 81*(1), 7–21.

Entman, R. (1993). Framing: Toward clarification of a fractured paradigm. *Journal of Communication, 43*(4), 51–58.

Entman, R. (2007). Framing bias: Media in the distribution of power. *Journal of Communication, 57*(4), 163–173.

Gamson, W. A., & Modigliani, A. (1989). Media discourse and public opinion on nuclear power: A constructionist approach. *American Journal of Sociology, 95*(1), 1–37.

Goffman, E. (1974). *Frame analysis: An essay on the organization of experience.* New York: Harper & Row.

Hardin, M., Simpson, S., Whiteside, E., & Garris, K. (2007). The gender war in U.S. sport: Winners and losers in news coverage of Title IX. *Mass Communication & Society, 10*(2), 211–233.

Hudson, H. H. (1931). The tradition of our subject. *Quarterly Journal of Speech, 17*(3), 320–329.

Keum, H., Hillback, E. D., Rojas, H., De Zuniga., H. G., Shah, D., & McLeod, D. M. (2005). Personifying the radical: How news framing polarizes security concerns and tolerance judgments. *Human Communication Research, 31*(3), 337–364.

Kinder, D. R. (2007). Curmudgeonly advice. *Journal of Communication, 57*(4), 155–162.

Kuypers, J. A. (Ed.). (2005). *The art of rhetorical criticism.* Boston: Allyn & Bacon.

Kuypers, J. A. (2006). *Bush's war: Media bias and justifications for war in a terrorist age.* Lanham, MD: Rowman & Littlefield.

McCombs, M. E. (1992). Explorers and surveyors: Expanding strategies for agenda-setting research. *Journalism Quarterly, 69*(4), 813–824.

McLeod, D. M., & Detenber, B. H. (1999). Framing effects of television news coverage of social protest. *Journal of Communication, 49*(3), 3–23.

Minsky, M. (1975). A framework for representing knowledge. In P. H. Winston (Ed.), *The psychology of computer vision* (pp. 211–277). New York: McGraw-Hill.

Nelson, T. E., & Willey, E. (2001). Issue frames that strike a value balance: A political psychology perspective. In S. D. Reese, O. H. Gandy, Jr., & A. E. Grant (Eds.), *Framing public life* (pp. 245–266). Mahwah, NJ: Erlbaum.

Pan, Z., & Kosicki, G. M. (1993). Framing analysis: An approach to news discourse. *Political Communication, 10*(1), 55–76.

Price, V., & Tewksbury, D. (1997). News values and public opinion: A theoretical account of media priming and framing. In G. A. Barnett & F. J. Boster (Eds.), *Progress in communication sciences: Advances in persuasion* (Vol. 13, pp. 173–212). Greenwich, CT: Ablex.

Reese, S. D. (2001). Prologue—Framing public life: A bridging model for media research. In S. D. Reese, O. H. Gandy, Jr., & A. E. Grant (Eds.), *Framing public life* (pp. 7–32). Mahwah, NJ: Erlbaum.

Reese, S. D. (2007). The framing project: A bridging model for media research revisited. *Journal of Communication, 57*(1), 148–155.

Reese, S. D., Gandy, O. H., Jr., & Grant, A. E. (Eds.). (2001). *Framing public life.* Mahwah, NJ: Erlbaum.

Scheufele, B. (2004). Framing-effects approach: A theoretical and methodological critique. *Communications, 29*, 401–428.

Scheufele, D. (1999). Framing as a theory of media effects. *Journal of Communication, 49*(1), 103–122.

Scheufele, D. (2000). Agenda-setting, priming, and framing revisited: Another look at cognitive effects of political communication. *Mass Communication & Society, 3*, 297–316.

Scheufele, D., & Tewksbury, D. (2007). Framing, agenda-setting, and priming: The evolution of three media effects models. *Journal of Communication, 57*(1), 9–22.

Schank, R. C., & Abelson, R. P. (1977). *Scripts, plans, goals and understanding: An inquiry into human knowledge structures.* Hillsdale, NJ: Erlbaum

Shah, D. V., Kwak, N., Schmierbach, M., & Zubric, J. (2004). The interplay of news frames on cognitive complexity. *Human Communication Research*, *30*(1), 102–120.

Simon, A. (2001). A unified method for analyzing media framing. In R. P. Hart & D. S. Shaw (Eds.), *Communication in U.S. elections: New agendas* (pp. 75–89). Lanham, MD: Rowman & Littlefield.

Tewksbury, D., Jones, J., Peske, M. W., Raymond, A., & Vig, W. (2000). The interaction of news and advocate frames: Manipulating audience perceptions of a local public policy issue. *Journalism & Mass Communication Quarterly*, *77*(4), 804–829.

Tuchman, G., (1978). *Making news: A study in the construction of reality*. New York: Free Press.

Van Gorp, B. (2007). The constructionist approach to framing: Bringing culture back in. *Journal of Communication*, *57*(1), 60–78.

Weaver, D. (2007). Thoughts on agenda-setting, framing, and priming. *Journal of Communication*, *57*(1), 142–146.

Wicks, R. H. (2005). Message framing and constructing meaning: An emerging paradigm in mass communication research. *Communication Yearbook*, *29*, 331–361.

# Part I

# Perspectives on Frame Building and Frame Definition

# Chapter 2

# Finding Frames in a Web of Culture

## The Case of the War on Terror

*Stephen D. Reese*

The framing concept brings an intuitively appealing and provocative openness, a bridging model that resists being pinned down to any one paradigm, a program of research made useful by its theoretical diversity (D'Angelo, 2002; Reese, 2007). My own definition of frames broadly captures this diversity and bridging quality: "organizing principles that are socially shared and persistent over time, that work symbolically to meaningfully structure the social world" (Reese, 2001, p. 11). This idea suggests that frames manifest themselves in a number of different sites and across a number of domains: policy, journalistic, and public. Other definitions have focused on the idea that in framing certain aspects of the world can be communicated "*in such a way* as to promote a particular problem definition, causal interpretation, moral evaluation, and/or treatment recommendation" (Entman, 1993, p. 52). I am especially interested in the "in such a way" aspect, the way in which frames accomplish these results, which is determined by the nature of the organizing principle.

As the goal of this volume suggests, framing analysis can take place in a number of locations or sites. Given the eclecticism and multiple perspectives, the definitive framing study will never be found. So, the researcher doing framing analysis must make some well-informed choices about the best point of entry to answer the question at hand. Many of these decisions are implicit or taken for granted, but in this chapter I would like to think about them more explicitly within the context of a particular case study. In doing so, I call to mind the emphasis placed on the researcher's own decisions about how to go about a study—the practical, conceptual, and methodological decisions that must be made before and during any framing analysis. I have experienced these decisions first-hand through working with students in seminars devoted to framing research, which inevitably yield a few predictable questions: Where does the frame reside (in text, culture, or the cognitions of the perceiver)? How does one convincingly establish that a frame exists (or is it the subjective construction of the researcher)? Is framing a subset of agenda-setting or vice versa?

Where do topics and themes leave off and frames begin? What is the unit of analysis; that is, what is to be counted or examined? Regardless of how these issues are resolved, one inevitably reaches the moment of truth when frames must be empirically identified so they can be usefully examined. Taking the term *empirical* broadly, one must engage with real materials and evidence whether making a quantitative codification or taking a more interpretive, qualitative approach.

In my particular case example, I consider the interpretive, qualitative approach, which tends to give greater emphasis to the cultural and political content of news frames and how they draw upon a shared store of social meanings. In this light, because frames are specific and explicit agents of ideological processes, they tend to be more general and encompassing than news themes, topics, and issues. Frames organize and structure, and thus are bigger than topics. This leads naturally to exploring how they are connected to other systemic features that give them support and reinforcement. So, for me framing relates to my interest in media sociology, connecting media production and content (Reese, 2008). Understanding the routines and values of news work, for example, helps explain how certain frames are favored over others. Journalists occupy a significant role in the propagation of news frames and don't just simply relay ideas from political leaders to citizens. They participate in frame construction, just as do others in the deliberative arena.

Thus, as the title of this chapter indicates, I regard frames as embedded in a web of culture, an image that naturally draws attention to the surrounding cultural context and the threads that connect them. Much as Tuchman (1978) conceived the "news net" as a dynamic phenomenological structure, ensnaring events and new concepts, the web idea alerts us to how certain frames are connected to an underlying structure—a historically rooted but dynamic cultural context. Frames don't just arise as free-standing entities. Of course, the challenge then becomes how to draw boundaries—isolating and foregrounding frames for analysis from their surrounding context. Although I don't address framing effects in any depth, this approach speaks to those questions too, and I will examine their implications. Framing effects analysis (what I will later call the "how" of framing research) should rely more firmly on work that has identified frames in their cultural environments, which is what I will call the "what" of framing. Too many effects analyses now rely on vague notions of "considerations" (e.g., Zaller, 1992) or "attributes of issues," without locating them in this larger web.

## Critical Constructionist Perspective

In working through my own research, I have regarded framing as a valuable analytical approach to answering the questions I have about media phenomena. So, rather than try to organize a theory about framing, I have borrowed some ideas from this area that help organize my own thinking about large-scale political influence. As D'Angelo (2002) advocated, framing research benefits from working across paradigms, which he identifies as cognitive, constructionist, and critical. My own interests span the constructionist and critical: critical in the sense that I see frames as expressions and outcomes of power, unequally distributed with public opinion dominated and enlisted accordingly; and constructionist in the sense that I grant participants, such as journalists, some professional autonomy and take them seriously, using frames as "interpretive packages" in creating understandings of the social world.

I have been particularly interested in how the government has helped organize public opinion about the risks of war and terrorism, beginning with the invasion of Kuwait by Iraq in 1990 and the subsequent success of the first Bush administration in mobilizing public opinion in favor of Desert Storm. I characterized the media jingoism and marginalization of dissent in that period as the "routine" framing and militarization of local television (Reese & Buckalew, 1995). By introducing American troops into the Middle East, the Persian Gulf conflict helped feed the ideology of Osama Bin Laden and lead to his subsequent attacks of September 11, 2001, in New York City and Washington, DC. I revisited these concerns several years later in view of the globalization of dissent and media (Reese, 2004) and was concerned personally with the way the second Bush administration located terrorism within a broader political framework of the War on Terror—again, with effective impact on public opinion (Christie, 2006). I began thinking of how best to approach this question—with great difficulty, it turned out, given the breadth and elusive quality of this particular framing. Later in this chapter I will discuss the steps taken in this study regarding the measurement of frames and its theoretical implications.

## The "What" vs. the "How" of News Framing Analysis

A major dividing line in news framing research it seems to me is whether the emphasis is on the what vs. the how of frames. In my own research, I have been particularly interested in the way issues are organized *in such a way* that they guide policy and opinion. The what perspective is more frame-centric; it is concerned with frame building and involves the dissection of the content of the frame, specifically the network of concepts and the unique narrative and myths that make it work. As Gamson and Modigliani (1989) pointed out, an important step in a framing analysis is the identification of framing devices, which are specific linguistic structures such as metaphors, visual icons, and catchphrases that communicate frames. In addition, the what of framing (analysis) leads the researcher to examine latent aspects of the text, such as reasoning devices (e.g., problem definition and moral evaluation; see also, Entman, 1993) as well as specific keywords that constitute the concepts underlying frames (e.g., the words *game* and *competition* are integral discourse elements of a strategy frame in political campaign news; see Cappella & Jamieson, 1997). In all, an analysis of the what of frames emphasizes the special configuration of discourse elements that articulate culture. If the what of frames are explored, it encourages an analysis that delves into the contextualization of topics—social, historically, culturally—and urges the framing researcher to look closely at the particular features of the frame. Some have pointed out that this approach to studying framing leads to ad hoc analyses applicable only to a particular topic or issue (Tankard, 2001). Still, the specificity that is engendered by the what of a framing study helps in the end to uncover the culturally relevant and resonant theme that illuminates unique social and political understandings. And these are the sorts of frames that have the greatest implications for understanding the how of framing.

One can also conceive of frames uncovered in the way just described as strategic resources, constructed and wielded by an individual or group (including journalists), along with everything else the individual or group has at its disposal. This emphasis underlies a more process-centric, or "how" research orientation. Here, frames are situated in competitive social and political environments; frames are constructed and promoted to achieve some predetermined outcome. In these environments, elites compete against elites, as in the struggle over the Clinton health care policy (Pan & Kosicki, 1993). And whereas groups may utilize frames to mobilize themselves internally and to compete against each other in the public arena (Snow & Benford, 1988), they may also, as in the case of social movements, seek to construct frames—often using media—that resonate with the life experiences of a target group (Benford & Snow, 2000). In other instances, elites may be said to compete with the public, such as with the nuclear freeze issue where elite frames were at variance with public opinion (Entman & Rojecki, 1993). In each of these cases, a focus on the how of framing encourages researchers to examine the features of frames associated with success—and the role, too, of the news media in this process. Along these lines, some experimental framing research is criticized for its often exclusive emphasis on the how of framing. These studies take the what for granted, focusing instead on how cognitive processes interact with (news) frames to produce effects (e.g., Carragee & Roefs, 2004). In the larger picture, both the what and the how are important facets of doing framing analysis, as long as the what is not given short shrift. Privileging the what leads to deeper inspection of frames in the social arena; that is, to identifying the key organizing principles and most relevant values that inevitably help guide the how studies that are more concerned with examining specific effects.

The what of frames opens to analysis the internal structure both of frames themselves and their connections to the surrounding web of culture—and in doing so more likely leads to the level of analysis question. The significance of frames increase as they become more overarching and broadly reaching, and the bigger the frame, of course, the more difficult it can be to isolate and measure the social influence process. Gamson (2001) observed that frame analysis brings the "vexing problem" of level of analysis: events, issues, master frames, and worldviews yield frames within frames (p. x). In this respect, frames can be macro (e.g., Cold War, War on Drugs) or smaller in scope (e.g., pro-life/pro-choice). Depending on the level, different questions come into play. At the lower level, one is more likely to examine the "how" of frames, the specific political and marketing decisions made to mobilize sufficient support to win the policy conflict—frames as part of the deliberative process toolbox. At the larger level, we are more likely to consider how frames are connected to the surrounding culture, and how sponsors may go about exploiting these connections. Macrocultural frame analysis may not lend itself to precise measurement and codification, but it is an important part of the overall project. Putting the what before the how provides a valuable foundation for selecting more specific frames for further effects analysis, because their importance within the overall society has been more clearly demonstrated and understood.

## Critical Effects of Frames: Constructing Culture

One of the tendencies for communication scholars grappling with framing is in being drawn into the traditional sender–receiver model of message, audience, and effect. We substitute "frame" for some other stimulus and measure its effects as we would with other persuasive appeals, information emphasis, or agendas. Broadening that view to include the conceptually prior media and journalistic factors that shape the creation of frames opens up other questions but retains the linear, process model of effects. The idea of framing certainly suggests a linear transmission of influence from one location to another, exemplified by the agenda-setting model with its compelling matrix for tracking the correspondence of objects and attributes in media to audience. A set of objects and attributes in the media find their correspondence in the minds of the audience.

Frames, as a semantic equivalency, refer to structures in various locations (cultural, symbolic, and psychological), raising the often confusing question of where does the frame reside? Based on my own definition of frames as organizing principles, the frame is always an abstraction and finds its manifestation in various locations. But using the "frame" concept to apply to both cognitive and textual phenomena can be confusing. In the how orientation of framing, exemplified by the agenda-setting tradition, a frame is conceived as a multisited structure which moves from textual structures to mental structures. A change is found in the receiver, an effect, and attributed to some cause.

In the case of the political psychologists (who contribute to an expansive area of framing research), the effect is not so much the movement of emphasis from media to public, but in the making of some values and facts more relevant to the receiver for issue reasoning. Framing is the interaction between the incoming message structure and the psychological characteristics of the receiver. In Nelson's work, for example, frames work to establish hierarchies among values (Nelson & Willey, 2001). A message can activate mental frames, but how did those frames become effective? People differ in their responses to facts when certain values are prioritized for them, but this doesn't help explain the most relevant configuration of values. The how shouldn't take precedence over the what, the important aspect of frames that arises from their cultural rootedness. Frames articulate and maintain ways of reasoning about public issues, creating issues in discourse (e.g., Pan & Kosicki, 1993). To emphasize the effects *of* frames, or effects *on* frames, draws our attention away from this rootedness. That's why the cultural approach means approaching the issue of framing effects in a different way, namely, to consider how social actors participate in the creation and maintenance of certain frames, the ongoing construction of the discursive environment, and the interests that are served in the process. Disaggregating the frame into merely an emphasis on certain values over others has the effect of taking attention away from the cultural origins of specific frames. So, the effects, in the broad sense, that interest me are suggested by big swings in public opinion that imply someone has won a framing contest. This focuses attention on the public generally, how significant social frames emerge, and less on specific individual-level processes. We must be careful to examine those frames of greatest import and resist the tendency to focus on the strong effects caused by relatively insignificant issues.

## Background to the Case Study: War on Terror

As a case study illustration, I will review the conceptual and empirical decisions involved in analyzing the frames surrounding the War on Terror (Reese & Lewis, 2009).[1] War frames are highly significant in directing national policy, and I chose an inductive qualitative approach to help understand the constitutive components and narratives binding them together. Rather than narrow the scope of such frames to particular short-term policy options, we should also be concerned with more macroframing that subsumes those options within terms of the Administration's own choosing. Research for me is always a process of linking my own normative concerns to the language and tools of investigation, and I had been thinking about this particular issue for several years. After the president declared "war on terror" in 2001, I was immediately concerned about his resurrecting this phrase (used previously in the Reagan administration) as a guide for thinking about the issues surrounding 9/11. In an op-ed I wrote for the local newspaper about a year later, shortly before the Iraq invasion, I argued that the framing regrettably conditioned the public to think about the solutions as primarily military.

> Patriotic post 9/11 television news graphics provided related shorthand frames, with "America strikes back" mutating into "America's new war." Placing the issue primarily in the military realm privileges armed strength at the expense of the international political, diplomatic, and law enforcement arenas, where conflicts may also be mediated. We are led to ask simply whether we will win, not whether we are in the right fight with the right strategy. (Reese, 2002, p. A13)[2]

Even within the national security community, Record (2003) argued that the Global War on Terror's insistence on moral clarity lacked strategic focus, that its open-ended quest for absolute security was not politically sustainable and risked involving the military in conflicts it was not designed to fight, much less win.

Any study begins with the justification of its importance, and to me this frame was particularly compelling. In their life and death implications, war frames are highly significant in the way they direct vital debates on national policy. The Bush administration was successful in obliging policy actors to approach the debate over military conflicts within terms of its own choosing. Opponents of the war in Iraq, for example, have found it difficult to respond to the administration's claims of moral legitimacy without reframing it in their own terms (Lakoff, 2006). As political violence has taken on global proportions, it is more important than ever to understand how the policy has been structured, its validity, and the role of the news media in allowing the expression of a clear and appropriate role for the U.S. in the world community.

## Content of "War on Terror" Frames

If we are to examine the War on Terror it means we must take its frame construction seriously. Beyond observing whether the media treat an issue using, say, a "war" frame compared to a "diplomacy" frame, it is helpful in this case to open up this analysis to examine precisely what were the elements of the frame and how were they organized. This makes me vulnerable to the ad hoc frame criticism, which, as I mentioned, argues that rather than proliferate more frame categories, research should identify a consistent set of frames generalizable over many cases. But here I examine an already established framing and don't create one as an analytical category.[3] In this respect, I understand frames to have structured content; they're not just "considerations" or varying "contexts" for the same nucleus of facts (e.g., Zaller, 1992). As I've argued throughout this essay, in opposition to the psychological approach that often treats them as an easily manipulated element within a news story, divorced from a context of production and usage, frames should be treated in a more holistic and integrated fashion. In this sense, I favor Hertog and McLeod's (2001) approach, which regards frames as "structures of meaning made up of a number of concepts and the relations among those concepts" (p. 140). Master narratives are among the devices that structure these concepts, providing rules for processing new content, which is organized on the basis of the more central network of concepts. This gives frames their dynamic quality as they operate over time to assimilate and reconstitute new facts and concepts. That is, frames are not static and immutable as the "agenda" or issue approach often implies.

This perspective lends itself to both quantitative and qualitative approaches (although Hertog and McLeod place more emphasis on the latter). The network of concepts, with notions of center and periphery, could be tackled with semantic association analysis and the identification of nodes, links, and structure. The basis for these links, however, lies in the societal associations of meaning and their historical evolution, and draws on a different tradition. This approach to framing traces to the concept of ideology, a lineage provided by Hackett (1984), who regards framing as the application of "deep structure," the naturalized, taken-for-granted beliefs by members of society about what goes together. In that respect, the examination of the myths, metaphors, and narratives calls for a more qualitative, interpretive approach. The ultimate frame may not be plainly visible from a simple inspection of the manifest content and terminology that it invokes. Rather, it must be interpreted in its latent message.

## Examining the Global War on Terror

In this analysis, I'm not interested in terrorism per se, but in how the meaning of terrorism has been constructed for political ends. Terrorism has been examined before as a form of political "theater," with the media seen as a vital link for terrorists to produce their desired impact— sending demands and relying on public fear to accomplish their goals. These earlier scholarly concerns seem almost quaint by comparison to the megaterrorism made possible by global coordination and access to technologically advanced weapons of mass destruction. The terrorist is no longer some aggrieved party seeking dramatic redress, someone with whom authorities may negotiate. Instead, destruction on a broad scale is possible on behalf of groups who seek to wound a society, literally and symbolically, and don't necessarily desire any immediate concession.

To examine the War on Terror frame, I began with a close reading of the policy documents produced by the administration and the various critiques of policy in academic and media commentaries (Gordon & Trainor, 2006; Isikoff & Corn, 2006; Ricks, 2006). This immersion helps alert the analyst to the problematic nature of the targeted frame. Deconstructing the War on Terror begins with the component concepts, beginning with the metaphor of war itself, which follows in the tradition of other social problems that government is led to "declare war" on, including poverty and drugs (Lule, 2001). Invoking a war metaphor allows frame sponsors to marshal other comparisons and to define abstract challenges as more concrete "fronts." Traditional war involves conflict between armies, with the boundary between them labeled a front. By definition, asymmetric warfare has no "front," but President George W. Bush insisted on declaring Iraq the "front line." Arguing that point is made easier when located already within the metaphor. "War" also connects with other conflicts, which are deeply rooted in the American psychology. The War on Terror, thus, becomes linked to World War II, Pearl Harbor, and the Axis of Evil slogan recalls the Fascist Axis forces. Unlike the War on Terror, however, traditionally defined wars have specific identifiable enemies, and they have determined phases of time during which they are fought until one side has defeated the other and declared victory. In this respect, the policy takes a concept understood by all and applies it to a new and less familiar domain. Of course, the policy involved an actual war beginning with the conflict in Afghanistan, but the larger metaphor was controlling for all other related initiatives, including domestic surveillance and other measures.

Regarding the more problematic concept of terrorism, many definitions reinforce the role of government as the protagonist, leaving aside the possibility of state-sponsored terrorism. For example, Nacos (2002) defines "mass mediated terrorism" as "political violence against non-combatants/innocents that is committed with the intention to publicize the deed, to gain publicity and thereby public and *government* attention" (p. 17). In this way it is easy to render terrorism a status quo concept, with Nacos even including within her definition antiglobalization dissent! Others have properly adopted more encompassing definitions. Norris, Kern, and Just (2003), for example, call it "the systematic use of coercive intimidation against civilians for political goals" (p. 6), containing the nature of the techniques, the targets, and the goals, and including violence perpetrated by state *and* nonstate actors.

In various addresses by President Bush and other policy documents, the strategy was explicitly organized by marshalling core American values. Recognizing that some frames may be accused of being superficial "spin," Bush declared that the "war on terror is not a figure of speech. It is an inescapable calling of our generation" (Stevenson, 2004). Indeed, the frame slogan is deeply rooted in the strategic plans of the government. The National Strategy for Combating Terrorism (The White House, 2003), defined the attacks of 9/11 as "acts of war against the United States of America and its allies, and against the very idea of civilized society." It identified the enemy as terrorism, an "evil" threatening our "freedoms and our way of life. Freedom and fear are at war" (p. 1). Calling the defeat of terrorism "our nation's primary and immediate priority" (p. 19), this terrorism strategy as outlined argued that the nation could not wait for terrorists to attack before responding. As such, it took on even greater significance by being coupled with and expanding upon the National Security Strategy of the United States (The White House, 2006), which outlined a doctrine of unilateral preemptive strike capability that ran counter to historical norms of containment, deterrence, and international cooperation. Indeed, the National Security Strategy was developed years before 9/11, but was not palatable policy until the rationale of preventing terrorism was available. The War on Terror and national strategy are thus crucially linked (Armstrong, 2002).

Within the broad national strategy, terrorism was seen as crucially connected to rogue nations and weapons of mass destruction. If nation-states can be defined as sponsors of terrorism, then these two strategies combine into a powerful rationale for interventions at home and abroad. The frame fits the government's national security strategy in setting up a clear demarcation between us and them. Terrorism is linked to rogue states, which are defined in part as those states that "display no regard for international law...and callously violate international treaties...." Rogue states "reject basic human values and hate the United States and everything for which it stands" (The White House, 2006). As seen in these documents, specific security threats (nations and groups) were named and discussed, but beyond that broad culturally potent concepts are invoked to justify the political objectives of the government. A war is outlined with on one side arrayed the forces of civilization, rule of law, freedom, democratic values, prosperity, security, way of life, security, human dignity, tolerance, and even open economies; on the other side is the enemy: terror, fear, violence, fascism, and the destroyers of civilization. Speaking on the first anniversary of the start of the Iraq war, Bush declared, "There is no neutral ground—no neutral ground—in the fight between civilization and terror because there is no neutral ground between good and evil, freedom and slavery and life and death" (Stevenson, 2004, p. A7). The irony, of course, is that the administration had created a strategy that led to our own country revoking international multilateralism in order to oppose others for violating international law. The War on Terror sealed off the government from criticism. It was right, and those who opposed it were wrong.

This rationale was used as the basis for the invasion of Iraq, locating it within the frame. As one article reported, a year before the invasion, "President Bush acted to leave no doubt Thursday that his warnings to Iraq, Iran and North Korea to shape up or face U.S. retaliation are part of an expansion of the War on terrorism" (Keen, 2002c, p. A6). He underscored that link the following year in proclaiming a military success: "The battle of Iraq is one victory in a War on terror that began on Sept. 11, 2001, and still goes on" (quoted in McQuillan & Benedetto, 2003, p. A1). Connecting the ongoing occupation with terrorism, he declared that the "defeat of violence and terror in Iraq is vital to the defeat of violence and terror elsewhere." He further declared that for the "the first time, the civilized world has provided a concerted response to the ideology of terror" (Bush, 2004a, p. A11). Although no specific evidence linked Saddam Hussein to the 9/11 attacks, the Bush administration continued to link the invasion of Iraq to the War on Terrorism, leading a majority of Americans to believe that there was such a connection. In an article concerning casualties in Iraq a month after the beginning of the conflict, the 88 American dead were compared to the 3,000 who died on September 11, 2001. "Those, to me, are casualties of this same war, which is a war against terrorism, " said Daphne Scholz, co-owner of a gourmet food store in the Park Slope section of Brooklyn. "We took the first casualties, and the balance of dead is still on our side" (Wilgoren & Nagourney, 2003, p. B1).

## Inductively Finding the "What" of Frames

Following an intensive period of following news media accounts, I began to consider how best to operationalize the framing in some kind of more systematic measurement scheme. An early hypothesis was that a news article making reference to the War on Terror would have certain characteristics; in particular, the story would likely accept the prevailing assumptions of the administration embodied in the frame. Perhaps such stories would be more likely to emphasize military language and strategy than a reference to the issue couched in other language. After much reading of media texts from both U.S. and international news organizations, however, it became apparent that the War on Terror was used in ways difficult to predict and classify. For example, I assumed that international media would be far less likely to use the frame than U.S. news organizations, but this was not the case. The terminology of the administration was picked up by a variety of international officials, who found in the campaign a way to direct U.S. policy toward their own goals. The Israelis found in the War on Terror support for their dealings with the Palestinians, the Russians confirmation of their strategy toward Chechnya, and the Chinese against the Falun Gong. Subsumed within the phrase was a variety of local problems and political needs. Domestically, even critics of the administration found themselves using the phrase, even if ironically. Michael Ignatieff, for example, warned in the *New York Times* of the nation becoming decadent and repressive in combating the problem, giving up democratic liberties, but he also continued to use the metaphor, referring to the "front lines" of the war on terror (Ignatieff, 2004).

I observed a variety of evidence, however, to suggest that the response to terrorism had particular American features. In Madrid following the bombings of March 11, 2004, I observed that the Spanish response was to reassert the importance of democracy, looking internally to rearticulate those values. The American response to 9/11 had been a much more externally focused response, aimed at attacking the perceived source of the threat. The War on Terror, although cast in terms of upholding the American "way of life," is first and foremost a reconfiguring of relationships in the service of U.S. security policy, with new allies, enemies, and bases for international coalitions. Rojecki (2005), for example, noted that American support for promoting human rights and other liberal international initiatives was at a low ebb before 9/11. Afterwards, he found that press coverage of globalization and its connection with terror did little to change it—creating an issue culture emphasizing state security as an "unfortunate but necessary drag on global prosperity" (p. 77).

I discussed some of my preliminary impressions in Reese (2007), making the point that the War on Terror had become an institutionalized way of seeing the world, but I had yet to settle on a specific research design to pursue that claim. During that same spring and following discussion of these issues, one of my doctoral seminar students, Seth Lewis, carried out an analysis of the Associate Press and how it covered the War on Terror. I was particularly struck by a graph he produced showing that over the period from 2001 to 2006, the war on "Terrorism" declined in frequency of mentions in news articles, with a visible rise in the preference for the war on "Terror." As often happens in the research process, a striking pattern or result emerges that can spur the imagination for a larger analysis. It seemed that in these contrasting trends lay an illustration of how the policy had become internalized by the press. The "War on (or against) Terrorism" is the phrase used by national security policy statements, including the National Strategy for Combating Terrorism, released by the White House on February 14, 2003 (although in his remarks about it the President said, "The war against global *terror* will be hard and long"). The phrases have been used interchangeably, but they have a different connotation relevant to the process of internalization. "Terrorist" and "terrorism" suggest a specific actor and action, while "terror" conveys a condition, an ideologically laden term often contrasted with "freedom" or "civilization." Moreover, a war on *terror* fashions itself as a war against fear, a more global condition that affords wide latitude in defining "enemies" and justifying tactics. Thus, I would argue that a preference for "terror" by journalists suggests a naturalization of the frame over time.

Over the period it was clear that the administration had been successful in framing the response to 9/11 in a way that successfully enlisted public opinion, with no clear competing frame. During this time Entman (2003) proposed a "cascading activation" model that assumed the administration's success in dominating the public discourse, examining how various "counter-framing" emphases (war with Iraq vs. war with Saudi Arabia) were challenged or not by influential journalists such as Thomas Friedman and Seymour Hersh. My own preference, however, was to see how the entire macroframe was absorbed by the press. So after this extensive exposure to news texts, my primary question was still rooted at the professional level: to what extent did U.S. journalists absorb the administration's framing and take for granted the policy, which should rightly have been contested? Given the debacle of the war in Iraq that unfolded even as I had been thinking about this framing issue, one of the key areas for fault-finding was a compliant press corps. The question for me became how this happened within a framing context, and how the communication of the War on Terror could reveal a crucial aspect of the press's role in the process.

Taking an inductive approach, I began to more systematically examine coverage by identifying a sample of news texts from *USA Today*, which I took to be a representative national news organization, that contained as the sampling unit the various combinations of War on/against Terror(ism), whether mentioned in headline or main text (N=226), selected from the middle full week of each month of the period. The main time period of interest lay between the attacks of 9/11 and the 3-year anniversary of the beginning of the Iraq war in the first quarter of 2006. This period encompasses the declaration by President Bush of the "War on Terrorism," Afghanistan, and the most controversial expression of that policy—the Iraq invasion and its aftermath. I assume here that the entire discourse was relevant, so I didn't make any distinctions between editorials or news articles when selecting the excerpts. Here the unit of analysis was the excerpt rather than the entire article, based on my view that frames are embedded across a body of discourse and speakers, rather than cleanly identified within a single article.

In examining such excerpts I've found that some kind of electronic tool is helpful to keep track of the analysis and classification, especially when the amount of content is large. This time I used a software application called Tinderbox, an organizer for "notes, plans, and ideas," which allowed me to retain the original electronic full text of the news item, highlight the excerpt containing the target phrase, and then link those excerpts to categories as they developed. Throughout the analysis it was helpful to be able to quickly refer back to the original article for context in deciding how to evaluate the particular excerpts. Lists of journalists could also be kept with quick reference to one or all of their articles.

I made the assumption that a mention of the War on Terror signaled an engagement with the administration framing, a framing that had already been well established in the policy documents and speeches. Given my research question, I was particularly concerned about how journalists handled the frame, and what indications that could provide about their own internalization of the organizing principle. As I reviewed the 226 excerpts selected from the middle full week of each month of the period, some patterns began to emerge and I tagged them electronically into several working categories. Later, I consolidated these categories into: transmission, reification, and naturalization. A fuller description and analysis of these is found in Reese and Lewis (2009)

In my reading I tried to keep in mind what was journalistically realistic. A number of articles referred to the War on Terror because that was what Bush called it, and it would have been awkward to call it anything else. Critics now may refer to the so-called War on Terror, but this distancing from administration terminology cuts against the objectivity norm. So, "transmission" was indicated when the frame was passed along as a reasonable proxy description of the policy itself, and about half the excerpts were in that category. Here are two examples:

> In his State of the Union address, President Bush made clear that "the war on terrorism is only beginning." (Deats, 2002, p. A11)

> Bush asked for support from wavering Democrats and vowed to prosecute the war on terror. (Page, 2004, p. A1)

"Reification" was indicated when the excerpt seemed to treat a contested policy as a material fact. Beyond simple transmission, the usage in many instances became uncritically routine, with the frame and its underlying assumptions taken for granted. The newspaper editorial grouping of stories under the heading "War on Terror," or as *USA Today* might do, "What Happened Wednesday in the War against Terrorism," exemplifies this kind of handling: "It's a touchy topic because Bush advisers don't want people to think he's coasting while the war on terrorism and economic jitters continue" (Keen, 2002a, p. A4).

Echoing the television graphics of "America strikes back," the more muted print response was still to turn Bush's policy into "America's" policy, another aspect of this reification. Two examples:

> The two nations need much from each other. The United States needs Russia's oil, its help in the war on terror and its support in curbing nuclear ambitions in Iran and North Korea. (Dorell, 2005, p. A5)

> Intelligence is one of America's most important tools in the global war on terror. (Di Rita, 2005, p. A12)

Journalists naturally follow a "horserace" angle when covering politics, a tendency that allows them to insert themselves into the story without appearing biased. In the case of the War on Terror, the organizing principle often appeared taken for granted as news reports proceeded to consider who could exploit the policy with greatest success. Republican frame sponsors, of course, considered that it favored their interests (as they continue to do).[4] For example,

> Bush advisers say *his stewardship of the* War on terrorism *will help GOP candidates* [italics added], and he mentions it in each speech. (Keen, 2002b, p. A10)

Later these attributions seem to drop by the wayside as the idea became absorbed into the "common wisdom." Following are four examples:

> To some degree, *Republicans will benefit* [italics added] from the president's association with the War on terrorism. (Shapiro, 2002, p. A14)

> Crowd reactions to President Bush's new campaign speech provide more evidence that *his management of the* War on terrorism *is his best political asset* [italics added]. (Keen, 2004, p. A5)

> *Bush's popularity is rooted in the* War on terrorism [italics added]. He is the commander in chief leading the assault on the forces that traumatized us on 9/11. (Wickham, 2003, p. A15)

> Even Defense Secretary Donald Rumsfeld, who *has gotten high marks for leading the* War on terrorism [italics added], faced criticism before then for alienating generals, defense contractors and members of Congress because of the way he put together a defense overhaul plan. (Page, 2002a, p. B1)

Bush has emphasized a moral dimension of the War on Terror (Spiel-vogel, 2005), with his "steadfastness" by definition becoming a measure of its success. News reports seemed to have internalized this advantage:

> Bush succeeded in his first term when *he displayed his strong con-victions and acted decisively* [italics added]—as he did after the 9/11 attacks in launching the war on terrorism. (Gannon, 2005, p. A15)

> Some Democrats have suggested that the Bush administration is play-ing politics with the threats to bump Democratic presidential nomi-nee John Kerry from the headlines and boost *Bush, who is viewed as a strong leader in the war against terrorism* [italics added]. Are they right? (Hall, 2004, p. A10)

Vice President Cheney's so-called "one percent doctrine" argued that U.S. action was justified given even a minute chance of danger to the nation (Suskind, 2006). By that logic, the absence of terrorism would seem to vindicate any action taken prior to that absence, a fallacious post hoc reasoning mirrored in the following analysis provided for "context."

> Context: The war on terrorism remains a success for the Bush administration by its most basic measure: The United States has not been attacked since 9/11. (Dorell, Drinkard, Kiely, Kirchhoff, & Ko, 2006, p. A7)

Another form of reification lay in what I originally regarded as a sepa-rate "execution" frame: the tendency, especially among election candi-dates, to compete on who could be the toughest prosecutor of the War on Terror.

> Democratic presidential nominee John Kerry said Monday that Pres-ident Bush has dragged his feet in the war against terror and failed to make America as safe as it could be since the Sept. 11 attacks. "I believe I can fight a more effective, more thoughtful, more strategic, more proactive, more sensitive war on terror" than Bush, he said. (Lawrence, 2004, p. A2)

Bush, of course, was only too happy to oblige, given that Kerry was playing within his definitional boundaries.

> Our biggest difference is found in our approach to the war on terror. I will always make America's security my top priority. Sen. Kerry would be satisfied if terrorism were just a "nuisance." (Bush, 2004b, p. A17)

These are not journalists directly making these statements; rather, they are only reflecting what the candidates themselves said. So, execution seems to be better regarded as an aspect of the reification process. Given that news media track, or "index" (Bennett, Lawrence, & Livingston, 2006) the partisan campaign discourse, the absence of a viable counterframe from the Democrats meant that the War on Terror was reified through the balance routine, reinforcing the notion that the only decision on the table was how to be most effective.

Surveys of public opinion struck me early on as an example of reification in that they took a clearly problematic concept and turned it into an unproblematic subject for polling. In 2002, for example, a Pew Center survey reported that the public "continues to be disposed to use military force in the war on terrorism" (cited in Hess & Kalb, 2003, p. 262). In a circular process, the issue is defined by administration labeling, the public asked to respond to it, and the predictable results fed back to the country through the media as accepted wisdom. In constructing the poll questions, the language of "war" itself becomes a given with predictably favorable effect on opinions about its militarization. Journalists further confirm this when they reproduce these results through reification: "Mr. Bush has consistently received a much higher public trust rating on the war on terror than the Democrats" (Luce, 2006, p. 11).

The most obvious form of internalization that I sought was the frame at its most embedded. In ideological analysis, this process is suggested by the concept of naturalization, in which the War on Terror was no longer policy but "way of life." These expressions were often found in "analysis" or other nonbreaking news commentaries, where it seemed the frame had become the institutional common sense:

Our view: Even after deadly surprises of Sept. 11, convention reigns. From the opening salvo of airliners assaulting buildings to anthrax attacks that come in the mail, the war on terrorism has proved to be one of unexpected turns. (USA Today, Editorial, 2001)

Bush can change that course simply by reverting to the policies of earlier Republican administrations, notably his father's. If that gets in the way of smaller party agendas, so what? The war on terror is the top priority. (USA Today, News Analysis, 2004b, p. A26)

Bin Laden showed new strengths and fallibilities in his tape. They revealed, too, the antidote: determination in the war on terror. That begins with hunting down bin Laden, but it also includes much more. (USA Today, Editorial, 2004a, p. A20)

Others like George Lakoff (2002) and Pancake (1993) have examined how often military conflict is likened to natural events (e.g., "Desert Storm"), so I was looking for expressions of this literal "naturalization." Bush himself had encouraged this by depicting the War on Terror in terms of natural events, claiming that "We do not know the day of final victory, but we have seen the turning of the *tide*" (Bush, 2003, p. A2). Like a force of nature, it just "happened" to us (on 9/11). Indeed, after Hurricane Katrina, Bush couldn't resist trying to link that natural disaster to the War on Terror, suggesting that America's enemies were pleased to see the devastation (Sanger, 2005)![5] In this respect, likening the War on Terror to an "event" (natural or otherwise) seemed another way to naturalize it, by taking a political policy over which there should be debate and likening it to an event over which there is little public input and control.

> A *series of raw events* [italics added], including the economic downturn, "the elusive War on terrorism, the impending war against Iraq and now the shuttle accident" are a challenge to a nation "grown comfortable with predictability, prosperity and superficiality," he said. (Grossman, 2003, p. A5)

Other references suggested that how long the War on Terror lasts was something beyond our control. Like a natural event, it lasts as long as it lasts. Excerpts like the following pose the question as a matter of duration, a formulation that left no one in charge.

> The economic impact of the War on terrorism *will depend on how long it lasts*, [italics added] how much it costs and whether it slows the trend toward globalization. If this war continues for years, as President Bush warns it will, analysts say it could have the most far-reaching effects on the U.S. economy of any event since World War II. (Page, 2002b, p. A4)

## Journalists and the War on Terror

My original sense, following the AP data trends, was that journalists would follow a stage model, handling the frame objectively early on but over time absorbing it more completely. There were fewer of these "naturalization" references than I had expected, and they did not necessarily fall toward the end of the period. But the "organizing principle" definition of framing suggests that these structures can be manifested in a number of ways, not just as embedded in news texts, which led me to want to corroborate these results with another source. With a background in journalism education, I've spoken to a number of professionals as a "reality-check" about my concerns about media handling of the War on Terror. I'm reluctant to attribute explanations for their behavior based solely on their work (a frequent academic tendency, given the easy availability of electronic news retrieval systems). At the same time, their ability to reflect on why they do what they do is often limited by their time and perspective. Journalists are among the most closely scrutinized professionals, and they naturally become defensive when second-guessed about press failings. Nevertheless, I thought it was important to have their views as further evidence for the internalization hypothesis.

Seth Lewis and I identified from their bylines several of the journalists behind the articles in our sample, eventually interviewing 13 of them in a semistructured interview format by phone. In spite of the number of requests they must receive, we got a surprising response from an initial e-mail identifying ourselves and requesting an opportunity to speak with them. The challenge was to find words to describe the project without unduly influencing their responses, or provoking an automatic professional defense mechanism. Here's how I prefaced our interview request:

> I've been taking a look recently at how issues surrounding 9/11, Afghanistan and Iraq have been covered in the press, specifically how post-9/11 security policy has been characterized in the print media. The focus is on a broad sample of reporting at the national level, including the Associated Press and *USA Today*. Academics often stop at just reading news articles, so I wanted if possible to go directly to the source and get your insight about the subject.... We both have already done a thorough review of news articles on these issues spanning the last six years. So, at this point we are following up by getting journalists' reflections on their reporting, now with the benefit of hindsight.

Asking someone to reflect on work from several years previous has its own problems, but where necessary we could read back their phrasing and ask for their thinking at the time. There's a balance in interviews with expert respondents between essentially trying out one's hypothesis and using their responses as evidence for it. We said we were particularly interested in the War on Terror and we asked what they thought people meant by the phrase, what qualms they may have about it, and whether the administration and media were more or less talking about the same thing when using it. A fuller analysis of the interview results is described in Lewis and Reese (2009).

Given their status as professionals at one of the nation's top news organizations, these were thoughtful and often self-critical respondents. They recognized that the War on Terror had become something of a cliché, politicized, and propagandistic, which does not seem like a group that has internalized an administration framing. One noted that the War on Terror was the wording of Bush, and therefore would likely be used in that context. This was supported by the number of transmission-style excerpts in *USA Today*. On the other hand, numerous other examples (including references continuing to the present day in elite publications such as the *New York Times*), show otherwise, indicating that it has become disassociated from the frame sponsor. Closer examination of their responses suggested, however, that they objected primarily to the frame having been invoked to invade Iraq, and that objection came after the fact, as suggested by the following response:

> I think there would be more of a reluctance [on the part of the press] to extend it to that war (Iraq) because the linkages are not as clear.

Another journalist was more specific:

> I think some press aren't using that phrase anymore, or are using it less. They've become more sensitive to it, especially since the revelations that have come out about the reasons for going to war.... The administration tries to confuse people and just lumps Iraq and Afghanistan and 9/11 and everything else in the same package, and I don't necessarily think they go together.

Thus, the phrase proved to be context-dependent, with a meaning that shifted over time, as a third journalist indicated:

> So, I don't think it has one meaning. It has an infinite number of meanings, and that only serves to confuse people.... It's all in the context of what they're saying. It can mean very different things.... It's sort of thrown out there and left for the audience to interpret what they mean by that.

This sense that "we all know what we mean" when we say the War on Terror, that it means what we want it to mean, speaks to the embedded quality of the frame, that it has passed into the realm of being regarded as common sense and is taken for granted. Occasionally, one can find deconstructions of the frame in the mainstream press, but these are rare.[6] The War on Terror was accepted from the beginning, with its weakness as an organizing principle revealed primarily with respect to Iraq—but that was only after it became recognized as a foreign policy debacle.

I don't provide further analysis of these interviews here, but for me their main value was to show some of the professional context of the internalization process. To the extent that the frame has been undermined in recent years, post-Iraq, underscores the extent to which it was accepted uncritically in the early days post 9/11. Frame contestation in this case was not a linear process of slowly winning over the news media and public, progressing from transmission to reification and naturalization. Each of these processes was going on throughout the period. Here was a case where the country was immediately caught up in a particularly compelling macrolevel organizing principle, and the discourse that followed took place within those boundaries. Given their professional constraints, journalists were ill-equipped to mount their own frame challenge when the opposition party gave them little to index, when they emphasized horse-race style strategy flowing from the frame, and when they themselves felt obliged to transmit and amplify the framing they already implicitly accepted as a way of viewing the world.

## Summary

Within the framing project one could approach the War on Terror from a number of different directions. In this case, taking the frame as a cultural "structure of meaning" leads to examining the network of concepts and underlying narrative that gives it power as an organizing principle—which has worked to shape profoundly U.S. foreign policy. Militarizing the policy response and drawing on definitions of terrorism cast as a threat to the status quo, and with a benign view of state-sponsored violence, has warped our ability to think clearly about the real problem. But how has this frame been propagated by the U.S. press? To answer that question has meant taking a close look at the construction of the frame and how journalists participated in this process, not as a passive recipient (as the critical paradigm might suggest). This construction is seen in specific content, but also in the surrounding cultural context of social values and professional norms to which it must be connected (a construction I still can regard in a critical context). The frame that eventually works to affect public opinion, invoking and altering certain values hierarchies, must be created. The what of the frame must be understood before the how of its effectivity on citizens. In between, it must be processed through institutional machinery, and that's where another "how" question comes in: the professional context of journalism. In examining news texts and asking journalists themselves to articulate their own understandings about those texts, I hoped to triangulate an understanding of cultural framing—how journalists participate in the construction of the War on Terror.

Taking a more qualitative and interpretive approach can be difficult when it appears that definite categories are not immediately presenting themselves and no easy coding scheme into which textual units can be sorted is evident. But in sifting through texts and allowing these insights to emerge, the subtle power of large macroframes can be discerned. For me, that's where frames get interesting—the "in such a way" aspect of their internal structure. For such an important issue, which has filled the media for years with commentaries and investigations, an interpretive framing study of the War on Terror makes a stimulating way to merge the public debate with scholarly questions. For such issues, the news is always full of grist for the mill, and the research task takes on a journalistic style in trying to get to the bottom of a story. But the academic task is to be systematic and provide the careful analysis not available elsewhere. Stepping back with that kind of imagination is all the more important when it seems the entire society is captive to the power of a deeply embedded organizing principle.

## Notes

1. Various phrases have been used in this context, including the "war on terrorism," the "war against terror," and the "war on terror." Henceforth, the capitalized "War on Terror" will be used when referring to the frame itself and otherwise a lower-case "war on terror(ism)" when quoted or paraphrased in its use by others.
2. Suggesting something of what concerned me about journalists, the op-ed editor changed the headline of my piece from "Framing the War on Terror" to "Framing Our Country's War on Terrorism."
3. Based on Smith's (2005) cultural sociology perspective, I would argue that the War on Terror approximates his most extreme genre, "apocalyptic," which pushes the good and bad guys to their most divergent and, according to him is the only narrative capable of mobilizing mass support for warfare by making it culturally acceptable.
4. In the 2008 presidential race, an official in the McCain campaign claimed that a terrorist attack would benefit McCain, an assumption with clear ties to Bush's success in framing terrorism to the advantage of Republicans.
5. Echoing this force-of-nature perspective, White House adviser Karl Rove said of the War on Terror: "We didn't welcome it, we didn't want it, but it came" (Kelly, 2004).
6. A number of articles have revealed the internal struggles within the administration over terminology (e.g., Stevenson, 2005). In the summer of 2005, reporters noticed the administration's transition in the "catchphrase," quoting officials as saying the slogan had outlived its usefulness by overemphasizing military response. Instead, the plan was to introduce a more positive alternative of democracy and freedom, while, in the words of Defense Department spokesman Lawrence Di Rita, denying that it represented a "shift in thinking, but a continuation of the immediate post-9/11 approach" (Schmitt & Shanker, 2005). In fact, the alternative, "global struggle against violent extremism," was still cast by Defense Secretary Donald Rumsfeld as an apocalyptic conflict "against the enemies of freedom, the enemies of civilization." Not long afterwards, however, Bush reasserted his preferred label cast in military terms, repudiating any notion that the policy had changed: "We're at war with an enemy that attacked us on Sept. 11, 2001" (Stevenson, 2005).

# References

Armstrong, D. (2002, October). Dick Cheney's song of America: Drafting a plan of global dominance. *Harper's, 305*, 76–83.

Benford, R., & Snow, D. (2000). Framing processes and social movements: An overview and assessment. *Annual Review of Sociology, 26*, 611–639.

Bennett, W. L., Lawrence, R., & Livingston, S. (2006). None dare call it torture: Indexing and the limits of press independence in the Abu Ghraib scandal. *Journal of Communication, 56*(3), 467–485.

Bush, G. W. (2003, May 2). Bush: "Enemies of freedom are not idle, and neither are we." *USA Today*, p. A2.

Bush, G. W. (2004a, April 14). President Bush's opening statement on Iraq. *New York Times*, p. A11.

Bush, G. W. (2004b, November 2). Why you should vote for me today. *USA Today*, p. A17.

Cappella, J., & Jamieson, K. (1997). *Spiral of cynicism: The press and the public good*. New York: Oxford University Press.

Carragee, K. M., & Roefs, W. (2004). The neglect of power in recent framing research. *Journal of Communication, 54*(2), 214–233.

Christie, T. B. (2006). Framing rationale for the Iraq War: The interaction of public support with mass media and public policy agendas. *International Communication Gazette, 68*(5–6), 519–532.

D'Angelo, P. (2002). News framing as a multiparadigmatic research program: A response to Entman. *Journal of Communication, 52*(4), 870–888.

Deats, R. (2002, February 1). Bush "doctrine" too narrow. *USA Today*, p. A11.

Di Rita, L. (2005, August 5). Don't tie our hands: Congress shouldn't set limits on interrogating captured terrorists. *USA Today*, p. A12.

Dorell, O. (2005, May 5). Bush visit puts focus on concerns over Russia's path. *USA Today*, p. A5.

Dorell, O., Drinkard, J., Kiely, K., Kirchhoff, S., & Ko, S. (2006, February 1). The key points and their context: The State of the Union. *USA Today*, p. A7.

Entman, R. M. (1993). Framing: Toward clarification of a fractured paradigm. *Journal of Communication, 43*(4), 51–58.

Entman, R. M. (2003). Cascading activation: Contesting the White House's frame after 9/11. *Political Communication, 20*(4), 415–432.

Entman, R. M., & Rojecki, A. (1993). Freezing out the public: Elite and media framing of the U.S. anti-nuclear movement. *Political communication, 10*(2), 151–167.

Gamson, W. A. (2001). Foreword. In S. D. Reese, O. H. Gandy, & A. E. Grant (Eds.), *Framing public life: Perspectives on media and our understanding of the social world* (pp. ix–xi). Mahwah, NJ: Erlbaum.

Gamson, W. A., & Modigliani, A. (1989). Media discourse and public opinion on nuclear power: A constructionist approach. *American Journal of Sociology, 95*, 1–37.

Gannon, J. P. (2005, November 3). How Bush can right the ship. *USA Today*, p. A15.

Gordon, M. R., & Trainor, B. E. (2006). *Cobra II: The inside story of the invasion and occupation of Iraq.* New York: Pantheon Books.

Grossman, C. L. (2003, February 3). President draws on the Bible to comfort a grieving nation. *USA Today,* p. A5.

Hackett, R. (1984). Decline of a paradigm? Bias and objectivity in news media studies. *Critical Studies in Mass Communication, 1*(3), 229–259.

Hall, M. (2004, August 5). Questions about terror threat answered. *USA Today,* p. A10.

Hertog, J. K., & McLeod, D. M. (2001). A multiperspectival approach to framing analysis: A field guide. In S. D. Reese, O. H. Gandy, & A. E. Grant (Eds.), *Framing public life: Perspectives on media and our understanding of the social world* (pp. 139–161). Mahwah, NJ: Erlbaum.

Hess, S., & Kalb, M. L. (Eds.). (2003). *The media and the war on terrorism.* Washington, DC: Brookings Institution Press.

Ignatieff, M. (2004, May 2). Lesser evils: What it will cost us to succeed in the war on terror. *New York Times Magazine,* 46–51, 86, 94.

Isikoff, M., & Corn, D. (2006). *Hubris: The inside story of spin, scandal, and the selling of the Iraq War.* New York: Crown.

Keen, J. (2002a, August 1). Bush won't be all play and no work *USA Today,* p. A4.

Keen, J. (2002b, November 4). President's all-out campaigning for GOP a gamble. *USA Today,* p. A10.

Keen, J. (2002c, February 1). Stern Bush repeats warning to "axis." *USA Today,* p. A6.

Keen, J. (2004, August 2). Talk on terrorism draws cheers; Tough stance revs up crowds. *USA Today,* p. A5.

Kelly, M. (2004, May 15). Rove lauds Ill. GOP for voter registration. *The Baltimore Sun,* p. A2.

Lakoff, G. (2002). *Moral politics: How liberals and conservatives think.* Chicago: University of Chicago.

Lakoff, G. (2006). "War on terror," rest in peace. Retrieved from http://www.rockridgeinstitute.org/research/lakoff/gwot_rip

Lawrence, J. (2004, August 3). Kerry criticizes Bush's pace in war on terrorism. *USA Today,* p. A2.

Lewis, S., & Reese, S. D. (2009). What is the War on Terror? Exploring framing through the eyes of journalists. *Journalism & Mass Communication Quarterly, 86*(1), 85–102.

Luce, E. (2006, March 11). How Republicans and Democrats alike are out-Bushing Bush. *The Financial Times,* p. 11.

Lule, J. (2001). *Daily news, eternal stories: The mythological role of journalism.* New York: Guilford Press.

McQuillan, L., & Benedetto, R. (2003, May 2). Bush hails win, looks ahead. *USA Today,* p. A1.

Nacos, B. L. (2002). *Mass-mediated terrorism: The central role of the media in terrorism and counterterrorism.* Lanham, MD: Rowman & Littlefield.

Nelson, T., & Willey, E. (2001). Issue frames that strike a value balance: A political psychology perspective. In S. D. Reese, O. H. Gandy, & A. E. Grant

(Eds.), *Framing public life: Perspectives on media and our understanding of the social world* (pp. 245–266). Mahwah, NJ: Erlbaum.

Norris, P., Kern, M., & Just, M. R. (2003). Framing terrorism. In P. Norris, M. Kern & M. R. Just (Eds.), *Framing terrorism: The news media, the government, and the public* (pp. 3–23). New York: Routledge.

Page, S. (2002a, August 7). Corporate credentials weigh down Bush's team. *USA Today*, p. B1.

Page, S. (2002b, May 3). The new new economy. *USA Today*, p. A4.

Page, S. (2004, November 1). Swing states lean to Kerry; Democrat ties Bush nationally. *USA Today*, p. A1.

Pan, Z., & Kosicki, G. M. (1993). Framing analysis: An approach to news discourse. *Political Communication, 10*(1), 55–75.

Pancake, A. S. (1993). Taken by storm: The exploitation of metaphor in the Persian Gulf War. *Metaphor & Symbolic Activity, 8*, 281–295.

Record, J. (2003). *Bounding the global war on terrorism*. Carlisle, PA: Strategic Studies Institute, U.S. Army War College.

Reese, S. D. (2001). Framing public life: A bridging model for media research. In S. D. Reese, O. H. Gandy, & A. E. Grant (Eds.), *Framing public life: Perspectives on media and our understanding of the social world* (pp. 7–31). Mahwah, NJ: Erlbaum.

Reese, S. D. (2002, December 16). Framing our country's war against terrorism. *Austin American-Statesman*, p. A13.

Reese, S. D. (2004). Militarized journalism: Framing dissent in the Persian Gulf wars. In S. Allan & B. Zelizer (Eds.), *Reporting war: Journalism in wartime* (pp. 247–265). New York: Routledge.

Reese, S. D. (2007). The framing project: A bridging model for media research revisited. *Journal of Communication, 57*(1), 148–154.

Reese, S. D. (2008). Media production and content. In W. Donsbach (Ed.), *International encyclopedia of communication* (pp. 2982–2994). Malden, MA: Blackwell.

Reese, S. D., & Buckalew, B. (1995). The militarism of local television: The routine framing of the Persian Gulf War. *Critical Studies in Mass Communication, 12*(1), 40–59.

Reese, S. D., & Lewis, S. (2009). Framing the War on Terror: Internalization of policy by the U.S. press. *Journalism: Theory, Practice, Criticism, 10*(6).

Ricks, T. E. (2006). *Fiasco: The American military adventure in Iraq*. New York: Penguin Press.

Rojecki, A. (2005). Media discourse on globalization and terror. *Political Communication, 22*(1), 63–81.

Sanger, D. E. (2005, September 22). Bush compares responses to hurricane and terrorism. *New York Times*, p. A24.

Schmitt, E., & Shanker, T. (2005, July 25). New name for "war on terror" reflects wider U.S. campaign. *New York Times*, p. A7.

Shapiro, W. (2002, November 1). Democrats may have edge, but it won't be a sharp one. *USA Today*, p. A14.

Smith, P. (2005). *Why war? The cultural logic of Iraq, the Gulf War, and Suez*. Chicago: University of Chicago Press.

Snow, D., & Benford, R. (1988). Ideology, frame resonance, and participant mobilization. *International Social Movement Research, 1*, 197–217.

Spielvogel, C. (2005). "You know where I stand": Moral framing of the war on terrorism and the Iraq War in the 2004 presidential campaign. *Rhetoric & Public Affairs, 8*(4), 549–569.

Stevenson, R. W. (2004, March 20). President, marking anniversary of war, urges world to unite to combat terrorism. *New York Times*, p. A7.

Stevenson, R. W. (2005, August 4). President makes it clear: Phrase is "war on terror." *New York Times*, p. A12.

Suskind, R. (2006). *The one percent doctrine: Deep inside America's pursuit of its enemies since 9/11.* New York: Simon & Schuster.

Tankard, J. W. (2001). The empirical approach to the study of media framing. In S. D. Reese, O. H. Gandy, & A. E. Grant (Eds.), *Framing public life: Perspectives on media and our understanding of the social world* (pp. 95–106). Mahwah, NJ: Erlbaum.

Tuchman, G. (1978). *Making news: A study in the construction of reality.* New York: Free Press.

*USA Today.* (2001, November 5). [Editorial] Defense plan doesn't adapt to new face of war. *USA Today*, p. A14.

*USA Today.* (2004a, November 1). [Editorial] Bin Laden's message. *USA Today*, p. A20.

*USA Today.* (2004b, November 4). [News Analysis] GOP challenge: Small wins or enduring dominance. *USA Today*, p. A26.

The White House. (2003). *National strategy for combating terrorism.* Washington, DC: Government Printing Office.

The White House. (2006). *National security strategy of the United States of America.* Washington, DC: Government Printing Office.

Wickham, D. (2003, May 6). Democratic herd needs culling. *USA Today*, p. A15.

Wilgoren, J., & Nagourney, A. (2003, April 8). While mourning dead, many Americans say level of casualties is acceptable. *New York Times*, p. B1.

Zaller, J. (1992). *The nature and origins of mass opinion.* New York: Cambridge University Press.

# Chapter 3

# Knowledge Into Action
## Framing the Debates Over Climate Change and Poverty

*Matthew C. Nisbet*

In February 2008, I appeared on a panel about news coverage of climate change at the meetings of the American Association for the Advancement of Science (AAAS). Close to 300 attendees packed the convention hall, including journalists, scientists, and science policy advocates. The sense of urgency in the room was electric. Historically, these groups have played separate, though complementary communication roles, but on climate change traditional boundaries no longer appeared to apply. Regardless of their professional background, the great majority of attendees wanted to understand how to use the media to motivate and empower citizens to actively participate in policy debates over climate change.

Yet despite this common purpose, most of the discussion focused on a well-intentioned but incomplete strategy for achieving this shared communication goal. Journalists, scientists, and advocates alike defined the way forward as "covering the science of climate change better" and "getting more coverage of climate science" out to the public. If the public only better understood the science of climate change, reasoned many attendees, then they would view the urgency of the problem as experts do. As I explain in this chapter, this misplaced line of thinking was unfortunately predictable, deriving from decades-old false assumptions among journalists, advocates, and scientists about how to effectively engage the public on pressing social problems.

As limited as climate change communication assumptions might be, the debate over how to effectively engage the public on solutions to domestic poverty borders on the divisive. In fact, even the label *poverty*, used as a collective umbrella term to refer to issues related to income disparity, low wage work, and quality jobs, remains contested. Moreover, the stories and meanings that many journalists and advocates believe are effective at building public concern and consensus—what has been called a "sympathy for the poor" frame—may actually reinforce harmful stereotypes and false beliefs.

Almost a year before the AAAS meeting, in the spring of 2007, I was invited to participate in a roundtable discussion at the Brookings Institution in Washington, DC, on the use of documentary film campaigns to mobilize the public around complex policy problems.[1] After the meeting, I was approached by Margy Waller, director of the nonpartisan Mobility Agenda. In her work, Waller had been drawing upon framing research to communicate about poverty in new ways. Yet while she often discovered a receptive audience for these innovative strategies among state-level and community-based groups, in the nation's capital she found that major advocacy coalitions were still locked in a decades-old language of "poverty." Hoping to shape this internal struggle among progressive organizations over communication strategy, Waller commissioned me to author an analysis of how framing research can be applied to the topic.

This chapter is intended as a primer for practitioners—journalists, experts, or advocates—who wish to understand what it takes to break through the perceptual paralysis that plagues complex policy problems. Drawing on insights from my research and experience working with a variety of organizations, experts, and journalists, my goal is to translate past research on framing and media influence into meaningful communication principles, using the case studies of climate change and poverty as examples.

My recommendations in this chapter derive from a fairly basic premise: To overcome the communication barriers of human nature, partisan identity, and media fragmentation requires tailoring messages to a specific medium and audience, using carefully researched metaphors, allusions, and examples that trigger a new way of thinking about the personal relevance of a gridlocked problem. Whether it is climate change, poverty, or another issue, the public and policymakers require frameworks for connecting the dots on otherwise apparently isolated events, trends, and policy solutions. Applying research on framing to help individuals and groups see clearly the linkages between their everyday lives, their specific values, and these problems is by no means a magical key to catalyzing action, but it is a first step. This chapter offers a few modest ways forward.

## Why Framing Matters

As I review in this chapter, framing is an unavoidable reality of the public communication process. The choice as a journalist, expert, or advocate is not whether to employ framing, but rather how to effectively frame a message for your audience. From many conversations and talks on the topic, I know that some journalists and experts are likely to read the recommendations in this chapter and dismiss them as out of bounds, preferring to follow perceived traditions of "objectivity," "impartiality," and "neutrality." Though the meaning and usefulness of these norms have always been debated, they are perhaps even more challenged in today's world, where pressing problems such as climate change are decided within a dramatically different media and political landscape from just a decade ago.

While traditionalists among journalists and experts may be slow to apply lessons from framing research, an avant-garde among these groups are pushing ahead with innovative approaches. Confronted by a profusion of think tanks and disinformation campaigns, many journalists are actively seeking ways to move beyond the trap of "false balance," even if it cuts against conventional definitions of objectivity or independence (Cunningham, 2003; Mooney, 2004). This shift has occurred in part out of professional necessity, as many veteran reporters have been forced to leave their jobs at major news organizations while early career journalists encounter limited job prospects (Russell, 2006). As an alternative career path, some journalists have joined with universities or foundations to forge a new brand of not-for-profit journalism where reporting and commentary merge in outlets such as blogs, interactive Web sites, books, and documentary films. The focus at these outlets is not only to inform but also to alert and mobilize the public, with media produced in collaboration with scientists, experts, and nonpartisan advocacy groups (Brainard, 2008; Lewis, 2007). In other initiatives, leading organizations, such as the National Academies, have already put framing theory and principles into practice, commissioning audience research to inform the framing of their background materials and public outreach on the teaching of evolution in schools (Nisbet, 2009a).

Of course, if research on framing is transformed into a communication technology and strategy, it needs to be used responsibly. Journalists, experts, and advocates alike must respect the uncertainty that is inherent to any technical question and resist engaging in hyperbole or offering concrete answers when there are none. If these groups stray from accurately conveying what is conventionally known about an issue, they risk losing public trust. Moreover, if framing appears to serve overtly partisan purposes, then there is the risk that expertise will be quickly and easily reinterpreted by the public through partisan lenses. The result will be increased polarization rather than increased engagement.

Finally, journalists, experts, and advocates are not the only ones who struggle with the nature and application of framing research: Scholars remain challenged by the many strands of theorizing and approaches. This is not surprising given that the process of framing is frustratingly subjective and therefore difficult to map out and measure. Many framing studies are just poorly done: either they are conceptually and operationally weak or they fail to offer enough of a context for the issue analyzed.

In other cases, solid research is not packaged in a way that is professionally relevant or that gains notice.

Scholars also have a tendency to "reinvent the wheel" in identifying and labeling the frames that exist in any debate. Not only does this lead to a troubling level of inconsistency in understanding the nature of disputes in a policy sector such as science, the environment, or social policy, but it also leads to major differences in the measurement of media trends and in the observation of any influences. Scholars often overlook that in each policy sector, there is likely to exist a generalizable typology of latent meanings that are directly applicable to understanding a specific issue or major event. In the section on climate change, one of my chief goals is to show how an existing typology developed to explain debates over nuclear energy and biotechnology can also be used to explain the specific communication dynamics of what many experts consider to be the most pressing problem of our generation.

## What is News Framing?

My description of past work has been sharpened by way of my experience translating this research for nonspecialists, including journalists, scientists, policy advocates, and communication strategists. Over the past 3 years, I have also engaged in many debates over these themes at my blog[2] and in dozens of talks at various universities and interdisciplinary meetings.[3]

The concept of framing turns on what observers have understood for centuries: in storytelling, communicators can select from a plurality of interpretations. The storyteller's preferred meanings are filtered by the predispositions of the audience, which, in turn, shape their judgments and decisions. The origin of framing research in the study of communication is commonly attributed to the work of Erving Goffman (1974). In his ethnographic research that examined how individuals make sense of their environment and interpersonal interactions, he described frames as "schemata of interpretation" that allow individuals to locate, perceive, identify, and label issues, events, and topics. Words, according to Goffman, are like triggers that help individuals negotiate meaning through the lens of existing cultural beliefs and worldviews.

Attesting to the various intellectual roots of framing research, in the 1970s and 1980s, cognitive psychologists Daniel Kahneman and Amos Tversky applied framing in experimental designs to understand risk judgments and consumer choices (cf. Kahneman & Tversky, 1979). They concluded in their Nobel Prize-winning research that perception is reference dependent. If individuals are given an ambiguous or uncertain situation to consider, the different ways in which a message is presented or framed can result in very different responses, depending on the terminology used to describe the problem or the visual context provided in the message. (For many members of the public, as I will discuss later, given its complexity and creeping nature, climate change is likely to be the ultimate ambiguous situation.)

The now classic definition of a frame by the sociologist William Gamson and colleagues—a frame organizes central ideas on an issue—places framing research more squarely within the realm of news discourse and audience reception. According to Gamson and Modigliani (1989), frames endow certain dimensions of a complex topic with greater apparent relevance than the same dimensions might appear to have under an alternative frame. Frames are used by audiences as "interpretative schema" to make sense of and discuss an issue; by journalists to condense complex events into interesting and appealing news reports; by policy-makers to define policy options and reach decisions; and by experts to communicate to other experts or to broader audiences (Nisbet, 2009a; Scheufele, 1999). In each of these contexts, frames simplify complex issues by lending greater importance or weight to certain considerations and arguments over others. In the process, they help communicate why an issue matters; how it can be differently defined; who or what might be responsible for problems associated with the issue; and what should be done about these problems (Entman, 1993; Ferree, Gamson, Gerhards, & Rucht, 2002).

### How Does News Framing Work?

In terms of psychological accounts of the influence of news framing, Price and Tewksbury's (1997) applicability model argues that a message frame is only effective if it is relevant—or "applicable"—to a specific existing interpretive schema acquired through socialization processes or other types of social learning. Put another way, frames appearing in the media or as part of communication campaigns are most influential when they resonate with an audience's strongly held "perceptual lenses," which typically mean strong feelings about another issue suddenly made relevant, or with value constructs such as religious beliefs, political partisanship, or ideology.

Media frames work by connecting the mental dots for the public. They suggest a connection between two concepts, issues, or things, such that after exposure to the framed message, audiences accept or are at least aware of the connection. An issue has been successfully framed when there is a fit between the line of reasoning a message or news story suggests on an issue and the presence of those existing mental associations within a particular audience (Scheufele & Tewksbury, 2007). For example, as I will review in the section on climate change, by emphasizing the religious and moral dimensions of the issue, several scientists have convinced religious leaders that understanding the science of climate change is directly applicable to questions of faith. Moreover, books and news stories that emphasize these religious dimensions have captured attention from religious audiences, readers who might not otherwise pay attention to environmental issues if framed in more traditional ways.

Alternatively, if a frame draws connections that are not relevant to something a segment of the public already values or understands, then the message is likely to be ignored or to lack personal significance. For example, as later reviewed, climate change advocates compare distortion of climate science to the George W. Bush administration's misuse of evidence in making the case to go to war against Iraq, or in formulating policy on stem cell research. Among liberals and science enthusiasts, this connection activates negative emotions, yet for many Americans the frame either cuts against their partisan leanings, and is therefore likely to be rejected, or does not hold strong personal significance, ignored as inside-the-beltway bickering.

Complementing these psychological accounts, sociologists such as William Gamson have promoted a "constructionist" explanation of news framing. According to this research, in order to make sense of political issues, citizens use as resources the frames available in media coverage, but integrate these packages with the frames forged by way of personal experience or conversations with others. Media frames might help set the terms of the debate among citizens, but rarely, if ever, do they exclusively determine public opinion. Instead, as part of a "frame contest," one interpretative package might gain influence because it resonates with popular culture or a series of events, fits with media routines or practices, or is heavily sponsored by elites (Gamson, 1992; Price, Nir, & Cappella, 2005).

As Pan and Kosicki (2005) concluded, the social constructivist approach to framing also highlights that "effects do not occur without citizens' active mental engagement and that their susceptibility to framing influences do not make them ignorant dupes" (p. 191).[4] Many members of the public hold their own applicable lay theories based on personal experience, culture, or conventional wisdom. In combination with media coverage, these lay theories enable people to reason and talk about a complex policy issue in their own familiar terms. This allows citizens to participate in a "bottom up" framing of issues. Grassroots social movements, for example, use frames to mobilize members and connect groups into advocacy coalitions (see Croteau, Hoynes, & Ryan, 2005, for an overview). With new forms of user-centered and user-controlled digital media such as blogs, online video, and social media sites, "bottom up" alternative frames may be gaining greater influence in the discursive contest that surrounds issues such as climate change and poverty. I return to the implications of this important new trend in user-centered digital media in the conclusion to this chapter.

### The Anatomy of Frames: From Events and Sources to News

Before moving to specific case studies, a few more key details need to be covered. First, the identification and application of frames as general organizing devices—whether as shaping the meaning of advocacy campaigns or a news story—should not be confused with specific policy positions. As Gamson and his colleagues describe, individuals can disagree on an issue but share the same interpretative frame (cf. Gamson & Modigliani, 1989), which means that any frame can include pro, anti, and neutral arguments (see Ferree et al., 2002; Tankard, 2001). For example, as will be reviewed, though some conservatives have used the economic consequences frame to oppose action on climate change, many environmental advocates now seek to turn this interpretation in their favor by emphasizing instead the opportunity to revitalize the economy through investment in clean energy technology.

Consider as an alternative example the debate over embryonic stem cell research, which I have reviewed in other research (Nisbet, Brossard, & Kroepsch, 2003; Nisbet & Scheufele, 2007). A dominant frame is that the debate is really a question of "morality/ethics." Both sides use this frame to argue their case in the debate. Research opponents say it is morally wrong to destroy embryos, since they constitute human life. Research supporters say it is morally wrong to hold back on research that could lead to important cures. Or alternatively, think about the debate over gay marriage. Both sides often argue their position via the interpretative lens of "fairness and equality." Many progressives demand that gay couples receive equal legal status and benefits, whereas many conservative opponents question why gay couples should be granted "special rights" (Price et al., 2005).

Second, the latent meaning of any frame is often translated instantaneously by specific types of framing devices such as catchphrases, metaphors, sound bites, graphics, and allusions to history, culture, or literature (Gamson, 1992). Many studies often confuse frames and frame devices. For example, they might track in news coverage or test in an experiment a slogan such as Al Gore's "climate crisis," but never carefully consider the underlying interpretative meaning ("runaway, impending disaster"), of which the slogan is just one among many possible triggers. We will return to climate change later, but for now, consider just a few prominent and successful examples of such devices that have been used to alter the frame of reference in other policy debates:

Republicans have used the frame device "death tax" to recast estate tax policy in populist terms and to trigger wider public concern.

Democrats have used the phrase "gun safety" to shift the traditional debate over "gun control" away from a focus on civil liberties and instead toward an emphasis on public health.

Greenpeace has used the term "frankenfood" to redefine food bio-technology in terms of unknown risks and consequences rather than the industry-promoted focus on solving world hunger or adapting to climate change.

Religious conservatives have relabeled the medical procedure known as "dilation and extraction" as "partial birth abortion," pushing decision making on whether to use the procedure away from doctors and into the hands of Congress and the courts.

Antismoking advocates have promoted the term "big tobacco," which is a headline-friendly phrase that immediately emphasizes considerations of corporate accountability and wrongdoing.

Antievolutionists have coined the slogan "teach the controversy," which instantaneously signals their preferred interpretation that there are holes in the theory of evolution and that teaching rival explanations for life's origins is really a matter of intellectual freedom.

While pointing out central themes (and several common mistakes) from the literature, my synthesis of the scholarship on news framing, public opinion, and policy influence is by no means comprehensive. Instead, it is meant to establish common ground and a basic framework for understanding the dynamics of the two major case studies covered next, the frame contests over climate change and poverty.

## Failed Strategies, Consistent Meanings

At the opening of this chapter, I described how the attendees at the AAAS panel on climate change communication all shared the uncontroversial goals of boosting public attention to the issue while motivating and empowering citizens to become involved in the policy process. Yet the attendees defined the best way to achieve these goals as "covering the science of climate change better" and "getting more coverage of climate science" out to the public. This decades-old "deficit model" paradigm assumes that when debates over science occur, ignorance is at the root of conflict or public inaction. The goal, then, of public communication is to fill in the "deficit" in knowledge, with the hope that if the public only understood the facts of the science, then they would be more likely to see the issues as experts do. The strategy is to inform the public by way of popular science outlets such as television documentaries, science magazines, newspaper science coverage, and more recently, science Web sites and blogs (Bauer, Allum, & Miller, 2007; Nisbet & Goidel, 2007).

Any failures in this science communication process are blamed on inaccuracies in news coverage and the irrational beliefs of the public. Yet as communication researchers will recognize, this model ignores a number of realities about audiences and how they use the media to make sense of public affairs and policy debates. First, individuals are naturally "cognitive misers" who rely heavily on mental short cuts, values, and emotions to make sense of a science-related issue. These "shortcuts" work in place of paying close attention to news coverage of science debates and in lieu of scientific or policy-related knowledge (see Downs, 1957; Popkin, 1991). Second, as part of this miserly nature, individuals are drawn to news sources that confirm and reinforce their preexisting beliefs. This tendency, of course, has been facilitated by the fragmentation of the media and the rise of ideologically slanted news outlets (Mutz, 2006). Third, in a media environment with many choices, if individuals lack a strong preference or motivation for quality science coverage, then they can completely avoid such content, instead focusing narrowly on their preferred news topics or entertainment and infotainment (Prior, 2005).

As I explained at the AAAS panel, given these challenges and realities, instead of focusing on getting "more of the facts out there," depending on the targeted demographic, information about climate change needs to be repackaged around core ideas and values that resonate with the background of the intended audience while remaining true to the underlying science. As the next section details, the communication challenge for journalists and scientists is to shift climate change from the mental box of "uncertain science," an "unfair economic burden," or a "Pandora's box" of disaster toward a new cognitive and cultural reference point that connects to something the specific intended audience already values or understands. Recent examples include recasting climate change in terms of clean energy and "green collar jobs," redefining the debate as a matter of public health, or emphasizing the issue as a matter of moral and religious duty.

First though, a few more key details about framing need to be explained. Developing a framing strategy on climate change—or in any policy sector—should be approached both deductively and inductively. Drawing on previous work, studies usually work from a set of frames that appear to reoccur across science-related policy debates. Originally identified by sociologists Gamson and Modigliani (1989) in a framing study of nuclear energy, the typology of frames, which include *public accountability* and *progress*, was further adapted in studies of food and medical biotechnology in Europe and the United States (Dahinden, 2002; Durant, Bauer, & Gaskell, 1998; Nisbet & Lewenstein, 2002). In my recent research, I have also been applying this typology to other science-related issues such as the teaching of evolution, climate change, and an updated look at the nuclear energy debate (Nisbet, 2009a, 2009b). Second, after identifying the frames that exist around a specific policy debate and that might resonate with an intended audience, researchers can use focus groups, sophisticated experimental designs, and survey research techniques to specifically test these frames along with the types of frame devices that instantly trigger their underlying meaning.

In Table 3.1, I outline this generalizable typology of frames, defining the latent meanings of each interpretation. These frames consistently appear in science policy debates, though as we will later see in the case of climate change, unique issue-specific frames can also emerge. (With the reader in mind, throughout the next section, references to frames from the typology are italicized and frame devices are in quotes.)

*Table 3.1* Frames that Consistently Appear Across Science Policy Debates

| Frame | Defines Science-Related Issue As… |
|---|---|
| Social progress | …improving quality of life, or solution to problems. Alternative interpretation as harmony with nature instead of mastery, "sustainability." |
| Economic development/ competitiveness | …economic investment, market benefits or risks; local, national, or global competitiveness. |
| Morality/ethics | …in terms of right or wrong; respecting or crossing limits, thresholds, or boundaries. |
| Scientific/technical uncertainty | …a matter of expert understanding; what is known versus unknown; either invokes or undermines expert consensus, calls on the authority of "sound science," falsifiability, or peer-review. |
| Pandora's box / Frankenstein's monster / runaway science | …call for precaution in face of possible impacts or catastrophe. Out-of-control, a Frankenstein's monster, or as fatalism, i.e. action is futile, path is chosen, no turning back. |
| Public accountability/ governance | …research in the public good or serving private interests; a matter of ownership, control, and/or patenting of research, or responsible use or abuse of science in decision-making, "politicization," |
| Middle way/ alternative path | …around finding a possible compromise position, or a third way between conflicting/polarized views or options. |
| Conflict/strategy | …as a game among elites; who's ahead or behind in winning debate; battle of personalities; or groups; (usually journalist-driven interpretation.) |

## The Framing Dynamics of Climate Change

Survey analyses depict the American public for the most part as still largely disengaged from the climate change. A majority of Republicans continue to dispute the validity of the science and the urgency of the matter, while also believing that the media have greatly exaggerated the problem (Dunlap & McCright, 2008; Pew, 2008). Even among Democrats and Independents, a majority of whom say they accept the science and are concerned about global warming, the issue still rates as a second or third tier political priority (Nisbet & Myers, 2007; Pew, 2009). Other survey research shows that regardless of party affiliation, less than a majority has adopted important personal or household behaviors related to reducing greenhouse emissions or conserving energy (Maibach, Roser-Renouf, & Taylor, 2008).

What explains the perceptual difference between the objective reality of climate change and its perceived subjective conditions? As I argued in an essay in the journal *Science*, if mainstream news attention and scientific consensus alone drove public responses, then we would expect increasing public confidence in the validity of the science and decreasing perceptual gridlock. However, instead of scientific reality, ideologically friendly frames are providing the perceptual cues for the public (Nisbet & Mooney, 2007a).

### A Matter of Uncertainty and Economic Burden

Several conservative think tanks, political leaders, and commentators continue to hew closely to their decade-old playbook for downplaying the urgency of climate change, which includes questioning that human activities are driving climate change while also arguing that any action will lead to dire economic consequences. Even over the past several years, as Republican leaders such as U.S. Senator John McCain (R-AZ) and California Governor Arnold Schwarzenegger have urged the need for action on global warming, the strength of these decade-old frames linger as salient in popular culture, political discourse, and the memory store of many audiences.

During the 1990s, based on focus groups and polling, Republican consultant Frank Luntz helped shape the climate skeptic playbook, recommending in a strategy memo that the issue be framed as *scientifically uncertain*, using as evidence the opinions of contrarian scientists. He also wrote that the "emotional home run" would be an emphasis on the dire *economic consequences* of action, impacts that would result in an "unfair burden" for Americans if other countries such as China and India did not participate in international agreements (Environmental Working Group, 2003).

This framing strategy was effectively incorporated into talking points, speeches, white papers, and advertisements by conservative think tanks and members of Congress to defeat major policy proposals and the adoption of the Kyoto Protocol, a treaty that would have committed the United States to cutting greenhouse gas emissions (Dunlap & McCright, 2008). The communication campaign also promoted distortions in news coverage. As political reporters applied their preferred *conflict and strategy* frame to the policy debate, focusing on which side was winning, the personalities involved, and their message strategies, they also engaged in the same type of false balance that has been common to coverage of elections and other political issues (Boycoff & Boycoff, 2004).

U.S. Senator James Inhofe (R-OK), former chair of the Senate Committee on Environment and Public Works, remains the loudest voice of climate skepticism. In speeches, press releases, and on his Senate web log, Inhofe casts doubt on the conclusions of the Intergovernmental Panel on Climate Change and other major scientific organizations by selectively citing scientific-sounding evidence. To amplify his message, Inhofe takes advantage of the fragmented news media, with appearances at television outlets such as Fox News, on political talk radio, and via Web traffic driven to his blog from the Drudge Report.[5]

For example, on a February 2007 *Fox & Friends* segment titled "Weather Wars," Inhofe deceptively argued that global warming was in fact due to natural causes, adding that mainstream science was beginning to accept this conclusion. Inhofe, unchallenged by host Steve Doocy, asserted that, "those individuals on the far left, such as Hollywood liberals and the United Nations" want the public to believe that global warming is manmade. Similar frames of scientific uncertainty and economic consequences continue to be pushed by other conservative commentators, including influential syndicated columnists George Will (2008), Charles Krauthammer (2009), and Tony Blankley (2008).

An adaptation of these familiar frames is offered by Danish political scientist Bjorn Lomborg, author of *The Skeptical Environmentalist* (2001) and *Cool It* (2008). While accepting that human activities have contributed to climate change, Lomborg questions the severity of impacts, arguing that the resources spent on dealing with climate change are better spent on problems such as malaria and poverty. These novel contrarian views provide fresh fodder for skeptic commentators such as George Will (2009).

### A Pandora's Box of Looming Disaster

In contrast, former U.S. Vice President Al Gore, many environmentalists, and even some scientists have attempted to counter the uncertainty and economic consequences frames by emphasizing a *Pandora's Box*

of looming "climate crisis." To instantly translate their preferred interpretation, these advocates have relied on depictions of specific climate
impacts, including hurricane devastation, polar bears perched precari-
ously on shrinking ice floes, scorched, drought-stricken earth, blazing
wild fires, and famous cities or landmarks under water due to future
sea-level rise.

Publicity for Gore's documentary on climate change's effects, *An
Inconvenient Truth*, dramatized climate change as an environmental
Frankenstein's monster, including a hurricane-shaped plume spewing
from a smoke stack on its movie poster and a trailer telling audiences to
expect "the most terrifying film you will ever see." With an accent on
visual and dramatic effects, the catastrophe strategy triggered similarly
framed news coverage. For example, a 2006 *Time* magazine cover featured a polar bear on melting ice with the headline, "Global Warming:
Be Worried, Be VERY Worried."[6]

This line of communication only plays directly into the hands of climate skeptics and further reinforces the partisan divide in climate change
perceptions. Andrew Revkin, who has covered climate change for nearly
20 years for the *New York Times*, argues these claims are effectively
countered by critics such as Inhofe as liberal "alarmism," since the error
bars of uncertainty for each of the climate impacts are much wider than
the general link between human activities and global warming. These
challenges, which are easier when the target of ridicule includes a former
political figure such as Gore, quickly reactivate a focus on scientific uncertainty and the heuristic of partisanship (Revkin, 2007). In addition, the
public is likely to translate these appeals to fear into a sense of fatalism,
especially if this information is not accompanied by specific recommendations about how they can respond to the threats (Maibach et al., 2008).

Revkin and others worry that the news media have moved from an
earlier era of false balance to a new phase of overdramatization, one that
skeptics, such as Inhofe, can easily exploit to dismiss climate change as
a problem. Polls suggest that the public has picked up on critiques of the
media by conservatives, likely filtering this information through their
preferred partisan lens and their belief in liberal media bias. Such filtering results in Republicans who not only discount the climate change
problem but who also agree that the mainstream news media are exaggerating its severity (Dunlap & McCright, 2008).

### Public Accountability and "A War on Science"

Many journalists, advocates, and scientists have focused on *public
accountability* as an additional engagement strategy on climate change.
Various opinion articles, books, and news reports depicted the George
W. Bush administration as putting politics ahead of science and expertise

on a number of issues, including climate change. For example, in the 2004 election, Democratic presidential candidate U.S. Senator John Kerry (D-MA) made strategic use of the public accountability frame, comparing distortions on climate change to the administration's use of intelligence to invade Iraq.[7]

In 2005, journalist Chris Mooney's best-selling *The Republican War on Science* helped crystallize the public accountability train of thought, turning the "war on science" into a partisan rallying cry. In 2007, Hillary Clinton, in a speech marking the 50th anniversary of Sputnik, promised to end the "war on science" in American politics, highlighting the prominence of this frame device.[8] In a late 2008 transition speech, President Obama similarly invoked the public accountability frame and Gore's film while announcing his science policy advisers:

> Because the truth is that promoting science isn't just about providing resources—it's about protecting free and open inquiry. It's about ensuring that facts and evidence are never twisted or obscured by politics or ideology. It's about listening to what our scientists have to say, even when it's inconvenient—especially when it's inconvenient.[9]

The public accountability frame has outraged and intensified the commitment of scientists, environmental advocates, and many Democrats, motivating them to label climate skeptics as "deniers" and to engage in ever sharper rhetorical attacks on political opponents. Yet for other members of the public, "war on science" claims are likely ignored as just more elite rancor or to further alienate Republicans on the issue.

### An Economic Opportunity Rather Than a Burden

Not every citizen cares about the environment or defers to the authority of science. To generate widespread engagement with the ongoing policy debate, news coverage of climate change needs to shift away from traditional frames and devices toward new perceptual contexts that resonate with a broader and more diverse audience of Americans. Over time, these new meanings for climate change are likely to be key drivers of public engagement and, eventually, policy action.

In *Break Through: From the Death of Environmentalism to the Politics of Possibility*, environmentalists Ted Nordhaus and Michael Schellenberger (2007) advocate a move away from the "pollution paradigm," which offers a familiar storyline of dire environmental consequences if greenhouse gas emissions are not radically reduced. Instead, they offer an alternative communication strategy, which involves turning the *economic development* frame in favor of action, recasting climate change as an opportunity to grow the economy. The two authors argue that only by refocusing messages and building broad-based coalitions in support of "innovative energy technology" and "sustainable economic prosperity" can meaningful action on climate change be achieved.

With this framing strategy, Nordhaus and Schellenberger seek not just to engage the wider public, but also catalyze a more diverse social movement—perhaps even activating support for energy policies among both Republicans, who think predominantly in terms of market opportunities, and labor advocates, who value the possibility of job growth.

Both 2008 U.S. presidential candidates emphasized this frame, which was strongly echoed in news coverage. The Obama administration continues to promote this frame through the sound bite of "creating green jobs" and fueling economic recovery. Yet the techno-optimism of the clean energy solution is also open to the counter frame of *uncertainty*. The case of corn-based ethanol is a warning to any politician or journalist not to oversell any path forward, with public trust and continued confidence in the possibility of feasible energy solutions at stake (Russell, 2008). In this case, the gasoline substitute was initially heralded as a way to benefit the economy and to reduce greenhouse emissions, but subsequent research determined that the increased agricultural land use would actually boost emissions while also increasing food costs (Searchinger et al., 2008).

### A Religious and Moral Call to Action

E. O. Wilson (2006) offered a second potentially unifying interpretation in his best-selling book, *The Creation: An Appeal to Save Life on Earth*. Wilson frames environmental stewardship as not only a scientific matter, but also one of *morality and ethics*. In penning the book as an open letter to a Baptist minister, he acknowledged that as an atheist, he might hold a different belief regarding the origin of the earth, but that he shares a common value and respect for nature, what the Bible symbolically calls "creation." In this manner, he has engaged Christian readers and media outlets that might not otherwise pay attention to popular science books or appeals related to climate change. Paralleling Wilson's interpretation, an increasing number of Christian leaders, including Pope Benedict XVI and evangelicals such as Richard Cizik and Rick Warren, are emphasizing the religious duty to be "stewards" of God's creation.

The *morality and ethics* frame is also featured in Gore's WE campaign, which launched in spring 2008. The WE campaign to "repower America" attempts to unify U.S. citizens by framing climate change as a solvable and shared moral challenge. For example, in television and print advertisements, the WE campaign aims to break the gridlock of partisan perceptions by pairing unlikely spokespeople, such as Speaker of the House Nancy Pelosi (D-CA) with Republican and former Speaker of the House Newt Gingrich, and self-professed respectively liberal and conservative clergymen Al Sharpton and Pat Robertson,.

Other WE ads compare action on global warming to the U.S. Civil Rights Movement, to World War II, and to the recovery from the Great Depression. More recent WE TV spots, which feature actors as ranchers, construction workers, and auto workers, stress the economic development frame, emphasizing job creation and growth. Importantly, these ads are placed during daytime talk shows and entertainment programming and in leisure magazines, which all reach non-news audiences who might not otherwise pay attention to coverage of climate change.

Similar to the Pandora's Box metaphor widely used in 2006, as a way to dramatize the complexity of climate change in a novel way, journalists have also started to echo this *morality and ethics* frame in their coverage of climate change. For example, *Time* magazine devoted its 2008 Earth Day cover to that interpretation. Calling to mind the iconic Iwo Jima flag-raising photograph, the cover featured an illustration of soldiers struggling to plant a tree and the headline, "How to Win the War on Global Warming."[10] Acknowledging an overt public agenda-setting goal, managing editor Richard Stengel (2008) described the cover as "Our call to arms to make this challenge—perhaps the most important one facing the planet—a true national priority."[11]

### When Issue Specific Frames Emerge

Since the beginning of this decade, the *public health* implications of climate change have emerged as a potentially powerful interpretative resource for experts, journalists, and advocates (Frumkin, Hess, Luber, Malilay, & McGeehin, 2008). This trend is an example of how a unique issue-specific frame may emerge that is not predicted by the general typology for science debates outlined in Table 3.1. The *public health* frame stresses the potential for climate change to increase the incidence of infectious diseases, asthma, allergies, heat stroke, and other salient health problems, especially among the most vulnerable populations, such as the elderly and children. In the process, the public health frame makes climate change personally relevant to new audiences by connecting the issue to health problems that are already familiar and perceived as important. The frame also shifts the geographic location for impacts, replacing visuals of remote arctic regions, animals, and peoples with more socially proximate neighbors and places across local communities and cities. Coverage at local television news outlets and specialized urban media is also generated.

As this section details, framing analysis can not only be used to describe and track the communication dynamics of the climate change debate, it can also be used to identify new meanings and stories that can be told by experts, advocates, and journalists. In the conclusion, I return to specific recommendations on how this type of framing analysis can be further developed and used in collaborative initiatives among these groups. First, however, I review the case of poverty, which offers additional insight on how framing can be applied to break through to the public on gridlocked policy debates.

## Beyond a Language of Poverty

Few Americans seem to be aware that over 40 million jobs in the United States—or about one in three—pay low wages. The great majority of low wage jobs lack benefits such as health insurance or retirement accounts and provide little or no chance for career advancement. These conditions translate into 35 million Americans who earn poverty-level incomes, while millions more struggle to make ends meet (Boushey, Fremstad, Gragg, & Waller, 2007). Yet, in the face of this urgent problem, many antipoverty advocates and media commentators express great optimism about achieving effective policy solutions. They argue that a confluence of economic trends and focal events—ranging from the devastation of Hurricane Katrina to the 2008 presidential campaign to the economic recession—have created the opportunity to mobilize public support for policies that improve the lives of low wage workers, reduce poverty, and strengthen the country.

Seizing upon this policy moment, these advocates have pitched a variety of specific proposals. The menu includes raising the minimum wage; increasing access to health, disability, and life insurance; requiring retirement benefits and paid time off; offering job training and education; subsidizing child care; expanding housing vouchers and the Earned Income Tax Credit; increasing unemployment benefits; expanding Pell Grants for college; promoting unionization; and modernizing the food stamp and TANF programs.

The labels, themes, and language used to promote these ideas are equally diverse. For example, the Center for American Progress echoes a traditional progressive emphasis on a "fair economy" with its "Task Force on Poverty" and its lead report, entitled "From Poverty to Prosperity: A National Strategy to Cut Poverty in Half." *American Prospect* magazine has echoed this call to action, with its special May 2007, issue on "Ending Poverty in America." Yet, other organizations, such as the Ford Foundation and the think tank Inclusion have argued for a different message and set of labels, emphasizing instead low wage work, responsible economic planning, or "social inclusion."

While many innovative policy ideas have emerged, in order to build public consensus and energize widespread concern, advocates, experts, and journalists need to go beyond traditional stories about poverty and make meaningful otherwise apparently isolated problems and solutions. Currently there is no agreed upon blueprint or story format for communicating the "big picture" on how the minimum wage, for example, is connected to Pell grants for college, housing vouchers, or increased unionization. Moreover, for many Americans, news coverage still inadvertently places the roots of poverty in the same problematic mental boxes related to race, individualism, and moral failings.

### Conflicting Values and Deep Ambivalence

During the 1990s, there was an explosion of research in political science, communication, and sociology on the factors that shape public opinion and media coverage of poverty-related issues. While this past research mainly focused on attitudes or news coverage specifically about welfare reform, multiple strands of evidence demonstrate that the same general principles still apply today, despite changes in the political and media environment. These factors include the stubborn perceptual screen of individualism and belief in limited government, lingering racial stereotypes, and patterns in how the news media, particularly TV news, cover issues related to poverty and low income work.

When reaching judgments about poverty, Americans actively draw upon a few core cultural values. In particular, many survey analyses have identified a belief in individualism as guiding preferences about social spending and policies. The assumption underlying a belief in individualism is that economic opportunity in the United States is widespread and that anyone who tries hard enough can succeed (Gilens, 1996a). Yet other values also play a role. In particular, individualism is balanced in the minds of many Americans by humanitarianism, or the belief that government has an obligation to assist those who are most in need (Kuklinski, 2001).

In one classic study demonstrating this ambivalence, political scientists John Zaller and Stanley Feldman (1992) analyzed the open-ended answers of survey respondents about whether or not the government should spend more on social services, including education and health. Respondents who opposed increased spending offered thoughts that drew almost exclusively on individualism and a corresponding belief in limited government, emphasizing personal effort, responsibility, and hard work while opposing increased taxes and bureaucracy. In contrast, supporters of increased government emphasized the core value of humanitarianism—mentioning a duty to help others and the need for the government to provide social assistance—but they *also* somewhat ambivalently warned against increased taxes and bureaucracy, emphasizing that before receiving assistance, individuals should always try to get along on their own.

More recent work demonstrates the ability of news frames to activate the core values of either individualism or humanitarianism as the criteria by which audiences evaluate anti-poverty initiatives. In an experiment with college students, Shen and Edwards (2005) asked student subjects to fill out an initial questionnaire that measured their orientations towards both individualism and humanitarianism. Subjects were then asked to read one of two different versions of a newspaper article about poverty. After finishing the article, they were instructed to write down any thoughts that came to mind. As depicted below, the first article by way of the headline and lead paragraph framed the issue in terms of individualism and the second article framed the issue in terms of humanitarianism.

> *Headline:* Welfare Reform Must Require Strict Work Requirements.
>
> Americans remain sharply divided on whether welfare reform should expand work requirements or increase aid to low income families. Welfare critics argue that recent welfare reform legislation doesn't go far enough to require recipients to work for their benefits. They would like to see tougher work requirements on welfare benefits.
>
> *Headline*: Tough Welfare Restrictions Said to Hurt the Poor and Children.
>
> Americans remain sharply divided on whether welfare should expand work requirements or increase aid to low income families. Welfare supporters and defenders warn that further restrictions on welfare benefits would hurt children and the poor. They argue that welfare reform should aim to reduce poverty and assist needy families.

Not surprisingly, for subjects who read the first article, they recorded significantly more thoughts that were in line with individualistic objections to welfare (Shen & Edwards, 2005). In comparison, the subjects who read the second article were more likely to write down thoughts that were in line with a humanitarian support for welfare. Yet more importantly, among readers of the first article who also scored high on individualistic values, they generated significantly more opposing statements about welfare than readers who did not score high on this value orientation. In other words, the news article's selective emphasis on individual accountability triggered the application and intensification of this core value in evaluating welfare reform. A similar amplification, however, was not found for subjects reading the second article who also scored high on humanitarianism.

Consistent with the study by Feldman and Zaller (1992), these experimental findings provide further evidence that Americans' views about poverty are developed on an uneven playing field. In comparison to humanitarianism, the core value of individualism exists as a far more potent schema, always ready to be triggered by way of selectively framed arguments and news coverage.

### Black Stereotypes in White America

While core values and their activation by news frames play a significant role in structuring American views about poverty, the issue is by no means "race neutral." In fact, based on analyses of multiple national surveys, the political scientist Martin Gilens (1995, 1996b, 1999) concludes that among Whites, the belief that "black people are lazy" is the most important source of opposition to spending on welfare and to programs that provide direct assistance such as food stamps and unemployment benefits.

In one survey analysis, Gilens determined that holding negative perceptions of White welfare mothers led to some increase in opposition to welfare spending, but the increase was limited. In contrast, holding negative views of Black welfare mothers resulted in substantial increases in opposition (Gilens, 1996b, 1999). He also compared the relationship between the real world incidence of Blacks in poverty to shifts in news magazine and TV portrayals, examining any corresponding changes in the public's perception of poverty's racial composition. Between 1985 and 1991, while the actual percent of poor who were Black remained relatively constant at about 29%, the percent of Blacks featured in media portrayals of poverty increased from 50% to 63%; and public estimates of the percent of the poor who were Black increased from 39% to 50%.

Other research is consistent with Gilens's conclusions. For example, Gilliam (1999) traces the stereotype of the "black welfare queen" to a story recited in stump speeches during the 1976 presidential campaign by Ronald Reagan. Gilliam argues that the image has become a common script found in TV news coverage. In his experiments testing the effects of these stereotypes, Gilliam finds that when White viewers watch TV news portrayals of Black mothers on welfare, exposure leads viewers to oppose welfare spending and to endorse beliefs that Blacks are lazy, sexually promiscuous, law breakers, and undisciplined. Similarly, in a separate study analyzing Chicago-area TV news coverage, Entman and Rojecki (2000) found that the dominant visuals in TV stories related to poverty featured Blacks. Moreover, beyond images of race, they found that poverty itself was seldom the direct subject of a news story, with reports rarely focused on low income, hunger, homelessness, low housing quality, unemployment, or welfare dependence. Instead, the focus was on symptoms associated with poverty, particularly racial discrimination and problems of health or health care.

### TV News and Attributions of Responsibility

In combination with core values and stereotypes, the public tends to reach decisions on political issues by reducing them down to questions of responsibility and blame. In answering these questions, the public relies heavily on the news, especially television. Across a series of studies, Iyengar (1991) finds that the mode of presentation across TV reports of poverty can alter viewers interpretations of causal responsibility (i.e., judgments about poverty's origins), and treatment responsibility (i.e., judgments relative to who or what has the power to alleviate poverty).

Based on his analysis of TV reports from the late 1980s, Iyengar (1991) concluded that most reports tended to be packaged in "episodic" terms, focused on a particular event or individual, defining poverty relative to concrete instances. (An example would be a story filed during an especially cold winter in Chicago depicting a single mother struggling to afford the cost of heating.) Far less common were "thematic" TV stories that took the form of more general backgrounders, placing poverty in the context of social conditions or institutions.

In experiments, Iyengar (1991) discovered that, in contrast to thematic reporting, episodic stories led White middle class viewers to assign the causes and treatments of poverty to individuals rather than societal conditions and government institutions. Race also played a role. News coverage of Black poverty in general, and episodic coverage of Black mothers specifically, heightened the degree to which White middle class viewers held individuals responsible for their economic plight.

Gilliam (n.d. [a]) notes that while the natural tendency for journalists and advocates alike is to tell personal stories about issues with the goal of capturing interest and stirring emotion, episodic presentations are likely to lead viewers to "miss the forest for the trees." Overwhelmed by personal stories, viewers miss out on any greater understanding of the systemic causes of poverty. In other words, memorability and vividness in news portrayals of poverty likely come at the expense of support for public policy. If journalists and advocates want to focus on institutional fixes to the problem, thematic TV news stories are likely to favor the effort to build public support for these goals.

### The Decade After Welfare Reform

In a series of published analyses, political scientists Sanford Schram and Joe Soss identified each of the previously described factors as contributing to the passage in 1996 of welfare reform legislation. Yet, they explained, while many centrist Democrats predicted that the victory would pave the way for more meaningful antipoverty policies, the intensive communication campaign needed to build support for the historic legislation might have inadvertently delivered many self-inflicted wounds. In the public's mind, there remains the interpretation that poverty is fundamentally a problem anchored in personal responsibility and race. Despite many recent focusing events and powerful economic forces, public perceptions today are little changed from the 1980s.

For decades, in attacking the welfare system, conservatives claimed that symptoms associated with poverty such as crime, teen pregnancy, and drugs were in fact the result of a permissive system that allowed lifelong dependency on government assistance. Poverty, in fact, was an outcome of big government. By the early 1990s, centrist Democrats had concluded that conservatives had successfully used welfare to turn the public against any public spending and to stoke the flames of racism. Yet they reasoned that if Democrats could reform welfare and make government aid recipients appear to "play by the rules," then they could claim political credit, undercut racism, and mobilize the public in support of more effective antipoverty policies. Soon after his election, Clinton set the agenda for these efforts, vowing in his 1993 State of the Union address to "end welfare as we know it" (Soss & Schram, 2007).

Playing on the public's conflicting orientations toward individualism and compassion for the "deserving poor," both conservatives and centrist Democrats recast policy initiatives in terms of "welfare to work," and labeled bills using frame devices such as "personal responsibility," "temporary assistance," and "family self-sufficiency." Uglier, more tacit messages evoked the myth of the "Black welfare queen" or similar race codes, while the news media's episodic presentation style and skewed depictions of race further reinforced individual attributions (Schram & Soss, 2001).

This message campaign successfully redefined welfare for the public as a social crisis. In 1992, only 7% of the public named welfare as the most important problem facing the country, but by 1996, this number had crested to 27% (Soss & Schram, 2007). In fact, by 1996, given magnified media attention and selective interpretations that played on public values and racial attitudes, more than 60% of Americans supported handing responsibility for welfare over to the states, and a similar number supported capping welfare benefits at 5 years. In August 1996, following successful Congressional passage of the Personal Responsibility and Work Opportunity Reconciliation Act, more than 80% of the public said that they supported Clinton signing the bill into law (Shaw & Shapiro, 2002).

In the decade since 1996, the emphasis on ending "long term dependency" continues to serve as the primary criterion by which many elites

and the news media define the success of welfare reform. Specifically, journalists have focused almost exclusively on statistics showing a decrease in
welfare caseloads and an increase in the number of individuals who have
left welfare to take low wage jobs (Schramm & Soss, 2001).

### Tipping Point or Illusion?

By making welfare more "morally demanding," centrist Democrats
hoped to reinstill confidence in the ability of the government to help the
poor. Strategists, pundits, and several prominent scholars had predicted
that welfare reform would set in motion a powerful policy feedback
effect, removing the taint of racism, and opening up the public to support for more effective policies.

Unfortunately, in a systematic analysis comparing multiple indicators
of polling data gathered between 1998 and 2004 with data from the late
1980s, Soss and Schramm (2007) find no evidence for this impact. The
tendency for Americans to blame poverty on a lack of effort has held
steady, feelings toward the poor have grown slightly cooler, willingness
to aid the poor has stayed the same or diminished, and racial attitudes
still color support for assistance to the poor.

Yet, pointing to more recent polling data, influential progressives
remain optimistic that the public is finally ready to get behind a campaign against poverty (Halpin, 2007; Teixeira, 2007). In particular, a
widely talked about analysis by Pew (2007) indicates a roughly 10%
shift between 1994 and 2007 in the public's agreement that the government should take care of people who can't take care of themselves,
guarantee food and shelter for all, and help more needy people even if it
means government debt.

However, as Soss and Schramm (2007) point out, any comparison
to 1994 is misleading, since these polls were taken at the height of the
welfare reform campaign. During this period, news attention to welfare
soared, with this coverage overwhelmingly negative in tone. By 1998,
however, news attention and negativity had both sharply declined (Schneider & Jacoby 2005). In reality, absent very salient messages attacking
welfare programs, *what the 2007 polls reveal is a normalization of public attitudes about poverty to their pre-Clinton era levels, rather than
any turning point in public sentiment.*

A more recent analysis by Dyck and Hussey (2008) supports these
conclusions. Although news attention to welfare policy declined between
1999 and 2004, in this coverage, Blacks remained dramatically overrep-
resented as the face of America's poor. Blacks during these years consti-
tuted roughly 25% of Americans in poverty, yet more than 40% of news
magazine pictures of poor people at *Time, Newsweek,* and *US News
& World Report* featured blacks. With this racial stereotype remaining

salient and few counterstereotypes available in news coverage, Dyck and Hussey find in their analysis of 2004 survey data that the belief among Whites that "Blacks are lazy" remained among the strongest predictors of opposition to welfare spending.

Today, these enduring misconceptions about individual responsibility and work ethic as causal agents of poverty continue to be reinforced by leading political figures, even by moderates such as New York City Mayor Michael Bloomberg.[12] Though he might be celebrated in the press for promoting innovative antipoverty policies, Bloomberg's language and definition of the problem is decidedly old-fashioned. In speeches, he argues for restoring the "dignity of work" and "ending dependency" by "restoring personal responsibility" through a program that "incentivizes personal decisions" (Bloomberg, 2007). Each of these phrases serve as powerful triggers, setting in motion a train of thought that narrowly places responsibility for poverty on the individual rather on society and its institutions.

### Reframing the Problem and the Solutions

The realities of income disparity, low wage work, and economic insecurity span partisan, ideological, and racial boundaries. Yet in news media portrayals and political messaging, most policy solutions continue to be framed in ways that trigger the perceptual lens of individualism, limited government, and racial bias.

To date, the most comprehensive research on the re-framing of low wage work and poverty was funded by the Ford Foundation and carried out by Meg Bostrom and her company Public Knowledge LLC. In a series of analyses conducted in 2001, 2002, and 2004, Bostrom identified several alternative frames that might be able to break through the public's persistent belief that poverty is a matter of individual failure, establishing a train of thought that focuses instead on systemic problems and solutions. Bostrom (2004) developed and tested several rival interpretations to the traditional *sympathy for the poor* frame that focused on moral appeals, individual stories, and solutions. She examined the influence of these frames as experiments embedded in a nationally representative telephone survey (n = 3205). Across subsamples of survey respondents, she tested the traditional *sympathy for the poor* frame, a new *responsible economic planning* frame, and a slightly different *responsible community planning* frame.

Within subsamples, these alternative frames were first presented as part of an introductory script. After that, they were reemphasized in selectively worded questions that asked generally about issue priority, issue concern, news attentiveness to the issue, the perceived cause of a decline in wages, followed by an agree/disagree attitudinal question regarding what should be done in terms of policy. This innovative design ensures that across the survey a specific train of thought is established for the respondent before answering a series of neutrally worded key indicator questions. At the end of the survey, these key indicator questions served as dependent variables to test the relative effects of the three frame conditions. Respondents were asked about the perceived opportunity to get ahead; preferences for government action on the economy; the priority of specific economic policies; beliefs relative to how the economy works; and perceptions regarding who is to blame for poverty. Table 3.2

*Table 3.2* Description of Frames Tested on Poverty

| Frame | Script Read to Survey Respondents |
|---|---|
| Sympathy for the Poor | In a weak economy the working poor have to take any job they can get…Imagine the plight of a single mother working a low wage job. Even at $10/hour she earns only about $20,000 a year with few benefits like healthcare and paid leave. Who could support a family on $20,000 a year? The working poor frequently need to choose between buying food and paying the rent. We need to ask our government officials to find a way to address these problems and help those in need. |
| Responsible Economic Planning | The nation is relying too heavily on low-wage service sector jobs from national companies without insisting that they pay workers good wages and benefits…Creating prosperity tomorrow requires responsible planning today. Too many companies and decision makers focus on short-term profits and short term thinking to the detriment of our workforce. And when we allow one part of the workforce to weaken and struggle, it weighs down the economy for us all, resulting in a lower standard of living. Our nation needs to change its short-term thinking and start building good-paying jobs with benefits, and a strong economy for the long term. With better planning we can repair the nation's economic engine and create a future with a strong economy and good-paying jobs for our workers. |
| Responsible Community Planning | Communities are relying too heavily on the low-wage service sector jobs that national companies bring to an area without insisting that the national companies invest back into the community by paying workers good wages and benefits… Creating prosperous communities tomorrow requires responsible planning today. Too many companies and decision makers focus on short-term profits and short term thinking to the detriment of our communities. And when we allow one part of the community to weaken and struggle, it weighs down the economy for us all, resulting in a lower standard of living. Our nation needs to change its short-term thinking and start building good-paying jobs with benefits, and strong communities for the long term. With better planning we can repair the nation's economic engine and create a future with a strong economy and good-paying jobs and strong communities. |

summarizes the language used in each frame's corresponding introductory script to set the train of thought for respondents on the issue of low income work and poverty.

Among the frames tested from Table 3.2, the most effective interpretation for activating support across diverse audiences was the *responsible economic planning* frame. In the survey analysis, when presented in this context, policies were supported by net margins 4 to 11% higher than when framed in traditional terms of *sympathy for the poor*. Moreover, the *responsible economic planning* frame also rated as more credible than other well worn arguments such as "breaking a cycle of childhood poverty" and the emphasis on a "fair economy" where "people who work hard shouldn't be poor."

Perhaps most importantly, in the survey analyses, the economic planning frame was able to generate added support for low wage work issues among nontraditional segments of the public, audiences for whom the typical *sympathy for the poor* frame might actually activate increased opposition. These groups included the self-identified "working class," noncollege educated and older men, union voters, and older voters without a college education. The frame even appeared to soften opposition to proposals among traditional Republican voters.[13] Table 3.3 reproduces the key differences and points of emphasis that Bostrom identifies between the *responsible economic planning* frame and the *sympathy for the poor* frame. In the conclusion to this chapter, we will return to a discussion of what these findings mean not only for the media strategy of advocates, but also for journalists who want to break through entrenched audience filters on the issue.

### Lessons from UK's Social Inclusion Movement

The ability of the *responsible economic planning* frame to unify public support reflects closely the successful efforts in Great Britain by Tony Blair and the New Labour party to redefine antipoverty initiatives in terms of "social inclusion." Instead of alleviating the *condition* of poverty and its implied moral and racial underpinnings, the new social inclusion direction in government was about improving "prospects and networks and life chances" rather than simply raising the dollar amount of wages or redistributing wealth through cash welfare benefits or taxes (Fairclough, 2000).

The language and metaphors of social inclusion are designed to focus attention on the structures and processes that exclude certain groups of individuals from full participation in society, and may offer important clues for advocates in the United States. Similar to the *responsible economic planning* frame, the logic emphasizes that in a competitive global marketplace, the nation is stronger, more secure, and better off if more

*Table 3.3* Key Elements of Poverty-Related Frames

| Responsible Economic Planning | Sympathy for the Poor |
| --- | --- |
| The issues are the economy, jobs, and the future of prosperity | The issues are poverty, the poor, and the working poor. |
| The relevant values are responsibility, vision, stewardship, interdependence. | The relevant values are sympathy, disparities, the Golden Rule, and generosity. |
| The economy is a system that can be influenced; humans have power to influence economic conditions. | The economy is irrelevant, or it is cyclical, uncontrollable. |
| Trends, broader influences are integral to the story. | Profiles of sad individuals are integral to the story. |
| The reader's relationship to the problem is connective; it is about "us" | The reader's relationship to the problem is separate; it is about "them." |
| Solutions are the focus; the problem is manageable | Problems are the focus; the issue is overwhelming. |
| Responsibility for fixing the problem lies with citizens collectively. Strengthening communities is one of the objectives for action. | Responsibility for fixing the problem rests with the individuals who are having the problem. |

of its population can participate fully in the labor force and economy. The metaphor of the "caravan of the desert" has been offered as a frame device to quickly and vividly translate the meaning of social inclusion:

> One can picture our nation as a convoy crossing the desert. Everyone may be moving forward, but if the distance between those at the back and [the] rest of the convoy keeps growing there comes a point at which it breaks up.[14]

### A Work in Progress: The Reframing of Poverty

A few recent policy reports and legislative proposals incorporate elements of the *responsible economic planning* frame. For example, in 2007, Margy Waller's Mobility Agenda applied the frame to their own reformulation of the definition and measure for low wage work (Boushey et al., 2007). This approach defines low wage work as a job that pays less than two-thirds of the median wage, or typical job, held by men. In analyses and graphical displays of data, this recalibration of jobs away from the traditional measure of either below or above the poverty line more accurately and effectively communicates how structural problems in the economy and society are pulling workers apart. This "much less than the rest" approach shows that for low wage workers their inflation adjusted wages today are roughly equivalent to what they were in 1979. As the authors of the report argue, while remaining accurate, this new metric also fits better with a message that might mobilize broader segments of the public to care about low wage issues. Echoing the *economic planning frame* as well as social inclusion's "caravan in the desert" metaphor, the authors' emphasize that:

> An economy that leaves a substantial segment of workers far behind the rest of the workforce is contrary to the national belief that the United States is "one nation, indivisible...." As a nation, we are stronger and more cohesive if we have an economy that does not allow those at the back to fall so far behind that the essential unit of the nation breaks apart. (Boushey et al., 2007 p. 5)

Though for the most part, still focusing on moral calls to action that employ a *sympathy for the poor* appeal, the Center for American Progress (CAP) has also begun to shift to a *responsible economic planning* frame, connecting poverty to national economic recovery. For example, in a white paper entitled "The Price of Poverty," CAP argues that if generations of children remain in poverty as adults, then the trend grows the overall cost of social services and leads to additional costs to the economy in terms of lost tax revenues from adults who would otherwise be working. The report concludes: "Many believe that the moral case for ending child poverty is already clear. But this research makes clear that failing to tackle poverty today imposes substantial financial costs on society as well."[15] Other CAP reports have defined programs such as food stamps and home energy assistance and retrofitting as benefiting efforts at economic stimulus, emphasizing that these "investments" create private sector jobs in the food and housing industry while freeing up money for consumer spending among low income households.[16]

In terms of shifts in news coverage, analyses of print coverage show that there has been some decline in racial stereotypes about poverty (Dyck & Hussey 2008) and an increase in thematic depictions of structural problems and solutions (Gould Douglas, 2001, 2007). Yet there is little research indicating whether or not national TV news has shifted from its preferred package of episodic coverage. There is also scant data on racial bias in national TV news, and almost no data on how local television news frames low wage issues. Specific to amount of attention, these recent analyses show that even as of 2006, media attention to the "working poor" or "low wage jobs" was still relatively limited in comparison to other major policy issues. The 2008 presidential campaign and more recent debate over economic recovery have focused, somewhat vaguely, on "relief for the middle class" with little explicit mention of low wage workers. In addition, few stories about poverty-related issues appear on national television news. Finally, even when poverty or low wage work is mentioned, news attention is frequently incidental to a broader focus on issues such as either health insurance or housing generally (Gould Douglas, 2007).

A 2007 seven-part series by the *Columbus (OH) Dispatch* offers a leading example of how news coverage can successfully reframe poverty and low wage work around *responsible economic growth*. In a state ravaged by urban job losses and unemployment, instead of focusing anecdotally on individual stories of struggle, the *Dispatch* editorial team framed the problem in terms of communities, specifically Ohio's seven largest cities. In doing so, the newspaper evaded the all too familiar trap of characterizing job loss and poverty as an "us" (the suburbs) versus "them" (the inner cities) problem. Consider the train of thought generated by *Dispatch* editor Benjamin Marrison in his editorial launching the series. Reflecting on his experience as a young reporter covering Toledo City Hall, Marrison recounted how he asked the then city manager why "anyone in the suburbs should care about Toledo?" As Marrison described:

> "A region is like a piece of fruit," said [the city manager]. "The core is the city. If the core rots, it's only a matter of time until all the fruit is rotten." That exchange forever changed my view of cities. It made sense. Although many of us live in the suburbs, we depend on cities for things that are important to us. We also take them for granted.... We should all pray for their success. While many of us live and work in the suburbs, the quality of life for all Ohioans will deteriorate if our major cities continue to decline.

Finally, the biggest impact on how poverty and low wage work will be framed by both advocates and the news media will be the message set by President Obama and his administration. However, if Obama's major campaign speeches and policy papers on the topic are any indication, then it appears as if Obama is not unlike the rest of the progressive policy community: He still lacks a consistent storyline.

For example, in the opening of his speeches, Obama has heavily emphasized a *sympathy for the poor* moral imperative, telling the story of Bobby Kennedy's encounter with a hungry child in 1968 and Kennedy's tearful reaction to reporters: "How can a country like this allow it?" He then uses the story and question as a recurring theme throughout the speech (Obama , 2007). On urban poverty, Obama has also emphasized traditional themes of personal responsibility, arguing the "difference it makes when people start caring for themselves," admonishing fathers that "responsibility does not end at conception," and asserting that "it makes a difference when a parent turns off the TV once in awhile, puts away the video games, and starts reading to their child, and getting involved in his education" (Obama, 2007).

In addition, simply by way of its politically safe title, the administration's "Task Force on the Middle Class," led by Vice President Joe Biden, risks deflecting further attention away from the needs of low income workers. For example, while several progressive advocates stress that the administration's affiliated "green jobs" programs be heavily focused on low-income urban youth, the Vice President officially launched his Task Force initiative with news coverage and an op-ed in the *Philadelphia Inquirer* headlined "Green jobs Are a Way to Aid the Middle Class," a frame device that immediately calls to mind a very different focus and target for the jobs program (Biden, 2009).

Still, in a positive sign for low wage advocates, Obama has also emphasized in his public remarks the systemic causes of poverty. In a message that echoes the *responsible economic planning* frame, he consistently attributes part of the blame for poverty to more thematic realities of the economy:

> Today's economy has made it easier to fall into poverty. The fall is often more precipitous and more permanent than ever before.... You used to be able to count on your job to be there for your entire life. Today almost any job can be shipped overseas in an instant.... Everyone American is vulnerable to the insecurities and anxieties of this new economy (Obama, 2007).

Another promising framing strategy is the explicit connection that the Obama administration has made between addressing climate change and his "Making Work Pay" program, a plan to provide up to $500 in subsidy to low income individuals and $1,000 to families. To pay for the program and to reduce the burden on the federal deficit, the Obama administration proposed in its 2009 Federal budget to allocate $60 billion from revenue generated by a still yet to be passed carbon cap-and-trade bill (Eilperin & Mufson, 2009).

The strategy is risky, but in real policy terms, it starts to connect the dots for the public around a new model for an environmentally sustainable and socially responsible economy. As Nordhaus and Schellenberger (2007) have argued, this type of move bridges policy coalitions, tying the goals of poverty advocates with those of environmental groups. The strategy also activates incidental media attention to climate change and poverty across news beats and audiences. Environmental reporters have begun to include in their climate coverage mention of low wage work policies and similarly, political reporters have begun to mention climate policy in the context of their focus on economic recovery programs.

## Conclusion

This chapter is written as a primer for journalists, experts, and advocates who want to understand the relevance of framing research for engaging the public on complex policy problems. Yet it is also a call to action for scholars in our field to provide communication solutions to the perceptual gridlock surrounding these issues.

### A Deductive Foundation for Research

On climate change, despite two decades of ever-stronger scientific consensus and record amounts of news coverage, Americans are still locked in a deep divide over the issue, particularly along partisan and ideological lines. While there have been several innovations in communication strategy, many scientists, advocates, and journalists still focus on frames that are easily dismissed as alarmism, are not personally relevant to a diversity of Americans, or that might actually further alienate Republicans, the very group they need to mobilize behind policy action.

Recent large scale survey and market segmentation techniques have begun to examine what specific groups in society want to know about the issue, their political interpretations, the perceived implications for their daily lives, the resonance or conflict with their values and social identity, where they are most likely to receive information, and who or what they are looking to for answers (Leiserowitz, Roser-Renouf, & Maibach, 2008; Maibach et al., 2008). If framing research is going to be combined with these audience segmentation techniques, researchers will require a solid and valid starting point.

In this chapter, I note that the framing literature has a general tendency to "reinvent the wheel" in identifying and labeling the frames that exist in any debate. Not only does this lead to inconsistency in understanding the nature of disputes such as climate change, but it also leads to major differences in the measurement of media trends and in the observation of any influences.

As I argue, what is often overlooked is that in any policy arena—whether science, foreign policy, or social policy—there likely exists a generalizable typology of latent meanings that are directly applicable to understanding a specific issue or major event. In my analysis of climate change, one of my chief goals was to show how an existing typology developed to explain debates over nuclear energy, biotechnology, and more recently evolution, can also be used to explain the specific communication dynamics of climate change. Across policy sectors, research could strongly benefit from a similar synthesis of research that identifies and conceptualizes common and recurring frames.

Additional research using in-depth interviews, focus groups, and sophisticated survey and experimental techniques needs to further explore, identify, and test these frames across various and well-defined audiences. A careful understanding of the frame contest that exists in the real world is especially important for experimental researchers. This would not only bolster consistency in stimulus design and the possible triangulation of results, but also increase external validity and boost the relevance to professional practice, matching frames as they are tested in the lab with the reality of how they appear in public discourse and are used by journalists in the news media.

On poverty, more than a decade after welfare reform, the tendency for Americans to blame poverty on a lack of effort has held steady. Moreover, feelings toward the poor have grown slightly cooler, willingness to aid the poor has stayed the same or diminished, and racial attitudes still color support for assistance to the poor. Even though recent events and trends offer opportunities for policy action, advocates, political leaders, and journalists still lack a consistent frame on the issue. In fact, many continue to emphasize frames or racial stereotypes that actually undermine support for policy action.

Ford Foundation-funded work by Meg Bostrom has identified the *responsible economic planning* frame as an alternative and more effective focus for advocates and journalists seeking to build public consensus. This research also points to innovative methods for combining focus group research with split-ballot survey tests of alternative frames on a policy issue. More recent work has applied similar principles and methods to understanding how to reframe related debates over race (Gilliam, n.d. [b]) and the role of the government in managing the economy.[17]

One challenge that merits additional research is how to break the tyranny of the news peg in coverage of poverty and low-wage work. In other words, based on the principles reviewed in this chapter, what types of staged news events and story pitches successfully generate both print and television news attention, result in an emphasis on preferred frames, and reach key targeted audiences? For example, in her report, Bostrom (2004) concludes with a few ideas about several possible news angles that might activate in coverage a *responsible economic planning* frame. More work in this area needs to be done. These research efforts can be completed by bringing organizations, journalists, and media producers together to participate in a "communication summit" on low-wage work. Similar strategies should be applied to climate change.

### Social Media and "Bottom Up" Framing

In thinking about news framing, it is important to also expand the scope of research and applications beyond the mainstream media to include new interactive forms of digital media as well as new genres of documentary film, especially when these films are a complement to coalition-driven communication campaigns. In terms of new forms of digital and interactive media, recent proposals have focused on building a "participatory" public media infrastructure at the local and regional level (Aufderheide & Clark, 2008; Miel & Farris, 2008). With cutbacks in coverage at local and regional newspapers, many communities lack the type of relevant news and information that is needed to adapt to challenges such as climate change or to reach collective choices about economic development, low wage work, and poverty.

As a way to address these local-level information gaps, government agencies and private foundations are being called upon to fund public television and radio organizations as digital media hubs. These initiatives would partner public media with for-profit media outlets to share digital content that is interactive and user-focused. The digital portals would feature in depth reporting, blogs, podcasts, shared video, news aggregation, user recommendations, news games, social networking, and commenting. Proponents argue that these new models for nonprofit citizen-focused media are an integral part of the infrastructure that local communities need to adapt to climate change, to move forward with economic development, and to solve problems such as poverty. As proponents observe, a community without a quality source of public affairs information—packaged in a way that is accessible and relevant to most members of that community—is ill prepared to make collective decisions about these issues.

These new forms of interactive digital media also shift the focus away from a transmission model of traditional news framing effects to a more interactive, social constructivist, and "bottom up" model of framing. As lay citizens become active contributors, creators, commentators, sorters, and archivers of digital news content, new possibilities *and* new demands arise for framing research and its professional applications.

Related to interactive digital media hubs, with increasing frequency, new genres of documentary film such *An Inconvenient Truth* are serving as the foundation for "social media campaigns," bringing together filmmakers with partner foundations, journalists, and progressive organizations. As I reviewed specific to Gore's documentary and his more recent WE campaign, the framing of the film and the social media campaign matters to their reach, either connecting with and mobilizing a base audience of support or potentially reaching new audiences, expanding the scope of activity and engagement with an issue. On poverty-related issues, a relevant example was the film *Waging a Living*. Released as part of the 2006 season of the PBS series POV, the film chronicled the stories of minimum-wage workers. Leading up to its appearance on local affiliates, POV specifically targeted media efforts at news outlets in 17 states that had minimum-wage initiatives on the ballot in the 2006 election.

Comparative case study examinations of similar social media campaigns would provide valuable insight into how films can be used systematically and strategically and the role that framing plays in this process.

### A Bridging Model for Knowledge into Action

What is common to the issues, media portrayals, initiatives, and new media forums reviewed in this chapter is that framing and storytelling plays an integral, foundational role. Yet, despite the heavy focus of most scholarly work in the field, the issues and themes addressed do not fit neatly—or even very well—into a narrow media effects paradigm. Instead, as Stephen Reese (2001, 2007) suggests, the reality of framing fits better when thought of as a "bridging model" of media scholarship and application, bringing together qualitative, quantitative, and interpretative methods; and psychological, sociological, and critical traditions; while connecting the academic and professional communities through media initiatives that address social problems.

What is important, however, is that there is internal consistency within this diverse arena of bridging approaches. In this direction, university scholars benefit from working with professionals, who can help scholars recognize relevant research questions and encourage them to articulate their conclusions in accessible language and formats, both of which abet the search for funding. Government agencies, experts, and nonpartisan advocacy groups can use the results of this bridging model of framing research to systematically design and target their messages, to structure their public education materials, to effectively engage with journalists and editors, and to organize more interactive public dialogue initiatives such as deliberative forums and town meetings, whether face-to-face or virtual. Journalists, film makers, and social media designers can use this information to craft novel, accessible, and relevant narratives for nontraditional audiences across media formats, expanding their audience reach and impact.

## Notes

1. For background on these types of film campaigns, see a 2007 report from the Center for Social Media, available at http://www.centerforsocialmedia.org/files/pdf/ docs_on_a_mission.pdf.
2. My blog, *Framing Science*, can be found at www.scienceblogs.com/framing-science.
3. These talks were launched in part by the articles on the framing of science debates that I published in *Science*, the *Washington Post*, *The Scientist*, and *Environment*, respectively (Nisbet, 2009b; Nisbet & Mooney, 2007a; Nisbet & Scheufele, 2007).
4. Pan and Kosicki (1993) work from a "constructivist" perspective, which holds a different epistemological stance about the nature of frames than

constructionism, the perspective from which Gamson and Modigliani (1989) work. The full nature of this debate does not concern us here, but constructivists hold that framing analysis "does not assume the presence of frames in texts independent of readers of the texts"—a view that differs from the constructionist stance that how an issue culture is produced and changed "needs to be accounted for in its own right, regardless of any claims that one might make about its causal effect on public opinion" (Gamson & Modigliani, 1989, p. 2).

5. See Inhofe's Senate Office "Skeptics Guide to Global Warming," new releases, and blog. Retrieved from http://epw.senate.gov/public/index. cfm?FuseAction=Minority. WelcomeMessage.

6. The *Time* cover is available at http://www.time.com/time/covers/ 0,16641,20060403,00.html.

7. For example, see the transcript of the second 2004 Presidential Debate. Retrieved from http://www.washingtonpost.com/wp-srv/politics/debat-ereferee/debate_1008.html.

8. More on Clinton's speech can be found at the Washington Post. com. Retrieved from http://blog.washingtonpost.com/44/2007/10/04/ clinton_vows_to_end_assault_on.html.

9. The Office of the President Elect (2008), "The Search for Knowledge, Truth and a Greater Understanding of the World Around Us." Retrieved from http://change.gov/newsroom/entry/ the_search_for_knowledge_ truth_and_a_greater_understanding_of_the_world_aro/

10. The *Time* cover can be retrieved from http://www.time.com/time/covers/ 0,16641,20080428,00.html.

11. "War" is a commonly used metaphor and frame device across American politics. When the threat is defined as originating from a social group within American society, such as liberals' alleged "war on Christmas" or conservatives' alleged "war on science," the metaphor polarizes views, communicates the differences between "us" and "them," and rallies a particular social movement or ideological base. When used to point to an external existential or real threat such as the "war on terror," "the Cold War," "the war on cancer," or the "war on global warming," the metaphor results in national and societal unity, transcending ideological divisions, as Americans join to defend common values and self-interests (Nepstad, 2005).

12. Bloomberg (2007, August 28). Address to the Brookings Center, Washington, DC. News from the Blue Room. Available at www.nyc.gov.

13. In terms of activating core supporters for low income proposals, Democrats responded positively to all three frame treatments; in comparison, the responsible community planning frame generated slightly stronger support for specific policy.

14. Greg Clark, "Poverty is Too Important an Issue to Leave to the Labour Party," Conservative Home Blogs (see http://www.tinyurl.com/wkjlo). Clark's convey image is borrowed from journalist Polly Toynbee's book *Hard Work: Life in Low-Pay Britain* (London: Bloomsbury, 2003; see also Polly Toynbee, "If Cameron Can Climb on My Caravan, Anything is Possible," *The Guardian*, November 23, 2006. Retrieved from http://www. guardian.co.uk/ Columnists/Column/0,1954790,00.html). Somewhat ironically, in 2007 the UK Labour Party, under pressure from Conservatives, seemed to shift its frame toward a more traditional U.S definition of the issue, putting forward a proposal titled "Reforming Welfare to Reward Responsibility" and introducing "work for the dole" programs,

language that mirrors directly the mid-1990s U.S. welfare reform debate. This shift is an example of how frames often translate across national contexts, especially when there is shared political culture (see report at http://www.americanprogress.org/issues/2008/08/uk_welfare.html).

15. Retrieved from http://www.americanprogress.org/issues/2008/11/price_of_poverty.html.
16. Retrieved from http://www.americanprogress.org/issues/2009/02/basic_needs_brief.html.
17. See the collected research of Demos and The Frameworks Institute. Retrieved from http://www.demos.org/publicworks

## References

Bauer, M., Allum, N., & Miller, S. (2007). What can we learn from 25-years of PUS research? Liberating and expanding the agenda. *Public Understanding of Science, 16*(1), 79–95.

Biden, J. (2009, February 27). Green jobs are a way to aid the middle class. *Philadelphia Inquirer.* Retrieved from http://www.philly.com/philly/opinion/20090227_Green_jobs_are_a_way_to_aid_the_middle_class.html

Blankley, T. (2001). Bush raises temp on global warming, April 16, 2008. Retrieved January 23, 2009, from http://townhall.com/columnists/Tony-Blankley/2008/04/16/bush_raises_ temp_on_global_warming

Bloomberg, M. (2007, August 28). Speech at the Brookings Institution. Retrieved from http://www.brookings.edu/~/media/Files/.../2007/.../20070828bloomberg.pdf

Bostrom, M. (2002a). *Responsibility and opportunity.* Economy that Works Project of the Ford Foundation. Retrieved from http://www.economythatworks.org/reports.htm.

Bostrom, M. (2002b). *Responsible planning for the future.* Economy that Works Project of the Ford Foundation. Retrieved from http://www.economythatworks.org/reports.htm.

Bostrom, M. (2004). *Together for success: Communicating low-wage work as economy, not poverty.* Economy that Works Project of the Ford Foundation. Retrieved from http://www.economythatworks.org/reports.htm.

Boushey, H., Fremstad, S., Gragg, R., and Waller, M. (2007). *Understanding low-wage work in the United States.* Inclusionist.org. Retrieved from http://www.inclusionist.org/files/ lowwagework.pdf.

Boykoff, M., & Boykoff, J. (2004). Bias as balance: Global warming and the U.S. prestige press. *Global Environmental Change,14*(2), 125–136.

Brainard, C. (2008, Dec. 8). A one-stop shop for climate information? *Columbia Journalism Review Online.* Retrieved December 11, 2008, from http://www.cjr.org/theobservatory/ climate_central.php?page=all.

Cunningham, B. (2003, July/August). Rethinking objectivity. *Columbia Journalism Review.* Retrieved December 11, 2008, from http://cjrarchives.org/issues/2003/4/objective-cunningham.asp.

Croteu, D., Hoynes, W., & Ryan, C. (Eds.) (2005). *Rhyming hope and reason: Activists, academics, and social movement scholarship.* Minneapolis: University of Minnesota Press.

Dahinden, U. (2002). Biotechnology in Switzerland: Frames in a heated debate. *Science Communication*, 24, 184–197.

Downs, A. (1957). *An economic theory of democracy*. New York: Harper.

Dunlap, R. E., & McCright, A. M. (2008). A widening gap: Republican and Democratic views on climate change. *Environment* (Sept./Oct.). Retrieved September 1, 2008, from http://www.environmentmagazine.org/Archives/Back%20Issues/September-October%202008/dunlap-full.html

Durant, J., Bauer, M. W., & Gaskell, G. (1998). *Biotechnology in the public sphere: A European sourcebook*. Lansing: Michigan State University Press.

Dyck, J. J., & Hussey, L.S. (2008). The end of welfare as we know it? *Public Opinion Quarterly*, 72(4), 589–618.

Eilperin, J., & Mufson, S. (2009, Feb. 26). Budget expects revenue from limits on emissions. *Washington Post*, A04.

Entman, R. M. (1993). Framing: Toward clarification of a fractured paradigm. *Journal of Communication*, 43(4), 51–58.

Entman, R., & Rojecki, A. (2000). *The Black image in the White mind*. Chicago: University of Chicago Press.

Environmental Working Group. (2003). Luntz Memo on the Environment. Retieved January 2009, from, http://www.ewg.org/node/8684

Fairclough, N. (2000). *New Labour, new language?* London: Routledge.

Ferree, M. M., Gamson, W.A., Gerhards, J., & Rucht, J. (1992). *Shaping abortion discourse: Democracy and the public sphere in Germany and the United States*. New York: Cambridge University Press.

Frumkin, H., Hess, J., Luber, G., Malilay J., & McGeehin, M. (2008). Climate change: The public health response. *American Journal of Public Health*, 98, 435–445.

Gamson, W. A. (1992). *Talking politics*. New York: Cambridge University Press.

Gamson, W. A., & Modigliani, A. (1989). Media discourse and public opinion on nuclear power: A constructionist approach. *American Journal of Sociology*, 95, 1–37.

Gilens, M. (1995). Racial attitudes and opposition to welfare. *Journal of Politics*, 57, 994–1014.

Gilens, M. (1996a). Race and poverty in America: Public misperceptions and the American news media. *Public Opinion Quarterly*, 60(4), 513–535.

Gilens, M. (1996b). Race-coding and White opposition to welfare. *American Political Science Review*, 90, 593–604.

Gilens, M. (1999). *Why Americans hate welfare: Race, media, and the politics of anti-poverty policy*. Chicago: University of Chicago Press.

Gilliam, F. D. (n.d. [a]). Vivid examples: What they actually mean and why you should be careful using them. Frameworks Institute E-Zine. Retrieved from http://www.frameworksinstitute.org/ezine33.html.

Gilliam, F.D. (n.d. [b]). The architecture of a new racial discourse. Frameworks Institute Message Memo. Retrieved from http://www.frameworksinstitute.org/ assets/files/PDF_race/message_brief_race.pdf.

Gilliam, F. D. (1999). The "welfare queen" experiment. *Nieman Reports*, 53(2), 49.

Goffman, E. (1974). *Frame analysis: An essay on the organization of experience.* New York: Harper & Row.

Gould Douglas & Co. (2001). *Between a rock and a hard place.* Economy that Works Project of the Ford Foundation. Retrieved from http://www.economythatworks.net/reports/index.htm

Gould Douglas & Co. (2007). *Working press: An analysis of media coverage on low wage work.* Economy that Works Project of the Ford Foundation. Retrieved from http://www.economythatworks.net/reports/index.htm

Halpin, J. (2007, April 26). *Reducing poverty is the right goal.* Center for American Progress. Retrieved from http://www.americanprogress.org/issues/2007/04/halpin_poverty.html

Iyengar, S. (1991). *Is anyone responsible? How television frames political issues.* Chicago: University of Chicago Press.

Kahneman, D. (2003). Maps of bounded rationality: A perspective on intuitive judgment and choice. In T. Frängsmyr (Ed.), *Les Prix Nobel: The Nobel Prizes 2002* (pp. 449–489). Stockholm, Sweden: Nobel Foundation.

Kahneman, D., & Tversky, A. (1979). Prospect theory: An analysis of decision under risk. *Econometrica, 47,* 263–291.

Kuklinski, J. H. (2001). *Citizens and politics: Perspectives from political psychology.* Cambridge, UK: Cambridge University Press.

Leiserowitz, A., Roser-Renouf, C., & Maibach, E. (2008). *The six Americas of climate change: An audience segmentation.* Yale School of Forestry and the Center for Climate Change Communication. Retrieved from http://environment.yale.edu/uploads/ SixAmericas.pdf

Lewis, C. (2007, September/October). The nonprofit road. *Columbia Journalism Review.* Retrieved from http://www.cjr.org/feature/the_nonprofit_road.php

Lomborg, B. (2001). *The skeptical environmentalist: Measuring the real state of the world.* New York: Cambridge University Press.

Lomborg, B. (2008). *Cool it: The skeptical environmentalist's guide to global warming.* New York: Viking.

MacLeavy, J. (2006). The language of politics and the politics of language: Unpacking "social exclusion" in New Labour Policy. *Space and Polity 10*(1), 87–98.

Maibach, E. W., Roser-Renouf, C., & Leiserowitz, A. (2008). Communication and marketing as climate change intervention assets: A public health perspective. *American Journal of Preventive Medicine, 35*(5), 488–500.

Maibach, E. W., Roser-Renouf, C., & Taylor, M. (2008) What are Americans thinking and doing about global warming: Results of a national household survey. Retrieved from http://climatechange.gmu.edu

Marrison, B. (2007, December 2). Everyone has stake in fate of Ohio's cities. *Columbus Dispatch* (OH). Retrieved from http://www.dispatch.com/live/content/insight/stories/2007/12/02/ben2.ART_ART_12-02-07_G1_U78KJBM.html

McCright, A. M., & Dunlap, R. E. (2003). Defeating Kyoto: The Conservative movement's impact on U.S. climate change policy. *Social Problems, 50*(3), 348–373.

Mooney, C. (2004, Nov./Dec.). Blinded by science. *Columbia Journalism Review.* Retrieved December 11, 2008, from http://cjrarchives.org/issues/2004/6/mooney-science.asp.

Mooney, C. (2005). *The Republican war on science.* New York: Basic Books.

Mutz, D. (2006). How the mass media divide us. In P. Nivola & D.W. Brady (Eds.), *Red and blue nation?* (Vol. 1, pp. 223–263). Washington, DC: Brookings Institution.

Nepstad, E. (2005). The continuing relevance of Coser's theory of conflict. *Sociological Forum, 20*(2), 1573–7861.

Nisbet, M. C. (2009a). Framing science: A new paradigm in public engagement. In L. Kahlor & P. Stout (Eds.), *Understanding science: New agendas in science Communication.* New York: Taylor & Francis.

Nisbet, M.C. (2009b). Communicating climate change: Why frames matter to public engagement. *Environment, 51*(2), 12–23.

Nisbet, M. C., Brossard, D., & Kroepsch, A. (2003). Framing science: The stem cell controversy in an age of press/politics. *Harvard International Journal of Press/Politics, 8*(2), 36–70.

Nisbet, M. C., & Goidel, K. (2007). Understanding citizen perceptions of science controversy: Bridging the ethnographic-survey research divide. *Public Understanding of Science, 16*(4), 421–440.

Nisbet, M. C., & Lewenstein, B. V. (2002). Biotechnology and the American media: The policy process and the elite press, 1970 to 1999. *Science Communication, 23*(4), 359–391.

Nisbet, M. C., & Mooney, C. (2007a). Policy forum: Framing science. *Science, 316,* 5821–5856.

Nisbet, M. C., & Mooney, C. (2007b, April 15). Thanks for the facts, now sell them. Washington Post, B3. Retrieved from http://www.washingtonpost.com/wp-dyn/content/article/2007/04/13/AR2007041302064_pf.html

Nisbet, M. C., & Myers, T. (2007). Twenty years of public opinion about global warming. *Public Opinion Quarterly, 71* (3), 444–470.

Nisbet, M. C., & Scheufele, D. A. (2007). The future of public engagement. *The Scientist, 21*(10), 39–44.

Nordhaus, T., & Schellenberger, M. (2007). *Break through: From the death of environmentalism to the politics of possibility.* New York: Houghton Mifflin.

Obama, B. (2007, July 18). Changing the odds for urban America speech. Retrieved from http://www.barackobama.com/2007/07/18/remarks_of_senator_barack_obam_19.php

Pan, Z., & Kosicki, G. M. (1993). Framing analysis: An approach to news discourse. *Political Communication, 10,* 55–75.

Pan, Z., & Kosicki, G. M. (2005). Framing and understanding of citizenship. In S. Dunwoody, L. Becker, G. Kosicki, & D. McLeod (Eds.), *The evolution of key mass communication concepts: Honoring Jack M. McLeod* (pp. 165–204). Cresskill, NJ: Hampton Press.

Pew Center for the People and the Press. (2007). Trends in political values and core attitudes: 1987-2007. Retrieved from http://people-press.org/reports/display.php3?ReportID=312.

Pew Center for People and the Press. (2008, May 8). A deeper partisan divide on global warming. Pew Research Center for the People and the Press. Retrieved November 15, 2008, from http://people-press.org/report/417/a-deeper-partisan-divide-over-global-warming.

Pew Research Center for People and the Press. (2009). Economy, jobs trump all other policy priorities in 2009. Retrieved August 17, 2009, from. http://people-press.org/report/485/economy-top-policy-priority

Popkin, S. L. (1991). *The reasoning voter*. Chicago: University of Chicago Press.

Price, V., Nir, L., & Cappella, J. N. (2005). Framing public discussion of gay civil unions. *Public Opinion Quarterly, 69*(2), 179–212.

Price, V., & Tewksbury, D. (1997). News values and public opinion: A theoretical account of media priming and framing. In G. A. Barnett & F. J. Boster (Eds.), *Progress in the communication sciences* (Vol. 13, pp. 173–212). New York: Ablex.

Prior, M. (2005). News vs. entertainment: How increasing media choice widens gaps in political knowledge and turnout. *American Journal of Political Science, 49*(3), 577–592.

Reese, S. D. (2001). Prologue—Framing public life: A bridging model for media research. In S. D. Reese, O. H. Gandy, & A. Grant (Eds.), *Framing public life: Perspectives on media and our understanding of the social world* (pp. 7–31). Mahwah, NJ: Erlbaum.

Reese, S. D. (2007). The framing project: A bridging model for media research revisited. *Journal of Communication, 57*(1), 148–154.

Revkin, A. (2007). Climate change as news: Challenges in communicating environmental science. In J. C. DiMento & P. M. Doughman (Eds.), *Climate change: What it means for us, our children, and our grandchildren* (pp. 139–160). Boston: MIT Press.

Russell, C. (2006). *Covering controversial science: Improving reporting on science and public policy*. Working Paper, Joan Shorenstein Center on the Press, Politics, and Public Policy, Harvard University. Retrieved December 11, 2008. from http://www.hks.harvard.edu/presspol/research_publications/papers/working_papers/2006_4.pdf

Russell, C. (2008, July/August). Climate change: Now what? A big beat grows more challenging and complex. *Columbia Journalism Review*. Retrieved Januaru 23, 2009, from http://www.cjr.org/feature/climate_change_now_what.php

Scheufele, D. A. (1999). Framing as a theory of media effects. *Journal of Communication, 49*(1), 103–122.

Scheufele, D. A., & Tewksbury, D. (2007). Framing, agenda-setting, and priming: The evolution of three media effects models. *Journal of Communication, 57*, 9–20.

Schneider, S. K., & Jacoby, W. G. (2005). Elite discourse and American public opinion: The case of welfare spending. *Political Research Quarterly, 58*, 367–379.

Schram, S. F., & Soss, J. (2001). Success stories: Welfare reform, policy discourse, and the politics of research. *The Annals of the American Academy of Political and Social Science, 557*, 49–65.

Searchinger, T., Heimlich, R., Houghton, R. A. Dong, F., Elobeid, A., Fabiosa, J., et al. (2008). Use of U.S. croplands for biofuels increases greenhouse gases through emissions from land-use change. *Science 319*(5867), 1238–1240.

Shaw, G. M., & Shapiro, R. Y. (2002). The polls—trends: Poverty and public assistance. *Public Opinion Quarterly, 66,*105–128.

Shen, F. Y., & Edwards, H. H. (2005). Economic individualism, humanitarianism, and welfare reform: A value-based account of framing effects. *Journal of Communication, 55*(4), 795–809.

Soss, J., & Schram, S. F. (2007). A public transformed? Welfare reform as policy feedback. *American Political Science Review, 101*(1), 111–127.

Stengel, R. (2008, April 17). Why we're going green. *Time*. Retrieved November 20, 2008, from http://www.time.com/time/magazine/article/0,9171,1731899,00.html

Tankard, J. (2001). The empirical approach to the study of media framing. In S. D. Reese, O. H. Gandy, & A. Grant (Eds.), *Framing public life: Perspectives on media and our understanding of the social world* (pp. 95–106). Mahwah, NJ: Erlbaum.

Teixeira, R. (2007, April 27). *Public opinion snapshot: Americans extend helping hand to the poor.* Washington, DC: Center for American Progress.

*Waging a Living.* (2006). POV series. Public Broadcasting System. Information about film. Retrieved from http://www.pbs.org/pov/wagingaliving

Will, G. (2007, Oct. 22). An inconvenient price. *Newsweek*. Retrieved January 23, 2009, from http://www.newsweek.com/id/43352

Wilson, E. O. (2006). *The creation: An appeal to save life on earth.* New York: Norton.

Zaller, J., & Feldman, S. (1992). The political culture of ambivalence: Ideological responses to the welfare state. *American Journal of Political Science 36,* 268–307.

# Chapter 4

# Strategies to Take Subjectivity Out of Framing Analysis

*Baldwin Van Gorp*

My interest in the framing concept is rooted in my background as a journalist. When I returned to academic research and began a PhD project on my former professional occupation, Watson (1998) directed me to the work of Entman (1991, 1993), which highlighted the functionality of frames in the news: namely, "to select some aspects of a perceived reality and make them more salient in a communication text, in such a way as to promote a particular problem definition, causal interpretation, moral evaluation, and/or treatment recommendation" (1993, p. 52). Over time, I realized what I had been dealing with as a journalist: looking for frames that could turn events into news stories by suggesting an explanation for what happened in the surrounding world.

The line of thought that is the basis of my conceptualization of framing was developed in these key works: Bateson (1955/1972), Entman (1991, 1993), Gamson and Modigliani (1989), Goffman (1974), James (1890/1950, pp. 283–324), Schutz (1945/1964), and Tuchman (1978). The decisive *Aha-Erlebnis* came when I tried to merge insights of narrative analysis with the constructionist approach to framing as formulated by Gamson and colleagues (Gamson, 1992; Gamson, Croteau, Hoynes, & Sasson, 1992; Gamson & Lasch, 1983; Gamson & Modigliani, 1989). Constructionism deals with the process in which individuals and groups actively create social reality from different information sources (Neuman, Just, & Crigler, 1992; Wicks, 2005). Journalists are in the middle of this dynamic process of meaning construction in that they present additional layers of interpretation of issues and events in the form of a news story. They cannot tell stories effectively without preconceived notions about how to order story elements and about what meanings they could or should impose upon those story elements.

Another conceptualization of framing that informs my work comes from Swidler's (1986) notion of culture as a tool kit of symbols from which people may select to devise communication strategies and solve problems. At the cultural level, frames also are conceptualized as a tool kit from which journalists draw upon to do their job, much as individuals use news stories as a tool kit to understand their social and political environments (cf. D'Angelo, 2002, p. 877). Thus, one way of approaching news framing *analysis*—the approach taken in my work—is to understand journalistic practice by identifying the cultural notions that working journalists apply in order to frame the behaviors and motivations of news sources and to explain the origins of an issue, both of which suggest to the audience members how an event can be interpreted.

Various scholars have argued that journalists employ common understandings to cover news events, such as myths and archetypes (e.g., Bird & Dardenne, 1997; Coman, 2005; Lule, 2001), narratives (e.g., Bennett & Edelman, 1985; Roeh, 1989), and values (e.g., Gans, 1979). These authors did not yet situate their thoughts within the framing tradition, but it is hard not to conclude that, for instance, the "situation-defining symbolic forms" (Bennett & Edelman, 1985, p. 156), the "macroanalytic features of narrative" (Gurevitch & Kavoori, 1994, p. 14), and "platforms, frameworks, and rules" (Manoff & Schudson, 1986, p. 5) are in fact news frames.

As a result, my research focuses on news frames that express culturally shared notions with symbolic significance, such as stereotypes, values, archetypes, myths, and narratives. These phenomena are interwoven with each other, but they refer to different aspects of a news story. Myths are related to narratives, but whereas a myth deals with "the *deep truth* of human experience" (Silverblatt, Ferry, & Finan, 1999, p. 144; italics in original), a narrative stands for a script structure with a development in different stages, from problem to resolution. Values are reproduced in myths and embodied by archetypes. Archetypes are motifs and characters that help to structure stories; stereotypes refer to the simplified characteristics of a group of actors.

My contribution to this book explicitly elaborates on a theoretical essay in which I expound upon a constructionist view of framing (see Van Gorp, 2007)—a view that weaves together these strands of literature and clarifies the nature of culturally embedded frames. Locating frames on this level would seem to be an inherently subjective enterprise, owing to their latent presence in news texts. However, in this chapter, I wish to present some methodological guidelines for doing framing analysis that will help to take the subjectivity out of finding these sorts of frames in news discourses. I argue for an approach that combines, on the one hand, inductive framing analysis, in which a repertoire of frame packages is reconstructed, and, on the other hand, techniques for validating the reliability of the results in a deductively executed content analysis.

## Culturally Embedded Frames

I'll first illustrate culturally embedded frames by describing an ongoing study on poverty in the news (e.g., Van Gorp, Blow, & Van de Velde, 2005). The news frames we identified are all rooted in common cultural themes, such as the archetypes of villain, victim, and tragic hero, the stereotype of the vagabond, and the conviction that each individual has a pregiven destiny. In this study, my colleagues and I hold that journalists express these frames in news discourse, and that the meaning of the issue changes fundamentally according to the chosen frame.

Specifically, a number of archetypes may function as a frame. If the archetype of the villain is used, then poverty can be viewed as the result of certain individuals who make use of, or abuse, the social welfare system to which they do not financially contribute. The poor lack the will to work and that is why they live in poor conditions. A more positive usage of this frame results in a stereotypical portrayal of the jolly vagabond who feels very strongly about complete freedom and opts for voluntary poverty. Next, poor people can be portrayed as victims of a demanding socioeconomical system. Some succeed in beating the system and become heroes when they combat poverty. Other poor people do not succeed, because they try to change what is unalterable and fight in vain a pitiless and demanding society. Persons who are familiar with Cervantes' novel may recognize in these idealistic poor Don Quixote, who frequently appears in the media in many guises. Seen from this perspective, poor people are disposed to escape poverty, but they fail because they do not benefit from equal opportunities. The popular wisdom that "fate will catch up with you" is a second type of frame that leads to an interpretation of poverty as the result of misfortune and repeated setbacks, such as a bankruptcy, an accident, or sickness. If one is poor, it is the result of an inescapable destiny that can turn anyone into poverty.

The examples demonstrate that journalists have at their disposal a repertoire of frames that can be useful to construct a news story—in this case, a story about poverty. Organizational factors, external conditions, and journalistic sources may influence the selection of a frame. As such, the sequential use of frames may follow a framing cycle, with an emergence phase, a conflict phase, and a resolution phase (Miller & Riechert, 2001). For instance, in our analysis we found that in the news homeless people are less blamed for poverty during the cold winter months than in summer time when they may bother tourists (Van Gorp, Blow, & Van de Velde, 2005). Other contextual factors may influence the selection of a frame. In a framing analysis of news on asylum seekers I noted that journalists particularly tend to adopt the frames from their sources with regard to unfamiliar and unexpected topics (Van Gorp, 2005). However, soon after the first coverage, news media introduced their own frames and apparently neglected the frame as offered by their sources. Thus, the process of frame-building, in which media frames are formed and change over time (Scheufele, 1999), can be understood as a process in which journalists frame events and issues not only by applying news values, but also by being sensitive to cultural themes.

Values, narratives, and archetypes are couched in almost any form of communication, both popular and informative, "because they embody the fears, hopes, and prejudices of the cultures in which their audiences live" (Bennett & Edelman, 1985, pp. 157–158). Journalists already make themselves familiar with these culturally shared elements in the process of socialization that precedes their journalistic training and experience. Therefore, they are often not aware of adopting, using, and reproducing them in the news.

Culturally embedded frames are appealing for journalists because they are ready for use. On the basis of their narrative ingredients it is possible to assign roles to the principal actors of an issue (e.g., good-bad, advocate-opponent), specify what the problem is and who is responsible, and so forth, all of which contributes to the dramatization and the emotional appeal of the news (Van Os, Van Gorp, & Wester, 2008). As a result, frames sometimes "overproblematize" an event and that adds to its endurance. On the other hand, the selection of a particular frame can contribute to the perceived solution of a problem, in the sense that the media attention for an issue decreases. I noted such a resolution phase in the Belgian newspaper coverage of asylum when there was a shift in frames from the intruder frame to the victim frame, whereas the objective conditions, reflected in the number of asylum applications, did not follow that trend (Van Gorp, 2005).

There are two reasons why I give preference to these types of frames over issue-specific frames and generic frames, such as the omnipresent conflict frame. First, they possess an outspoken defining capacity. By placing new events in these familiar molds constructive insights can be introduced into social life. Second, frames that resonate with cultural themes have a natural advantage over other types of frames (Gamson & Modigliani, 1989, p. 5). Because such frames make an appeal to ideas the receiver is already familiar with, their use appears to be natural to those who are members of a particular culture or society. Such "cultural resonance" makes the association between a frame and the issue seem transparent and obvious (Benford & Snow, 2000; Schudson, 1989). In this vein, Hertog and McLeod (2001, p. 141) invoked a cultural explanation of the power of news frames by emphasizing their symbolic meaning, their potential to evoke other familiar stories, and their widespread recognition. In sum, culturally embedded frames form universally understood codes that implicitly influence the receiver's message interpretation, which lends meaning, coherence, and ready explanations for complex issues.

Because the organizational routines of journalistic practice encourage the use of culturally embedded frames to tell stories about many topics and issues, their capacity to define issues and events remains largely unnoticed both within news culture and, to an extent, within the scholarly study of news framing (Gamson et al., 1992). This causes a problem for the frame analyst, precisely because the person who does a frame analysis belongs most often to the same culture as in which the news is produced. Conceivably, the most obvious frames are overlooked. Therefore, in classroom situations, I advise students to start their framing analyses by looking at newspaper articles or TV news items about the issue from earlier years. These former frames may look weird and unusual today, but they were normal and obvious at that time. The same is true for the frames the news media employ today.

## Between Constructionism and Constructivism

The approach to frames as cultural phenomena does not imply that all cultural concepts are frames by definition (cf. Fisher, 1997). They only become frames when someone applies them for their defining capacity. Accordingly, each culture or subculture has a limited set of commonly used frames that are institutionalized in various ways and prized and protected for their ability to explain important issues (Entman, 1993, p. 53; cf. Goffman, 1981, p. 63). In Western societies, for instance, the idea that each person must have will power and is able to exercise control over the body has become a norm that governs our social behavior and forms the basis of parenting, education, and jurisdiction (cf. Lakoff, 1995). Thus, frame-building in the media, including (and perhaps, especially) in the news media, is at its core a process in which cultural values and norms are reproduced.

Journalists, along with their sources and audiences, draw upon the stock of frames that culture provides to them. Although the cultural repertoire is formed and reformed in the interaction between groups of people, some parts of it may be rarely employed or ignored (cf. Swidler, 1986). In that respect one could state that some alternative frames already exist and wait to be used or reused (cf. Hartley, 1982, p. 28).

The idea of a cultural repertoire of frames seems to situate frames outside the individual. In line with their constructionist approach to framing, Gamson and Modigliani (1989) argued that this cultural level indeed follows a logic of its own, which runs parallel to the cognitive level of individual meaning construction. They conclude that the social construction of meaning resides in the interaction of the cultural system and the individual system, and that the former can be examined in its own right, regardless of its causal effect on individual opinion formation. However, Pan and Kosicki (1993, p. 58), who adhere to the constructivist approach, do not assume that the presence of frames in the news can be analyzed independent of the interpreting individual. This apparent ontological contradistinction is rooted in the debate between structuralism and symbolic interactionism that followed from Goffman's *Frame analysis* (Goffman, 1974; see, e.g., Denzin & Keller, 1981; Hazelrigg, 1992). As seen from the first perspective, news texts are complex systems of meaningful elements, whereas in the second perspective this meaning structure only reveals itself in the interaction between the text and its reader.

To return to the poverty example, a TV report about a homeless person who was sleeping on a bench in a public park with a bottle of liquor in his hand led to a discussion during the analysis in which we tried to relate the TV reports to the question of who is to blame for poverty (Van Gorp et al., 2005). One interpretation started from the particular individual and his apparent alcohol addiction, which may be the cause of his poverty. Also, the degradation and dangerous nature of public spaces may be evoked by the image. My colleagues, however, exercised restraint in blaming a homeless man for his poverty. For them, structural circumstances are ultimately the cause of poverty. From a constructionist approach, however, there is some inherent structure in the portrayal: the homeless man, the bottle, and the park tell the story of someone who is not willing to work. From a constructivist perspective there is both a victim and a villain who are sleeping on that bench. It depends on the interaction between the receiver's prior knowledge and the TV report whether the victim frame or the villain frame is used to ascribe meaning to the report.

In earlier work I suggest a middle position (Van Gorp, 2007). On the one hand, frames are part of a culture and not purely individual, and, on the other hand, individuals are needed as an agent to make a connection between a text and the cultural stock of frames. Thus, the cultural stock of frames is not above people but among them, because culture originates through communication and it is articulated in the mass media and in discourse. The theoretical decision to opt for a somewhat external positioning beyond the individual rests on the incapacity of the individual to change or create myths, stereotypes, values, and so forth. For the most part, the life spans of cultural motifs exceed the life expectancy of the individual. Furthermore, the extraindividual conception of culture gives more power to culture than when it is internalized (Kubal, 1998; Swidler, 1995). However, individuals can mediate the persuasive power of frames by *using* them: by articulating cultural themes in socially situated conversations individuals can indeed reconfigure these themes. Talking with frames (not about them per se) integrates these frames with personal experiences and associations, not all of which are consistent with the external manifestations of the cultural theme (cf. Edy & Meirick, 2007). Thus, the social and cultural claim made by the constructionist approach held here does not completely rule out a psychological mechanism within framing. Quite the reverse, it acknowledges that the individual cognitive level and the social cultural level are interdependent and mutually responsive.

## Content Analysis in Framing Analysis

Concern about reliability and validity in framing research on the basis of content analysis is regularly expressed in the literature (e.g., Matthes & Kohring, 2008; Tankard, 2001). For the most part, this concern is expressed owing to the difficulty to demonstrate the relationship between the abstract frame and the pattern of elements within a news text that are able to evoke the core frame on the side of the receiver—a point made even more complicated by the fact that we do not know in principle how many frame elements in a text need to be present in order to generate an effect (Hertog & McLeod, 2001).

From the position that there is an underlying meaning structure that can be observed independently from the interpreting subject, it is possible to turn to content analysis to reveal this hidden structure. If this structuralist perspective is rejected, you cannot but turn to the receivers and regard each personal interpretation as an additional "insert" into the original text. In that case, you also need to scrap the ambition to reveal what journalists say "between the lines" on the basis of a content analysis.

The very first attempt I made to do a framing analysis was labeled as being too impressionistic. Therefore, much of my further effort was devoted to meeting the standards of validity and reliability that are traditionally expected from a content analysis. Although I tried to do this by systematically taking into account all techniques to assure that the results were sufficiently reliable, I found out that some level of subjectivity was unavoidable. After all, the linkage between the explicit elements of the news text and the central framing idea, which is part of a larger cultural level, requires some interpretation by the person who is doing the analysis. The researchers who are doing a frame analysis are also individuals and it is difficult for them to withdraw from their own cognitive knowledge. Taking this into account, the aim of the chapter is to present a number of methodological considerations and a practical guide that can be helpful in reconstructing the frames that are applied in the news. Systematic techniques for doing content analysis can help to limit the subjective involvement of the person who is doing the framing analysis and improve the reliability and validity of the results.

## The Reconstruction of Frame Packages

In framing research a deductive strategy is regularly used. Namely, a pre-defined and limited set of frames is invoked and the empirical aim of the study is to decide to what extent these frames are applied in the news, in campaigns, in TV series, on Web sites, in political communication, and so forth, and which effects they produce (for an overview of approaches see Matthes & Kohring, 2008). But where do those frames come from? On what level and by which techniques are they to be observed? These are questions that are frequently left open in deductive analyses. They can be satisfactorily answered via an inductive framing analysis in which the spectrum of conceivable frames that are relevant for the topic under scrutiny is identified.

Gamson and colleagues (Gamson & Lasch, 1983; Gamson & Modigliani, 1989) coined the notion of "media package," but because it suggests that the package is a product of media routines, and not of a broader culture or society, I prefer the term *frame package* (Van Gorp, 2007). Each reconstructed frame is presented by a frame package; that is, by an integrated structure of framing devices and a logical chain of reasoning devices that demonstrates how the frame functions to represent a certain issue. The manifest elements in a text that function as demonstrable indicators of the frame are the framing devices. Metaphors, historical examples from which lessons are drawn, catchphrases, depictions, and visual images are five framing devices Gamson and Modigliani (1989) referred to. Other devices that can be taken into account are themes and subthemes, types of actors, actions and settings, lines of reasoning and causal connections, contrasts, lexical choices, sources, quantifications and statistics, charts and graphs, appeals (emotional, logical, and ethical), all of which contribute to the narrative and rhetorical structure of a text (see Kitzinger, 2007; Pan & Kosicki, 1993; Tankard, 2001). The number of words and pictures, the layout of a text, the placement of a news article on a page, and the editing of an audiovisual production, are not considered as being framing devices but are, rather, formatting devices. These, too, are important because they provide cues about how readers and viewers of news perceive the salience and importance of the topic being framed.

The reasoning devices refer to the defining functions of frames, as identified by Entman (1993), and they form a route of causal reasoning which may be evoked when an issue is associated with a particular frame. The most important difference between framing devices and reasoning devices is that the reasoning devices do not need to be explicitly included in a mediated message. During the interpretation of the message, when a mental connection is made between the text, the frame, and the individual schema, the reader may come up with causal inferences that are in line with the reasoning devices.

A core function of framing is to define issues. Sometimes these are problematic issues and other times they are not. To make this point clear, Edelman (1988) refers to the social issues of racism and sexism that remained unproblematic for a long period of time, until the application of certain frames altered the situation. Other crucial defining functions of framing are to indicate what the cause of the problem is, what has to be done, who is responsible for causes, consequences, and solutions, and to convey moral judgments (Entman, 1993). A frame may be more suitable to indicate the origins of an issue, and others the consequences, but all frames have the ability to promote a specific interpretation.

The example of poverty further illustrates the importance of these reasoning devices. For this topic, the most important reasoning device regards who is to blame for poverty. This can be an abstraction, such as faith or structural and societal forces, or a human agent, in extremity the poor people themselves. Most often, this causal reasoning is not explicitly touched upon in the news. However, the incorporation of explicit framing devices in the news may implicitly promote a certain causal reasoning. For instance, Iyengar (1991) demonstrated that viewers are inclined to blame the victim when poverty is portrayed in an episodic news format, without a thematic elaboration of the issue. They hold the portrayed poor responsible for their poverty-stricken position.

In a framing analysis of the American youth series *The O.C.* we found the value of self-control as an important frame in the portrayal of alcohol consumption (Van den Bulck, Simons, & Van Gorp, 2008). The idea expressed through the frame sounds as if a person must always be able to exercise control over the body, and therefore it is a matter of willpower to withstand the temptation of alcohol. The same holds true for the homeless man sleeping on a bench in the park with a bottle of French brandy in his hand.

In my conceptualization, the heart of a framing analysis is to identify the framing and reasoning devices and to relate them to a condensing symbol, which is part of a shared culture. The frame molds the frame package to an internally consistent whole. The intention of an inductive framing analysis is to reconstruct the frames that are useful to define a certain topic. A systematic analysis of the framing and reasoning devices that relate to a specific frame makes it possible to instruct independent coders to identify the presence of the frame in a subsequent deductive phase, thus limiting, or even eliminating, subjectivity from the framing analysis. Procedures that can be useful in the reconstruction of frame packages and in their verification are explained in the following paragraphs.

## Inductive Phase

### The Construction of a Frame Matrix

The end product of the inductive phase is a *frame matrix* (Gamson & Lasch, 1983; see also, Pan, Lee, Man Chan, & So, 1999; Van den Bulck et al., 2008; Van Gorp, 2005; Van Os et al., 2008). Each row in the matrix represents a frame package and each column an enumeration of framing and reasoning devices by which the frame manifests itself. For example, I defined the moral basis of the victim frame as the duty to help people in affliction, whereas compassion forms the emotional basis (Van Gorp, 2005). With regard to the issue of undocumented immigration, the frame matrix can be completed with the type and role of the illegal immigrant who frequently falls into the hands of human traffickers and who is in need of help. The problem definition is oriented toward the question of how to receive these anxious refugees who are forced to leave their country. The main cause of the problem is the gap between rich and poor countries. The countries that live in comfort shoulder the responsibility to develop a flexible migration policy that is cautiously and effectively applied.

Frame packages gradually take shape during the process of simultaneously collecting, coding, and analyzing texts. I use the constant comparative method (Glaser & Strauss, 1967/1971) as the central methodological principle. The repeated examination of the source material offers the opportunity to support and document the preliminary findings. The inductive coding takes place during three coding procedures: open coding, axial coding, and selective coding (cf. Strauss & Corbin, 1990). These steps are not necessarily sequential, but rather are iterative. For instance, the use of a certain frame can be dominant and the constituent elements obvious, thus allowing the frame matrix to be filled in an early stage of the analysis. Other frames may be nascent or may have escaped notice during the first steps of the analysis. I have found that it is regularly necessary to go back to the source material, reexamine it, and to do some additional observations in order to gain further insight into the newly identified frame.

Because the purpose is to reconstruct the underlying, culturally embedded frames in a text, the question is raised as to whether the researcher should be a member of a cultural group. All the examples in this chapter stem from my West European cultural background and reflect the usefulness of a level of familiarity with this cultural heritage. Still, it is important to maintain some distance from personal thinking patterns in order to grasp the striking and natural characteristics of a (sub)culture. Ideally, therefore, members of a cultural group and outsiders to that group should work together to do the job. For instance, I can benefit from being a Belgian citizen working at a university in the Netherlands when I discuss Dutch media messages with my students because I can bring in my perspective as a relative outsider.

### Procedures of Analysis

*Step 1: Collect Source Material*   Because frames are part of a culture they enjoy wider circulation than simply being in news stories. Certain frames that circulate in public debate may not be picked up by the news media, whereas other frames are typically applied by the media or by a specific frame advocate. Therefore, do not limit this phase of the analysis to the news media. Frames are used in different places, in different circumstances, and in different periods of time. Some frames are applied only by advocates, others only by their opponents. It is also possible that one time a frame is used to argue in favor of an issue, while another time it is used to argue against the issue.

It is advisable to strategically collect sources of "frame sponsors" who use frames for strategic purposes, including, for instance, pressure groups, NGOs, and political parties (see Kruse, 2001). In frame advocates' press releases, pamphlets, and brochures, one frame often dominates, and on that basis, it can be easily identified. Of course, owing to the balance norm, the news media may apply more than one frame to cover a given issue (Van Gorp, 2005).

*Step 2: Open Coding of the Texts*   To do an open coding means that texts are analyzed without the use of a predefined coding instrument. The different elements of the strategically collected set of texts are compared in order to make an inventory of empirical indicators that may contribute to the readers' interpretation of the text. The most important guideline is not to focus on what a text is about, but on how the story is told. Essentially, when one creates a story one is making choices. With regard to the news, framing is not about the core facts of a news event, but about what selections the journalist has made. When a news story is just about core facts and the journalist's only choice is whether to write the story or not, there is probably no frame applied. It depends on how frames are conceptualized, but if they are reflected in how a news story is told, then at times, news stories can be considered "frameless." This may happen within short informative messages—for instance, a brief newspaper story about a car accident in the paper's Metro section. Even if the number of casualties is mentioned, this does not necessarily mean a (victim) frame has been used.

Table 4.1 contains a short excerpt taken from a newspaper article published in the Canadian daily *National Post*. It shows that some elements are worth listing as feasible framing or reasoning devices. Part

Table 4.1  Framing and Reasoning Devices in a Newspaper Article About Poverty

| Source text | Framing devices | Reasoning devices |
|---|---|---|
| [...] The Christians and the crack addicts meet for breakfast every Thursday in a downtown park. [...] | Contrast of actors: Christians vs. crack addicts; description of visual scene: having breakfast as an everyday activity | |
| It is not a happy scene. Sadly, it is too familiar. [...] | Emotional appeal: sadness, compassion | 'Familiar' refers to omnipresence of poverty |
| But here in B[ritish] C[olumbia]'s bible belt, feeding the poor and the afflicted is cause for concern. [...] | Context: Bible Belt refers to the ascetic Protestants. Lexical choice: afflicted | Feeding the poor as iconic and ultimate act of charity |
| "Cheerios build relationships." According to others, Cheerios cause trouble. [...] | Symbol / synecdoche: A brand of cereals is used as 'pars pro toto', a symbol for charity | Seemingly illogical causal relationship between harmless charity and problems |
| The place is overrun with pushers and drug users. [...] | Lexical choices: overrun, pushers, and drug users | Drug users cause problems just by being there (no actual examples of them causing trouble are given); do drug users belong to the poor people? |
| Even with its stunning scenery, the mountains and the rich farmland that surround it, it is like any other community in Canada: Threatened by drug user use and uncomfortable with the rising tide of homelessness. | Description of visual scene with contrast: idyllic scenery vs. misery; metaphor 'rising tide' that refers to an unstoppable overwhelming force | Drug users but also homeless people are perceived as threatening |

Note. From "Please don't feed the homeless," by B. Hutchinson, May 24, 2008, National Post, pp. A7, A8.

of the next step in the analysis is to locate them within frame package where they belong.

*Step 3: Arranging the Codes Around "Axes" of Meaning*  The next step of the analysis is to look for patterns of devices by linking them to overarching ideas. Whereas in the second step the inventory of devices is made for each separate text, in the third step similarities, differences, and contrasts between the devices are indicated and reduced to dimensions.

The level of abstraction increases as soon as the framing devices and the reasoning devices are separated from the specific news stories. The coded elements in the example in Table 4.1 could result in at least one dimension, namely, that some poor people deserve help whereas others do not. Furthermore, the metaphor of the 'rising tide' (Table 4.1, row 6) suggests that poverty can turn into something that is unstoppable and threatening.

In this phase, it is also advisable to turn to the literature. During open coding this should be avoided, because it may hinder keeping an open mind about possible framing devices within the text. By contrast, during the axial coding, the distinction between *God's poor*, who deserve our charity, and the *devil's poor*, the undeserving poor (cf. Gamson & Lasch, 1983; Golding & Middleton, 1982), is helpful to make because it aids in identifying which textual elements coming from the open coding are indicative of what is at stake with regard to the drug users in the example.

*Step 4: Selective Coding*   The next step in the analysis is to sort out the codes by filling in the cells of a frame matrix. Ultimately, the row entries represent a frame package and the column entries refer to the central reasoning and framing devices. Each row is a logically and integrated cluster of devices that refers to the same organizing frame. Each column summarizes the diversity of a framing function, such as definitions of an issue. Some elements from the axial coding will be left out; others are included in the matrix because they can adequately reflect the frame. Therefore, the first task is to complete the matrix, one column after another. Then, search for logical combinations across the columns: definition, causal responsibility, solutions, treatment responsibility, and so on. The purpose is to look for a limited number of frame packages that are mutually exclusive and in which each link is meaningful.

Most often, the analysis of only one text is not sufficient to complete the entire matrix. However, the news story that serves as our example (see Table 4.1) contains an interesting pair of competing frames. The journalist has chosen to construct the story as a fight between good and evil. The drug users are framed as the villains or as the Devil's poor, a stereotype that rather naturally conflicts with the Christian value of charity that is used as a frame for the event. The value of charity is put into question. Unselfish intentions are criticized because the Devil's poor benefit. The charitable institution is responsible and should be more careful about those to whom it distributes a free breakfast.

Naming the frame package involves the researcher in making an association with a cultural motive that can function as the core idea, thus fusing the framing devices into a coherent unit. Students experience this step as being the most difficult one to take. Mainly, this is because the subjective interpretation of the frame analysis—to express the central structuring idea in a frame package—is introduced in the analysis. Indeed, giving a name to a frame involves a kind of framing on the part of the researcher (Tankard, 2001, p. 89).

In some instances, naming a frame can be rather easily done when the journalist explicitly mentions the frame. For instance, a newspaper article may refer to genetically engineered trees as "Frankentrees" (Little, 2008). Frankenstein's monster, who has become an internationally applied symbol for the threats associated with genetic engineering (Hitchcock, 2007), suggesting that something intended to be beautiful is in reality dangerous and unmanageable. With this famous fictional character it is easy to suggest that these trees can endanger life on earth, even without explaining how exactly the trees may cross-breed with natural forests and endanger biodiversity. In a different example, a *Washington Post* journalist (Spivack, 2008) conjures the David vs. Goliath frame by suggesting that huge developers clash with players in the real estate market when plans for city extension are unfolded. As the journalist suggests, sometimes it is a struggle among two giants, "Goliath vs., well, Goliath." Most often, however, journalists are rather inexplicit about the applied frame; to be otherwise they would first need to be aware that the selection of frames is part of their daily routine. Table 4.2 provides a list of culturally embedded frames that can be useful to identify the core concept at the heart of a frame.

### Evaluating the Frame Matrix

Once a repertoire of frames is defined, two questions need to be answered. First, is the list of frames complete? Second, are these frames the most dominant ones? An exercise that can be helpful to determine whether or not to carry out an additional coding cycle is to sort the texts according to the applied frame. A text that cannot be put on any pile is either frameless or points to a frame that has not yet been identified.

There are three criteria that can be helpful to evaluate the suitability of a frame: (1) the thickness of the frame description; (2) the degree of abstraction; and (3) the applicability of a frame to define other issues. First, can the frame package be fully described with an extensive list of framing and reasoning devices? If the answer is yes, then the frame potentially promotes a specific meaning. The thickness of the description is also an indicator for the dominance of the frame in the news. Second, is the chain of reasoning devices, from problem definition to (policy) solution, complete and logically consistent? Some frames have the ability to define an issue as not being problematic and, as a matter of course, to absolve some agents of responsibility. For instance, the location of a new reception center for asylum seekers in a residential area

Table 4.2 Overview of Cultural Frames

| Type of frame | Examples of frames | Example of application |
|---|---|---|
| Metaphor | The building; the runaway train; the flood; the game; war; disease and recovery | Current food production methods undermine the foundations of the food system which puts the worldwide ecological system at risk (Aubrun & Grady, 2006) |
| Value or norm | Altruistic democracy, responsible capitalism (Gans, 1979); free speech vs. disruption of public order (Nelson, Clawson, & Oxley, 1997); good governance; sacredness of life | All people have equal rights, so the same is true for gay people, for example with regard to marriage and the adoption of children. Perceived from the idea that only what is 'natural' is normal, gay people or abnormal and cannot claim equal rights (Brewer, 2002) |
| Virtue or sin | Sexual restraint; temperance; satisfaction with one's lot; "punishment can be good for you" (Lakoff, 1995) | People who get drunk do not have the power to exercise self control, this internal evil has to be overcome (cf. Van den Bulck, Simons, & Van Gorp, 2008) |
| Myth | The myth of science; the American dream; the pact with God; the Apocalypse; Oedipus; the Tower of Babel; the destruction of Sodom and Gomorrah; Pandora's box; good vs. evil, heaven and hell (see Silverblatt, Ferry, & Finan, 1992) | Biotechnology will lead to catastrophes, just as Pandora opened the box that contained all the evils of mankind (Dahinden, 2002). Scientists who do stem cell research destroy human life. They take on the role of God and violate divine will (Nisbet, 2005) |
| Narrative | Man's inhumanity to man (Gurevitch & Kavoori, 1994); Cinderella, Frankenstein, Snow white, the Beauty and the Beast, Faust | The cigarette brought the smoker to a higher-class position, but with the workplace smoking ban, smoking 'Cinderella' would loose her class position (Handley, 2008) |
| Archetype | The victim, the villain, the hero, the donor (Propp, 1928/1958); the Good Mother (Lule, 2001); the angry wife, the invisible, the wise one, the merciless warrior | Mods and rockers, two youth cultures from the sixties, became synonymous with villains, from the moment the British press used a melodramatic vocabulary to portray the youngsters as a mob of "folk devils" that "besieged" and "destroyed" a small coastal village (Cohen, 1976) |
| Stereotype | A deep distrust of anything official (Knight, 2000); the foreigner as barbarian, women as being helpless, the innocent child, the stingy Dutchman | In women's magazines the victims are blamed for domestic violence, first, because, the women seem to provoke the abuse, and, second, because it is a matter of courage to get out of the abusive relationship (Berns, 2004). |

can be framed as a "gift" of the government (the donor) to the neighborhood because it creates jobs, enables storekeepers to gain customers, and stimulates cultural exchange (Van Gorp, 2006). A third question is: Are the frames sufficiently abstract? The main challenge here is to decide upon the appropriate level of abstraction. To meet this criterion the frames must be applicable to definitions of other issues. An issue or event can be presented from different perspectives (i.e., framed differently), and each frame may be used to give meaning to different issues or events. This is a rule of thumb that I always keep in mind when evaluating a frame analysis. Each frame has to be abstract enough in order to be applicable to other issues that likely lie beyond the scope of the specific research topic.

## Deductive Phase

### Validation of Inductively Reconstructed Frames

The framing devices and the manifest reasoning devices are crucial in the deductive phase of a framing analysis because they are recognizable, demonstrable, and countable, and because they can be arranged and manipulated (Pan & Kosicki, 1993). The deductive phase is based on principles of doing quantitative content analysis which deal with measuring the extent to which inductively reconstructed frame packages are actually applied in a representative sample of texts. Instead of taking a random sample it can be sensible to focus on the news coverage of particular key events which can cause a frame shift.

### Procedures of Analysis

*Step 1: Make a Codebook of the Frame Matrix*   One way to put down the frame in coding instructions is to think of a limited number of questions that grasp the core idea expressed by the frame. Although the procedures are meant to remove subjectivity, it is inevitable to sacrifice some reliability, because frames are hidden meaning structures. Reliability is a necessary condition for validity, but for a framing analysis to be valid it cannot be limited to just the most easily quantifiable aspects of a text.

Experience leads me to conclude that there are four rules of thumb for securing the reliability of the results. First, limit the deductive phase to frames that are clearly mutually exclusive. Tankard (2001) even suggested taking just two frames in order to reach acceptable levels of intercoder reliability.

Second, to achieve good reliability restrict to a minimum the coders' need to interpret the material. Simple yes/no questions seem to work out the best. Semetko and Valkenburg (2000; see also d'Haenens & de

Lange, 2001) developed a list of questions—such as, "Does the story suggest that some level of the government is responsible for the issue/problem?"—in order to identify a number of generic frames in the news. Although such questions require some interpretation, those researchers reported good levels of reliability.

Careful and thorough coding instructions are indispensable. So, third, provide for sufficient time to train coders. To rephrase this advice in framing terminology: training sessions are used to bring to coders' minds the cognitive schemas that are in line with the propositional content of the frame. The best results seem to be attained when only two coders do all the work. During training they write up their coding experiences and discuss them in detail. After coders reach satisfactory agreement on coding protocols they can commence to independently code the complete sample.

Fourth, do not expect to reach a high level of coder agreement for framing devices that are only occasionally applied in a text. This is especially so when using Cohen's kappa, which overcorrects for chance agreement when the distribution of the categories (present–not present) diverges from 50/50 (Potter & Levine-Donnerstein, 1999). Therefore, try to focus on framing devices that are regularly used in texts, such as lexical choices and metaphors. However, these framing devices may turn out to be not the strongest indicators to identify a frame. For instance, in a frame analysis of asylum seekers I expected that the lexical choice of "asylum seeker" would be a negative portrayal, as if asylum seekers ask for something they are not entitled to. This contrasts with the notion of "refugee," which evokes a positive and legitimate connotation (Kaye, 2001). Ultimately, this hypothesis was rejected because both terms were equally applied in the news, both when asylum seekers were portrayed as innocent victims as well as in stories which implicitly portrayed them as intruders (Van Gorp, 2005).

*Step 2: Look for Clusters in the Coded Devices*   Instead of separately formulating a coding instruction for each framing device and reasoning device, it is worth considering simultaneously coding of those framing devices. This means that coders should be trained to recognize the framing and reasoning devices and to code not for the individual devices but for the frame package as a whole (see Van Os et al., 2008). In that way this second step of the deductive phase could be skipped. However, it is indispensable to find out to what extent the elements within the identified frame packages actually constitute clusters held together by a latent frame. The most convincing way to do that is by using coders that are blind to the manner in which the distinct framing devices and reasoning devices on the coding sheet refer to the core frame. The coders determine whether an unordered list of characteristics shows up in a text. Afterwards, a factor analysis or a cluster analysis can be applied to ascertain that the variables relate to some underlying dimensions. Ideally, these underlying dimensions should correspond to the predefined frames.

For example, Semetko and Valkenburg (2000) used a factor analysis (principal components, varimax rotation) to determine whether the underlying questions reflect the presence of the frame in the study material. Matthes and Kohring (2008) applied a hierarchical cluster analysis by which they identified clusters of topics, definitions, causal attributions, moral and treatment evaluations with regard to biotechnology.

An alternative method is provided by multiple dimensional scaling (Van Gorp, 2005). A homogeneity analysis generates a plot by calculating for each framing or reasoning device coordinates on at least two dimensions. The distance between the devices indicates the strength of their relationship. Devices that regularly occur simultaneously within one text are plotted close to each other, whereas devices that do not show up simultaneously in any of the texts are plotted far apart. Subsequently, it is possible to determine whether or not the frame packages stand for actual clusters of textual elements. Graphical representations of factors can be helpful to succeed in the final evaluation of the frame matrix. If the factor or cluster analysis does not show the same underlying dimensions as assumed, the frame analyst can reinterpret the elements that do form a factor and define some alternative frames.

*Step 3: Considering the "Weight" of the Frame Packages*   A next step consists of determining the extent to which the identified frame packages are found in the data collection. This step is taken by counting for each item the number of framing and reasoning devices that belong to a particular frame package, as confirmed by the cluster analysis. The higher the number the higher the chance the different devices within a particular text are able to evoke a schema in the mind of the reader that is in line with the frame to which the devices refer.

The result of this calculation is a number of indexes per item in the data set that can be used to determine whether only one frame dominates or whether multiple frames are encoded in a (news) text. For instance, an analysis of the use of the intruder frame and the victim frame in the Belgian press showed that in about 50% of the newspaper articles only one of the frames was applied, whereas the other half of the sample held devices of both frames (Van Gorp, 2005). Further, it is possible to compare averages and to determine, for instance, in which kind of medium or in what period of time the application of the identified frames comes into vogue, increases, diminishes, or fades away. In that respect, the analysis can offer insight into frame attention cycles (Miller & Riechert, 2001).

In sum, the suggestion is simply to count the number of devices within a frame package that shows up in a text. There are, however, at least three conceptual questions with which the frame analyst has to deal before doing the calculations. Each question engenders a different approach. First, is it necessary to factor in the relative frequency of a single framing device? Second, how will the relative position of the texts in the data set be determined? (This question arises because some texts may attract the attention more easily than others.) Third, does a framing device applied by the producer of the text, for instance a journalist, carry more weight than the devices that slip into the text because they are mentioned by a source, for instance an interviewee? I will answer these questions in order, arguing from a theoretical viewpoint.

It is not necessary for a framing device to be frequently repeated in order to be capable of activating a frame. Entman (2004, p. 6) argued that this is particularly true for frames that are highly salient in a culture. Still, in other cases, the impact of a frame will stem from the prominence and repetition of its framing devices. The strategic integration of a single framing device can be sufficient to evoke a complex narrative of which, except that one element, nothing is explicitly mentioned in the text (cf. Lippmann, 1922/1997). For instance, stating that Saddam Hussein was even worse than Adolf Hitler sufficed for President George Bush to explain what was going on in Iraq (The Museum at the George Bush Presidential Library, 1990).

It seems reasonable to take into account the prominence of the particular framing and reasoning devices in a news story. The difficulty, however, is to determine what stylistic aspects are able to make a framing device more salient, because salience is not a characteristic of a text but an attribution in the mind of the reader. One way to manage this is to code, for each item in the data set, the extent to which demonstrable style characteristics increase the chance that the framing devices become salient in the perception of the audience member. For instance, a front-page newspaper article that is located above the fold, has an eye-catching headline, and is illustrated with photographs, receives a higher score on the scale than a small unillustrated article at the bottom of the page. This scale score can be used as a weight coefficient in further calculations for determining the prominence of the frame package in the data set.

An additional weight coefficient that can be used to calculate the indexes is the source of the framing devices. Sources make the news, perhaps particularly so when they disagree. Some frames have been processed in communication utterances by frame sponsors and other actors, which is a matter of framing *through* the media (Van Gorp, 2007). In that instance it may be unfair to conclude that a medium uses a particular frame. In order to make a distinction between, for instance, the statements made by frame advocates and the journalistic handling of them, the coders need to answer additional questions, such as whether or not the journalist agrees with the point of view expressed by his or her sources. The affected framing devices may then get a negative sign in the calculation. However, I personally hold the position that framing devices originating from a source that are included in the news make a positive contribution in the evocation of a frame. A statement or element originating from an external source and the prominence the journalist gives to it in a news story are part of the framing process and have to be included in the analysis regardless of its origin.

## Conclusion

The title of this contribution suggests, first, that a distinctive character- istic of framing analyses is that they are to a certain extent subjective; second, that it is advisable to phase out this subjectivity; and, third, that it is possible to achieve this goal when certain procedures are strictly followed. Some may even argue that this cultural approach to framing brings subjectivity *in* rather than it takes subjectivity *out*, as the title suggests. Indeed, some degree of subjectivity is inevitable. Moreover, in an inductive framing analysis, I strongly advise researchers to make the most of the analysts' gifts of observation and perceptive mind, precisely to get a grip on the subtlety of some frames. In this first stage, reading between the lines is permitted and even indispensable. In the next stage, however, additional procedures have to be followed to take subjectivity out of the identification and to attain acceptable levels of reliability.

Despite some useful exceptions (e.g., Kitzinger, 2007; Pan & Kosicki, 1993; Semetko & Valkenburg, 2000; Tankard, 2001), the framing liter- ature offers rather little on which to draw to objectively identify frames. The procedures presented in this chapter are designed to aid framing researchers in conducing more systematic inquiry into the content of frames in news stories.

Specifically, the main purpose of the technique is to gain insight into the simultaneous manifestation of multiple textual characteristics that fit together. Here the main difference with a linguistic approach such as discourse analysis is to be found. To determine how framing devices and reasoning devices work together under the heading of an overarch- ing idea is the core of a framing analysis. Further, from the perspective of discourse analysis, frames would stand for the interests of political and economic elites. As D'Angelo (2002) argued, the constructionist approach does not link news framing to a form of media bias or label it as contributing to hegemonic processes. Each frame provides a view- point that can help to understand issues. Therefore, the aim of a fram- ing analysis should always be to identify a variety of alternative frames.

When an important social issue is dominated by just a single frame, there should be some alternatives that lead to a better understanding of what the issue is about. Only when multiple frames are identified does framing become socially relevant.

The procedures as expounded in this chapter, however, do have certain drawbacks. The strategies put forward, particularly those for the inductive procedures, are difficult to repeat, as Semetko and Valkenburg (2000) indicated, partly because they are based on principles for qualitative research. Furthermore, the approach is time consuming, especially because the researcher has to start with an inductive frame analysis in order to construct a repertoire of frames. When advising graduate students, I impress on them that a qualitative framing analysis of a specific issue is both challenging and time consuming. I tell them, as well as undergraduate students, to begin a framing analysis with a limited number of news articles in order to inductively reconstruct the applied frames. This is a valuable experience that familiarizes students with the framing approach. Going though the admittedly inductive stage is necessary in order to then "take subjectivity out" in later stages.

The idea that there is a cultural stock of frames and the goal of reliably reconstructing those frames by means of a framing analysis ultimately underlies my conceptualization of framing. Although an anonymous reviewer once ridiculed this idea as a "Wal-Mart in the sky" from which journalists and individuals would pick whatever frame they like, I still believe that the identification of a repertoire of frames offers some opportunities. First, it engenders new insights into the coverage of certain socially relevant issues in the news. Second, it opens the door to alternative perspectives, which, in turn, can be used to convince journalists that how they cover the news is not suggested by the events themselves, but rather, by the result of *their* choices. The reason why journalists unconsciously use frames is that they are unfamiliar with alternatives. Third, a pluralistic repertoire of frames implies a larger tool-kit or a broader range of perspectives through which citizens understand issues and events. Not only journalists, but also professional communicators, policy makers, advocate groups, and scientists can be provided with alternative points of view to communicate about an issue. By redefining the terms of the debate they can constructively contribute to the public understanding of complex issues. Undocumented immigration, poverty, and genetic engineering are only some of the issues that rank high on the public agenda, and they are sufficiently complex to be beyond the understanding of laypeople. However, people require a clear explanation why things happen, partly because they want to have the feeling that they can control their environment. Frames can help to fulfill this need.

# References

Aubrun, A. & Grady, J. E. (2006). *Towards a cross-cultural simplifying model for food systems: Findings from French talkback research*. Brussels: King Baudouin Foundation.

Bateson, G. (1972). A theory of play and fantasy. In G. Bateson (Ed.), *Steps to an ecology of mind: A revolutionary approach to man's understanding of himself* (pp. 177–193). New York: Ballantine Books. (Original work published in 1955)

Bartlett, F. C. (1964). *Remembering: A study in experimental and social psychology*. Cambridge, England: Cambridge University Press. (Original work published in 1932)

Benford, R. D., & Snow, D. A. (2000). Framing processes and social movements: An overview and assessment. Annual *Review of Sociology, 26*, 611–639.

Bennett, W. L., & Edelman, M. (1985). Toward a new political narrative. *Journal of Communication, 35*(4), 156–172.

Berns, N. (2004). *Framing the victim: Domestic violence, media, and social problems*. New York: Aldine de Gruyter.

Bird, S. E., & Dardenne, R. W. (1997). Myth, chronicle and story: Exploring the narrative qualities of news. In D. Berkowitz (Ed.), *Social meanings of news: A text reader* (pp. 333–350). Thousand Oaks, CA: Sage.

Brewer, P. R. (2002). Framing, value words, and citizens' explanations of their issue opinions. *Political Communication, 19*, 303–316.

Cohen, S. (1976). Mods and rockers: The inventory as manufactured news. In S. Cohen & J. Young (Eds.), *The manufacture of news: Social problems, deviance, and the mass media* (pp. 226–241). London: Constable.

Coman, M. (2005). News stories and myth—The impossible reunion? In E. W. Rothenbuhler & M. Coman (Eds.), *Media anthropology* (pp. 111–120). Thousand Oaks, CA: Sage.

Dahinden, U. (2002). Biotechnology in Switzerland: Frames in a heated debate. *Science Communication, 24*, 184–197.

D'Angelo, P. (2002). News framing as a multiparadigmatic research program: A response to Entman. *Journal of Communication, 52*, 870–888.

Denzin, N. K., & Keller, C. M. (1981). Frame analysis reconsidered. *Contemporary Sociology, 10*(1), 52–60.

d'Haenens, L., & de Lange, M. (2001). Framing of asylum seekers in Dutch regional newspapers. *Media, Culture and Society, 23*, 847–860.

Edelman, M. (1988). *Constructing the political spectacle*. Chicago: University of Chicago Press.

Edy, J. A., & Meirick, P. C. (2007). Wanted, dead or alive: Media frames, frame adoption, and support for the war in Afghanistan. *Journal of Communication, 57*, 119–141.

Entman, R. M. (1991). Framing U.S. coverage of international news: Contrasts in narratives of the KAL and Iran Air incidents. *Journal of Communication, 41*(4), 6–28.

Entman, R. M. (1993). Framing: Toward clarification of a fractured paradigm. *Journal of Communication, 43*(4), 51–58.

Entman, R.M. (2004). *Projections of power: Framing news, public opinion, and U.S. foreign policy.* Chicago: University of Chicago Press.

Fisher, W. R. (1984). Narration as a human communications paradigm: The case of public moral argument. *Communication Monographs, 51,* 1–22.

Fisher, K. (1997). Locating frames in the discursive universe. *Sociological Research* Online, 2(3), Article 4. Retrieved May, 18, 2000, from http://www. socresonline.org.uk/socresonline/2/3/4.html

Gamson, W. A. (1992). *Talking politics.* Cambridge, England: Cambridge University Press.

Gamson, W. A., & Lasch, K. E. (1983). The political culture of social welfare policy. In S. E. Spiro & E. Yuchtman-Yaar (Eds.), *Evaluating the welfare state: Social and political perspectives* (pp. 397–415). New York: Academic Press.

Gamson, W. A., Croteau, D., Hoynes, W., & Sasson, T. (1992). Media images and the social construction of reality. *Annual Review of Sociology, 18,* 373–393.

Gamson, W. A., & Modigliani, A. (1989). Media discourse and public opinion on nuclear power: A constructionist approach. *American Journal of Sociology, 95,* 1–37.

Gans, H. J. (1979). *Deciding what's news: A study of CBS Evening News, NBC Nightly News, Newsweek, and Time.* New York: Pantheon Books.

Glaser, B. G., & Strauss, A. L. (1971). *The discovery of grounded theory: Strategies for qualitative research.* Chicago: Aldine-Atherton. (Original work published in 1967)

Goffman, E. (1974). *Frame analysis: An essay on the organization of experience.* Boston: Northeastern University Press.

Goffman, E. (1981). A reply to Denzin and Keller. *Contemporary Sociology, 10*(1), 60–68.

Golding, P., & Middleton, S. (1982). *Images of welfare: Press and public attitudes to poverty.* Oxford, UK: Martin Robertson.

Gurevitch, M., & Kavoori, A. P. (1994). Global texts, narrativity, and the construction of local and global meanings in television news. *Journal of Narrative and Life History, 4*(1–2), 9–24.

Handley, R. L. (2008, May). *"This is a workfree smokeplace": Public policy change and the resilience of cultural frames.* Paper presented at the annual meeting of the International Communication Association, Montréal, Canada.

Hartley, J. (1982). *Understanding news.* London: Methuen.

Hazelrigg, L. (1992). Reading Goffman's framing as provocation of discipline. *Human Studies, 15,* 239–264.

Hertog, J. K., & McLeod, D. M. (2001). A multiperspectival approach to framing analysis: A field guide. In S. D. Reese, O. H. Gandy, & A. E. Grant (Eds.), *Framing public life: Perspectives on media and our understanding of the social world* (pp. 139–161). Mahwah, NJ: Erlbaum.

Hitchcock, S. T. (2007). *Frankenstein: A cultural history.* New York: Norton.

Iyengar, S. (1991). *Is anyone responsible? How television frames political issues.* Chicago: University of Chicago Press.

James, W. (1950). *The principles of psychology* (Vol. 2). New York: Dover. (Original work published in 1890)

Kaye, R. (2001). "Blaming the victim": An analysis of press representation of refugees and asylum-seekers in the United Kingdom in the 1990s. In R. King & N. Wood (Eds.), *Media and migration: Constructions of mobility and difference* (pp. 53–70). London: Routledge.

Kitzinger, J. (2007). Framing and frame analysis. In E. Devereux (Ed.), *Media studies: Key issues and debates*. Los Angeles: Sage.

Knight, P. (2000). *Conspiracy culture: From Kennedy to "the X-Files."* New York: Routledge.

Kruse, C. R. (2001). The movement and the media: Framing the debate over animal experimentation. *Political Communication, 18*, 67–88.

Kubal, T. J. (1998). The presentation of political self: Cultural resonance and the construction of collective action frames. *The Sociological Quarterly, 39*, 539–554.

Lakoff, G. (1995). Metaphor, morality, and politics or, why conservatives have left liberals in the dust. *Social Research, 62*(2), 177–213.

Lippmann, W. (1997). *Public opinion* (2nd ed.). New Brunswick, NJ: Transaction. (Original work published in 1922)

Little, M. (2008, May 30). Canada blocks bid to outlaw "Frankentrees." *The Epoch Times*, p. 1.

Lule, J. (2001). *Daily news, external studies: The mythological role of journalism*. New York: Guilford Press.

Manoff, R. K., & Schudson, M. (1986). Reading the news. In R. K. Manoff & M. Schudson (Eds.), *Reading the news* (pp. 3–8). New York: Pantheon Books.

Matthes, J., & Kohring, M. (2008). The content analysis of media frames: Toward improving reliability and validity. *Journal of Communication, 58*, 258–279.

Miller, M. M., & Riechert, B. P. (2001). The spiral of opportunity and frame resonance: Mapping the issue cycle in news and public discourse. In S. D. Reese, O. H. Gandy, & A. E. Grant (Eds.), *Framing public life: Perspectives on media and our understanding of the social world* (pp. 107–121). Mahwah, NJ: Erlbaum.

The Museum at the George Bush Presidential Library. (1990). Remarks at a Republican party fundraising breakfast in Burlington, Massachusetts 1990-11-01. Retrieved June 2008, from http://bushlibrary.tamu.edu/research/public_papers.php?id=2379&year= 1990&month=11

Nelson, T. E, Clawson, R. A., & Oxley, Z. M. (1997). Media framing of a civil liberties conflict and its effect on tolerance. *American Political Science Review, 91*, 567–583.

Neuman, W. R., Just, M. R, & Crigler, A. N. (1992). *Common knowledge: News and the construction of political meaning*. Chicago: University of Chicago Press.

Nisbet, M. C. (2005). The competition for worldviews: Values, information, and public support for stem cell research. *International Journal of Public Opinion Research, 17*, 90–112.

Pan, Z., Lee, C. C., Man Chan, L., & So, C. Y. K. (1999). One event, three stories: Media narratives of the handover of Hong Kong in cultural China. *Gazette, 61*, 99–112.

Pan, Z., & Kosicki, G. M. (1993). Framing analysis: An approach to news discourse. *Political Communication, 10*, 55–75.

Potter, W. J., & Levine-Donnerstein, D. (1999). Rethinking validity and reliability in content analysis. *Journal of Applied Communication Research, 27*, 258–284.

Propp, V. J. (1958). Morphology of the folktale. Bloomington: Indiana University. (Original work published in 1928)

Roeh, I. (1989). Journalism as storytelling, coverage as narrative. *American Behavioral Scientist, 33*(2), 162–168.

Scheufele, D. A. (1999). Framing as a theory of media effects. *Journal of Communication, 49*(1), 103–122.

Schudson, M. (1989). How culture works: Perspectives from media studies on the efficacy of symbols. *Theory and Society, 18*, 153–180.

Schutz, A. (1964). On multiple realities. In A. Schutz, *Collected papers* (Vol. 1, pp. 207–259). Den Haag, the Netherlands: Martinus Nijhoff. (Original work published in 1945)

Semetko, H. A., & Valkenburg, P. M. (2000). Framing European politics: A content analysis of press and television news. *Journal of Communication, 50(2)*, 93–109.

Silverblatt, A., Ferry, J., & Finan, B. (1999). *Approaches to media literacy: A handbook*. Armonk, NY: M.E. Sharpe.

Spivack, M. S. (2008, April 29). Bethesda zoning dispute is case of Goliath vs., well, Goliath. *The Washington Post*, p. B01.

Strauss, A. L., & Corbin, J. (1990). *Basics of qualitative research: Grounded theory procedures and techniques*. Newbury Park, CA: Sage.

Swidler, A. (1986). Culture in action: Symbols and strategies. *American Sociological Review, 51*(2), 273–286.

Swidler, A. (1995). Cultural power and social movements. In H. Johnston & B. Klandermans (Eds.), *Social movements and culture* (pp. 25–40). Minneapolis: University of Minnesota Press.

Tankard, J. W. (2001). The empirical approach to the study of media framing. In S. D. Reese, O. H. Gandy, & A. E. Grant (Eds.), *Framing public life: Perspectives on media and our understanding of the social world* (pp. 95–106). Mahwah, NJ: Erlbaum.

Tuchman, G. (1978). *Making news: A study in the construction of reality*. New York: Free Press.

Van den Bulck, H., Simons, N., & Van Gorp, B. (2008). Let's drink and be merry: The framing of alcohol in the prime time American youth series The OC. *Journal of Studies on Alcohol and Drugs, 69*(6), 933–940.

Van Gorp, B. (2005). Where is the frame? Victims and intruders in the Belgian press coverage of the asylum issue. *European Journal of Communication, 20*, 485–508.

Van Gorp, B. (2006). *Framing asiel: Indringers en slachtoffers in de pers.* [Framing asylum: Intruders and victims in the press]. Leuven, Belgium: Acco.

Van Gorp, B. (2007). The constructionist approach to framing: Bringing culture back in. *Journal of Communication, 57*, 60–78.

Van Gorp, B., Blow, H., & Van de Velde, M. (May, 2005). *Representation of poverty in TV reports in Belgium: Who is to blame?* Paper presented at the annual meeting of the International Communication Association, New York.

Van Os, R., Van Gorp, B., & Wester, F. (2008). Successful joint venture or out of control? Framing Europe on French and Dutch websites [Une intreprise commune réussi ou non? Cadrer l'Europe sur les sites web français et hollandais]. Retrieved from *Electronic Journal of Communication/La Revue Electronique de Communication, 18*(1).

Watson, J. (1998). *Media communication: An introduction to theory and process.* London: Macmillan.

Wicks, R. H. (2005). Message framing and constructing meaning: An emerging paradigm in mass communication research. In P. Kalbfleish (Ed.), *Communication Yearbook 29* (pp. 333–360). Mahwah, NJ: Erlbaum.

# Chapter 5

# Of Spreading Activation, Applicability, and Schemas

## Conceptual Distinctions and Their Operational Implications for Measuring Frames and Framing Effects

*Bertram T. Scheufele and Dietram A. Scheufele*

Overall, the framing approach still has conceptual shortcomings, especially with respect to the relevance and role of schemas in news framing research. Our heretofore separate metatheoretical considerations (e.g., B. Scheufele, 2004; D. Scheufele 1999) have elaborated upon various aspects of the so-called framing-effects approach. An area of common interest in those considerations is the cognitive structures that enable journalists to make news and that enable audiences to understand and use news in their everyday lives. This chapter synthesizes our work to produce a model of cognitive structures: in showing how schemas work with frames on the cognitive level, we shed light on the construction of news on the textual level and on the development and transformation of cognitive frames on the discourse level.

We begin by explaining our two complementary models of framing. The first model (B. Scheufele, 2004, 2006) provides a vertical and horizontal matrix for studying frames, framing, and framing effects from a static perspective. The second model provides a four-cell matrix of independent and dependent variables, and media and individual frames, from a more dynamic perspective (D. Scheufele, 1999). The first model clarifies many of the conceptual questions surrounding news framing research, in particular for our purposes here, the differences between the terms *schema* and *frame*. The second model also clarifies framing effects research, doing so, among other ways, by distinguishing frame-building and frame-setting as distinct, dynamic processes in media effects research. A summary of both of these models segues into a discussion of how each one complements and extends the seminal work of Price and Tewksbury (1997). Their view that applicability is the core mechanism of framing effects is amended here by drawing on ideas associated with mental models and spreading activation and leads to a broader view of framing effects.

After laying out these preliminary classifications and arguments, the chapter proceeds to explore how schemas and frames are integrated both on the level of cognition and on the level of text. We follow this with a case study that examines how journalists' schemata are vital in constructing frames on the level of news texts. We end with a call for theory-based framing effects research.

## Two Metatheoretical Models of News Framing Research

Previous research has offered diverse and sometimes contradictory conceptual definitions of *frame* and *framing* (e.g., Entman, 1993; Gamson & Modigliani, 1989; Gitlin, 1980; Pan & Kosicki, 1993; Reese, 2001; B. Scheufele, 2004; D. Scheufele, 1999; Tankard, 2001). Regardless, most framing researchers trace the lineage of the frame concept, at least in part, to work on the structure and function of memory, assuming that cognitive schemas enable an individual to efficiently classify and process information encountered within social environments.

Our approach calls for conceptually distinguishing frames from schemas in order to more accurately observe how frames resonate with schemas when an individual watches or reads news (cf. Price & Tewksbury, 1997) and subsequently makes an evaluation, forms a decision, or articulates an opinion about a person or issue covered in the story (e.g., Gamson & Modigliani, 1989; Iyengar, 1991; Price et al., 1997; B. Scheufele, 2004; D. Scheufele, 2000). We will return to this point shortly. But before we do, let us briefly summarize our respective models of news framing.

### Model 1: The Horizontal–Vertical Matrix for Frames, Framing, and Framing Effects

The first model of news framing (B. Scheufele, 2004, 2006) delineates frames and framing along a horizontal and a vertical dimension. Frames (and framing) occur in different *arenas* (horizontal perspective): in the media system, in the political system, in society, and among counter publics. In addition, frames can be located at different *levels*: on the vertical perspective, frames are cognitive tools for information processing (cognitive level), which emerge and change in discourse (discursive level) and manifest themselves in discourse products (textual level), such as newspaper articles or party platforms. Using this classification, we can identify three approaches to theorizing framing.

The first approach concerns the agents (social groups, political players, etc.) that promote specific frames in order to gain public support for their interests, positions, and concerns. We refer to this as a *public discourse* or *social movement approach to framing* (e.g., Gamson, 1992; Johnston & Noakes, 2005; Snow & Benford, 1988). This approach treats the news media mostly as a "carrier" for frames promoted by public agents and considers media content to be an indicator of public discourse. As a result, many of these studies approach framing from both an intraorganizational and interorganizational level, examining, for example, how sponsors frame their activities to gain maximum coverage by the news media.

The second approach to theorizing news framing is concerned with cognitive frames journalists rely upon when they produce news content. How do these cognitive frames influence news production? How are these cognitive frames reflected in media content? Answers to such questions are provided by what we call the *journalistic approach* to framing. One strand of this research tradition deals with journalists' cognitive frames as criteria of news production (e.g., Gitlin, 1980; Tuchman, 1972, 1978; B. Scheufele, 2006). Similar to their audiences, journalists are susceptible to perceptual biases and are more likely to focus on information, events, or statements that match their own cognitive frames. At the same time, they are likely to pay less attention to frame-discrepant information, events, or statements. Empirical studies in this area have examined how *journalists' cognitive frames* (cognitive level) influence news production and are reflected as *media frames* in news reporting (textual level). The second strand of research in this subfield can be labeled "coverage studies" (e.g., Entman, 1991; Pan & Kosicki, 1993), and focuses on delineating the media frames within news stories.

The third approach to theorizing news framing deals with the effects of individuals' exposure to news frames. We call this the *media effects approach* (e.g., Cappella & Jamieson, 1997; Iyengar, 1991; Nelson, Oxley, & Clawson, 1997; Park & Kosicki, 1995; Price et al., 1997). This approach explores the impact of media framing on recipients' schemas, attitudes, decisions, and emotions. Previous research has classified potential *framing effects* into four groups (B. Scheufele, 2004): (1) audience schemas can be activated because individuals deem these schemas applicable to the frame(s) that they encounter (activation or applicability effect); (2) audience schemas can be modified by media framing (transformation effect); (3) if there is no schema available, cumulative and consonant media framing can establish such a schema (establishing effect); and (4) media framing can alter recipients' attitudes or opinions (attitudinal effect).

All three of these approaches—public discourse, journalistic, and framing effects—dovetail with subprocesses described and developed by the second metatheoretical model, which will be summarized next.

### Model 2: The Dependent–Independent–Variables Matrix for Framing Research

The second approach to categorizing framing effects is based on a somewhat different set of categories (D. Scheufele, 1999, 2000), but arrives at similar conclusions. While it lacks some of the details of the horizontal–vertical matrix, the second classification scheme adds a time dimension which the first model lacks. The second model delineates four subprocesses: frame building, frame setting, individual-level effects of framing, and feedback loops that model journalists as members of the audience who are susceptible to framing effects.

These four subprocesses form an interconnected four-cell typology (D. Scheufele, 1999). Any particular framing study can be located within this typology. The typology locates frames as independent vs. dependent variables that are studied at social and individual levels of analysis. News framing analyzed at the *social level* is mostly concerned with how frames are created and promoted in social discourse, a level that dovetails with B. Scheufele's public discourse approach to news framing. Much of the research in this area has dealt with competition among policy makers, interest groups, NGOs, journalists, and other groups over establishing dominant frames to influence public attitudes or policy outcomes.

At the *individual level*, frame analysis deals with questions about the structure of frames used by citizens to make sense of the world around them, as well as the impact of these frames on attributions of responsibility or other behavioral outcomes. This level parallels B. Scheufele's *journalistic approach* to framing; that is, it can focus on the cognitive frames that journalists, to one extent or another, "infuse" into their news stories. Thus, relevant questions here include: Do journalists' individual-level frames, for instance, manifest themselves within media frames? But the individual level also refers to the audience. Here, a relevant question is: How do more short-term, issues-specific audience frames differ from long-term underlying audience schemas (Price & Tewksbury, 1997)?

D. Scheufele's (1999) model goes beyond the somewhat static horizontal–vertical matrix by emphasizing the dynamic nature of framing as a social process. Specifically, the dependent–independent–variable matrix outlines four different subprocesses that represent causal relationships at various levels of analysis. First, *frame building* refers to the idea of linking frames in social discourse as independent variables to media frames as dependent variables. How effective are efforts by interest groups, policy makers, and elite media to establish frames that will be adopted by journalists in their news coverage (for an overview, see Nisbet, Brossard, & Kroepsch, 2003)? What are the factors that make frame adoption likely? This includes not only characteristics of new items themselves, which are equivalent to news values (Galtung & Ruge, 1965), but also journalistic norms and practices (Shoemaker & Reese, 1996).

*Frame setting*, the second subprocess, shifts the focus to media frames as the independent variable and audience frames as the dependent variable. It is concerned with the degree to which the frames audiences use when describing issues mirror the frames provided to them by mass media (Huang, 1995, 1996).

Third, a large body of research has focused on *individual-level effects of framing*. This research has examined the impact of media frames on citizens' judgment about issues. Experimental research often merges frame setting and frame building into a single design by exposing captive audiences to mediated frames and then testing the behavioral or attitudinal effects of these frames, assuming that they have been adopted by the participants (Iyengar, 1991). The picture in the real world, of course, is much more complex, and frames only influence behavioral or attitudinal outcome variables if they (1) are prevalent enough to get adopted by citizens over other, competing frames and (2) resonate with underlying long-term audience schemas (Price & Tewksbury, 1997).

Finally, the dependent–independent–variable matrix models a *feedback loop* from individual-level framing effects to journalists and other actors in the policy arena who—of course—are also audiences for their own framing efforts. This is particularly important, given phenomena like the CNN effect, which refers to the idea that policy actors often react to their own *perceptions* of the effects that the ubiquitous coverage on 24-hour news channels may have on audiences, rather than the real impacts that this coverage *does* have. Based on their lay perceptions of framing efforts, it is therefore reasonable to assume that policymakers, journalists, and other actors in the policy arena also translate these perceptions into conclusions about which frames to emphasized or revise during a policy debate.

### Integrating the Metatheoretical Models

A suitable site from which to integrate our metatheoretical models is the seminal work by Price and colleagues (e.g., Price & Tewksbury, 1997; Price et al., 1997). According to Price and colleagues, framing is a matter of *applicability*. For instance, the "Iraqi Freedom" frame is more applicable to some underlying audience schemas (e.g., "freedom") than others (e.g., "economy"). Consequently, the freedom schema is more likely to be activated than the economic one. Once a schema is activated (activation effect), it is more likely to be considered when judging, say, the job performance of (former) President George W. Bush. Based on this model, this kind of framing effects is not a simple adoption of media frames. Rather, Price and Tewksbury (1997) speak of an interactive effect of a framed message that resonates with an underlying, culturally shared audience schema. Of course, there are individual differences with respect to applicability effects, based on factors such as people's value systems, predispositions, and preexisting knowledge levels. Recipients may like or dislike a politician, or they may already have knowledge about an issue.

D. Scheufele (1999) intimated the vital importance of examining how audience frames may mediate the effects of media frames (see p.

117). In distinguishing the mechanisms of agenda-setting and priming effects from framing effects, D. Scheufele (2000) stated, "Framing influences how audiences think about issues, not by making aspects of the issue more salient, but by invoking interpretive schemas that influence the interpretation of incoming information" (p. 309). In a similar vein, B. Scheufele specified how exposure to news stories can alter cognitive schemas via cumulative and consonant media framing (transformation and evaluation effects). In addition, he argued that many of the images and opinions held by audience members have in fact been created by prior media coverage (establishing effect), a point that matches with D. Scheufele's (1999, 2000) frame-setting stage.

As outlined by B. Scheufele (2004), the theory of *mental models* (see Johnson-Laird, 1980, 1989) helps to explain how news frames transform or establish audience schemas (transformation and establishing effect). A mental model is a temporary cognitive representation of a problem or situation. In the context of framing effects, a mental model can also be considered to be the *cognitive frame* temporally applied to an issue by an audience member. For instance, readers of a newspaper report about the War in Gaza have specific ideas or mental models of the Middle East conflict before starting to read ($t_1$). When starting to read, the recipients' mental models at $t_1$ predominantly draw on their schemas. But media framing can change this current mental model. If the headline and lead text of the newspaper report frame the Gaza War in a specific way (e.g., "Innocent people killed in Gaza"), then the story is more applicable to certain of a reader's interpretative schemas (e.g., "humanitarian concerns" or "anti-Semitic stereotypes") rather than others (e.g., "self-defense"). D. Scheufele (2000) characterized this aspect of framing effects in terms of attributions of causal and treatment responsibility that are made after audience frames have been shaped by media frames (see p. 307). Back to B. Scheufele's (2004) nomenclature, the mental model at date $t_2$ is now more heavily influenced by the media frame.

In the case of cumulative and consonant media framing—that is, many reports framing the issue in a consistent fashion—an audience member's mental model will be modified in a step-by-step fashion consistent with the predominant framing of the issue in mass media. After a while, audience members will also adjust their more stable cognitive schemas. As a result, media framing can alter audience schemas (transformation effect). The Price and Tewksbury (1997) idea of an interactive effect between a framed message and an underlying audience schema matches this view of a mental model nourished by a media frame and audience schemas, as well as the view that individual-level consequences of exposure to a media frame—attributions of causal and treatment responsibility (D. Scheufele, 2000)—are engendered by media frames acting upon audience frames.

## Cognitive Schemas, Cognitive Frames, and Media Frames

Recall that, according to the horizontal–vertical matrix, frames can be located at three levels. One can explore (1) the cognitive frames of journalists (cognitive level); (2) the frames emerging and changing in news room discourse (discursive level); and (3) the media frames in, say, a television news broadcast (textual level). As a prelude to our case study, this section discusses frames on the cognitive level and the textual level.

### Cognitive Schemas and Frames

At the *cognitive level* we are interested in the cognitions of journalists, recipients, or politicians. Framing literature suggests a lot of alternative terms like *cognitive schema, script, cognitive representation* or *mental model* (see D. Scheufele, 1999; B. Scheufele, 2004). Many researchers (e.g., Entman, 1993; Gitlin, 1980; Valkenburg, Semetko, & de Vreese, 1999) do not distinguish between a cognitive frame and a cognitive schema. Quite often they simply adopt schema definitions and replace "schema" by "frame." This, however, reduces the frame construct to a synonym of schema and makes it more or less obsolete. In earlier publications (B. Scheufele, 2004, 2006) we presented a more convincing conceptualization for *cognitive frames* and *cognitive schemas*. This conceptualization integrates both constructs by drawing on schema theory, cognitive network theories, and the aforementioned theory of mental models.

A *cognitive schema* is a cognitive representation of an object or relation between objects (see Fiske & Taylor, 1991; Higgins, Herman, & Zanna, 1981; Wicks, 1992). For instance, we all have a schema for terrorist acts; that is, each of us has an idea of what a typical terrorist act looks like. Since the attacks of 9/11 most of us probably think of Islamist suicide attacks, significant civilian casualties, and so on. Following the model of template schemas (e.g., Hastie, 1981; Tesser, 1978), a schema is broadly defined as a configuration of salient attributes that helps us process subsequent information. A terrorist schema, for instance, is a cognitive representation of terrorists with attributes like "Islamist background," "anti-Western," and "having military training." This means that many audience members usually connect these attributes to terrorists. But we also have a schema for the causes of terrorism and a schema for policy measures against terrorism. The latter include military action or border security. Each of these schemas refers to a specific object or relation—to terrorists themselves, to the causes of terrorism, or to potential ways of fighting terrorism.

This notion of schemas is also consistent with Price and Tewksbury's (1997) model of framing effects, which shows that by framing an issue in a particular fashion, media make some schemas more applicable than others. For example, if mass media portray inhabitants of the Gaza Strip as terrorists ("terrorism frame"), this frame is applicable to a range of terrorism-related audience schemas, including treatment schemas or causal schemas. As a consequence, recipients will support measures like military action, since their treatment-of-terrorism schema is activated by the "terrorism frame" in news reports. If the media frame life in the Gaza Strip in humanitarian terms ("humanitarian frame"), however, very different schemas are made applicable. As a result, audience members may support humanitarian aid since their treatment schema represents international aid to be the appropriate treatment against poverty, hunger, and illness in the world's poor regions.

When dealing with the interplay between schemas and frames, four aspects warrant a more detailed discussion. First, there are individual differences among audience members in terms of the schemas they hold and in terms of the schemas that media frames may be applicable to. But as social cognition approaches in social psychology have shown (cf. Fiske & Taylor, 1991), many schemas are *socially shared*. Since 9/11, for example, many people share the belief that terrorist acts are often attacks by Islamist extremists.

Second, schema theory (e.g., Higgins et al., 1981; Wicks, 1992) also discusses *schema hierarchies*. Schema hierarchies refer to the notion that people sometimes cannot apply a general schema since the particular news item is too unique or specific to fit the general schema. Thus, people either treat this case as an exception from the rule or establish a subschema. Third, theories of *cognitive networks* (e.g., Lindsey & Norman, 1977; Rummelhart & Norman, 1978) conceptualize knowledge about a topic as a network of different related schemas. This can be illustrated using a simple metaphor. Imagine a wood board with light bulbs mounted to it, representing the recipient's brain (see Figure 5.1). Each bulb represents a schema which is connected to other schemas by spreading activation from one schema to another. These connections are indicated by the dashed lines on the top level ("Recipient's network of cognitive schemas") in Figure 5.1. Some network theories (e.g. Clark, 1989; McClelland & Rumelhardt, 1986) suggest even more complex structures with waves of activation. If media framing is applicable to all or parts of these schemas, all other, related schemas are likely activated as well. For instance, if a news report resonates with the "act of terrorism" schema, the "causes of terrorism" schema and the "treatment of terrorism" schema are activated as well due to spreading activation.

This leaves us with an important question: What is a *cognitive frame*? The answer is also outlined in the mental models approach depicted in Figure 5.1. If a newspaper article, for instance, frames inhabitants of the Gaza Strip as terrorists ("Media frame" at the bottom level in Figure 5.1),

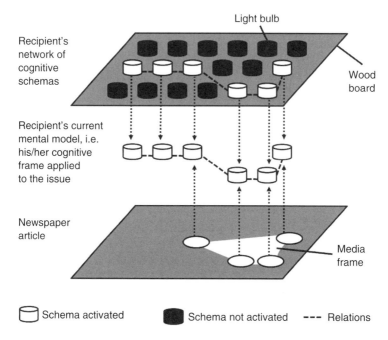

*Figure 5.1*    Light bulbs on wooden board as a simple model of a cognitive frame.

terrorism-related cognitive schemas ("white bulbs" at the top level) are made more applicable than other schemas ("dark bulbs") in the recipient's cognitive network. In Figure 5.1 the media frame activates four of the recipient's terrorism-related schemas by means of applicability. The media frame in Figure 5.1, however, is not applicable to the other two terrorism-related schemas (on the left at the middle level of Figure 5.1). In this example, these unrelated schemas are nonetheless activated by spreading activation.

As a result, the specific mental model applied to the Gaza Strip issue, as per our running example, is a function of the media frame and its applicability to a respondent's cognitive schemas. This specific, temporary mental model is nothing else than the current cognitive frame that the recipient (individual-level) applies to the Gaza Strip issue. In other words, a cognitive frame is a consistent set of activated cognitive schemas (see B. Scheufele, 2004, 2006). This conceptualization of cognitive frames can also serve as a theoretical explanation for sets of individual-level frames held by recipients, journalists, politicians and so on. Expanding on the different sets of framing models offered in the recent literature (for an overview, see D. Scheufele, 1999, 2000; Scheufele & Tewksbury, 2007), our conceptual model draws clear conceptual distinctions between cognitive frames and cognitive schemas. At the same time, it integrates both of them into a consistent model of framing effects that should serve as a blueprint for future empirical work in this area.

### Media Frames (Textual Level)

This conceptualization of cognitive frames also matters for how we think about framing at different levels of analysis, either along a dependent–independent–variable matrix or a horizontal–vertical matrix. Our conceptualization of media frames, therefore, starts from *journalists' cognitions.* Journalists themselves are recipients of news when scanning reports from news tickers or relying on other opinion-leader media. Reports from these sources will resonate with some of the journalists' schemas (white bulbs at the top level in Figure 5.1) thereby shaping his or her issue-specific cognitive frame.

When writing a newspaper article about the Gaza Strip, for example, the journalist may adopt facts from the ticker report, but will also present his or her perspective on the topic for the readers by framing the article in certain way—consciously or unconsciously. In other words, *journalists' cognitive schemas* enter new stories in the form of *media frames.* Thus, it is reasonable to postulate a more or less pronounced correspondence (see Figure 5.2) between cognitive levels (a journalist's schemas) and textual levels (media frames). Based on B. Scheufele's framing model

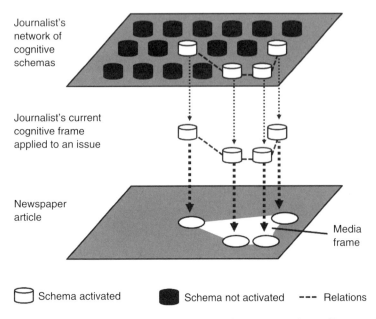

*Figure 5.2*   Correspondence between a journalist's cognitive schemas/frame and the media frame in a newspaper article.

of news production (2006), journalists' individual-level frames and schemas establish and change in *newsroom discourse*. As a result, they serve as working routines for the workaday activities of doing journalism (e.g., Gitlin, 1980; Tuchman, 1972, 1978). Their cognitions are not static, but rather change based on frame building efforts from media opinion leaders, politicians, protest groups, and so on (D. Scheufele, 1999; Walgrave & Manssens, 2005).

If there is a correspondence between the cognitive and the textual level, it is reasonable to assume that the cognitive schemas that shape journalists' cognitive frames also match the *elements of media frames*. In other words, if journalists think about problems, ask for causes, or recommend treatments (cognitive level), they also apply these ways of thinking about an issue to their articles (textual level). For example, journalists think about a political problem in a particular way. In the case of terrorism, this could be a broader schema for the problem of terrorism, but it could also be a schema for thinking about its origins; for example, the "causes of terrorism" schema.

Accordingly, the problem definition and its causal interpretation are likely to be core elements of a media frame at the textual level (e.g., a newspaper article). As far as distinctions between different types of textual frames go, this is also consistent with Entman's (1993) definition of framing, which is, "to select some aspects of a perceived reality and make them more salient in a communicating text, in such a way as to promote a particular problem definition, causal interpretation, moral evaluation, and/or treatment recommendation" (p. 52). These *frame elements*, amended by values, were already suggested by Neidhardt and Rucht (1993). Even earlier, Snow and Benford (1988) addressed similar frame elements when they distinguished between diagnostic, prognostic, and motivational framing.

## Measuring Journalists' Cognitions and Media Frames: A Case Study

These conceptual foundations have important implications for measuring both journalists' frames/schemas and media frames. Those implications are presented next, followed by a case study that illustrates how they work in an actual framing analysis.

### Measuring Journalistic Frames and Media Frames

The best way to explore *journalists' cognitions* would be representative surveys among journalists. Yet, in many cases—for example, for less recent issues—it is difficult to survey journalists retrospectively and tap their cognitive schemas or frames. We will discuss this problem in greater detail later on.

The measurement of *media frames* is somewhat more straightforward, and B. Scheufele (2003) has outlined a series of suggestions for measuring these types of frames. All of these approaches can be divided into qualitative and quantitative techniques (B. Scheufele, 2003). Recently, Matthes and Kohring (2008) presented a similar classification.

The *qualitative approach* splits up into hermeneutic-qualitative and systematic techniques (B. Scheufele, 2003). Most studies applying *hermeneutic-qualitative procedures* (e.g., Fair & Astroff, 1991) provide little systematic information on why and how specific media frames were used in the analyses. Tankard (2001) and others have rightfully criticized many of these studies as being somewhat arbitrary and unsystematic in their approach. But there are some exceptions to the rule: Some qualitative approaches use very systematic techniques, such as careful analyses of syntactical, thematic, rhetorical, and script structures (e.g., van Dijk, 1988; Pan & Kosicki, 1993) or analyses of "framing devices" and "reasoning devices" (Gamson & Modigliani, 1989). Unfortunately, it is difficult to use these more qualitative procedures with larger amounts of material. And in many cases, it is difficult to identify from these more qualitative approaches how framing devices "are woven together to signify a [media] frame" (Reese, 2001, p. 16).

The *quantitative approach* splits up into holistic and device-oriented techniques (B. Scheufele, 2003). *Global techniques* often approach the analysis of media frames by coding for a set of predefined frames previously identified in a qualitative study (e.g., Hendrickson, 1993; Nisbet et al., 2003). Some authors (e.g., Eilders & Lüter, 2000) follow the conceptual definition of framing offered by Snow and Benford (1988), for instance. But the question of how and why specific frames or the interplay between them were included in the analyses often remains unanswered (e.g., Shah, Kwak, Schmierbach, & Zubric, 2004). In fact, one danger of global techniques is that the choices of categories may in fact be influenced by the researchers' own cognitive frames and schemas instead of those actually occurring in media content (for an overview of this problem, see B. Scheufele, 2006).

Studies relying on *device-oriented techniques* code for indicators or elements of frames, rather than predefined categories of frames. Framing devices can be simple indicators like key words (e.g., Entman, 1991; Miller & Andsager, & Reichert, 1998) or can be argumentative structures (e.g., Rössler, 2001; Shanahan & McComas, 1999). Other studies develop categories similar to Entman's (1993) frame elements in a content analysis, conduct a cluster analysis of these frame elements, and then interpret these statistical clusters as media frames (e.g., van Gorp,

2005). Expanding on these techniques, Matthes and Kohring (2008) suggest latent class analysis which is similar in that it promotes clustering procedures to be the best solution for measuring media frames. The key advantage of this method is consistency. In other words, coding very manifest frame elements in text is highly reliable. Unfortunately, the advantages of coding of manifest content come with trade-offs as far as validity is concerned. In fact, it is unlikely that these clusters adequately tap into media frames, which would require coding of latent content.

The potential disconnects between the results of clustering techniques and what they intend to measure are illustrated in Figure 5.3. The clusters that emerge from an analysis of frame elements may *overlap* with media frames to some degree, but it is unlikely that they fully *match* them. In other words, a cluster analysis or similar technique may provide us with a ballpark estimate of what certain media frames or combinations of frames may look like, but it does not measure a media frame in its *pure form*. For example, "agricultural benefit" and "agricultural pros/cons" may be perfectly separating clusters, but definitely do not represent media frames for biotechnology. And "scientific progress" is likely a pure media frame applied to biotechnology, whereas "ethical aspects of scientific progress" is a *statistical artifact* or *mélange* of two pure media frames ("scientific progress" frame and "ethics").

In short, statistical procedures like cluster analysis are merely exploratory tools. As Reese (2007) noted, "[h]ighlighting simple description of media frames is tempting, and a frequent approach given the easy availability of media texts, but this risks reifying them" (p. 149). As a result, scholars have "often identified unique sets of frames with each new study" (Tewksbury & Scheufele, 2009, p. 28) and paid significantly less attention to identifying larger theoretical and potentially more meaningful underlying distinctions.

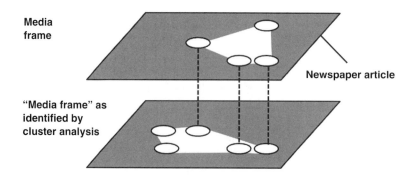

*Figure 5.3*   Why cluster analysis does not measure media frames appropriately.

### Case Study: Applying "Frame Analysis" and "Framing Analysis"

We have empirically tested an alternative to cluster analysis with some success (see B. Scheufele, 2003, 2006). The coding effort goes beyond simple coding of manifest content. But the benefits in terms of meaningful, valid results make up for the initial effort. In the following sections, we present the design, the methods, and selected results from a case study. The case study encompasses a frame analysis and a framing analysis.

The *frame analysis* identified journalists' individual-level cognitions. The editorial staff of a newspaper likely holds similar cognitive schemas, with continuous frame building influences from the "outside" world (e.g., politicians promoting their own frames, interest groups, NGOs, etc.). When reporting about xenophobia or violence against foreigners, for example, journalists working together on a news desk likely have similar schemas for making sense of xenophobic attacks, of the causes of xenophobia, and of appropriate policy measures for fighting xenophobia. In other words, within any given news organization, it is reasonable to expect significant overlaps among journalists with respect to their cognitive perspectives or frames for an issue, such as xenophobia (refer to Figure 5.2). The *framing analysis* explored whether these cognitive schemas/frames served as working routines and entered media coverage in the form of *media frames*.

As outlined earlier, systematic surveys among journalists would be the best way to identify journalists' cognitions. Unfortunately, surveys are restricted to data collections of current events and limited in their ability to assess phenomena retrospectively. Since the case study focused on xenophobia during the early 1990s in Germany, we had to apply a different method. For our *frame analysis* we therefore retrieved journalists' cognitions from editorials published by the two leading national papers, the *Frankfurter Allgemeine Zeitung* (FAZ) (published nationally and located in Frankfurt, Germany) and the *Sueddeutsche Zeitung* (SZ) (published nationally and located in Munich, Germany). Editorials express journalists' cognitive schemas and frames in a condensed form.

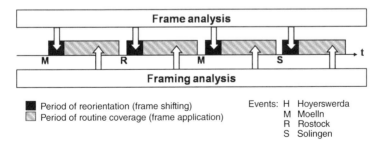

*Figure 5.4*   Study design: Frame analysis and framing analysis.

We did not analyze all commentaries, only those published directly after the four most high-profile xenophobic attacks (Hoyerswerda, Rostock, Moelln, Solingen) that took place in Germany in the early 1990s. We expected that journalists' cognitions were "reformatted" within 2 weeks of each event. We call this a *period of reorientation* (see Figure 5.4).

Our frame analysis explored how journalists' cognitive schemas and frames shifted after each event. For instance, several foreigners had been killed in Moelln. As a consequence, commentaries published directly after Moelln showed that journalists no longer thought of xenophobia as the result of failed asylum policies and too many asylum seekers entering Germany ("asylum frame"), but as a problem of rising levels of right-wing and neo-Nazi extremism in Germany ("Nazi frame").

For our *framing analysis* (i.e., analysis at the textual level) we tested whether journalists also applied these modified or new cognitive schemas/frames in the news articles they wrote about xenophobia. Here, we content analyzed *news articles* published in so-called *routine periods* subsequent to each period of reorientation (see Figure 5.4).

The overall design was not circular since our frame analysis applied a qualitative coding technique and the framing analysis was based on a large-scale quantitative content analysis. In addition, we focused on different time periods for the frame analysis and for the framing analysis (see Figure 5.4). Finally, the frame analysis sample comprised editorials whereas the framing analysis explored news articles.

*Frame Analysis*   As outlined earlier, our frame analysis focused on the two leading national papers in Germany: the *Frankfurter Allgemeine Zeitung* (FAZ) and the *Sueddeutsche Zeitung* (SZ). We selected eight commentaries dealing with xenophobia for each paper in each of the four periods of reorientation (see Figure 5.4), which comprised a total of 64 commentaries. The commentaries were not selected randomly but by means of thematic variance. In order to retrieve journalists' cognitions from their commentaries, we developed a frame identifying technique which included several steps.

The starting point was a qualitative coding of the commentaries, which we consider a good indicator of journalists' cognitive schemas in a condensed form. Coders analyzed the commentaries by applying a semi-open *coding scheme* and answering such coding questions as "Which causes of xenophobia are mentioned in the commentary?" or "Which attributes of perpetrators are mentioned in the commentary?" The coding questions tapped references to cognitive schemas and to relationships among them; that is, to objects such as perpetrators or victims of violence, as well as to relational references such as the causes of xenophobia or the effects of xenophobia on society.

Second, the analysis of the completed coding manuals identified the presumed *references to cognitive schemas*. We applied Mayring's (2000, 2002) technique of summarizing, so all "answers" in the coding sheets were reduced and generalized in terms of the schema references mentioned. Table 5.1 presents the final list of schema references which were retrieved from the coding of the editorials. The classifications in Table 5.1 are based on the assumption that journalists had a schema for each schema reference. For instance, we assumed that journalists had a cognitive schema for xenophobic attacks, including a culprit-schema representing their interpretations of the perpetrators behind xenophobic crimes. But, as Table 5.1 indicates, journalists also held schemas about the likely causes of xenophobia, about the effects of attacks against foreigners (e.g., politicians publicly demanding tougher review criteria for asylum applications), and about the treatment necessary to fight xenophobia.

The third analytic step asked for the *schema attributes*, which builds on the idea of template schemas (e.g., Hastie, 1981; Tesser, 1978). Our assumption was that journalists' cognitive schemas would shift after each of the four very prominent xenophobic attacks (Hoyerswerda, Rostock, Moelln, and Solingen; refer to Figure 5.4). Based on this assumption, we compared all attributes for a specific schema reference (e.g., culprits). For example, we compared all attributes of culprits mentioned in the commentaries published directly after Hoyerswerda to all attributes of culprits mentioned in commentaries directly after Rostock, and so on. Comparisons were conducted separately within all schema references (e.g., culprits).

*Table 5.1   Schema References for Xenophobia*

| General schema reference | Schema type | Specific schema reference | Specific schema type |
|---|---|---|---|
| Event | Event schema/ script | a) Xenophobic attacks | a) Attack schema |
| | | b) Demonstrations against xenophobia | b) Demonstration-schema |
| Person/Group | Person/Group schema | a) Culprits | a) Culprit schema |
| | | b) Victims | b) Victim schema |
| | | c) Demonstrators | c) Demonstrator schema |
| | | d) Right-wing extremists | d) Right-wing extremists schema |
| Cause | Causal schema | Causes of xenophobia | Sub schemata for different spheres (e.g. political sphere) |
| Effect/Treatment | Effects/ Treatment schema | Effects/Treatment of xenophobia | Sub-schemata for different spheres (e.g. policy measures) |

An example is as follows. Directly after Rostock, journalists shared the culprit-schema "the savage mob." In other words, journalists' cognitive schemas were built on the assumption that xenophobic crimes or attacks were usually committed by right-wing circles which organized and instigated mass hysteria among violent young skinheads. After Solingen, however, their schemas shifted toward an interpretation that saw perpetrators as fanatic young Nazis, acting alone, and becoming murderers. After all rounds of coding and comparisons were completed, our analyses provided us with a systematic overview of which cognitive schemas were prevalent after each of the four events in Hoyerswerda, Rostock, Moelln, and Solingen. In addition to providing extremely valid assessments of journalists' prevalent cognitive schemas, the comparison strategy within schema references and between locations is also directly consistent with the technique of ideal typing that descends from the work of Max Weber (1984, 1988).

The fourth and final analytic step tapped into *cognitive frames*. As outlined earlier (see Figures 5.1 and 5.2), all currently applicable cognitive schemas make up a consistent cognitive frame. Thus, cognitive frames were derived from the schemas identified before in the final step. Let us illustrate this last step: All cognitive schemas that emerged from the editorials after Hoyerswerda were playing on a broader perspective related to political asylum. Asylum seekers were seen by journalists as the archetypical victims (victim-schema), the unsolved political problem of too many asylum seekers in Germany was seen as the major cause of xenophobia (causes-schema), and more restrictive regulations for obtaining political asylum were perceived to be the best way to stop xenophobic crimes (treatment-schema). Thus, the dominant cognitive frame after Hoyerswerda—and even after Rostock—was labeled the *"asylum frame."* After Moelln and Solingen, however, the overall perspective applied to xenophobia shifted to *"neo-Nazi extremism"* as the core cognitive frame underlying most of the cognitive schemas that emerged from our analysis of relevant editorials. Of course, there were other cognitive frames available in this period as well. For instance, journalists also framed xenophobia in terms of an integration of foreigners into the German way of life in the periods after Moelln and Solingen—but not in the periods after Hoyerswerda and Rostock. These cognitive frames, however, remained rather peripheral and secondary. We applied the same contrasting strategy within frames and between events that we had used for schema identification.

*Framing Analysis*   Framing analysis examined if journalists' cognitive schemas and frames—as retrieved from the commentaries in the periods of reorientation—matched the media frames in the articles being published in the succeeding period of routine coverage (see Figure 5.4). In short, our framing analysis tested how closely journalists' cognitions matched the subsequent framing of issues in media content. For the sake of this chapter, we only present findings for *schema-specific congruency*. For instance, we examine the degree to which journalists' culprit-schemas fit the culprit images presented in the news articles written about each event. Overall frame congruency was measured the same way. For calculating the *degree of schema-specific congruency* the framing analysis codebook had to be adjusted to the findings of the frame analysis. For this purpose the cognitive schemas—as identified by frame analysis—were broken up into their constituents. Practically, all schema attributes (e.g., all attributes of the culprit-schemas) were listed and then transferred into categories (e.g., categories for culprits) for the codebook of the framing analysis. The left part of Figure 5.5 outlines this procedure.

Breaking down schemas into categories allowed us to assign codes that indicated congruency for each category value (see right half of Figure 5.5). Let us illustrate this procedure with an example: If an article was published in the period of routine coverage after Moelln (refer to Figure 5.2) and mentioned a neo-Nazi culprit, this culprit attribute matched the corresponding cognitive schema among journalists which had emerged from the frame analysis after Moelln. This would be a case of schema *congruency*. If the *same* article would have been published in the period of routine coverage after Hoyerswerda, the culprit attribute "neo-Nazi" would not have matched the culprit-schema from

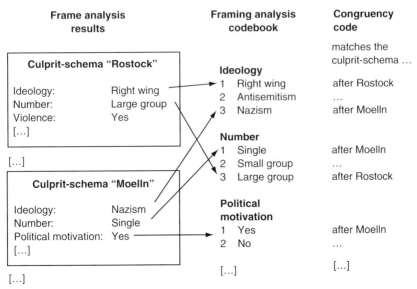

*Figure 5.5* Transforming cognitive schemas from frame analysis into codebook categories for the framing analysis (including congruency codes, exemplified by culprits of xenophobia).

the corresponding period of reorientation that emerged from the frame analysis after Hoyerswerda. This would be a case of schema *incongruency*. Accordingly, a binary *congruency code* was allocated for each category. Of course, this code was invisible for the coders. For instance, if a culprit-attribute was consistent with the corresponding culprit-schema, we assigned a congruency code of 1. If the attribute did not match, the congruency code was 0. This logic was applied to all schema attributes. Finally, an average of all culprit-attributes was calculated per article. This culprit-schema index indicated the *relative schema congruency* for each article and schema (e.g., culprits).

The *congruency-index for any given schema* (e.g., attack schema) was a ratio of all schema-consistent attributes and the total of attributes mentioned in an article. The closer this standardized index was to 1.00, the more schema-consistent attributes were mentioned ("Congruency"). An index value of 0.50 indicated an equal amount of schema-consistent and schema-discrepant attributes in the articles. In most of the cases we found schema-congruency (for more details, see B. Scheufele, 2006).

## Measuring Framing Effects: A Call for Theory-Based Research

As this chapter has shown, framing refers to the applicability of semantic or visual devices in communication to underlying culturally shared audience schemas. Cognitive frames (including those held by journalists) emerge as a combination of applicability (Price & Tewksbury, 1997) and spreading activation. Similar to a wooden frame around an oil painting, any given news frame will draw attention to certain *objects and relations* while downplaying others. In other words, framing is a function of simplifying an area of reality. Journalists, for example, may assume that mobs of angry, unemployed citizens—and not neo-Nazi fringe groups— are the main perpetrators behind most xenophobic crimes. But framing also means applying certain *standards* to these objects; that is, to the area of reality that is being focused on. Journalists, for instance, may interpret anti-immigration riots—and not arsonist attacks on foreigners' homes—as typical examples of xenophobic crimes. Here, different attributes are applied to the same class of objects; that is, to the xenophobic crimes. Taking all this into consideration, a cognitive frame can be defined as a *consistent set of cognitive schemata emerging in discourse* (e.g., among the editorial staff of a newspaper) *and becoming manifest in discourse products* (e.g., newspaper articles). Scholars should take their terminological work more seriously when it comes to frames and schemas. The theoretical reasoning presented in this chapter can serve as a blueprint for future empirical work.

Based on these multilevel definitions of framing, the case study out-lined in this chapter provides an overview of coding systems that can serve as a blueprint or as valid *and* reliable tests of framing processes. While our analyses focus on the link between journalists' cognitive frames and their impact on media frames, the theoretical premises of our work are applicable to other links in the independent–dependent matrix or the horizontal–vertical matrix outlined earlier. Exploring these other links, of course, raises other challenges, such as how to measure audi-ence schemas at a large scale without priming particular topics or arti-ficially establishing links between schemas in people's heads. And the answers to some of these questions may come from other, related areas of political communication research. Work on "knowledge structure density" (see Eveland, Cortese, Park, & Dunwoody, 2004), for example, may provide important insights into how to tap the contents and connec-tions within people's cognitive schemas in a reliable and cost-effective way in large scale surveys.

With these considerations in mind, we close with a few agenda items for future research. It is important to note that this section is not meant as a broader agenda for framing research. In fact, such an overview has been provided most recently by Tewksbury and Scheufele (2007; Tewks-bury & Scheufele, 2009). Rather, we will reiterate some of the method-ological implications of the work outlined in this chapter for measuring framing effects.

First, our theoretical models and also some of the results from the case study show clearly that analyzing media frames is much more method-ologically challenging than many previous studies have acknowledged. Purely deductive approaches that scan news coverage for predefined sets of categories face the problem that no consistent set of categories has emerged from the recent literature (Tewksbury & Scheufele, 2009). In other words, our field yet has to produce a commonly shared understand-ing of what kinds of consistent frames emerge across issues or cultures, or of the socially shared cognitive schemas to which they are applicable. Without this a priori theoretical framework, much of our understand-ing of media frames remains haphazard. In fact, without it any search for media frames is potentially contaminated by (a) a researcher's own cognitive schemas and ways of making sense of an issue; (b) the current media climate surrounding an issue, which can change significantly due to key events (see Fishman, 1978, 1982) like Moelln or Solingen in our analysis; and (c) medium-specific framing, such as Iyengar's (1991) find-ings related to episodic framing of local television news.

As our theoretical overview showed, however, purely *inductive* approaches are plagued by similar problems. Most importantly, explor-atory analyses of elements of frames are likely to produce thematic clusters that sometimes correspond to meaningful media frames, and sometimes do not. This lack of validity needs to be addressed in future research in a number of ways. First, if media frames can in fact be identified in a valid and generalizable fashion using exploratory tools for data reduction, it should also be possible to replicate the emerging clusters across issues using confirmatory tools of data analysis. Tests across multiple issues therefore need to be part of any study that tries to identify media frames based on exploratory cluster analysis of manifest content. Second, and more importantly, by focusing almost exclusively on manifest content, inductive clustering techniques make inevitable trade-offs in terms of validity. The multistage coding system outlined in our case study can provide important insights into how to cost-effectively analyze large amounts of coverage over time, while balancing concerns about validity and reliability.

The second implication is that most studies of framing effects operationally distinguish media frames at a single level, rather than exploring the possibility of frame hierarchies or, at least, multilevel conceptualizations of framing. This phenomenon is partly due to the parsimony and intuitive appeal of early psychological approaches to framing, such as prospect theory (Kahneman, 2003). Given the conceptual complexities of framing outlined earlier, however, the distinctions between *cognitive frames* and *cognitive schemas* is critical for future research in this area, since it helps avoid the rather oblique theoretical reasoning about cognitive structures in our field so far. Unfortunately, however, studies focusing narrowly on the psychological processes that underlie framing effects sometimes neglect to take into account important insights from the public discourse or social movement literature. These perspectives on framing (e.g., Gamson, 1992; Gamson & Modigliani, 1989; Snow & Benford, 1988) defined several frame elements, for example, problem definition, causal reasoning, solutions or values, even earlier than Entman (1993). It is assumed that there must be a consistent relation between all frame elements in order to form a powerful perspective. From our point of view, some frame elements (or combination of elements) may be more effective depending on the issue. For example, in the case of disasters, causal and responsibility considerations dominate public discourse. In other words, causal framing or messages may be more powerful than any other type of framing. In the case of scandals, political standards or social norms are violated. As a result, value framing may be more effective and predominant in public discourse. Future research therefore needs to compare framing effects of controversial issues and framing effects of routine issues. For the latter, recipients' cognitions likely moderate the effects of media framing, as suggested by findings on chronic accessibility in cognitive psychology (e.g., Higgins, 1989) and as modeled by the theory of mental models (e.g. Johnson-Laird, 1980, 1989).

We therefore urge scholars to integrate macroscopic sociological public discourse and social movement approaches (e.g. Gamson, 1992; Gamson & Modigliani, 1989; Snow & Benford, 1988) and microscopic psychological framing effects approaches in their thinking about framing and framing effects. Without this kind of conceptual integration, we are not fully capitalizing on the theoretical potential or the methodological opportunities that framing as a research domain provides.

## References

Cappella, J. N., & Jamieson, K. H. (1997). *Spiral of cynicism: The press and the public good*. New York: Oxford University Press.

Clark, A. (1989). *Microcognition: Philosophy, cognitive science, and parallel distributed processing*. Cambridge, MA: Harvard University Press.

Entman, R. M. (1991). Framing U.S. coverage of international news: Contrasts in narratives of the KAL and Iran air incidents. *Journal of Communication, 41*, 6–27.

Entman, R. M. (1993). Framing: Towards clarification of a fractured paradigm. *Journal of Communication, 43*, 51–58.

Eilders, C., & Lüter, A. (2000): Germany at war: Competing framing strategies in German public discourse. *European Journal of Communication, 15*, 415–428.

Eveland Jr., W. P., Cortese, J., Park, H., & Dunwoody, S. (2004). How web site organization influences free recall, factual knowledge, and knowledge structure density. *Human Communication Research, 30*(2), 208–233.

Fair, J. E., & Astroff, R. J. (1991). Constructing race and violence: U.S. news coverage and the signifying practices of Apartheid. *Journal of Communication, 41*, 58–74.

Fishman, M. (1978). Crime waves as ideology. *Social Problems, 25*, 531-543.

Fishman, M. (1982). News and nonevents: Making the visible invisible. In J. S. Ettema & D. C. Whitney (Eds.), *Individuals in mass media organizations: Creativity and constraint* (pp. 219–240). Beverly Hills, CA: Sage.

Fiske, S. T., & Taylor, S. E. (1991). *Social cognition* (2nd ed.). New York: McGraw-Hill.

Galtung, J., & Ruge, M. H. (1965). The structure of foreign news. *Journal of Peace Research, 2*(1), 64–91.

Gamson, W. A. (1992). *Talking politics*. New York: Cambridge University Press.

Gamson, W. A., & Modigliani, A. (1989). Media discourse and public opinion on nuclear power: A constructionist approach. *American Journal of Sociology, 95*, 1–37.

Gitlin, T. (1980). *The whole world is watching: Mass media in the making and unmaking of the New Left*. Berkeley, CA: University of California Press.

Hastie, R. (1981). Schematic principles in human memory. In E. T. Higgins, C. P. Herman, & M. P. Zanna (Eds.), *Social cognition: The Ontario Symposium, Vol. 1* (pp. 39–89). Hillsdale, NJ: Erlbaum.

Hendrickson, L. J. (1993, May). *Degrees of framing in media content*. Paper presented at the 43rd annual convention of the International Communication Association. Washington, DC.

Higgins, E. T. (1989). Knowledge accessibility and activation: Subjectivity and suffering from unconscious sources. In J. S. Uleman & J. A. Bargh (Eds.), *Unintended thought: The limits of awareness, intention and control* (pp. 75–123). New York: Guilford Press.

Higgins, E. T., Herman, C. P., & Zanna, M. P. (1981). *Social cognition: The Ontario Symposium* (Vol. 1). Hillsdale, NJ: Erlbaum.

Huang, K. S. (1995). *A comparison between media frames and audience frames: The case of the Hill-Thomas controversy.* Unpublished doctoral dissertation, University of Wisconsin-Madison.

Huang, K. S. (1996, May). *A comparison between media frames and audience frames: The case of the Hill-Thomas controversy.* Paper presented to the annual convention of the International Communication Association, Chicago.

Iyengar, S. (1991). *Is anyone responsible? How television frames political issues.* Chicago: University of Chicago Press.

Johnston, H., & **Noakes, J.** (Eds.). (2005). *Frames of protest: Social movements and the framing perspective.* Boston: Rowman & Littlefield.

Johnson-Laird, P. N. (1980). Mental models in cognitive science. *Cognitive Science, 4,* 71–115.

Johnson-Laird, P. N. (1989). Mental models. In M. I. Posner (Ed.), *Foundations of cognitive science* (pp. 469–499). Cambridge, MA: MIT Press.

Kahneman, D. (2003). Maps of bounded rationality: A perspective on intuitive judgment and choice. In T. Frängsmyr (Ed.), *Les Prix Nobel: The Nobel Prizes 2002* (pp. 449–489). Stockholm, Sweden: Nobel Foundation.

Lindsey, P. M., & Norman, D. A. (1977). *Human information processing: An introduction to psychology.* New York: Harcourt.

Matthes, J., & Kohring, M. (2008). The content analysis of media frames: Toward improving reliability and validity. *Journal of Communication, 58,* 258–279.

Mayring, P. (2000). *Qualitative Inhaltsanalyse. Grundlagen und Techniken* [Qualitative content analysis: Basics and techniques] (7th ed.). Weinheim, Germany: Beltz.

Mayring, P. (2002). Qualitative content analysis—Research instrument or mode of interpretation? In M. Kiegelmann (Ed.), *The role of the researcher in qualitative psychology* (pp. 139–148). Tübingen, Germany: Verlag Ingeborg Huber.

McClelland, J. L., & Rumelhardt, D. E. (1986). *Parallel distributed processing: Vol. 2. Psychological and biological models.* Cambridge, MA: Harvard University Press.

McCombs, M. E. (2004). *Setting the agenda: The mass media and public opinion.* Malden, MA: Blackwell.

Miller, M. M., Andsager, J. L., & Reichert, B. P. (1998). Framing the candidates in presidential primaries: Issues and images in press releases and news coverage. *Journalism & Mass Communication Quarterly, 75*(2), 312–324.

Neidhardt, F. & Rucht, D. (1993). Auf dem Weg in die „Bewegungsgesellschaft"? [Towards a "social movement society"?]. *Soziale Welt, 44,* 305–326

Nelson, T. E., Oxley, Z. M., & Clawson, R. A. (1997). Toward a psychology of framing effects. *Political Behavior, 19*, 221–246.

Nisbet, M. C., Brossard, D., & Kroepsch, A. (2003). Framing science: The stem cell controversy in an age of press/politics. *Harvard International Journal of Press-Politics, 8*, 36–70.

Pan, Z., & Kosicki, G. M. (1993). Framing analysis: An approach to news discourse. *Political Communication, 10*, 55–75.

Park, E., & Kosicki, G. M. (1995). Presidential support during the Iran-contra-affair: People's reasoning process and media influence. *Communication Research, 22*, 207–236.

Price, V., & Tewksbury, D. (1997). News values and public opinion: A theoretical account of media priming and framing. In G. A. Barett & F. J. Boster (Eds.), *Progress in communication sciences: Advances in persuasion* (Vol. 13, pp. 173–212). Greenwich, CT: Ablex.

Price, V., Tewksbury, D., & Powers, E. (1997). Switching trains of thought: The impact of news frames on reader's cognitive responses. *Communication Research, 24*, 481–506.

Reese, S. D. (2001). Prologue—Framing public life: A bridging model for media research. In S. D. Reese, O. H. Gandy, & A. E. Grant (Eds.), *Framing public life: Perspectives on media and our understanding of the social world* (pp. 7–31). Mahwah, NJ: Erlbaum.

Reese, S. D. (2007). The framing project: A bridging model for media research revisited. *Journal of Communication, 57*(1), 148–154.

Rössler, P. (2001). Between online-heaven and cyberhell: The framing of "the internet" by traditional media coverage in Germany. *New Media & Society, 3*, 49–66.

Rummelhart, D. E., & Norman, D. A. (1978). Accretion, tuning, and restructuring: Three models of learning. In J. W. Cotton & R. L. Klatzky (Eds.), *Semantic factors in cognition* (pp. 37–53). Hillsdale, NJ: Erlbaum.

Scheufele, B. (2003). *Frames—Framing—Framing-Effekte: Theoretische und methodische Grundlegung sowie empirische Befunde zur Nachrichten-produktion* [Frames—framing—framing effects: Theoretical and methodological foundation and empirical results on news production]. Wiesbaden, Germany: Westdeutscher Verlag.

Scheufele, B. (2004). Framing effects research: A theoretical and methodological critique. *Communications—European Journal of Communication Research, 29*, 401–428.

Scheufele, B. (2006). Frames, schemata and news reporting. *Communications—European Journal of Communication Research, 31*, 65–83.

Scheufele, D. A. (1999). Framing as a theory of media effects. *Journal of Communication, 49*, 103–122.

Scheufele, D. A. (2000). Agenda-setting, priming, and framing revisited: Another look at cognitive effects of political communication. *Mass Communication & Society, 3*(2&3), 297–316.

Scheufele, D. A., & Tewksbury, D. (2007). Framing, agenda setting, and priming: The evolution of three media effects models. *Journal of Communication, 57*(1), 9–20.

Shah, D. V., Kwak, N., Schmierbach, M., & Zubric, J. (2004). The interplay of news frames on cognitive complexity. *Human Communication Research*, *30*(1), 102–120.

Shanahan, J., & McComas, K. (1999). *Nature stories: Depictions of the environment and their effects*. Cresskill, NJ: Hampton Press.

Shoemaker, P. J., & Reese, S. D. (1996). *Mediating the message: Theories of influences on mass media content* (2nd ed.). White Plains, NY: Longman.

Snow, D. A., & Benford, R. D. (1988). Ideology, frame resonance, and participant mobilization. In B. Klandermans, H. Kriesi, & S. Tarrow (Eds.), *International social movement research: Vol. 1. From structure to action: Comparing social movement research across cultures* (pp. 197–217). Greenwich, CT: JAI Press.

Tankard, J. W. (2001). The empirical approach to the study of media framing. In S. D. Reese, O. H. Gandy, & A. E. Grant (Eds.), *Framing public life: Perspectives on media and our understanding of the social world* (pp. 95–106). Mahwah, NJ: Erlbaum.

Tesser, A. (1978): Self-generated attitude change. In L. Berkowitz (Eds.): *Advances in experimental social psychology* (Vol. 11, pp. 289–233). New York: Academic Press.

Tewksbury, D., & Scheufele, D. A. (2009). News framing theory and research. In J. Bryant & M. B. Oliver (Eds.), *Media effects: Advances in theory and research* (3rd ed., pp. 17–33). New York: Erlbaum.

Tuchman, G. (1972). Making news by doing work: Routinizing the unexpected. *American Journal of Sociology, 79*, 110–131.

Tuchman, G. (1978). *Making news: A study in the construction of reality*. New York: Knopf.

Valkenburg, P. M., Semetko, H. A., & de Vreese, C. H. (1999). The effects of news frames on readers' thoughts and recall. *Communication Research, 26*, 550–569.

van Dijk, T. A. (1988). *News as discourse*. Hillsdale, NJ: Erlbaum.

*Van Gorp, B. (2005)*. Where is the *frame*? Victims and intruders in the Belgian press coverage of the asylum issue. *European Journal of Communication, 20*, 484–507.

Walgrave, S., & Manssens, J. (2005). Mobilizing the white march: Media frames as alternatives to movement organizations. In H. Johnston & J. H. Noakes (Eds.), *Frames of protest: Social movements and the framing perspective* (pp. 113–140). Lanham, MD: Rowman & Littlefield.

Weber, M. (1984). *Soziologische Grundbegriffe* [Basic concepts of sociology]. Tübingen, Germany: J. B. Mohr. (Original work published 1921)

Weber, M. (1988). Die „Objektivität" sozialwissenschaftlicher und sozialpolitischer Erkenntnis [The "objectivity" of social sciences and sociopolitical knowledge]. In J. Winkelmann (Ed.), *Gesammelte Aufsätze zur Wissenschaftslehre* (7th ed., pp. 146–214). Tübingen: Mohr. (Original work published 1904)

Wicks, R. H. (1992). Schema theory and measurement in mass communication research: Theoretical and methodological issues in news information processing. In S. A. Deetz (Ed.), *Communication Yearbook* (Vol. 15, pp. 115–145). Newbury Park, CA: Sage.

# Chapter 6

# The Oppositional Framing of Bloggers

*Stephen D. Cooper*

As a new feature of the media system, the blogosphere is an extremely interesting subject for scholarly inquiry. One might spend research time along a variety of lines: why people blog, why people read blog content, the relationship of the blogosphere to the established media outlets, the who/what/when of blog content production and consumption, the subject matter of blog posts, the effects of exposure to blog content, the potential for and limitations on interactions, and so on, for quite a long list. Given that the blogosphere is a recent addition to the media mix, and itself a (presumably) unintended consequence of a technological innovation (computer-mediated communication, as a channel) and a heavy investment in infrastructure (the Internet, as an information transport resource), it is unsurprising that so much foundational inquiry into the blogosphere is warranted, and that the initial scholarly answers to the questions are so divergent! It seems fair, to me, to consider this situation as a real-life instance of the old joke about blind men arguing among themselves about what kind of thing an elephant is, each placing his hand on a different part of the elephant's anatomy.[1] We might be able to stipulate that the blogosphere has quickly become a social object of some degree of consequence and interest, but beyond that the insights we have into it will necessarily be shaped heavily by what aspects of the blogosphere we focus upon (the part of the elephant's body) and the tools we use to investigate it (our hand, and sense of touch). One of those body parts this blind man happened to touch was the way bloggers would share their understandings of the meanings of current events—the frames in which they understood the bare facts—and the hand with which I reached out was rhetorical framing analysis.

My personal interest in the blogosphere began when I noticed that bloggers would frequently take issue with some aspect of a news story—that a genre which seemed at first glance to be confined to trivial personal stories could in fact be a vehicle for substantive media criticism. Indeed, much of the content in the blogosphere is talk about hobbies, personal experiences and aspirations, relationship failures and successes, food and beverage preferences, specialized technologies and gadgetry fascinating to the blogger, self-promotion, and the like. And no doubt, there are substantial lines of inquiry to be pursued in this, related to questions about representation of oneself in cyberspace, representation of others in cyberspace, disclosure, deception, trust, interaction, uses and gratifications, political advocacy, and various other dimensions of computer-mediated interpersonal and mass communication. Perlmutter (2008), Kerbel and Bloom (2005), O'Donnell and McClung (2008), and Kaye (2005) are a few examples of such work.

The media criticism blogging seemed to me to be qualitatively different. This struck me as very much an instance of "talking back to power," in that an ordinary citizen with a relatively modest financial investment in a computer and Internet connection could take issue with professional journalists and the established news media outlets with whom they were affiliated. Not only could an ordinary citizen question the veracity of factual assertions in the news products, but—to the topic of this book— he or she could problematize the interpretations of facts routinely packaged with straight news reporting. I noticed that sometimes the media criticism was direct (as in, "Today's story in the [name of outlet] gets the issue completely wrong.") and other times it was indirect (as when a blogger drew facts from mainstream reporting and then built a different interpretation around them). In sum, it seemed to me that blogging could be a genuinely populist vehicle for critical analysis of the mainstream news media's framing, very much along the lines of the critical news framing paradigm D'Angelo (2002) described.

Viewing this as a version of consumer-to-producer feedback (i.e., the blogger as consumer of the mainstream outlet's news product), a strikingly new element is that the feedback is publicly available at the wish of the author of the feedback; put bluntly, the means of production are entirely in the hands of the blogger, and the mainstream outlet subject to the criticism is in no position to gatekeep the criticism. This is, of course, much different from a newspaper editor's power to run, edit, or reject a critical reader's letter to the editor, or a broadcaster's decision to take a call on air, or not. Moreover, a good number of blogs enable comment threads, and readers of the blog criticism can contribute their thoughts. There is an opportunity for the collaborative generation of critique in the blogosphere which seems to me to be an unprecedented feature in our media system.

In short, the evolution of the blogosphere offers both a rich subject to scholars interested in the relationship of the press and the public and a deep niche of media criticism to examine. And just as the innovation of computer-mediated communication suggested fresh questions (how is interpersonal communication different/similar when it goes through this new channel?) and rethought applications of time-proven methods of inquiry, so does this content innovation of serious media criticism in the blogosphere. In my opinion, qualitative inductive methods are a good choice in this situation, given the exploratory nature of the inquiry into a new communication phenomenon. That was the approach I chose for earlier work aimed at developing a typology of blog media criticism I was seeing and at sketching an analytical framework for the structural characteristics of blogosphere as a component of the public sphere (Cooper, 2006). I believe rhetorical framing analysis is a particularly useful tool for exploring this new body of mediated content widely available at minimal cost, and in the rest of this chapter I will try to show why.

It will be helpful to first describe a working definition of blogging and the blogosphere. To give a sense of the scope and nature of media criticism blogging, I will summarize a typology then supply a few concise illustrations of framing critique written by bloggers. This will lead to some observations about the unconventional authorial voice some bloggers use, and some thoughts about the suitability of a qualitative approach to this material.

Some readers may be unfamiliar with the blogosphere, and a Google search of "blog" is likely to come up with a large quantity of rather unimpressive material! I can recommend a number of blogs on which—in my opinion—there frequently appears thoughtful and thought-provoking commentary on the events of the day and the reporting of those events. No doubt others would put together a different list, and there are many others I could add to these! To best assess the media criticism blogging I would advise that one bracket off one's own political viewpoint, the better to focus on the substance of the argumentation the blogger is constructing. I mention this because in conversations with other academicians I have noticed that the blogger's politics is often the first thing they react to, and I think that can easily obscure the essential strengths and weaknesses of the argumentation. Put another way, I am of the mind that the quality of the media criticism a blogger makes (with regard to logic and evidence) is one matter, and whether the critique reinforces or goes contrary to one's personal ideology and political preferences is another. Another caution is that comment on the political issue of the day is not, in itself, media criticism; comment on the press's performance in covering the political issue of the day, including comment on the interpretations offered in the coverage, is media criticism.

That said, I believe the following blogs are useful starting points for a reader who wishes to get acquainted with media criticism blogging, as these authors often put up such posts:

Instapundit (http://pajamasmedia.com/instapundit/)
Power Line (http://powerlineblog.com/)
Hot Air (http://hotair.com/)

Patterico's Pontifications (http://patterico.com/)
Big Lizards (http://www.biglizards.net/blog/)
Protein Wisdom (http://proteinwisdom.com/)
QandO (http://www.qando.net/)
Back Talk (http://engram-backtalk.blogspot.com/index.html)

These are not necessarily the most visited sites; one can check the traffic statistics on Technorati to see which blogs get the most visits. However, these blogs give a good sense of the range of style and substance in this genre, particularly with regard to media criticism and argumentation.

## Defining Characteristics of the Blogosphere

Since preexisting meanings and current usage reciprocally influence each other in a living language such as English, it is unsurprising to find a degree of ambiguity in the terminology for a new phenomenon, even as the terminology finds its way into common usage. The nouns *blog* and *blogosphere* are no exception, and it will be helpful here to be as precise as possible about what they refer to, for the sake of clarity in the following discussion of their characteristics.

A blog is a variety of personal Web page formatted as a series of dated/time-stamped entries displayed in reverse chronological order. The entries are archived on the site, each having its own URL (called a permalink); hence each post is directly accessible.[2] The author may be a single individual or, as has become more common in the last few years, a small group of individuals. A good number of mainstream news outlets have added a "blog" feature to the online versions of their product, but I would distinguish these from the blogs produced by individual private citizens, even if they do share certain format or style characteristics. The issue is the degree of editorial independence of the blogger when the site is affiliated with an established corporate entity. That would be an interesting line of inquiry in itself, and my guess is that mainstream journalists enjoy somewhat more editorial independence when they blog than when they report for their parent news outlet, but presumably less editorial independence than a private citizen blogging on a Web site he or she owns and operates.

At the level of the media system, the independent blogger (sometimes called "citizen journalist") occupies a special niche in the media ecology. At a minimum this is a new channel for audience feedback. It is my view that the population of active bloggers and the document universe of their products (named the *blogosphere* by Bill Quick, 2001) have already evolved well beyond a simple feedback path into a decentralized and self-organizing institutional counterbalance to the established news out-

lets.[3] It is in the blogosphere that one finds news media criticism ranging from abusive, trashy, and shallow to courteous, professional, and
deeply insightful. Perhaps most intriguing is the media criticism which is
stylistically unrefined yet contains potent insights and substantive objections to the mainstream content. That is to say, the authorial voice may
be unorthodox, even transgressive. Yet the content is worthy of serious
consideration. In my view, it is crucial for the reader of blog documents
to clearly distinguish the style from the substance of the thinking, if one
is to fairly appraise the quality of the documents as intellectual works.
Style and substance are separate variables, and it is a mistake to assume
they are highly correlated in any easily operationalized way.[4] The examples later in this chapter serve to illustrate this point.

## A Typology of Media Criticism Blogging

*Watching the Watchdog* (Cooper, 2006) was my attempt to begin to see
regularities and patterns in the media criticism which was proliferating
in the blogosphere. Quite simply, I proceeded much as an ethnographer
might try to understand an unfamiliar culture, collecting artifacts and
gradually sorting them when I could perceive commonalities. I scanned
a good number of blogs daily (and still do!), followed their embedded
hyperlinks to both source material and other bloggers, and printed posts
which struck me as raising some substantive critical point. When the
criticism seemed to consist primarily of a personal attack (ad hominem,
ad feminam), to be factually unsupported, or to contain some clear logical weakness, I excluded it from the collection. Without a doubt, my
approach depended on me being a fair and impartial observer—but this
is true of qualitative methods in general, I believe.[5] This was explicitly an
inductive venture, aimed at reducing the huge volume of blogging which
made some critical reference to mainstream news product down to an
abstract typology of this particular subset of the blog docuverse.[6] No
doubt other researchers could choose a different approach and gain valuable insights into media criticism blogging, but I preferred a qualitative,
inductive approach for the reasons mentioned earlier and will return
to, later. (And I have no doubt that other researchers using a similar
approach might see a different pattern in the data!)

After a good amount of time sorting (and resorting) the pile of printed
blog posts,[7] I found that the criticism seemed largely to fall into four
categories with regard to the substance of the post. One could account
for nearly all of the posts, it seemed to me, with four major categories of critical problematics raised by the bloggers—and sometimes a
single post could contain more than one. To my eye, the critique could
center on these dimensions of the mainstream news product: (1) *accuracy* (facticity of the accounts of events); (2) *framing* (adequacy of the

interpretations offered); (3) *agenda-setting/gate keeping* (news judgment); and (4) *journalistic practices* (integrity of the production process). Within those categories there seemed to be subvarieties, much like the genus/species classification of living things. Framing is the subject of this book, so it is appropriate to go into greater detail about that category. Of the blog critiques of framing, there appeared to be these three varieties: (1) *disputing the frame* (arguing the supplied interpretation of facts was deficient, in some way); (2) *reframing a set of facts* (offering an alternative interpretation); and (3) *contextualizing* (offering additional relevant facts). Again, a single post could contain more than one variety of framing critique.

Of course, this two-level typology rests on some notion of what a *frame* is, as a construct applied to mediated information products. My understanding of news frames, as a phenomenon scholars can perceive and examine (Cooper, 2006, pp. 105-106), is congruent with that described by Kuypers in a number of works (Kuypers, 2002, p. 7; Kuypers 2006, p. 7; Kuypers & Cooper, 2005, p. 2; Kuypers, Cooper, & Althouse, in press ; Kuypers, in this volume). Put plainly, the frame of a news story is the storyline which subsumes the collection of raw facts into an interpretation of the meaning of events. Essentially, the frame is the short answer to a simple yet profoundly meaning-centered question: what's going on here? It is difficult for me to imagine a news story which does not offer some interpretation or meaning to the audience. My view is that news production inherently involves framing, no matter how scrupulously the reporter and editor may try to bright-line a distinction between straight news and opinion, and no matter how carefully they might try to remain neutral in reporting on some controversy.[8] It might be the case that the lede or headline is the straightforward statement of the frame; it might also be the case that the frame is best perceived as the "take-away" idea suggested by the complete story.[9] If the frame is essentially a holistic characteristic of a news product, this would suggest that a similarly holistic inquiry into framing is warranted.

Consider a hypothetical example in which the news/interpretation distinction might initially seem easy to make: a local news outlet reporting an armed robbery at a convenience store. True enough, the event itself is a simple fact: a holdup took place. But even in classic straight news style, beyond a one-paragraph recitation of names, place, and time the reporting will typically provide other information, such things as quotes from eyewitnesses, a narrative of the crime as it took place, a quote from the perpetrator's mother, some statistic about crime rates in the area, some sort of back story on the perpetrator or victim. These are all conventional elements of such reporting, and most likely readers would be dissatisfied with only a paragraph of cold facts. My view is that one can best perceive the frame by considering the totality of the information contained in the report with a close eye for word choice, supplementary detail, cause-and-effect assertions (especially implicit causal links), and use of sources, with good consideration for what might have been but was not included. The juxtaposition (or exclusion) of these other elements with the bare facts suggests the frame. In this hypothetical, for instance, the news story might frame the robbery as the savage act of a deranged or drug-impaired individual, the desperate act of a victim of structural injustice (social class, race), the rational and purposive act of a calculating professional criminal, a manifestation of general cultural decline, a tragic slice of life in a bad neighborhood, a symptom of the erosion of law and order, the consequence of trouble in the regional or national economy, a manifestation of simmering class/race tensions, evidence that some sort of government policy is working or not working, and so on.

All those are at least arguable understandings of the meaning of such an event, and one can imagine how the running text of the story would vary, depending on the reporter's own understanding of the meaning of the event. And one can certainly understand how readers might disagree with the reporter's understanding—or the understandings of the sources the reporter chose to include[10]—as embodied in the text of the reporting. As Kuypers (this volume) maintains, there is an intrinsically persuasive dimension to news reporting, which is why rhetorical framing analysis is indeed a useful scholarly tool which deserves a place among the other methodological approaches.

*Watching the Watchdog* examined a good number of examples of the varieties of blog media criticism, contemporaneous with the writing of the book. It will be helpful at this point to look at a few more examples of framing critique, current at the time of this writing. The reader is encouraged to obtain both the blog posts and the news stories which prompted the bloggers' critiques, the better to assess the framing in the news product, the blogger's objection to it, and my conceptualization of the relationship between the two. D'Angelo (2002, p. 876) identified the critical paradigm within scholarly framing studies as being characterized by its position that "frames are the outcome of newsgathering routines by which journalists convey information about issues and events from the perspective of values held by political and economic elites." While the authors of the posts are not, themselves, critical communication scholars,[11] these posts seem to me to nonetheless embody that problematization of elite values shaping news products, albeit in unconventional ways. The bloggers may accomplish that problematization explicitly by objecting to what they perceive as deficiencies in the framing of the mainstream news product; they may do this implicitly, by proposing an alternative frame they think makes better sense.

### Surgeon General Nominee Withdraws

In early March of 2009, the online version of the *Washington Post* ran a brief story (Shear & Kurtz, 2009) indicating that Sanjay Gupta, who had been offered the post of Surgeon General in the new Obama administration, had declined the position. The story does not appear obviously different from routine news reporting on Washington politics, in that it begins with a straightforward description of events, then proceeds to some background which suggests an interpretation of the withdrawal. The lede is this:

> Sanjay Gupta, CNN's chief medical correspondent, has told network officials [he] will not leave his television career to become the U.S. Surgeon General, according to sources familiar with his decision. Gupta, who had been described as the leading candidate for the public health post, withdrew his name even as President Obama hosted a health care summit at the White House today that Gupta did not attend.

On her eponymous blog, Ann Althouse dug into the background information contained deeper in the story, and offered a concise and tartly worded reframing in a post she titled, "What Happened with Sanjay Gupta?" (Althouse, 2009). She quoted from the *Washington Post* report, formatting the quote as a hyperlink to the story. Then she offered an alternative frame. In its entirety, this is her post:

> "Gupta, who was once named one of the 'sexiest men alive' by *People* Magazine, was never officially named to the post and continued to report on CNN. He did not issue a statement or explain his decision Thursday. Sources said the medical journalist told CNN executives that he wanted to devote more time to his medical practice and to his duties at the network. But one source close to him said he was very disheartened by Daschle's fate and fearful he was not going to get a prominent role in the health reform process."
>
> Okay. I understand. Thanks for the explanation, WaPo. He's rich and prominently sexy. He can't go into government without major flash and admiration. And some people were even going to pick at his credentials, maybe beat him up the way they did to poor little Tom. That won't do.

To my eye, the paragraph Althouse pulled from the *Washington Post* story does contain the frame for the event described in the story's lead. It is typical of mainstream news product, in that unnamed sources provide detail suggesting a motive for the action and thus predisposing a reader's interpretation of the withdrawal, beyond the simple fact that Guptay had declined the position. As is often seen in reporting on events such as this, there are two somewhat divergent explanations offered: that Guptay preferred not to leave his medical practice and network reporting (the "inside story"), and that he was reluctant to go through the confirmation process given the limited clout of the White House position he was offered (apparently the "inside inside story"). It seems fair to observe that this passage in the news story frames Guptay's withdrawal as primarily a career decision. In contrast, the blogger eschewed the polite language and refined syntax of elite journalism, reframing Guptay's withdrawal as an ego-based decision.[12]

### The Treasury Secretary Testifies

A Bloomberg News story described an appearance of the Treasury Secretary before the House Ways and Means Committee, concerning the state of efforts to stabilize the banking sector (Schmidt, 2009). In every respect, this is a straight news story summarizing the testimony of an administration official before a legislative committee charged with oversight of the official's function. The lede seems to me to clearly state the frame:

> Treasury Secretary Timothy Geithner said the U.S. bank rescue program may cost more than the $700 billion Congress approved, and he pledged to crack down on companies and individuals who try to avoid paying taxes. Testifying before the House Ways and Means Committee on the Obama administration's 2010 budget, Geithner pledged to work with Congress to "determine the appropriate size and shape" of further bailouts.

The story proceeds in a classic inverted pyramid format, adding supplementary detail about Geithner's testimony. The story caught the attention of Jim Geraghty, who writes the Campaign Spot blog attached to the *National Review Online* Web site. He posted a very concise critique by contextualization, at which he hinted in the title, "Tim Geithner, on the Case against Tax Cheats" (Geraghty, 2009).

> "Treasury Secretary Timothy Geithner said the U.S. bank rescue program may cost more than the $700 billion Congress approved, and he pledged to crack down on companies and individuals who try to avoid paying taxes." You mean those who try to avoid paying taxes like…Tim Geithner?

Geraghty's comment was a reference to an issue which had come up in Geithner's earlier confirmation hearing; he had agreed to pay a substantial sum in back taxes and penalties.[13] In an update, Geraghty relayed another contextual detail from his readers, that the chair of the House Ways and Means Committee, Charlie Rangel, had himself admitted owing back taxes.[14]

Patrick Frey piggybacked onto Geraghty's post with an even more concise reframing of the story (Patterico, 2009). In this case, the title of the post was itself the reframing: "Tax Cheat Tells Tax Cheat He'll Crack Down on Tax Cheats."

### A Prominent Columnist Reconsiders His Position

Humor is a staple of blog criticism, and an interesting example can be found in the criticism of a piece by *New York Times* opinion writer David Brooks. The exchange began with a Brooks column (2009a) in which he expressed serious misgivings about the fiscal initiatives of the new administration, even though he had supported the Obama candidacy during the general election campaign. As Brooks described it in a follow-up column a few days later (2009b), that piece had prompted the White House to contact him.

> On Tuesday, I wrote that the Obama budget is a liberal, big government document that should make moderates nervous. The column generated a large positive response from moderate Obama supporters who are anxious about where the administration is headed. It was not so popular inside the White House. Within a day, I had conversations with four senior members of the administration and in the interest of fairness, I thought I'd share their arguments with you today.

The piece proceeded to detail a number of lines of rebuttal those individuals took in the conversations; indeed, almost the whole column was devoted to the administration's rebuttal to Brooks's first piece. The last paragraph included this passage:

> Nonetheless, the White House made a case that was sophisticated and fact-based. These people know how to lead a discussion and set a tone of friendly cooperation.[15]

Ed Morrissey (2009) was troubled by Brooks's follow-up column, as the title of his Hot Air post indicates: "Revolt Over: White House Puts Brooks Back on the Leash." He was dissatisfied by Brooks's assertion that the follow-up column was an exercise in fairness, and raised a critical point about the nature of the opinion/news distinction (emphasis in the original):[16]

> We often complain about regular reporters injecting their opinions into what should be objective articles. This is the reverse of that problem. Brooks writes an opinion column, but the opinions are supposed to be *his*. In this column, he basically turns his newsprint space over to Rahm Emanuel and his staff and merely takes dictation. Had Brooks and the New York Times run this as an interview news piece, it might seem less obsequious than how it appears in Brooks's column today.

Ed Driscoll (2009) linked Morrissey's post and raised a tongue-in-cheek, but pointed, question about the appropriateness of the White House's contact with the journalist. The entire post, including the title, is this:

> When Luigi Met David
> Nice little career you've got there, Mr. Brooks—shame if something were to happen to it. We can guarantee that you won't get done over by Robert Gibbs[17] in a White House press conference for fifteen bob a week….

This example illustrates a number of common features in blog media criticism. The nature of the channel (computer mediation) facilitates a reader's access to earlier commentary and source material through hyperlinking; thus, there is a great deal of collaborative development of the critique, and supporting material can be referenced more concisely than in print format. In this case, Morrissey based his criticism largely in the traditional conception of the mainstream press standing apart from the political power structure (the Fourth Estate notion), with Driscoll highlighting the possibility of a certain degree of intimidation in the White House's contact with the journalist. Pop culture allusions also appear frequently, as in Driscoll humorously invoking the tone of dialog from a mobster movie. In this case, the humor was a concise but pointed reframing of Brooks's follow-up column: rather than being a story of "equal time," it was a story of intimidation. In turn, that suggests that the critique very much belongs in the critical paradigm, in that the blogger objected to what he saw as an illegitimate exercise of power by the political elite.

### Donations to the Palestinian Authority

A Reuters' analysis of external financial support for the Palestinian Authority (Entous, 2009) outlined a number of concerns about the precarious political and financial state of the Authority, and the reliability of the pledges made in fund-raising efforts. The story begins in this way:

> Rich states and investors have announced a record $14 billion to aid the Palestinians and their economy in a string of Western-backed meetings meant to boost President Mahmoud Abbas in his power struggle with Hamas. But diplomats said many of the pledges made at five donor and investor conferences held since December 2007, including one in Egypt on Monday, were counted more than once, have yet to materialize or were too vague to rely on.

The story goes on to give detail about the uncertainty of the financial support promised, the low Palestinian GDP, the low per capita income, and various contingencies affecting the actual provision of the promised support external support for the Palestinian Authority. It seems fair to say that the article itself is a critical reading of the state of affairs, focused on political tensions and economic difficulties.

Charles Johnson (2009) provided an alternative frame for the political and economic complexity described in the Reuters story. The post is a good example of a blogger reframing a set of facts; he did not take issue with the facts provided in the reporting, but provided a much different understanding of the situation. Apart from linking the story and quoting its lede, the bluntly worded post in its entirety is this:

> For decades, money has been pouring into the coffers of one Palestinian strongman after another, from Arab states and clueless Westerners, and all the Palestinians have to show for it is the ultimate welfare state—a death cult society whose main business is indoctrinating their children to hate and kill. So naturally, here come the deep pockets people again, pledging more than $14 billion that will go down the same hole of terrorism and hatred.

## Some General Observations on Blog Critique

One quickly sees that the authorial voice of bloggers is considerably more diverse than the authorial voice of mainstream journalists! Some bloggers strike a restrained tone with a good degree of detachment— quite similar to mainstream opinion journalism.[18] Others are restrained in wording, but more directly personal in their reflections on events and mainstream reporting.[19] Some seem to relish skillful use of irony and sarcasm,[20] and some take this confrontational style to a point some might find overly blunt.[21] I think the best explanation of this variety is simply that the authors see themselves as outsiders to the journalistic establishment. Their voices tend to be unconventional because they are private citizens rather than paid professionals drawing a salary from a commercial entity operating within a long-established social institution. At a minimum they thus are not bound by journalistic conventions in their authorial voice; at maximum, the voice they choose may be a direct statement of their oppositional stance to the media elite. And in general, I would characterize media criticism bloggers' voices as oppositional, sometimes to the point of being transgressive.

A visitor to the blogosphere expecting the detached, measured, restrained word choices of the professional journalists may indeed be put off by the more blunt style of many blog critics. This overtly argumentative tone (as opposed to the refined argumentative tone I see in much mainstream reporting) is unsurprising, in that the blogger is rebutting or countering the argument he or she perceives to be embedded in a piece of mainstream content. Put plainly, this is an outsider contesting the conventional wisdom of the insiders. In my view, it is important for a student of this genre to be mindful that the stylistic characteristics of blog critique are a textual variable independent of the fundamental quality of the thinking underlying the critique, and to look beyond the surface characteristics of the writing toward the underlying use of evidence and reason. Even if one does not enjoy the style of the expression, the quality of the thinking may be compelling.

The notion of quality requires further explanation here. I suggested earlier that congruence between the blogger's politics and the researcher's is not, in my opinion, sufficient as an indicator of the quality of the blogger's oppositional argumentation. Taking that position seems to me to reduce scholarly inquiry to tautology: opinion one likes is good, and one accepts it as insightful; opinion one dislikes is bad, and one rejects it as defective. What characteristics, then, might we use as indicators of quality? If blogging is a persuasive activity, then quality benchmarks from rhetorical analysis are applicable. Logical or argumentative fallacies diminish quality;[22] well-executed induction and deduction increase quality.[23] I believe Toulmin's model (2003)[24] is also helpful in this regard. A good fit of evidence and warrant, leading to a blogger's claim that events are better understood to mean something other than the mainstream product's frame, is an indicator of good quality. And particularly in the case of a critique by contextualization, the blogger may point out some powerful qualifier (i.e., a limitation) on the framing in the mainstream product; this, too, is an indicator of good quality in the critique.

Again, I am seeing both mainstream journalism and blogger critique of it as persuasive activities. Professional journalists implicitly or explicitly offer frames to their readers, and media bias is a perpetual issue in large part because of this complexity. News stories perforce provide framing, as it is impossible for journalists to decide the relative importance of various facts (as in the traditional inverted pyramid format) without having some background frame in mind, reflectively or reflexively. A journalist cannot lead a story or write the headline (or compose the background graphic, in broadcast news) with *everything* that will appear in it, all the complexity of the event or issue. The lede or headline may state the frame the story supplies to the reader, but again I would observe that the holistic frame of the story (the "take-away" sense of the meaning of events) is not necessarily coterminous with the lede or headline.

Often that frame is contestable, and bloggers do indeed contest it. When bloggers engage (presumably, intuitively) in framing critique, they may simply object to the frame they perceive in the mainstream content (argue, for instance, that there is a discontinuity of some sort in the Toulmin structure). Alternatively, they may reframe (replace the warrant and claim, based on the data/evidence as provided in the mainstream text) or they may contextualize (provide additional data/evidence, or replace the data/evidence in the mainstream text).[25]

By no means do I mean these concluding remarks to be taken as an argument against the utility or validity of quantitative approaches to the scholarly study of news framing and media criticism! I am very much of the mind that the variety of tools for scholarly inquiry is a disciplinary strength, and I enjoy learning about colleagues' work which differs from mine. Quantitative approaches are uniquely suited to measuring prevalence, proportion, and size; they can make use of excellent statistical tools, both descriptive and inferential. And certainly there are limitations on the knowledge claims one can make from a qualitative approach, particularly one rooted in rhetorical studies. My sense is that both qualitative and quantitative approaches are appropriate and useful for studying framing, as they have relative strengths and limitations that complement each other. With that important clarification in mind, there are reasons I prefer to use an inductive, qualitative, rhetoric-based analysis to examine blog media criticism.

Perhaps the biggest single reason is that blog criticism of mainstream news products is a new development in our media system. The factors which enabled the development of this content genre are recent: digital convergence in the dissemination of information products, the construction of the necessary access infrastructure (the Internet), and the declining cost of the required equipment (personal computers).[26] I do not believe it is safe to assume this particular content genre will in all crucial aspects mimic the media criticism which was available before. To the contrary, even a casual perusal of blog media criticism shows there are many differences. In general, I am of the mind that bottom-up (meaning, from phenomena toward theory) inquiry is appropriate when one lacks confidence that the phenomena are already understood with sufficient clarity. In a sense, a quasi-anthropological exploration of texts is a good choice when one encounters a novel body of texts. Granted, that there are important limitations on the knowledge claims one might make from this type of qualitative inquiry, but to me the overriding factor is that the texts are different from those with which we are already familiar.

An intrinsic task in a quantitative study of framing in some set of texts is the need to operationalize, and an unavoidable question is the validity of the coding scheme. To me this is essentially a *reasonable person* issue, in many respects similar to the reasonable person standard in common law.[27] Reliance on earlier works in the literature is no doubt appropriate, but nonetheless cannot offer complete assurance that the coding is impeccable, particularly when the texts of interest are something new. Chains of reliance from study to study could just as well result in the perpetuation of an error (i.e., mismatch between findings and the actual characteristics of the phenomena) as in continued quality assurance of the knowledge claims from the study. Again, it is important for me to emphasize that in no way am I dismissing the utility or validity of this kind of approach to the study of texts! Quite simply, I think a researcher must carefully consider the vulnerabilities of his or her method of choice; the fit of the method's strengths and limitations to the characteristics of the texts (as best they are known at the time) is crucial.

Particularly in the case of a quantitative study of framing, devising a coding scheme effectively presumes some sort of preliminary framing analysis on the part of the researcher, and hence requires the reasonable person judgment to have been made. If nothing else, which words or phrases are to be counted as textual units? And what clues would be recognizable as indicating the frame? Whether a researcher chooses to use a coding scheme from the literature or creates one from scratch, there is the presumption that the things being counted are, in fact, good indices of frames. Again, I have no fatal objection to this approach. I am simply pointing out that some sort of qualitative framing analysis is the foundational step, whether tacitly in the reliance on prior studies or de novo in the intuitive judgment of the researcher. In this light, the routine practice of training coders and measuring intercoder reliability is, at bottom, a check that the reasonable person standard has adequately been met.

The stunning complexity and subtlety of language—the many ways to express thoughts denotatively with a multiplicity of connotative meanings—is a caution that careful study of framing is by no means a simplistic venture. The use of sarcasm or irony in the text shows this clearly: the meaning a reasonable and fluent reader would construct from the passage may well run opposite to the actual wording. Sarcasm and irony are plentiful in blog media criticism, as the examples above suggest.

Lurking behind these thoughts is my foundational epistemological viewpoint—that theory ought not to be an end in itself and should never be taken as more than the current state of intersubjective knowledge. Rather, because theory is a tool with which one can gain insights into real life, theory development work optimally is the crafting of better tools with which to gain those insights. This is my personal touchstone when considering theoretical work: what does it tell me about reality? With how much fidelity (accuracy, validity), as best I can perceive it? And once again, I am left with what amounts to a reasonable person standard for the quality of scholarly knowledge.

Neither constructionism nor postmodernism contradict that position, in my view. Even if social reality is socially constructed in general—just as theoretical/scholarly reality is socially constructed within an elite academic group—the universe of actual human beings' interactions nonetheless is a thing apart from our abstract understanding of it. (I would not expect any great objection to the observation that the physical universe is a thing apart from our current version of astrophysics.) Hence, it is useful that some amount of scholarly attention proceed inductively from the microphenomena of human interactions and reciprocal influence (mediated, or not), groping toward an abstract understanding of the regularities which may be present in those phenomena. Indeed, this is an inherently reductionist venture—just as learning life lessons from our personal experiences is a reductionist effort, at bottom.

Kuypers (this volume) has made a strong case that rhetorical criticism is inherently viewpoint-centered and first-person in tone, and that it is inherently persuasive in nature. I would add that it is in the nature of an issue that is debated in the public sphere to give rise to competing ways for an individual to make sense of facts, and competing ways to assess the relevance and consequence of facts. If that were that not the case, there would be nothing to debate! The implication is that some of the most interesting things to study—public issues—necessarily entail disputation of frames. Further, the frame may well be an overall understanding or impression the reader derives from a text, and thus not readily identifiable in the form of specific word choices or phrases. Again I am left with the thought that a reasonable person interpretation of a text's frame is required, and that framing is best understood holistically.

I think I see a particularly good fit of this approach with blog media criticism. The blogosphere is a new channel, now becoming a structural component of the media mix. The barriers to entry into this space are minimal, and hence the blogosphere is a technological facilitator of citizen journalism of various sorts, including reportage, commentary, and critique. Thus there is a confluence of the channel characteristics and the author-centric nature of rhetorical criticism in general. This seems to me a good explanation for the proliferation of media criticism in the blogosphere, and the stylistic characteristics of the genre as it has evolved in the blogosphere's short existence. This also strikes me as a solid rationale for the use of rhetorical framing analysis as a way to begin to understand the genre.

## Notes

1. I hope no reader is put off by the use of the masculine pronoun in this passage. That is the way I heard the joke told, but in any case the knowledge problem is independent of gender. It would be the same for a group of blind women (or visually impaired sentient beings, of any particular cohort) trying to understand the nature of the mysterious thing in front of them! I am fond of the story, as it seems to me to contain a profound insight into the nature of inquiry: the tool does influence the finding.
2. A very helpful glossary of blog terms is available at the Samizdata site (http://www.samizdata.net)—a blog, itself—and I am indebted to the authors for bringing some clarity to the lexicon!
3. This point is elaborated much more fully in the last few chapters of *Watching the Watchdog* (Cooper, 2006).
4. That passage is a caution against taking an unorthodox style, in blog criticism, to indicate a deficiency in quality. I am of the mind that the corresponding error, regarding the content of mainstream news outlets, is taking the "professional" style to indicate good quality in the reporting— but that is an argument to be explored elsewhere.
5. Later in this article, I will take up the notion of "reasonable person" as a crucial element in any inquiry, whether qualitative or quantitative. My view is that neither qualitative nor quantitative methods can avoid the issue of the researcher's fairness and reasonable judgment, in arriving at the findings.
6. The online world is loaded with neologisms and metaphorical usage! If the term is unfamiliar, *docuverse* is the neologism for the metaphorical term, *document universe*.
7. This data-creation and data-reduction process in many ways resembled the way an ethnographer explores some unfamiliar cultural field in the hope of coming to an understanding of it. At first I just surfed the blogosphere, much as I would walk around a physical neighborhood, and printed posts that seemed striking and pertinent to my inquiry, much as I would make field notes of things that caught my eye. As best I was able, I "bracketed off" my familiarity with media and CMC theories and tried to remain free of preconceptions about what I would see in the posts. I followed embedded links much as I would ask informants to recommend others I should talk to, and over time came to think of some bloggers as "key informants" in that their work often pointed me toward other bloggers of interest or suggested some general insight. The posts I printed were something like interview transcripts, in that my goal was to surface the regularities in behavior (in this case, what became the typology of blog media criticism) and what seemed to be shared understandings among the natives (what counted as evidence and reasoning supporting the critique). The sorting process was much like the coding and pattern-identification process one might use to reduce a large batch of interview transcripts to a set of insights into the life-world of the informants (see Miles & Huberman, 1994, for an encyclopedia of techniques.)
   When I took the methods courses in graduate school, I didn't expect

I'd ever do an "ethnography" of texts, but this approach to blog media criticism seemed warranted for the reasons I mentioned earlier. Without a doubt, this was a heuristic venture! Lest it seem totally bizarre, consider that a qualitative inquiry into "blogger culture" probably wouldn't raise any eyebrows. A difference, here, was that I did not devise a data collection instrument, the way I would prepare an interview guide; I used the blog posts as the statements of the bloggers. Analytically, though, the task seemed much the same. And the same concerns about reliability and validity applied, as they would in any qualitative research (see Kirk & Miller, 1986, pp.13–59).

8. To my eye, that distinction has become quite blurry in recent years, in any case. One now finds overtly interpretive pieces on the front pages of newspapers, and "what does it mean?" features are a staple of broadcast content.

9. A narrative differs from a frame. Narrative includes some sort of plot line, events unfolding over time. A frame is shorter, in time—a snapshot organizing interpretation of a set of facts. While readers are used to complexity and ambiguity in narrative—as in, say, a novel or movie—they are more oriented to specificity in frames. That is why I think of the frame of a news story as the "take-away" idea which subsumes the facts detailed in the story.

10. My thought is that the reporter is framing events both by his or her word choice in the description of events, and also in the choice of sources to include in the story and choice of potential sources to leave out. In other words, a reporter acting as "conduit" for sources' frames is not just passively relaying the sources' frames to the audience, but actively selecting which sources' frames to relay in the first place, and actively deciding how prominently to feature them in the finished story. In the hypothetical armed robbery story, the reporter might choose to feature quotes from the perpetrator's mother, the perpetrator's lawyer, the police chief, a terrified bystander, the store owner, a neighborhood resident, a social worker or advocate, and so on. The reporter makes decisions about which potential sources to contact and where to place their quotes in the story. By my lights, this is framing by the reporter, every bit as much as the descriptive copy the reporter writes.

11. I find bloggers' biographies of interest, as oftentimes the bloggers have noteworthy credentials in professions other than journalism. In these examples, for instance, Ann Althouse is a law professor and Patrick Frey (a/k/a Patterico) is a county prosecutor. This is not meant as a slight to other bloggers who make their living in lower-status jobs, however. I am strongly of the mind that what matters in blog criticism is the strength of the critique, regardless of the critic's resume. The vigor of this marketplace of ideas convinces me of the strong democracy potential the blogosphere offers.

12. Lest the reader dismiss this post as the sniping of a die-hard opponent of the new administration, we should note that Althouse supported the Obama presidential run. One can see this, explicitly, in her posts during the 2008 campaign, which are available in her archive.

13. There was a one-sentence mention of this controversy in the Bloomberg article, about a third of the way into the copy, and no further reference to it in the balance of the article. To my eye, it is clear that the article had not emphasized this in a way that warrants considering it part of

the mainstream product's frame. In contrast, this fact (that Geithner had acknowledged a problem in his tax filings) was central in the bloggers' contextualization and reframing.

14. There was no reference to Rangel in the Bloomberg story.
15. An oddity about this column is that while the tone of copy is cordial to the verge of being deferential—Brooks raised no objection to four administration officials contacting him to discuss his earlier criticism of fiscal policy—the title has, to my eyes, a connotation more in keeping with the bloggers' critique. Brooks titled his follow-up column, "When Obamatons Respond."
16. This objection would fall into the *journalistic practices* category, in the *Watching the Watchdog* typology.
17. At that point in the post, Driscoll embedded a hyperlink leading to a story on the White House press secretary's recent jabs at media figures (Rick Santelli, Jim Cramer, and Rush Limbaugh) who had been critical of the new administration (Youngman, 2009).
18. For illustrations of this, see Power Line and Ed Morrissey's posts on Hot Air.
19. For illustrations, see Instapundit, Big Lizards, the Anchoress, and Althouse.
20. For illustrations, see QandO, Ed Driscoll, and Allahpundit's posts on Hot Air.
21. For illustrations, see Ace of Spades and Little Green Footballs.
22. An excellent summary of such problems is available in Weston (2000).
23. For good examples of bloggers utilizing induction and deduction in their critique of mainstream reporting, see this author's case study of blog critique of "fauxtography" (Cooper, 2007).
24. There are a couple Wikipedia entries which provide helpful summaries of this approach to arguments. See http://en.wikipedia.org/wiki/Stephen_Toulmin#The_Toulmin_Model_of_Argument; http://en.wikipedia.org/wiki/Practical_arguments.
25. *Watching the Watchdog* has a good quantity of examples of such critique.
26. For a more detailed discussion of economics of blogging, particularly the low barriers to entry, see chapter 6 in *Watching the Watchdog*.
27. A helpful overview of the reasonable person standard in common law is available at http://en.wikipedia.org/wiki/Reasonable_person_standard. The standard legal reference is Keeton, Dobbs, Keeton, and Owen (1984, pp. 173–193). While its primary use in law is in determining negligence, here I am arguing there is a similar reasonable person construct implicit in scholarly identification of news story frames, regardless of whether a qualitative or quantitative method is used. And in general, I would maintain that peer review is the academic enactment of the reasonable person standard!

# References

Althouse, A. (2009, March 6). What happened to Sanjay Gupta? Retrieved March 6, 2009, from http://althouse.blogspot.com/2009/03/what-happened-with-sanjay-gupta.html.

Brooks, D. (2009a, March 3). A moderate manifesto. *New York Times*, A27. Retrieved March 20, 2009, from LexisNexis Academic.

Brooks, D. (2009b, March 6). When Obamatons respond. *New York Times*, A27. Retrieved March 20, 2009, from LexisNexis Academic.

Cooper, S. D. (2006). *Watching the watchdog: Bloggers as the fifth estate.* Spokane, WA: Marquette Academic.

Cooper, S. D. (2007). A concise history of the fauxtography blogstorm in the 2006 Lebanon War. *American Communication Journal, 9*(2). Retrieved from http://acjournal.org/holdings/vol9/summer/articles/fauxtography.html

D'Angelo, P. (2002). New framing as a multiparadigmatic research program: A response to Entman. *Journal of Communication, 52*(4), 870–888.

Driscoll, E. (2009, March 6). When Luigi met David. Retrieved March 6, 2009, from http://pajamasmedia.com/eddriscoll/2009/03/06/when-luigi-met-david/

Entous, A. (2009, March 6). Record donor pledges to Palestinians raise questions. Retrieved March 20, 2009, from http://www.reuters.com/article/middleeastCrisis/idUSL4314212

Geraghty, J. (2009, March 4). Tim Geithner, on the case against tax cheats. Retrieved March 6, 2009, from http://campaignspot.nationalreview.com/post/?q=NzJhOTQ2YjczZWFjZDQ0ODgyYzg1MmMxMzcyMzE5MDY

Johnson, C. (2009, March 6). Another massive windfall for Palestinians. Retrieved March 6, 2009, from http://littlegreenfootballs.com/article/32989_Another_Massive_Windfall_for_Palestinians

Kaye, B. K. (2005). It's a blog, blog, blog, blog world. *Atlantic Journal of Communication, 13*(2), 73–95.

Keeton, W. P., Dobbs, D. B., Keeton, R. E., & Owen, D. G. (1984). *Prosser and Keeton on the law of torts.* St. Paul, MN: West.

Kerbel, M. R., & Bloom, J. D. (2005). Blog for America and civic involvement. *The Harvard International Journal of Press/Politics, 10*(4), 3–27.

Kirk, J., & Miller, M. L. (1986). *Qualitative Research Methods: Vol. 1. Reliability and validity in qualitative research.* Newbury Park, CA: Sage.

Kuypers, J. A. (2002). *Press bias and politics.* Westport, CT: Praeger.

Kuypers, J. A. (2006). *Bush's war: Media bias and justifications for war in a terrorist age.* Lanham, MD: Rowman & Littlefield.

Kuypers, J. A., & Cooper, S. D. (2005). A comparative framing analysis of embedded and behind-the-lines reporting on the 2003 Iraq War. *Qualitative Research Reports in Communication, 6*(10), 1–10.

Kuypers, J. A., Cooper, S. D., & Althouse, M. T. (in press). The President and the press: The framing of George W. Bush's speech to the United Nations on November 10, 2001. *American Communication Journal.*

Miles, M. B., & Huberman, A. M. (1994). *Qualitative data analysis.* Thousand Oaks, CA: Sage.

Morrissey, E. (2009, March 6). Revolt over: White House puts Brooks back on the leash. Retrieved March 6, 2009, from http://hotair.com/archives/2009/03/06/revolt-over-white-house-puts-brooks-back-on-the-leash/

O'Donnell, P., & McClung, S. (2008). MP3 music blogs: Their efficacy in selling music and marketing bands. *Atlantic Journal of Communication, 16*, 71–87.

Patterico (2009, March 4). Tax cheat tells tax cheat he'll crack down on tax cheats. Retrieved March 6, 2009, from http://patterico.com/2009/03/04/tax-cheat-tells-tax-cheat-hell-crack-down-on-tax-cheats/

Perlmutter, D. D. (2008). *Blogwars*. New York: Oxford University Press.

Quick, B. (2001, December 30). I propose a name Retrieved July 21, 2005, from http://www.iw3p.com/DailyPundit/2001_12_30_dailypundit_archive.php

Schmidt, R. (2009, March 3). Geithner says U.S. financial rescue "might cost more." Retrieved March 13, 2009, from http://www.bloomberg.com/apps/news?pid=20601087&sid= aQldZDIQpohE&refer=home

Shear, M. D., & Kurtz, H. (2009, March 5). Gupta steps aside. Retrieved March 6, 2009, from http://voices.washingtonpost.com/44/2009/03/05/gupta_steps_aside.html

Toulmin, S. E. (2003). *The Uses of argument* (Rev. ed.). Cambridge, UK: Cambridge University Press.

Weston, A. (2000). *A rulebook for arguments* (3rd ed.). Indianapolis, IN: Hackett.

Youngman, S. (2009, March 5). Gibbs knows the art of war. Retrieved March 20, 2009, from http://thehill.com/leading-the-news/gibbs-knows-the-art-of-war-2009-03-05.html

# Part II

# Perspectives on Framing Effects

# Chapter 7

# Studying the Effects of Framing on Public Opinion about Policy Issues

## Does What We See Depend on How We Look?

*Paul R. Brewer and Kimberly Gross*

In covering policy issues, the mass media provide more than "just the facts." They also provide frames that tell audience members how to understand particular policy controversies. As defined by Gamson and Modigliani (1987, p. 143), a frame is "a central organizing idea or story line that provides meaning to an unfolding strip of events, weaving a connection among them. The frame suggests what the controversy is about, the essence of the issue."[1] The frames for a given policy controversy exist within the public discourse surrounding that controversy—a discourse that is typically communicated to ordinary citizens through the mass media (e.g., Kinder & Sanders, 1996). Framing, in turn, involves the presentation of such organizing ideas or storylines. As Entman (1993, p. 52) writes, "To frame is to select some aspects of a perceived reality and make them more salient in a communicating text, in such a way as to promote a particular problem definition, causal interpretation, moral evaluation, and/or treatment recommendation."

In part, the media transmit elite debates over how to frame particular issues by serving as conduits for *partisan frames* developed by politicians and activists who advocate specific issue positions.[2] These frames are specific to a particular issue and its "issue culture" (Gamson, 1992; Gamson & Modigliani, 1987, 1989), though they may be revised and reintroduced into other issue cultures. As the name suggests, partisan frames highlight certain information and ideas in order to present one position (or set of positions) on an issue as being correct and other positions as being wrong. Such frames are typically introduced by actors seeking to move opinion in ways conducive to their particular position and their preferred policy solutions. For example, foes of affirmative action measures have justified their opposition by casting such policies as providing "unfair advantage" or creating "reverse discrimination," whereas supporters have framed them as "remedial action" to combat the legacy of discrimination (Gamson & Modigliani, 1987). Similarly, proponents of gay rights policies have framed these policies as promoting "equal rights," whereas opponents have framed them as promoting "special rights" and undermining "traditional moral values" (Brewer, 2003).

At the same time, the news media also rely on more general frames in telling stories about issues. Such frames are neither defined by a partisan stance in the context of a particular issue nor limited to a specific issue culture. Instead, these *news frames* are broadly applicable storytelling devices that can be used to present any number of issues. For example, the news media have used the episodic (or anecdotal) and thematic (or abstract) frames in covering a wide range of issues, including crime, terrorism, poverty, unemployment, and racial inequality (Iyengar, 1991). Likewise, the news media have used both the strategy or game frame (which emphasizes political maneuvering by self-interested politicians) and the substance or issue frame (which emphasizes the particulars of policy proposals) in covering health care reform (Cappella & Jamieson 1997; Fallows, 1997) and welfare reform (Lawrence, 2000). Although such news frames are not designed with the intent of moving public opinion toward or away from a particular position on an issue, they have implications for shaping public opinion nonetheless.

A burgeoning body of literature focuses on mapping the various partisan and news frames in public discourse, either through qualitative analysis or quantitative content analysis. Much of this research proceeds from a premise—sometimes explicit, sometimes implicit—that particular frames, by highlighting certain aspects of a controversy, will guide audience members' thoughts and feelings about that controversy in predictable ways, with predictable conclusions (e.g., Entman, 1993). As a consequence, the literature on framing in public discourse often (but not always; e.g., Gamson & Modigliani, 1987) conveys a portrait of powerful frames and malleable citizens.

To be sure, the presence of a frame in communication does not necessarily imply that exposure to it will influence the receiver. With this point in mind, scholars have used a range of methods to test for *framing effects*; that is, for evidence of the influence of frames on opinion about public policy. Research examining framing effects builds on the notion that frames lead a "double life" (Kinder & Sanders, 1996; see also Scheufele, 1999) as not only "interpretive structures embedded in political discourse" but also "cognitive structures that help individual citizens make sense of the issues that animate politics." Some studies—particularly those drawing on critical or constructivist models of framing effects—focus on framing and aggregate-level public opinion (e.g., Entman, 1991; Gamson & Modigliani, 1989), but many more draw on psychological models to look at individual-level framing effects (for further discussion, see Price, Nir, & Cappella, 2005). In the latter body of work, framing effects are typically defined as taking place when a person accepts a frame in communication and then uses it to form opinions

(Druckman, 2001a). Quantitative studies that conceptualize framing effects in this way have shown that exposure to partisan frames in media coverage can shape audience members' opinions about policy matters and that news frames for policy issues can do the same

At first glance, such findings seem to suggest that citizens respond to frames through psychological processes that are passive and automatic—and, thus, that public opinion about policy issues can be manipulated by political elites and news media (see Druckman, 2001a). Viewed from this perspective, evidence of framing effects could be interpreted as calling into question the notion that the public can offer a meaningful voice to guide policymaking. Then again, some recent studies—including our own research—point to a more optimistic account of framing and public opinion by demonstrating the limits of framing effects.

In this chapter, we argue that the decisions that researchers make regarding how to study the effects of frames on public opinion about policy issues may shape their conclusions about the nature and extent of such effects. As a result, the same decisions may also shape their conclusions about the implications of framing effects for theoretical models of framing and normative models of democracy. We illustrate these points by discussing past studies of framing effects that we and other scholars have conducted. In doing so, we consider research on both partisan frames and news frames for policy issues. Along the way, we highlight the strengths and limitations of a variety of approaches for studying framing effects, from experiments to qualitative methods such as in-depth interviews, focus groups, and participant observation. We then suggest ways in which future research on framing effects could draw on broader understandings of what constitutes a framing effect and use more diverse methodological approaches, including designs that combine the strengths of different approaches.

## Using Laboratory Experiments to Capture Framing Effects

Given that a large portion of the research on framing effects—including most of our previous research—draws on experimental data, we begin our methodological critique by discussing the strengths and weaknesses of the standard experimental approach to studying framing effects on policy opinions. All true experiments share two features: the researcher *controls* the conditions under study and *randomly assigns* participants to those conditions (see Iyengar & Kinder, 1987). The primary strength of experimentation is that it provides internally valid evidence of cause and effect. Put another way, researchers can conclude with a high degree of confidence that differences from one experimental condition to another reflect the impact of the treatment(s) to which participants have been exposed. Given this advantage, it is not surprising that scholars have turned to experimentation in studying framing effects. Nor is it surprising that much of the resulting research has taken place in laboratory settings that allow for easy control of conditions.

The seminal framing studies conducted by Nelson and his colleagues illustrate what we call the simple framing experiment (Nelson, Clawson, & Oxley, 1997). This design includes two conditions. In the first condition, participants are exposed to one frame; in the second condition, participants are exposed to a different frame. The experiments conducted by Nelson and his colleagues revolved around a Ku Klux Klan rally. In one condition, participants received a news story that framed the controversy as a free speech issue; in the other, participants received a news story that framed it as a public order issue.[3] Participants in both conditions then completed a posttest that included questions measuring their opinions about the controversy. Thus, the authors were able to capture the impact of exposure to alternative frames on public opinion by comparing opinion in the two conditions. Specifically, they found that support for allowing the rally was higher after exposure to the free speech frame than after exposure to the public order frame. Along the same lines, McLeod (1995) used a simple framing experiment to show that those exposed to a new story framing a social protest as deviant held different opinions than did those exposed to a story framing the protest in a more balanced and sympathetic manner.

### Individual-Level Mediators and Moderators of Framing Effects

With some modifications, the simple framing experiment can be used to examine not only framing effects but also the psychological processes through which the impact of framing on opinion flows. In other words, it can be used to explore the individual-level *mediators* of such effects. For example, Nelson and his colleagues used their experiments to test whether frames influenced opinion by shaping how accessible values were in receivers' memories (i.e., how easily they could call the values to mind) or by shaping how important receivers perceived those values to be (i.e., how much weight they attached to the values). Their results indicated that the impact of framing flowed through importance judgments rather than accessibility.

In addition, the simple framing experiment can be used to examine whether framing effects depend on the characteristics of the receiver. Put another way, it can be used to test the individual-level *moderators* of framing effects. For example, Nelson and his colleagues found that the impact of framing was greater among more knowledgeable receivers than among less knowledgeable ones (Nelson, Oxley, & Clawson, 1997; for evidence to the contrary, see Druckman & Nelson, 2003; Haider-

Markel & Joslyn, 2001; Jacoby, 2000). Likewise, Druckman and Nelson (2003) found that impact of framing depended on the individual receiver's "need to evaluate"; that is, the receiver's tendency to form opinions.[4] Last, but not least, the simple framing experiment can be used to test whether individual receivers' predispositions (e.g., partisanship, values, prior opinions about the issue) condition framing effects; that is, whether the impact of a frame depends on how it resonates with beliefs of the receiver. Thus, the simple framing experiment can demonstrate that framing does not affect everyone to the same extent or even necessarily in the same way. In doing so, it opens avenues for exploring the boundaries of framing effects.

### Adding a Control Group

Although the simple framing experiment is a powerful tool for capturing framing effects—as well as for studying some of the mediators and moderators of such effects—it is nevertheless limited in important ways. To begin with, the absence of a control group means that one cannot isolate the absolute impact of either individual frame. Instead, one can only draw conclusions about the impact of one frame relative to the other. As Chong and Druckman (2007a) observed:

> Although two opposing frames may be unlikely to push opinion in the same direction, it is possible that one of the frames will have the unintended consequence of causing recipients to counterargue with the frame and form an opinion that goes against the position advocated by the frame—thus rendering the frame *countereffective*. In such cases, both frames may have a significant influence on opinion yet not have contrasting effects. On the other hand, two frames may produce significantly different effects when only one of the frames is influencing opinions. In the case where one frame is effective and the other is *ineffective*, the contrast method of gauging framing effects requires that we judge both frames to be equally effective. (p. 105)

In short, studies based on framing experiments that depend on relative comparisons from one framing condition to another—rather than to a baseline—may overlook "boomerang effects" produced by frames and fail to distinguish between frames that move opinion and those that do not. If we derive our understanding of framing effects from simple framing experiments, then we may underestimate the impact of framing when the absence of a contrast across conditions results from a "boomerang effect." Similarly, we may misread the power of frames in cases where only one of the two frames is effective.[5]

To these points we would add another: if the two frames in a simple framing experiment produce opposing effects, then the contrast between the two will tend to reflect the maximum possible impact of those frames. If we base our understanding of framing effects on simple framing experiments with two competing frames that move opinion in opposite directions, then we run the risk of exaggerating the power of framing to shape opinion. As a consequence, the simple framing experiment may be better suited for demonstrating that framing can matter than for capturing the typical impact of particular frames.

One solution to the limitations of the simple framing experiment is the addition of a control group. The inclusion of a condition in which participants are not exposed to any frame provides a baseline for judging the impact of exposure to frames in other conditions and, thus, a tool for capturing the impact of each individual frame. In doing so, it allows the experimenter to assess whether one frame is more powerful than another in moving opinion, as well as to identify instances in which frames produce a backlash in opinion (Chong & Druckman, 2007a). The inclusion of a control group also gives researchers more leverage in examining what roles receiver characteristics and predispositions play in determining framing effects: if one can isolate the effects of specific frames, then one can also capture the extent to which the effects of specific frames vary across such characteristics and predispositions (Gross, 2001). In broader terms, the addition of control groups to framing experiments may yield a more balanced picture of the extent to which frames move public opinion.

### Contextual Factors and Framing Effects

Another weakness of the simple framing experiment is that it fails to capture the potentially crucial role of contextual factors in shaping framing effects, particularly the effects of partisan frames. For example, the simple framing experiment does not simulate competitive partisan framing environments. As several recent studies have observed (Brewer, 2002; Brewer & Gross, 2005; Chong & Druckman 2007a, 2007b; Sniderman & Theriault, 2004), real-world exposure to framing in public discourse frequently involves simultaneous exposure to two opposing frames rather than exposure to one frame or another. Elites who seek to sway public opinion often fight framing with framing, and journalists often seek to provide balanced accounts of policy controversies (Terkildsen, Schnell, & Ling, 1998). As a result, news media coverage of a given issue may include two or more clashing partisan frames. Accordingly, it is important to consider whether a partisan frame that moves opinion in the absence of competition can do the same when it is matched by a partisan counterframe.

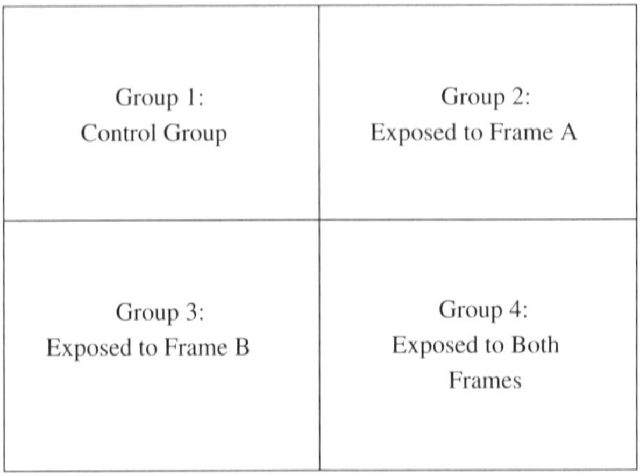

| | |
|---|---|
| Group 1:<br>Control Group | Group 2:<br>Exposed to Frame A |
| Group 3:<br>Exposed to Frame B | Group 4:<br>Exposed to Both<br>Frames |

*Figure 7.1*    A framing experiment with competition between frames.

The simple framing experiment with a control group can be expanded to explore this possibility. Several of our previous studies (Brewer, 2001, 2002; Brewer & Gross, 2005) revolved around framing experiments in which participants received (1) a frame for the issue at hand; (2) an alternative frame; (3) neither frame; or (4) both frames (see Figure 7.1; for similar approaches, see Chong & Druckman, 2007b; Sniderman & Theriault, 2004). This design allowed us not only to isolate the effects of each frame but also to capture the effects of the two frames when paired against one another. The results of our experiments and similar studies suggest that exposure to a rival frame can sometimes moderate or even neutralize the impact of a frame. Thus, framing effects that emerge in a simple framing experiment may disappear in an experiment that simulates a more competitive communication environment.

The simple framing experiment can also be modified to capture the role of message characteristics in shaping framing effects on opinion. For example, Druckman (2001b) conducted an experiment that replicated the one conducted by Nelson and his colleagues but added an additional manipulation: whether the frames appeared in a credible source (the *New York Times*) or a less credible source (the *National Enquirer*). The results indicated that framing moved opinion when it came from the credible source but not when it came from the less credible one. Along similar lines, Chong and Druckman (2007b) conducted a series of experiments in which participants were exposed to weak frames, strong frames, or both. They found that strong frames moved opinion in the direction of the frame when presented alone and dominated weak frames when presented alongside the latter.[6]

Furthermore, the simple framing experiment can be revised to capture the impact of other contextual factors that shape the effects of both partisan and news frames, including participation in interpersonal discussion, the passage of time, and repeated exposure to frames. To examine the first factor, Druckman and Nelson (2003) conducted an experiment in which participants who were exposed to frames subsequently talked with other participants who received the same frame, talked to participants who received different frames, or did not engage in any discussion with fellow participants. They found that conversations with participants exposed to different frames mitigated framing effects. To examine the second factor, the same authors surveyed participants 10 days after the initial treatment. Here, they found that the passage of time diminished the impact of framing on opinion.[7] To examine the third factor, Chong and Druckman (2007c) conducted an experiment in which some participants received multiple exposures to the same frame. The results suggested that repeated exposure to frames sometimes moved opinion among less knowledgeable participants who otherwise would not have absorbed the frames.

Taken as a whole, studies of contextual factors and framing effects show that more sophisticated laboratory experiments can help us determine what sorts of frames matter and when. In modifying the simple framing experiment, they also modify our understanding of framing effects: instead of pointing to the simple conclusion that framing matters, they point to the more complicated conclusion that *some* frames matter under *some* circumstances. Given that many of the initial experimental studies of framing effects involved exposure to strong frames from credible sources and did not involve exposure to competing frames, subsequent participation in interpersonal discussion, or the passage of time, it may be that these studies tended to overstate the impact of framing on public opinion. On the other hand, most studies of framing effects to date have only involved one-shot exposures to frames—a design feature that may lead to underestimating the impact of framing.

### The Limits of Laboratory Experiments

Having said all of this, even complex laboratory experiments share potentially important limitations when it comes to studying framing effects on opinion, particularly in terms of external validity (i.e., the degree to which one can generalize from the experimental results to the "real world"). One potential limitation to laboratory experiments revolves around the nature of the participants, who are often (but not always) college students. As Sears (1986) warned, the use of student samples in drawing conclusions about members of broader populations can be perilous if the psychological processes of the former tend to differ from the latter. With this concern in mind, some scholars have undertaken the costly endeavor of obtaining nonstudent samples for experimental studies of framing effects (e.g., Cappella & Jamieson, 1997; Iyengar, 1991).

To be sure, Sears himself acknowledged that the majority view in social psychology is that most psychological processes differ little from student populations to more general ones. Building on this point, a number of studies assert that findings of framing effects should generalize from student samples to the broader public (e.g., Druckman & Nelson, 2003; Nelson, Clawson, & Oxley, 1997). The results of experiments directly comparing framing effects in student samples and nonstudent samples support this claim (Druckman, 2004; Kühberger, 1998), and Druckman (2004) goes so far as to argue that participant samples "receive an inordinate amount of attention and criticism when it comes to the external validity of experiments" (p. 685).

Still, we should be cautious in basing our understanding of framing effects on student samples. As we have observed, individual receivers' characteristics and predispositions may shape framing effects. For example, framing effects may depend on how knowledgeable the receiver is or on what beliefs the receiver holds (e.g., Haider-Markel & Joslyn, 2001). If the participants in a given student sample are atypical in terms of characteristics or predispositions that may be relevant for the issue at hand, then the use of this sample may distort the experimental findings regarding the effectiveness of particular frames. Moreover, students often *are* atypical in key respects. As Cappella and Jamieson (1997, p. 88) noted, "College students are different in education, ideology, political knowledge and experience, and age from the voting public or the population as a whole."

The case of gay rights—the focus of an experimental study that one of us conducted—provides an illustration of this problem (Brewer, 2002). We know from our other research (Brewer, 2008) that one should expect college students to be more tolerant of gays and lesbians, less supportive of traditional morality, and more supportive of equality than members of the general public. Accordingly, it is plausible that they would be less receptive to anti-gay rights frames based on traditional morality and more receptive to pro-gay rights frames based on equality than would members of the general public. In such a case, research using student participants might lead us to draw different conclusions about the effectiveness of particular frames than would research using a more representative sample.

More broadly, it is important for researchers to think about how the specific issue and the specific frames under study may interact with the predispositions of a student sample. In some cases, obtaining a nonstudent sample may not be worth the effort and expense. In other cases, however, it may lend greater confidence to the conclusions that one draws. Most of our studies have used student samples, but one exception was an experiment that tested for framing effects on public opinion about world affairs (Brewer, 2006). Students from the George Washington University (where the study was conducted) might have been unusually well informed about international relations; after all, many of them come to the university to study the topic. In contrast, the nonstudent sample obtained by advertising in a local paper turned out to closely resemble the general public in terms of knowledge about world leaders. Thus, the nature of the participant pool strengthened the case that the effects of the specific frames under study would generalize to the American population.

Even if we leave aside the issue of nonrepresentative participants, two other threats to the external validity of laboratory experiments deserve consideration. One revolves around the realism of the treatments used to simulate exposure to framing in the mass media. Many experimental studies of framing effects address this issue by using either stimuli constructed from actual news stories or close facsimiles of such stories. Many of these studies, in turn, embed the presentation of the experimental treatments in a series of unrelated news stories to avoid undue attention to the news story of interest. Kinder (2007), however, criticizes experimental studies of framing effects for simulating exposure to frames in an "emaciated way," arguing that they "do not speak very convincingly to the presentation of frames in everyday life. Such presentations are characterized by repeated exposure through multiple venues over long periods of time—a whole curriculum of exposure" (p. 158). If this is so, then laboratory experiments may fail to capture the effects of the richer, more complex framing environments that citizens encounter "in the wild."

The other threat revolves around the artificiality of experimental settings. Kinder (2007) calls this issue the "major worry" regarding the external validity of framing experiments, arguing that such experiments are typically carried out in such a way that they "obliterate the distinction between the supply of information, on the one hand, and its consumption, on the other" (p. 157). As a consequence, he argues, these experiments avoid the obstacle of the inattentive audience and, thus, may overstate the power of framing to move opinion. Although it is also possible that the use of single exposures rather than a "whole curriculum of exposure" would limit the potential for experiments to detect framing effects, we agree with Kinder that artificiality of setting is one of the most significant worries regarding the external validity of experimental research. We also endorse his proposed solution: namely, for framing scholars to look to the "world outside" for evidence of framing effects. This is often no easy task, however, and only one of our studies to date (described below) has done so. Here, we must suggest, "Do as we say, not as we have mostly done."

## Studying Framing Effects Outside of the Laboratory

With Kinder's advice in mind, we turn to approaches for studying framing effects outside of the laboratory. One challenge in doing so is to preserve the key strength of experimental research—internal validity—while enhancing the external validity of the findings.

### Experiments Embedded in Surveys

Survey-experiments, which incorporate experimental manipulations into a survey interview, provide one tool for achieving random assignment and control over conditions with a large and representative sample of participants. Applied to the study of framing effects, this approach involves simulating exposure to framing by randomly assigning respondents to receive one form of the questionnaire or another, where the first form includes a frame in the wording of a question and the second includes an alternative frame in an otherwise identical question (Bleich, 2007; Keum et al., 2005; Kinder & Sanders, 1996; Nelson & Kinder, 1996). Like the simple framing experiment, such a survey-experiment can be expanded to include a control group that receives a version of the question that includes neither frame. Similarly, it can be expanded to include a group that receives competing frames (Sniderman & Theriault, 2004). The primary strength of survey-experimentation is that it produces results that are both internally valid and generalizable to the population from which respondents are drawn (assuming that these respondents are chosen through probability sampling). An additional advantage comes from the large samples that can be obtained through survey research: the greater the sample size, the more experimental conditions the researcher can include while maintaining the statistical power necessary to find evidence of framing effects and the more easily the experimenter can test whether framing effects are moderated by individual-level characteristics and predispositions.

The larger samples available through survey-experimentation also allow researchers to explore the impact of frames on the "ingredients" of policy opinions. For example, Nelson and Kinder (1996) found that when issues are framed in ways that draw attention to the beneficiaries of a policy, attitudes toward those groups play larger roles in shaping opinion about the policy. More generally, studies using survey-experimentation have shown that frames can enhance or diminish the roles of group resentments, political principles, and values in determining policy opinions (Kinder & Sanders, 1996; Nelson & Kinder, 1996). By shifting the focus from the question of whether frames change the overall balance of opinion to the question of whether frames alter the foundations of opinion, this research demonstrates that framing effects can occur even in the absence of shifts in the extent of policy support or opposition. In doing so, it suggests that conclusions about whether frames matter may depend not only on the design of the study in question but also the designer's conception of what constitutes a "framing effect."

Shifting experimental manipulations from the laboratory to a survey interview can carry costs, however, when it comes to other aspects of external validity. The realism of the treatments may be limited given that they must come in the form of a sentence or phrase in a survey question rather than a real or simulated news story: survey-experiments may mimic the catchphrases at the heart of elite frames but fail to fully capture the nuance of these frames as they appear in media accounts. Moreover, the setting of a survey-experiment—the unusual context of being interviewed about one's views by a stranger—may be just as artificial as the setting of a laboratory experiment. Thus, the use of survey-experiments to study framing effects allows for conclusions about how "real people" respond to frames but not necessarily for conclusions about how they do so in real-world situations. In particular, survey-experiments that incorporate framing manipulations into the same question that measures opinion about the issue of interest may exaggerate the prevalence of framing effects by virtually erasing the interval between exposure to framing and the expression of opinion.

### Field Experiments

Like survey-experiments, field experiments involve manipulations that occur outside of the laboratory. Unlike the former, the latter take place in naturalistic settings and involve realistic—or real—treatments. Field experiments tend to be rare in the field of public opinion research, but Cappella and Jamieson's (1997) work on the effects produced by strategy and issue framing provides one exception to this trend. In several of the authors' experiments, the participants read or watched framed news stories in their own homes rather than in a laboratory. One particularly novel design revolved around a 2-hour NBC news special on health care. A week before the program aired, participants were randomly assigned to be asked or not asked to watch the broadcast. After the program aired, they were surveyed regarding their views.

Although field experiments can address two key weaknesses in the external validity of experiments and survey-experiments—unrealistic treatments and artificial settings—they possess their own potential weaknesses. In particular, field experimentation often involves the surrender of some control over conditions. For example, only 76% of the participants in Cappella and Jamieson's study who were asked to watch the NBC health special subsequently reported watching the entire program (and some of these may have misrepresented or misremembered their viewing behavior). As the authors observe, reduced control "is the price of allowing people to consume news in the comfort of their homes and at their own pace" (Cappella & Jamieson, 1997, p. 108). Despite this trade-off, field experimentation can be a powerful tool for studying framing effects—one that researchers (including ourselves) should attempt to use more often. The primary obstacles to doing so are the costs and logistical challenges involved in conducting field experiments, which can be formidable.

### Natural Experiments

Natural experiments, or quasi-experiments, involve an even greater surrender of experimental control than do field experiments. Here, the researcher neither creates the conditions under study nor randomly assigns participants to conditions. Instead, the researcher treats naturally occurring conditions as though they were experimentally induced ones. Thus, natural experiments sacrifice a degree of internal validity for the sake of greater external validity. "In the case of framing," writes Kinder (2007, p. 158), "an exploitable natural experiment requires a decisive shift in the deployment of frames in some real-world setting taking place in such a way that the putative effects on public opinion—if such effects there be—are fortuitously captured." He goes on to note that studies employing natural experimentation are in "short supply," in part due to the fact that opportunities for such research are rare. For our part, we have never used this method to study framing effects; indeed, we cannot point to an example of a natural experiment in the entire literature on framing and public opinion about policy issues.

Like Kinder, we would advocate the use of this approach as a complement to traditional experimental research. Research on other sorts of media effects provide examples for framing scholars—ourselves included—to emulate (e.g., Krosnick & Kinder, 1990; Mondak, 1995; Putnam, 2000). One lesson from these previous uses of natural experimentation is that we must be ready and willing to seize opportunities provided by real-world events and be creative about finding data that might allow us to capture the effects of these events once they occur. Given that natural experimentation requires that researchers be positioned to capture something that they usually cannot anticipate, however, we remain skeptical that many such studies will emerge.

### Surveys in Conjunction with Content Analysis

Among the quantitative approaches to studying framing effects, the use of purely correlational survey research represents the end point of the progression away from true experimentation. This approach involves using patterns over time or across individuals in survey responses to create proxy measures for naturally occurring frame exposure and then infer evidence for framing effects. Given the absence of control and random assignment—or even a semblance thereof—the data provided by such research can yield only indirect evidence of cause and effect: these data can be used to establish relationships among variables, but correlation (as the truism goes) does not necessarily imply causation. On the other hand, survey findings can be high in external validity, as they come from representative samples and reflect naturally occurring phenomena. Building on these strengths, some scholars have used survey data in conjunction with content analysis of media coverage to develop circumstantial cases regarding framing effects on public opinion.

Some of the seminal works on framing and public opinion from critical or constructive perspectives implemented such an approach by looking for shifts over time in aggregate opinion that followed shifts over time in media framing (Entman, 1991; Gamson & Modigliani, 1987). One danger of this approach is that it may overstate causal inferences, though researchers have tried to use the approach in more nuanced ways that seek to account for other causal factors. Kellstedt's (2000) research on framing and public opinion about racial policy preferences provides a recent example of the approach in action. To obtain leverage on framing effects, the author combined time series content analysis data and public opinion data. The former came from measures of how often *Newsweek* stories on race mentioned two values—egalitarianism and individualism—from 1950 to the early 1990s. The latter came from 19 different racial policy preference survey items asked over the time period under study. Using these two data sets, Kellstedt was able to provide evidence that shifts over time in framing translated into shifts in public opinion. Another example comes from a study conducted by Shah, Watts, Domke and Fan (2002) that combined longitudinal content analysis of news media with polling data on presidential approval. The authors found that media framing helped to explain changes in Clinton approval over time. In particular, news media framing of the Lewinsky scandal in terms of the strategic actions of conservative elites helped to maintain approval of Clinton.

One of our studies used a different strategy to the same end (Brewer, 2003). Instead of drawing comparisons across time, it drew comparisons across values and individuals to capture framing effects on public opinion about gay rights. The first step was a content analysis, which found that one value—moral traditionalism—was uniformly framed as anti-gay rights in news coverage whereas another value—egalitarianism—was contested, with both a dominant pro-gay rights interpretation and a subordinate anti-gay rights interpretation appearing in news coverage. The next step involved identifying individuals who might be particularly likely to receive news media frames for the issue: namely, politically knowledgeable citizens (see Zaller, 1992). The final step involved using cross-sectional survey data to demonstrate that the impact of the uncontested value (moral traditionalism) on support for gay rights was greatest among the most knowledgeable citizens whereas the impact of the contested value (egalitarianism) did not vary with political knowledge. This pattern of results provides indirect evidence not only that framing shapes public opinion but also that competition between frames dampens framing effects "in the wild."

### The Limits of Quantitative Research Outside of the Laboratory

The approaches described in this section allow researchers to address potential weak spots in the external validity of laboratory experiments. As such, they provide tools for obtaining a richer understanding of framing effects in the real world. On the whole, it seems likely that finding framing effects outside of the laboratory will tend to be more difficult than finding them in the laboratory. As a result, evidence from non-laboratory settings can enhance our confidence that framing effects on opinion are politically important phenomena and not merely theoretical curiosities. Evidence from naturalistic settings may also enhance our confidence that the factors limiting framing effects in the laboratory also do so in real-world settings.

At the same time, the methods described in this section share other potential weaknesses of laboratory experiments. In particular, the existing quantitative research on framing and public opinion tends to emphasize demonstrating effects (or the absence thereof) at the expense of providing a more in-depth picture of how citizens respond to and use media frames, both individually and in group settings. Consequently, this research may fail to capture the full roles that individual critical thought and social interaction play in shaping the connections between media frames and public opinion.

## Using Qualitative Methods to Illuminate Framing Effects on Public Opinion

Although most previous research on framing and public opinion relies on quantitative methods, scholars have also used a variety of qualitative methods to shed light on the subject. The latter methods share a major limitation when it comes to the study of framing effects: they cannot provide clear evidence of cause and effect or even of relationships between exposure to media frames and issue opinions. Despite this limitation, the use of qualitative methods can expand and revise our understanding of how citizens use their reasoning skills, their experiences, their knowledge, and their conversations with fellow citizens to engage—and sometimes reconstruct—the frames that they encounter.

One qualitative approach to studying framing effects on public opinion about policy issues revolves around in-depth interviewing. Unlike survey research, which emphasizes a rigid uniformity in the interviewing protocol to generate responses that are readily quantifiable and comparable across large numbers of individuals, this approach sacrifices ease of analysis and generalizability of findings for flexibility in data collection and richness of data. A study conducted by Chong (1993) illustrates how in-depth interviewing can advance our understanding of framing and public opinion. The author's data came from 30 2-hour interviews of randomly selected citizens. The questions followed a structured protocol in which interviewees were "given ample time to think aloud and to speak freely" on a variety of topics (Chong, 1993, p. 867). He found that individual citizens approach issues with a variety of frames in mind and that they usually choose among these frames "off the top of their heads" (p. 869). He also found, however, that citizens turn to multiple frames when given time to think about the issue at hand and that they rely on public discourse to help them sort out which frames they should use to form opinions. Thus, he concluded that the interviews "highlight the difficulty of measuring public opinion...using conventional close-ended survey questions" (Chong, 1993, p. 870). We build on this point in arguing for a broader methodological approach to studying framing effects.

Gamson's (1992) use of focus group research provides a second illustration of how qualitative methods can contribute to our understanding of framing and public opinion. This approach shares the aforementioned weaknesses and strengths while also allowing the researcher to examine group dynamics. As Gamson (1992) explained, the "greatest advantage is that it allows us to observe the process of people constructing shared meaning, using their natural vocabulary" (p. 17). In doing so, it shifts the unit of analysis from the individual respondent (as in an experiment, survey, or in-depth interview) to the group conversation. Gamson conducted a series of focus group sessions in which four to six participants discussed policy controversies and responded to media discourse in the form of political cartoons provided by the facilitator. All of the discussions took place in naturalistic settings, highlighting another advantage of the approach. He found that citizens draw on popular wisdom, counterframes that challenge dominant media frames, and their own critical thinking skills when they encounter frames in public discourse. Moreover, he found that citizens use the frames they find in public discourse not only to form their own opinions but also to engage in discussion with their peers. Gamson (1992) calls such effects "effects *in use*" (p. 314; emphasis in the original), noting that when citizens "use elements from public discourse to make a conversational point of view, we are directly observing a media effect." In making this argument, he expands our notion of what can constitute a framing effect—another point that we revisit in advocating a broader methodological approach to studying such effects.

A third example of how qualitative methods can add to our knowledge of framing and public opinion comes from Walsh's (2004) participant observation research. Instead of assembling participants to discuss political issues, as Gamson did, she examined casual conversations about politics that took place in existing groups. Specifically, she observed groups such as the "Old Timers" who regularly met in a neighborhood corner store. Thus, she sacrificed control over the direction of the discussions in order to observe naturally occurring behavior. Her findings corroborate one of Gamson's key arguments: namely, that the links between framing and public opinion reflect bottom-up processes in addition to top-down processes. Although elite frames can shape public opinion, citizens can also engage in collective deliberation that transforms the meaning of media frames by filtering them through socially rooted identities. Moreover, groups can draw on firsthand knowledge to "circumvent" media frames. Walsh (2004) concluded that when public opinion shifts, much of the framing work "is likely done inch by inch in conversations among ordinary citizens" (p. 174).

Taken together, these qualitative studies of framing and public opinion suggest a revised portrait of framing and the public. In part, they expand our understanding of the psychological processes that govern the interplay between framing and public opinion. At the same time, they demonstrate that citizens are guided by sociological processes as well as psychological ones in responding to and using frames. By revising our understanding of framing and public opinion, qualitative research challenges the pessimistic account of framing and democracy that follows from the premise of a passive, socially isolated, and malleable citizenry. Although our own research has relied on quantitative methods to examine framing effects, the sorts of studies described in this section have shaped both our theoretical frameworks and our methodological choices (as we explain in the following section).

## A Broader Approach to Research on Framing Effects

All of the approaches to studying framing and public opinion that we have described are limited in one way or another—often in multiple ways (see Table 7.1). On the other hand, each approach also possesses advantages. Having discussed the strengths and weaknesses of the individual approaches, we now offer suggestions for how future research might modify and combine these approaches to provide a fuller picture of framing effects on public opinion.

*Table 7.1*   Research Methods Used to Study Issue Framing and Public Opinion

| Research Method | Examples | Strengths | Potential Weaknesses |
|---|---|---|---|
| Laboratory experiments | Iyengar (1991); Nelson, Clawson, and Oxley (1997) | Internal validity | External validity |
| Experiments embedded in surveys | Kinder and Sanders (1996); Kinder and Nelson (1996) | Internal validity; representative samples | Realism of treatments and setting |
| Field experiments | Cappella and Jamieson (1997) | Realism of treatments and setting | Internal validity (reduced control over conditions) |
| Natural experiments (quasi-experiments) | None | External validity | Internal validity (no control over conditions or random assignment) |
| Surveys in conjunction with content analysis | Kellstedt (2000); Brewer (2003) | External validity | Internal validity (ambiguity of causality in observed relationships) |
| In-depth interviews | Chong (1993) | Depth of analysis | Cannot demonstrate cause and effect; non-representative samples |
| Focus groups | Gamson (1992) | Depth of analysis; allows for study of group dynamics | Cannot demonstrate cause and effect; non-representative samples |
| Participant observation | Walsh (2004) | Depth of analysis; natural behavior | Cannot demonstrate cause and effect; non-representative samples |
| Combination | Price, Nir, and Cappella (2005) | May combine strengths of several approaches | May address the weaknesses of individual approaches |

## Using Open-Ended Measures in Quantitative Research

Building on qualitative studies of framing and public opinion, we recommend that quantitative studies pay more attention to how citizens express their opinions—and their responses to frames—in their own words.

The most common method of testing for framing effects in quantitative research is to draw comparisons across conditions using close-ended opinion measures (i.e., measures that provide respondents with a set of options from which to choose). Many experimental studies simply examine whether the mean response differs from one condition to another (e.g., McLeod & Detenber, 1999). As noted previously, scholars have also used close-ended opinion measures to examine the extent to which exposure to framing shapes the impact of "opinion ingredients" such values, interests, and partisan loyalties on issue opinions (Kinder & Sanders, 1996; Nelson & Kinder, 1996). Likewise, studies have used close-ended opinion measures to examine whether exposure to framing influences the likelihood that a respondent will offer an opinion or that a respondent will offer the same opinion at different points in time (Kinder & Sanders, 1996; Sniderman & Theriault, 2004), as well as to examine whether framing shapes the impact of issue opinions on other judgments, such as evaluations of political figures (Kinder & Sanders, 1996).

To be sure, analyses of close-ended opinion measures have been and will continue to be valuable in advancing our knowledge of framing effects. Still, an exclusive focus on such measures could lead researchers to overlook interesting sorts of framing effects. The qualitative studies described above suggest that citizens respond to framing in complex, critical, and even creative ways—ways that, say, a 5-point scale ranging from "strongly agree" to "strongly disagree" may not always capture. For this reason, scholars have also made use of open-ended opinion measures (i.e., measures that allow respondents to answer in their own words) to study framing effects (Price, Tewksbury, & Powers, 1997; Valkenburg, Semetko, & de Vreese, 1999). For example, Rhee (1997; see also Valentino, Beckman, & Buhr, 2001) found that experimental participants who were asked to write narratives differed in the extent to which they used strategic and issue interpretations depending on whether they were exposed to a strategy frame or an issue frame. Similarly, Shah, Domke, and Wackman (1996) found that exposure to an ethical frame for health care led experimental participants to provide ethical interpretations of the issue in their own words whereas exposure to a material frame led them to provide material interpretations.

Several of our own experimental studies have used open-ended measures to shed new light on framing effects. Our aim in using these measures has been to build on qualitative studies of framing effects by searching for evidence of active reasoning about partisan frames on the part of receivers. One study found that exposure to a pro-gay rights equality-based frame embedded in a news story led participants to invoke equality when using their own words to describe their thoughts about gay rights and that exposure to an anti-gay rights morality-based frame led them to invoke morality when describing their thoughts about the issue (Brewer, 2002). Although exposure to framing encouraged participants to interpret the values in ways that paralleled their uses in the story, it also encouraged them to interpret the values in ways that challenged their uses in the story. Thus, participants sometimes "borrowed" the values in the frames to make their own points about the issue. Such a finding—which resonates with the findings of qualitative research on framing effects—would not necessarily have emerged from an analysis of close-ended responses.

A second study that we conducted built on this study. Here, our goal was to capture how receivers reasoned about two rival partisan frames that revolved not around two competing values (as in the first study) but around two competing interpretations of the same value. We found that exposure to a pro-school vouchers equality frame encouraged participants to invoke equality when describing their thoughts about the issue and that exposure to an anti-school vouchers equality frame produced the same effect (Brewer & Gross, 2005). In addition, exposure to either frame led participants to provide fewer overall thoughts than did participants in a control condition. Neither effect, however, disappeared when participants received both frames; instead, the effects of the two frames were combined. Thus, the use of open-ended responses revealed two insights: first, that framing may work by simultaneously focusing and narrowing receivers' thought processes; and second, that competition between frames may sometimes magnify rather than diminish some sorts of framing effects.

### Expanding the Definition of Framing Effects

Another recommendation that follows from qualitative research on framing and public opinion is that quantitative studies of framing effects should follow a more expansive definition of what constitutes a framing effect. Following this recommendation, in turn, requires a broader conceptualization of public opinion itself—one that encompasses not only the expression of opinions but also the experience of emotions and the undertaking of behaviors. Put another way, it requires seeing public opinion as including not just what citizens believe but also what they feel and do.

One way in which we have attempted to expand the definition of framing effects is by focusing on how frames for policy issues shape emotions. To date, relatively little research has examined emotional responses to frames for political controversies (for further discussion, see Gross, 2008; Gross & Brewer, 2007; Gross & D'Ambrosio, 2004). Several of our experimental studies provide exceptions to this rule. One found that participants expressed more sympathy and pity when they were exposed to an opinion column that used an episodic frame to argue against mandatory minimum sentencing than when they were exposed to a column that used a thematic frame to the same end (Gross, 2008). Another study found that conflict-framed coverage of a defeat for campaign finance reform produced considerable anger and disgust among participants who favored such reform but virtually no anger or disgust among those who opposed it; meanwhile, both sorts of participants responded to substance-framed coverage with moderate levels of these emotions (Gross & Brewer, 2007). Yet another of our studies found that exposure to frames for the 1992 Los Angeles riots produced effects on anger, fear, and disgust that depended on the receivers' predispositions (Gross & D'Ambrosio, 2004). This study also found that frames could alter the content of emotional response as captured by open-ended measures even when they did not alter the overall levels of a specific emotion as captured by closed-ended measures—a result that reinforces our previous point about the value of using open-ended measures.

If previous research on framing effects has paid relatively little attention to effects on emotions, then it has paid even less to framing effects on behavior. This strikes us as a potentially crucial oversight. Although the expression of opinion is important in its own right, the impact of public opinion in the democratic process may often depend on the extent to which people act on their views. Given that such action can take a variety of forms, so, too, may framing effects on behavior. As Gamson (1992) observes, a framing effect can take the form of a citizen using a media frame in a conversation. By the same token, a framing effect could also take the form of a citizen using a media frame in deciding whether to wear a button, display a bumper sticker, donate money, become a volunteer, or vote on behalf of a cause or a candidate. One relatively easy way to test for such effects would be to include measures of behavioral intentions in experimental studies that manipulate exposure to frames. A more difficult—but potentially more revealing—approach would be to design experimental studies that measure actual behaviors following exposure to frames, through either firsthand observation of these behaviors or the subsequent collection of self-reports regarding them.

### Using Multiple and Combination Methods to Study Framing Effects

Our final recommendation is for scholars to design studies that incorporate the strengths of both quantitative and qualitative methods. One strategy for doing so is to design studies that use multiple methods in complementary ways. A study conducted by Neuman, Just, and Crigler (1992) provides a model of this strategy in action. The authors used a mix of quantitative and qualitative methods—experimentation, survey research, in-depth interviewing, and content analysis—to examine how the media and audience members constructed five different issues. Doing so allowed them to collect evidence that was strong in both internal validity and external validity, as well as in both breadth and depth (Neuman et al. 1992, p. 25). According to Neuman and his colleagues, this evidence supported the notion of an active audience for frames. "Individuals do not slavishly follow the framing of issues presented in the mass media," they conclude (1992, p. 77). "Rather, people...filter, sort, and recognize information in personally meaningful ways in the process of constructing an understanding of public issues." However, the normative implications of such active participation in the negotiation of meaning are not always reassuring. For example, the authors found that citizens were more likely than the media to draw on racist and xenophobic frames.

In addition to using multiple methods, researchers studying framing effects can design studies that combine features—and strengths—of two or more methods. We have already discussed one example of a combination method: experimentation embedded in a survey. Many other combinations are also possible, however, including ones that blend quantitative and qualitative approaches. A study by Price, Nir, and Cappella (2005) provides a striking illustration of how combining methodological approaches can open new windows into framing effects. The authors began by using survey research to collect a nationally representative sample. Next, they arranged for respondents to participate in online discussions about gay rights that yielded the depth of analysis and insight into social interactions provided by focus group research. Lastly, they randomly assigned the respondents to framing conditions defined by the composition of the group (conservative, mixed, or liberal) and the frame to which group members were exposed (a "civil unions/equal rights" frame or a "homosexual marriage/special rights" frame). Price and his colleagues found that the resonance of frames depended on the ideological composition of the group and that oppositional frames provoked particularly extensive and complex discussions among homogeneous groups. As the authors noted, their novel methodological approach highlights how citizens can respond to frames in active, complex, and socially negotiated ways—as well as how standard experimental approaches to framing effects may, by focusing on "short-term, isolated responses to news messages," lead us "toward overstating the capacity of media frames to direct public opinion" (Price et al. 2005, p. 205). Future research could develop other creative approaches for combining methods to expand our understanding of framing effects.

## Conclusion

As we noted at the beginning of this chapter, considerable evidence supports the conclusion that issue-specific partisan frames introduced by elites and broader storytelling frames used by journalists can influence public opinion on policy matters. Such evidence—which comes largely from quantitative research, particularly experiments—could be interpreted as suggesting that citizens are easily swayed by exposure to frames. Attention to research using more elaborate experimental designs points to more complicated conclusions, however: some frames matter, some of the time; citizens can be moved by framing but also resist it. Furthermore, qualitative studies reinforce the notion of citizens as active receivers of media frames.

Our review of the various approaches to examining framing effects suggests that both basic choices regarding methods and specific elements of study design can influence the conclusions that researchers draw about the nature and extent of framing effects—and, thus, their conclusions about the processes that govern such effects and the role of framing in democracy. At one extreme, the use of experimental designs that involve exposure to strong, one-sided frames from credible sources without allowing for the passage of time or interpersonal discussion and that focus on the analysis of closed-ended opinion items may tend to lead researchers to overestimate the power of framing (but may also lead them in some circumstances to underestimate the extent of framing effects). This tendency may be magnified by a bias toward publishing studies that demonstrate significant effects.

This is not to say that researchers should abandon experimental studies of framing effects. Not only does experimentation provide strong evidence of cause and effect, it can also yield insights into why and when framing effects occur. In recent years, sophisticated experimental studies involving multiple manipulations and large samples have helped to illuminate numerous factors that may limit framing effects, including receiver characteristics, message characteristics, and contextual factors (e.g., Chong & Druckman, 2007b, 2007c; Druckman & Nelson, 2003). By doing so, this research has led to a more cautious and complex assessment of how powerful framing is and what framing effects imply for democracy. New Internet-based technology, in turn, may lead to further experimental insights by allowing for the delivery of realistic treatments in a realistic context to representative samples drawn from the American public. At the same time, researchers should also look for ways to move their experiments outside the laboratory by conducting field experiments and by seizing opportunities for natural experiments. Though they do not allow for strong causal claims, nonexperimental studies that combine content analysis and survey data can provide another form of evidence regarding whether framing effects (and limitations on such effects) extend to the world outside the laboratory.

Nor should researchers neglect qualitative approaches to studying framing effects. Such approaches contribute to our understanding of the psychology of the framing process by emphasizing the ways in which individuals both use and challenge the frames that they encounter in media. Thus, qualitative methods allow researchers to explore the active role that citizens can play in constructing their opinions. These approaches also remind us that it is not only the "elite conversation" captured in the frames transmitted by the media that matters. Attention to conversations among citizens engaging with and making use of frames can enhance our understanding of framing effects by providing a richer picture of how individual critical thought and social interaction shape connections between media framing and public opinion.

Research that draws on multiple methodological approaches—particularly by incorporating both qualitative and quantitative approaches—holds great potential for generating new insights into framing effects. Scholars working within a particular methodological tradition can and should borrow from other traditions. This could take the form of using open-ended measures in quantitative research to better understand the processes by which citizens think about and make use of frames. It could also take the form of research that uses multiple methods or research that combines methods by building qualitative tools such as focus groups or in-depth interviews into experiments or surveys.

Finally, scholars should expand their definitions of what can constitute a framing effect on public opinion. In particular, we suggest that researchers go beyond the conception of framing effects in terms of enhancing or diminishing levels of support for specific public policies to look at effects on emotions and behavior. Doing so may prompt innovations in framing theory that produce deeper insights into the implications of framing effects for democracy.

## Notes

1. This definition allows for a broader conception of what constitutes a frame than do definitions that limit framing to the presentation of the same information in different ways (i.e., equivalency framing; see Druckman 2001a).
2. Nelson and Willey (2001) refer to such frames as "issue frames," but we prefer the term *partisan frame* given that news frames (see below) can also be applied to policy issues. Moreover, note that the term *issue frame* is sometimes used as a synonym for the "substance frame" (e.g., Cappella & Jamieson, 1997; Lawrence, 2000).
3. The experiments conducted by Nelson and his colleagues also included additional manipulations that did not revolve around exposure to frames.
4. Druckman and Nelson's experiment included a control group (see below), but the authors focus on comparisons between participants exposed to one frame and those exposed to an opposing frame.
5. In the first case, the absence of a difference in opinion across two opposing partisan frames may be interpreted as evidence of no framing effect when

in fact both frames may have moved opinion in a similar direction relative to a baseline (no frame) condition—one as a result of frame adoption and the other as a result of counterarguing a partisan frame. The inclusion of a control condition would allow us to see whether both frames influence opinion. In the second case—where there are significant differences in opinion across opposing partisan frames—researchers may assume that both frames moved opinion in opposite directions. In the absence of a control condition that provides an estimate of baseline unframed opinion, however, there is no way to determine the relative influence of each individual frame in moving opinion.

6. This second result shows that competitive framing environments do not always diminish framing effects (see also, Brewer 2002; Brewer & Gross 2005). Chong and Druckman also found that participants exposed to strong opposing frames expressed more moderate positions than did those exposed to one-sided strong framing.

7. In another study, Chong and Druckman (2007c) explored the interaction of the second and third contextual factors by looking at multiple exposures over time. They found that the effects of exposure to competitive framing over time differed from the effects of simultaneous exposure to competing frames. Specifically, strong frames offered later tended to dominate strong frames offered earlier.

## References

Bleich, S. (2007). Is it all in a word? The effects of issue framing on public support for U.S. spending on HIV/AIDS in developing countries. *Harvard International Journal of Press/Politics, 12*, 120–132.

Brewer, P. R. (2001). Value words and lizard brains: Do citizens deliberate about appeals to their core values? *Political Psychology, 22*, 45–64.

Brewer, P. R. (2002). Framing, value words, and citizens' explanations of their issue opinions. *Political Communication, 19*, 303–316.

Brewer, P. R. (2003). Values, political knowledge, and public opinion about gay rights: A framing-based account. *Public Opinion Quarterly, 67*, 173–201.

Brewer, P. R. (2006). National interest frames and public opinion about world affairs. *Harvard International Journal of Press/Politics, 11*, 89–102.

Brewer, P. R. (2008). *Value war: Public opinion and the politics of gay rights.* New York: Rowman & Littlefield.

Brewer, P. R., & Gross, K. (2005). Values, framing, and citizens' thoughts about policy issues: Effects on content and quantity. *Political Psychology, 26*, 929–948.

Cappella, J. N., & Jamieson, K. H. (1997). *Spiral of cynicism: The press and the public good.* New York: Oxford University Press.

Chong, D. (1993). How people think, reason, and feel about rights and liberties. *American Political Science Review, 37*, 867–899.

Chong, D., & Druckman, J. N. (2007a). A theory of framing and opinion formation in competitive elite environments. *Journal of Communication, 57*, 99–118.

Chong, D., & Druckman, J. N. (2007b). Framing public opinion in competitive democracies. *American Political Science Review, 101*, 637–655.

Chong, D., & Druckman, J. N. (2007c). *Framing effects over time*. Paper presented at the Annual Meeting of the American Political Science Association, Chicago.

Druckman, J. N. (2001a). The implications of framing effects for citizen competence. *Political Behavior, 23,* 225–256.

Druckman, J. N. (2001b). On the limits of framing effects: Who can frame? *Journal of Politics, 63,* 1041–1066.

Druckman, J. N. (2004). Political preference formation: Competition, deliberation, and the (ir)relevance of framing effects. *American Political Science Review, 98*(4), 671–686.

Druckman, J. N., & Nelson, K. R. (2003). Framing and deliberation. *American Journal of Political Science, 47,* 728–744.

Entman. R. M. (1991). Framing U.S. coverage of international news: Contrasts in the narratives of the KAL and Iran Air incidents. *Journal of Communication, 41,* 6–27.

Entman, R. M. (1993). Framing: Toward clarification of a fractured paradigm. *Journal of Communication, 43,* 51–58.

Fallows, J. (1997). *Breaking the news.* New York: Vintage.

Gamson, W. A. 1992. *Talking politics.* Cambridge, England: Cambridge University Press.

Gamson, W., & Modigliani, A. (1987). The changing culture of affirmative action. In R. Braungart (Ed.), *Research in Political Sociology* (pp. 137–177). Greenwich CT: JAI Press.

Gamson, W., & Modigliani, A. (1989). Media discourse and public opinion on nuclear power: A constructionist approach. *American Journal of Sociology, 95,* 1–37.

Gross, K. (2001). *Images of others: The effect of media coverage of racial unrest on public opinion.* Unpublished doctoral dissertation, University of Michigan, Ann Arbor.

Gross, K. (2008). Framing persuasive appeals: Episodic and thematic framing, emotional responses, and policy opinion. *Political Psychology, 29,* 169–192.

Gross, K., & Brewer, P. R. (2007). Sore losers: News frames, policy debates, and emotions. *Harvard International Journal of Press/Politics, 12,* 122–133.

Gross, K., & D'Ambrosio, L. (2004). Framing emotional response. *Political Psychology, 25,* 1–29.

Haider-Markel, D. P., & Joslyn, M. R. (2001). Gun policy, opinion, tragedy, and blame attribution: The conditional influence of issue frames. *Journal of Politics, 63,* 520–543.

Iyengar, S. (1991). *Is anyone responsible? How television frames political issues.* Chicago: University of Chicago Press.

Iyengar, S., & Kinder, D. R. (1987). *News that matters: Television and American opinion.* Chicago: University of Chicago Press.

Jacoby, W. G. (2000). Issue framing and public opinion on government spending. *American Journal of Political Science, 44,* 750–767.

Kellstedt, P. M. (2000). Media framing and the dynamics of racial policy preferences. *American Journal of Political Science, 44,* 245–260.

Keum, H., Hillback, E. D., Rojas, H., De Zuniga, H. G., Shah, D. V., & McLeod,

D. M. (2005). Personifying the radical: How news framing polarizes security concerns and tolerance judgments. *Human Communication Research, 31,* 337–364.

Kinder, D. R. (2007). Curmudgeonly advice. *Journal of Communication, 57,* 155–162.

Kinder, D. R., & Sanders, L. M. (1996). *Divided by color: Racial politics and democratic ideals.* Chicago: University of Chicago Press.

Krosnick, J. A., & Kinder, D. R. (1990). Altering the foundations of support for the president through priming. *American Political Science Review, 84,* 497–512.

Kühberger, A. (1998). The influence of framing on risky decisions. *Organization Behavior and Human Decision Processes, 75,* 23–55.

Lawrence, R. G. (2000). Game-framing the issues: Tracking the strategy frame in public policy news. *Political Communication, 17,* 93–114.

McLeod, D. M. (1995). Communicating deviance: The effects of television news coverage of social protest. *Journal of Broadcasting & Electronic Media, 39,* 4–19.

McLeod, D. M., & Detenber, B. (1999). Framing effects of television news coverage of social protest. *Journal of Communication, 49,* 3–23.

Mondak, J. J. (1995). *Nothing to read: Newspapers and elections in a social experiment.* Ann Arbor: University of Michigan Press.

Nelson, T. E., Clawson, R. A., & Oxley, Z. M. (1997). Media framing of a civil liberties conflict and its effect on tolerance. *American Political Science Review, 91,* 567–583.

Nelson, T. E., & Kinder, D. R. (1996). Issue frames and group-centrism in American public opinion. *Journal of Politics, 61,* 1040–1067.

Nelson, T. E., Oxley, Z. M., & Clawson, R. A. (1997). Toward a psychology of framing effects. *Political Behavior, 19,* 221–246.

Nelson, T. E., & Willey, E. A. (2001). Issue frames that strike a value balance. In S. D. Reese, O. H. Gandy, & A. E. Grant (Eds.), *Framing public life: Perspectives on media and our understanding of the social world* (pp. 245–266). Mahwah, NJ: Erlbaum.

Neuman, W. R., Just, M. R., & Crigler, A. N. (1992). *Common knowledge: News and the construction of political meaning.* Chicago: University of Chicago Press.

Price, V., Nir, L., & Cappella, J. N. (2005). Framing public discussion of gay civil unions. *Public Opinion Quarterly, 69,* 179–212.

Price, V., Tewksbury, D., & Powers, E. (1997). Switching trains of thought: The impact of news frames on readers' cognitive responses. *Communication Research, 24,* 481–506.

Putnam, R. D. (2000). *Bowling alone: The collapse and revival of American community.* New York: Simon & Schuster.

Rhee, J. W. (1997). Strategy and issue frames in election campaign coverage: A social cognitive account of framing effects. *Journal of Communication, 47,* 26–48.

Scheufele, D. A. (1999). Framing as a theory of media effects. *Journal of Communication, 49,* 103–122.

Sears, D. O. (1986). College sophomores in the laboratory: Influences of a narrow data base on psychology's view of human nature. *Journal of Personality and Social Psychology, 51,* 515–530.

Shah, D. V., Domke, D., & Wackman, D. B. (1996). "To thine own self be true": Values, framing, and voter decision-making strategies. *Communication Research, 23,* 509–560.

Shah, D. V., Watts, M. D., Domke, D., & Fan, D. P. (2002). News framing and cueing of issue regimes: Explaining Clinton's public approval in spite of scandal. *Public Opinion Quarterly, 66,* 339–370.

Sniderman, P. M., & Theriault, S. M. (2004). The structure of political argument and the logic of issue framing. In W. E. Saris & P. M. Sniderman (Eds.), *Studies in public opinion* (pp. 133–165). Princeton, NJ: Princeton University Press.

Terkildsen, N., Schnell, F. I., & Ling, C. (1998). Interest groups, the media, and policy debate formation: An analysis of message structure, rhetoric, and source cues. *Political Communication, 15,* 45–61.

Valentino, N. A., Beckmann, M. N., & Buhr, T. A. (2001). The spiral of cynicism for some: The contingent effects of campaign news frames on participation and confidence in government. *Political Communication, 18,* 347–367.

Valkenburg, P. M., Semetko, H. A., & de Vreese, C. H. (1999). The effects of news frames on readers' thoughts and recall. *Communication Research, 26,* 550–569.

Walsh, K. C. (2004). *Talking about politics: Informal groups and social identity in American life.* Chicago: University of Chicago Press.

Zaller, J. (1992). *The nature and origins of mass opinion.* Cambridge, England: Cambridge University Press.

# Chapter 8

# Framing the Economy
## Effects of Journalistic News Frames

*Claes H. de Vreese*

This chapter deals with the notion of journalistic news frames, an area of research that my colleagues and I at the Amsterdam School of Communications Research (*ASCoR*) have been engaged with since the 1990s. The starting point is that journalists and news organizations are not passive actors in the frame building process. Even as political elites, civil society actors, and other sources actively frame messages in order to achieve strategic goals, look favorable, and get news coverage, journalistic framing implies that journalists and news organizations inevitably add frames of their own; doing so, for example, by emphasizing some aspects of a topic while downplaying other aspects. With a few exceptions (e.g., Delli Carpini, 2005; Price, Tewksbury, & Powers, 1997), relatively little attention has been devoted to the ways in which journalistic routines translate into news frames, as Scheufele (1999, p. 115) has noted. But it stands to reason that these production processes are quite important. Public opinion is shaped by how the news media frame issues (e.g., Entman, 1991; Gamson & Modigliani, 1989). Also, journalistic production processes are central to understanding framing effects on the cognitive level, where they play a role in shaping individuals' thoughts, opinions, and attitudes.

In this chapter I first discuss journalistic news frames. After that, I outline my (still evolving) research agenda on a particularly interesting news frame, the *economic consequences frame*. I then report on data from an experiment which shows how framing effects occur when frames influence the relative importance of different considerations (Druckman, 2001a, 2001b; Nelson, 2004; Nelson, Clawson, & Oxley, 1997; Nelson & Oxley, 1999). The empirical study in this chapter is meant to show the reader how the various steps in my research agenda on journalistic frames—in particular, coverage containing the economic consequences frame and its effects upon readers and viewers—have come together. Thus, along with discussing issues surrounding the operationalization of the economic consequences frames, this chapter and the empirical study will address one of the most contentious issues in framing effects research: the underlying psychological responses to news frames. Along those lines, the empirical study constitutes a response to Kinder's (2003, p. 378) call for "clarification of psychological mechanisms that mediate mass communication influence." Such research is essential in explicating the full nature of the news framing process, which, in the end, is the goal of my research agenda on news framing.[1] Although previous research has demonstrated the influence of news frames on thoughts and opinions (e.g., Cappella & Jamieson, 1997; Iyengar, 1991; Valkenburg, Semetko, & de Vreese, 1999), there is little agreement on the specific mechanisms within more complex models of news framing effects.

## Journalistic News Frames

Previous research has discussed the presence and effects of a variety of news frames. The communication science framing research tradition has been systematized in three paradigmatic outlooks, called cognitive, constructionist, and critical (see D'Angelo, 2002). These paradigms are rooted in sociological work (cf. Gamson, 1992) as well as psychological research. In the latter tradition, seminal work includes Kahneman and Tversky's (1984) study that reverses the wording of identical information (equivalence frames). Equivalence framing is very useful in order to contrast scenarios that lend themselves to being reduced to risky choices that can be expressed in identical ways. The classical example of equivalence framing stems from the experiments of Kahneman and Tversky (1984) which stated the consequences of two disease-prevention programs on a disease expected to kill 600 people. A first group of participants was presented with a choice between Program A where they were told 200 people will be saved or Program B where they were told, there is a one-third probability that 600 people will be saved, and a two-thirds probability that no people will be saved. Seventy-two percent of participants opted for program A; 28% opted for Program B. The second group of participants was presented with the choice between Program C (400 people will die) and Program D (there is a one-third probability that nobody will die, and a two-third probability that 600 people will die). Seventy-eight percent preferred Program D; 22% preferred Program C. Faced with the reference state (600 people are expected to die) and possible gains, people were risk aversive and took the sure bet (Program A over Program B). However, faced with the same reference state and two possible losses, people took a gamble and chose Program D over C. So, even though options A and B were indistinguishable in real terms from options C and D, people were more risk avoidant in the first instance and more risk seeking in the second. Looked at differently, even though Programs A and C and programs B and D were identical, the choice resulting from these equivalence frames was very different.

In the world of news and politics, however, most issues are not so clear cut. News framing implies that political, economic, and social events and issues are presented to citizens as alternative characterizations of a course of action (Sniderman & Theriault, 2004). For example, when thinking about oil drilling, citizens may be presented with frames of reference such as gas prices, unemployment, environment, or U.S. dependency on foreign energy sources (Zaller, 1992). Such frames are parts of political arguments, journalistic norms, and social movements' discourse. They are alternative ways of defining issues, endogenous to the political and social world. They suggest that different aspects of an issue can be emphasized (de Vreese, 2002) and are therefore known as *emphasis frames*. They suggest that an issue can be related to different, often relatively distant and diverse, considerations. Journalists rely on such frames put forward by political elites and sources and they have the options of neglecting elite frames or negotiating the frames and thus reframe issues.

Emphasis frames go beyond the equivalence notion of framing in which only identical information is framed differently. In my view, doing news framing analysis by relying on equivalence framing alone is not sufficient. Accordingly, my work investigates the composition and effects of emphasis frames, which, in line with most scholars in communication and political science (e.g., Druckman, 2001a), are the kind of news frames that more realistically, and more frequently, are used by both political actors and journalists to present political reality. For example, when looking at the issue of welfare, pertinent frames encode considerations about who is to blame for a problem (individuals or society) and about the deservingness of welfare recipients. These are frames that offer a different emphasis of aspects of this issue rather than phrasing welfare as a choice between identical outcomes. Both of these frames can influence the willingness amongst policymakers and the public alike to provide welfare (Iyengar, 1991; Slothuus, 2007).

Although news framing can be considered in terms of equivalence and emphasis, it is also possible, and important, to distinguish conceptualizations of framing that pertain specifically to an issue under investigation. For example, the news framing of the final stages of the Clinton presidency was labeled as "Clinton behavior scandal," "Conservative attack scandal," and "Liberal response scandal" (Shah, Watts, Domke, & Fan, 2002). Another study examined the presentation of the U.S. national budget deficit in the press in terms of the chronology of the issue and found that "talk," "fight," "impasse," and "crisis," to be the relevant news frames (Jasperson, Shan, Watts, Faber, & Fan, 1998). Whereas these studies are examples of *issue-sensitive* news frames, other framing studies have addressed *generic* news frames that occur in relation to multiple topics. For example, Cappella and Jamieson (1997) labeled as *strategic news framing* the focus in political campaign news on politicians' performance and motives. Iyengar (1991, 1996) distinguished *episodic* and *thematic* news frames. Whereas the episodic frame depicts political issues as being tied to specific events, the thematic frame places incidents in a broader systemic context. His framing studies found there to be a strong preference for the episodic news frame in American news coverage of social issues, prompting the conclusions that Americans are given anecdotal and piecemeal information about important issues (p. 136) and that politicians are generally freed from political accountability because big picture stories about issues are mainly absent from news (pp. 142–143).

*Journalistic news frames* are generic news frames and emphasis frames. Journalistic production processes are certainly involved in the selection of topics that are the subjects of news coverage. But beyond that, these processes play a transformative role. As Gamson and Modigliani (1989) intimated, what journalists *do to* topics that their sources focus upon, or that are generated by other means (e.g., acts of nature), become a story's "organizing principle," or frame. In this vein, Neuman et al. (1992) identified *human impact, economics,* and *conflict* as common frames used both by the news media (and by audience members as well). Indeed, the journalistic imperative to frame topics and events in terms of conflict (e.g., De Vreese 2004; Huckfeldt, Johnson, & Sprague, 2004; Mutz & Reeves, 2005), and human interest (e.g., Price, Tewksbury, & Powers, 1997; Valkenburg et al., 1999) has been the subject of numerous framing studies (see also, Bennett, 1996; De Vreese, Peter & Semetko, 2001; Graber, 1997; McManus, 1994; Patterson, 1993; Semetko & Valkenburg, 2000).

## Building a Research Agenda on Journalistic News Frames

Close investigation of journalistic news framing will help us to understand how news norms and practices translate into patterns in news content that potentially affect public thinking and attitudes. I elaborate in this chapter upon a news frame that has interested me for a long time, the *economic consequences frame*, drawing upon my previous research as a guide to understanding this all-important frame.

Why the economic consequences frame? This frame focuses on the bottom line—economic implications, considerations, and prospects—and illustrates how journalistic selection processes translate into a template or structure of how to organize a news story in terms of which aspects of an issue to emphasize. Framing news in terms of its economic consequences for the audience is a translation of the journalistic news values proximity and relevance into the news (Gamson, 1992; McManus, 1994). In a more general sense, the focus on consequences is pertinent to journalists, who commonly allude to consequences of issues and actions in the grammar of news stories. This led van Dijk (1988) to conclude that consequences are part of news schemata and are engrained in journalistic practice. van Dijk suggested that the newsworthiness of an event "is partly determined by the seriousness of their consequences," adding, "by discussing real or possible consequences, a news discourse may give causal coherence to news events" (p. 54).

My research on the *economic consequences frame* developed from several sets of studies. In initial studies in the 1990s, I was concerned with establishing the presence and use of the economic consequences frame. My colleagues and collaborators at the University of Amsterdam, Holli Semetko and Patti Valkenburg, had demonstrated the existence of this frame in news coverage of European affairs. In a study of the introduction of the European common currency the euro, I demonstrated that economic consequences were among one of the most frequently used journalistic frames (de Vreese et al., 2001). The outcomes of our content analyses—in different countries, covering newspapers and television, different topics and different time periods—were important by themselves, but they also served as the impetus for the next stage in my research agenda: investigating and assessing the *effects* of such frames. My first research forays here found that the economic consequences frame could influence the focus of news readers' thoughts (Valkenburg et al., 1999). Later I found that economic consequences framing also affected the volume of references to economic considerations (de Vreese, 2004). These steps in the research were important because they formed a baseline for the research agenda. They demonstrated the presence of these frames (i.e., their validity) and that such frames matter.

In recent studies, I have extended this focus by acknowledging the inherent valence that such news frames can carry. In my view, valence is a key concept for understanding framing effects (see Schuck & de Vreese, 2006; Shah, Kwak, Schmierbach, & Zubric, 2004). From research on equivalence framing we know that individuals tend to be risk-seeking when an outcome is discussed in terms of potential negative losses but risk-averse when considering an outcome in positive ways; that is, in terms of potential gains (Kahneman & Tversky, 1984). This notion has been explored in health communication and campaign effectiveness research, generally demonstrating the superiority of negative frames above positive frames. When taking this knowledge into account in our attempt to understand the effects of journalistic news frames, we can extrapolate and assume that negative and positive frames affect individuals' judgments in different ways. Since economic consequences can be interpreted as positive or negative, I expect the effects of positive and negative economic news framing to be considerable and contingent upon whether or not the valence is positive or negative. This expectation embeds the knowledge from equivalence framing in research on emphasis framing.

Bringing together these reflections on frames and framing effects and the specific focus on the *economic consequences frame*, my research agenda on journalistic frames evolved in four stages. My starting point was an interest in understanding and assessing how journalistic practices and norms translate into patterns and templates of organizing news content. The existence of the journalistic news frames was assessed in media content analyses by ourselves and others and provided a first, important step toward developing questions that related to the *effects* of journalistic frames. In my view, there is a compelling need to ensure that media effects research in general and framing effects research in particular does not operate in a vacuum, meaning that effects that are discovered should stem from *assumptions* about the contents of the media rather than *knowledge* about the contents. In other words, to investigate *framing effects*, we first need to know more about *framing practices*. In practical terms, I have made, in a second stage, a clear link between the content analytic studies of journalistic news frames and subsequent experimental tests of the effects of these frames. In hindsight, the initial effects studies are rather straightforward in their design. Whereas the first content studies demonstrated the presence of the frames, the first effects studies set out to demonstrate in a rudimentary sense that "frames matter." In that vein, our main focus was to look for main effects of exposure to news stories that contained certain news frames on the content and direction of individuals' thoughts (e.g., de Vreese, 2004; Valkenburg et al., 1999).

In the third stage, my research has focused on the *valence* of news frames. The *economic consequences frame* is often applied by journalists in propositions that make both positive and negative claims, emphasizing, for instance, the implications of budget surpluses or deficits or economic pro's or con's of political actions (e.g., de Vreese & Boomgaarden, 2003). Again, evidence stemming from content analyses I conducted was applied in experimental designs, and these experiments showed that valenced frames had the capacity not only to affect cognitive responses but also to shift attitudes and economic assessments (e.g., de Vreese & Boomgaarden, 2003; Schuck & de Vreese, 2006).

In a fourth and still unfolding stage of the research, my focus has expanded (synchronous with a more general shift in framing effects research) to investigate in greater detail not only that frames matter, but how, under which conditions, and for whom. This involves building research designs that examine factors at either the individual level or at the contextual/situational level that *moderate* the effects of exposure to news frames. It also involves factors or variables the *mediate*, or come between, exposure to a frame and its effects (Baron & Kenny, 1986).

Extant research points to several individual-level moderator variables, such as knowledge (e.g., Nelson et al., 1997; Schuck & de Vreese, 2006) and values (e.g., Shen & Edwards, 2005). Other work has investigated contextual moderators, such as source characteristics (e.g., Druckman, 2001), interpersonal communication (e.g., Druckman & Nelson, 2003), and competitive framing (e.g., Chong & Druckman, 2007a, 2007b; Sniderman & Theriault, 2004). All of these moderator variables bring the study of framing effects closer to the sorts of real life contexts in which people consume news stories. My own work has focused on political knowledge as a moderator of susceptibility to framing effects (e.g., Cappella & Jamieson, 1997; Nelson et al., 1997; Price et al., 1997; Schuck & de Vreese, 2006; de Vreese et al., 2006). Still, to date, evidence on political knowledge as a moderator variable is divided. One group of scholars finds less knowledgeable individuals to be more susceptible to framing effects (e.g., Kinder & Sanders, 1990; Schuck & de Vreese, 2006), whereas a second group finds the opposite (de Vreese et al., 2006; Nelson et al., 1997; Krosnick & Brannon, 1993).

In terms of the mediators of framing effects research, a number of studies pay attention to the intermediary cognitive processes that are likely to underlie every news framing effect (e.g., Baden & de Vreese, 2008; Chong & Druckman, 2007b; Matthes, Wirth, & Schemer, 2007; Nelson et al., 1997; Slothuus, 2008). Because mediating variables are more germane to the empirical study on which I will report than moderating conditions, I will spend some time discussing mediation models in news framing research, doing so by touching on a current controversy surrounding psychological antecedents of framing effects.

## Mediating Framing Effects: Accessibility and Belief Importance

As I noted in the introduction to this chapter, an unresolved issue in framing effects research is the explication and identification of psychological antecedents of framing effects. When the existing literature is reviewed, two strands of research can be distinguished that address the effects of frames: *framing as an accessibility effect* and *framing as a consideration salience effect*. Both of these strands deal with the mediators of framing effects; that is, with the intervening cognitive processes through which frames have effects. Some of the first empirical studies conceived of framing effects almost entirely within the purview of the notion of *accessibility*. This was so because these studies viewed framing effects as an extension of priming effects. In discussing the priming effects of television news, Iyengar and Kinder (1987) noted that, "what information is accessible for presidential evaluations and what is not is a matter of circumstance," adding,

When circumstances change what comes to the citizen's mind most readily will also change. The circumstantial basis for judgments of presidential performance no doubt has many sources, but among the most important may be television news. We suggest that standards citizens use to judge a president may be substantially determined by which stories newscasts choose to cover and, consequently, *which considerations are generally made accessible* [italics added]. (p. 65)

Seen from this perspective, the notion of accessibility leads a double life, encompassing discursive features of news stories salient in communication and cognitive features of an individual's prior knowledge that can be easily brought to mind. In *News that Matters*, therefore, Iyengar and Kinder (1985) conducted experiments whose results were generated by what Iyengar (1991) later called an "accessibility bias"—the notion that "information that can be more easily retrieved from memory tends to dominate judgments, opinions, and decisions, and that in the arena of public affairs, more accessible information is information that is more frequently or more recently conveyed by the media" (pp. 130–131).

That framing effects should be differentiated from these various notions of accessibility is a perspective that has gained support in theoretical arguments (e.g., Price & Tewksbury, 1997; Scheufele, 2000) and in empirically based studies of framing effects (Druckman, 2001a; Nelson et al., 1997, Nelson & Oxley, 1999; Price et al., 1997). Price and Tewksbury (1997) articulated this position when they distinguished the ways in which knowledge is activated and used in subsequent political judgments and evaluations. In their view, framing is seen as an *applicability* effect whereas priming is seen as an *accessibility* effect. They maintained that framing effects are immediate effects that occur during initial message processing; that is, during initial interpretation and reaction to specific news stories (first-order effects). Salient attributes of a message affect the applicability of particular thoughts, resulting in their activation and use in evaluations. Priming effects, by contrast, are second-order effects with a temporal component: news stories render a construct applicable; once activated, that construct remains "temporarily accessible." Subsequently, when a person evaluates, say, a political actor in a news story, that construct is likely to be activated (Price & Tewksbury, 1997, p. 197).

These points presage work that more radically opposes the accessibility interpretation of framing effects, by Nelson and colleagues (Druckman, 2001a, 2001b; Nelson et al., 1997, Nelson & Oxley, 1999). Basically, they criticize the accessibility model for its dependency on memory for formulating attitudes. For example, Nelson and Kinder (1996) and Nelson et al. (1997) found no effect of framing manipulations on the cognitive accessibility of concepts induced by the news. Instead, framing effects stemmed from the *weight* and *importance* that citizens attached to certain considerations when asked to make political judgments. Framing effects, in other words, occurred through what I call a *consideration salience* mechanism. Nelson and colleagues found that news frames affected opinions and attitudes not by accessibility mechanisms—that is, through discursive features of news that miserly individuals use as cognitive shortcuts to getting informed and evaluating people in stories—but rather because news stories stressed specific values, facts, or other considerations, endowing them with greater relevance to an issue than under an alternative frame. Selectively enhancing the psychological importance and *weight* given to specific beliefs can be accomplished without accessibility of these concepts in memory (Nelson & Kinder, 1996; Nelson & Oxley, 1999). The salience attached to beliefs, which is activated by a news frame, is thus a strong *mediating variable* in predictions of effects of frames upon political attitudes such as tolerance.

In the next section I provide an example of research on how the economic consequences news frame operates and how, both directly and indirectly via applicability and accessibility mechanisms, this frame affects evaluations and opinions. The empirical study is meant to illustrate how the steps in my research agenda on journalistic frames have come together at an important junction of framing effects research, namely, the mediating mechanisms. Specifically, doing framing *effects* research now requires an assessment of the salience attached to considerations emphasized by a particular news frame (i.e., mediating mechanisms that operate via a combination of applicability principles and consideration salience principles) as well as an assessment of more *direct* routes of influence. A direct route of influence, too, merges applicability and accessibility principles: a frame may influence thoughts and opinions not merely as a result of how it renders considerations applicable to an individual who encounters the frame in a news story, but also as a result of its interaction with ideas that are chronically available to an individual (i.e., have a high baseline excitation; see Price et al., 1997). Framing effects occur via a combination of applicable constructs, accessible constructs, and what has been labeled "other factors" (Price et al., 1997), a process that is not fully understood. Therefore, research is needed to simultaneously assess several routes of the influence of frames in communication. In considering these complementary routes of influence, I respond to Kinder's (2003) and Nelson et al.'s (1997) call for more work that is focused on explicating the underlying psychological responses to news frames (see also Baden & de Vreese, 2008, for a recent overview of this literature).

## Study Context: Framing the European Economy

The topic of the study, European integration, is germane to my research. In fact, this topic has been central to my research agenda as a whole, even in work not specifically about framing and framing effects (see e.g., De Vreese & Boomgaarden 2005; De Vreese, Boomgaarden, & Semetko, 2008). On one hand, my interest in it stems from a desire to understand a topic that suffuses everyday life in Europe; thus, it is important for me to understand the impact of the media on public perceptions of, and support for, European integration. On the other hand, European integration is such a salient topic where I do research that it has proven to be a very suitable topic site to test aspects of framing effects theory (De Vreese & Boomgaarden, 2006; Peter, 2003). Our content analyses have shown (e.g., De Vreese et al., 2001) that the economic consequences frame is frequently used in the media's coverage of European integration. In these analyses we relied on multiple item indicators of the presence of different dimensions of the journalistic frames. In doing so, we have tried to unravel the degree to which frames were present. In addition, it opens the possibility that different frames can coexist within a single news story. In the case of the economic consequences frame, the indicators were: (1) "Is there a mention of the costs/degree of expense involved?" (2) "Is there a reference to economic consequences of pursuing or *not* pursuing a course of action?" and (3) "Is there a mention of financial losses or gains now or in the future?" (see De Vreese et al., 2001, p.112). In this and other studies in different countries and during different periods (cf. De Vreese, 2002) these items formed scales with consistently acceptable reliability coefficients.

In the literature on public opinion about European integration, several studies have emphasized the importance of utilitarian considerations as a key predictor for support for European integration, in addition to factors such as satisfaction with the government, national identity, and attitudes toward immigrants (De Vreese & Boomgaarden, 2005; Gabel, 1998). Citizens who perceive European integration to be financially beneficial to themselves or their country tend to support integration more strongly. Gabel and Palmer (1995) advanced the view that citizens perceive costs and benefits from integrative policies differently, and the utilitarian perspective was further supported in later analyses where different predictors for support for European integration were compared (see also, Gabel, 1998).

The enlargements of the EU are key developments in Europe. Ten countries ascended in May 2004, and more countries, including countries from the Balkans, and Turkey, are currently negotiating membership. With regard to the enlargement of the EU, utilitarian considerations and perceived benefits or costs are likely to influence public support. The role played by the news media in shaping perceptions of the potential economic gains and losses of integrative policies has not yet been investigated. This may seem surprising given that a vast majority of European citizens repeatedly identify the news media as their most important source of information about European integration (European Commission, 2004, pp. 51–70).

Media reports are influential in shaping citizens' perception of the economy. When the news media reported negatively about the economy—as was the case, for example, during the 1992 presidential election in the United States (Edwards & Swenson, 1997)—citizens' economic evaluations were affected. Controlling for personal economic assessments, party identification, support for the President, and engagement in politics, Hetherington (1996) found that media use was a significant predictor for negative evaluations of the national economy. Contrasting high and low media users, he furthermore found the media effect to be the strongest amongst the frequent users. In this study, I investigate the effects of positive and negative economic news framing on perceptions of the European economy and support for the enlargement of the EU. In the past, the issue of EU enlargement has received both positive and negative coverage in the news (Norris, 2000) and it is therefore worthwhile to investigate the potentially differential effects of positively and negatively framed news.

## Central Questions

Based in the research agenda outlined above, I will test the effects of economic consequences news framing on assessments of the economy and on public support for the enlargement of the EU, while simultaneously testing complementary hypotheses about the underlying mediating mechanisms. This is based on a distinction between accessibility-based framing effects, articulated by Iyengar (1991), and applicability, or importance-based effects, articulated by Price et al. (1997) and Nelson et al. (1997). I am also interested in valence—*positive* and *negative* interpretations of economic consequences news framing—and the role valence plays in framing effects.

I hypothesize that exposure to news that frames an issue in terms of its economic consequences affects citizens' assessment of the economy. Contrary to Hetherington (1996), who investigated retrospective national economic evaluations, this study looks at prospective evaluations, in particular economic expectations for the European economy. I also assess the effects on personal and national economic expectations but do not anticipate any effects on these measures. I am interested in the differential effects of positive and negative news framing on economic assessments and hypothesize (H1) that exposure to negative economic consequences news framing depresses prospective economic expectations compared to exposure to positive economic consequences news framing.

As mentioned, this study investigates the underlying psychological responses to news framing following the argument articulated by Price and Tewksbury (1997) and the empirical evidence provided by Nelson et al. (1997) and Druckman (2001a). I expect framing effects to be driven by the importance of certain considerations, independently of individuals' accessing their memory. I therefore hypothesize (H2) that the valence of journalistic news frames facilitates the applicability of different considerations. Specifically, I expect that exposure to positive interpretations of economic consequences news framing increases the salience attached to considerations such as stability and economic growth while exposure to negative interpretations of economic consequences news framing increases the salience of cost and risk considerations.

As stated in hypothesis 2, I expect framing effects to be mediated by the salience of certain beliefs and ideas. However, I also expect framing effects to be a *direct* effect that influences individuals in addition to, and independently from, either the accessibility of frame-related constructs or the importance of considerations (De Vreese, 2004; Price et al., 1997). In other words, I investigate the relative magnitude of effects of exposure to news framing both as a direct effect and as mediated by belief importance. Technically speaking, I expect that the variance in our dependent variable will be explained in part by applicable issue considerations, in part by a direct response to the frame. Because I have only limited previous knowledge (e.g., Slothuus, 2008) about the relative significance of the direct and the indirect paths of influence, I formulated a research question (RQ1) about the relative impact of this dual process of influence.

I am interested in the effects of news framing on support for the enlargement of the EU. Previous research has shown that utilitarian considerations are important predictors of support for the EU (Gabel, 1998). I test this relationship using a news story framed in terms of economic consequences. I investigate this relationship knowing that the media is the most important source of information about the EU. I therefore hypothesize (H3) that exposure to negative economic consequences news framing negatively affects support for EU enlargement.

## Designing the Study

A crucial step for framing effects research—and thus for this study—is the development of designs that establish linkages between actual news coverage and its effects upon readers and viewers. Again, for the economic consequences frame, I built upon on a rich body of studies demonstrating the use of this frame in different contexts. Here I investigate the *effects of negatively and positively valenced economic news framing*. To do so, I conducted an experiment that used a control group in a posttest only, between-subject design. Despite criticisms that experiments lack external validity, experimental research is the best way to crystallize the effects of manipulated independent variables (Kinder & Palfrey, 1993).

Participants were 177 undergraduate students enrolled at the Faculty of Social and Behavioral Sciences at the University of Amsterdam. The sample was reflective of the student population (age $M = 20.0$ years [$SD$ = 1.8]; 69% were female). Each participant was invited to The Amsterdam School of Communications (ASCoR) Research Lab to participate in a study of news. Upon arriving at the research site, each participant was randomly assigned to one of four conditions or to the control group.[2] All tasks were performed individually on personal computers in cubicles. Participants first completed a small task unrelated to the current study. An initial questionnaire addressed the participants' demographics, interest in news and current affairs, media use, political preference, and general political knowledge. In order not to cue participants, a pretest relevant to our dependent variables was not included. Participants were then asked to read three newspaper articles that appeared on a computer screen in the individual cubicles. The order of appearance of the articles was randomized to account for primacy and recency effects. After reading the experimental news articles, participants completed an online questionnaire. Upon completion of the questionnaire participants received their compensation and were debriefed.

### Stimulus Material

Each participant read two newspaper articles that had recently appeared in the news. This task was included in order to make the reading experience as close as possible to the reading of actual news articles. Participants in the control condition read a third article sampled from recent news coverage.[3] Participants in the experimental conditions read a third article about the enlargement of the EU framed in terms of economic consequences. The focal point of the story was the publication of a report by the European Commission on the state of affairs in the 10 countries that entered the EU in 2004. The article outlined the trajectory of preparations for the new countries and it reviewed the assessment criteria applied by the European Commission. The stimulus material was produced to reflect characteristics of the coverage of EU affairs as identified in available media content analyses (e.g., Kevin, 2001). For example, the story was written by the Brussels correspondent and referred to the European Commission as a stakeholder.

Both versions of the stimulus article described the economic situation in Europe following the enlargement, and the final paragraph dealt with unemployment in the ascension countries and the criteria defined by the European Commission.[4] The positively framed version interpreted the situation in terms of stability and did not attach an interpretation to the level of costs or the rate of unemployment. A second experimental article framed the economic consequences negatively. With the exception of the headline and the final paragraph this version was identical to the previous version. The negatively framed version interpreted the situation in terms of instability; it attached an interpretation to the level of costs (a number) and assessed the rate of unemployment as high. The full text of the stimulus material is in the Appendix.[5]

## Measures

*Economic Expectations*   Three questions were asked concerning personal, national, and European economic expectations so as to tap participants' prospective economic assessments. Each item ranged from 1 (a lot better) to 7 (a lot worse). Personal economic expectations ($M = 4.23$, $SD = 1.10$), national economic expectations ($M = 4.45$, $SD = 1.07$), and European economic expectations ($M = 4.25$, $SD = 1.11$).

*Consideration Importance*   Participants completed an importance-rating task. They were asked to "indicate how important they considered different ideas when thinking about the enlargement of the EU." They rated concepts such as stability, costs, unity, and risks on a scale ranging from 1 (not at all important) to 7 (very important).

*Support EU Enlargement*   To assess the effect of exposure to the experimental treatment, I used two measures. The first measure assessed the volume of negative versus positive reactions to the issue of enlargement of the EU. I used an open-ended thought-listing item:

> I am interested to hear how you think about the issue of the enlargement of the European Union. One of the news stories you read was about the enlargement of the EU. Please list your thoughts and feelings about the EU enlargement.[6]

The affective tone of each response, treated as the unit of analysis, was assessed as "positive" toward enlargement, "negative," "mixed," or "neutral." The thoughts were coded by two coders blind to the experimental condition. The intercoder reliability of the classification of thoughts ranged from $K = .89$ to $K = .95$. A second measure used to test the effect of the two frames on support for enlargement of the European Union included six positively and negatively worded agree–disagree items.[7] The responses to the statements were recoded and averaged to form a scale of "enlargement support" ranging from 1 to 5 ($M = 3.41$, $SD = .77$, $\alpha = .75$). I additionally assessed participants' support for the

EU in general (six items forming a reliable scale α = .67). I expected this index not to be influenced by the experimental intervention.

## Results

### Effects of News Frames on Economic Expectations

The results in Table 8.1 indicate that Hypothesis 1 was supported. Participants who were exposed to news that interpreted economic consequences of the EU enlargement negatively were less optimistic about the prospective European economy than participants that were exposed to positively framed news, $F(4, 176) = 5.06$, $p < .001$. Participants in the "negative" conditions were more pessimistic ($M = 4.47$ and $M = 4.79$) than participants in the control condition ($M = 4.32$) and participants in the "positive" conditions ($M = 3.79$ and $M = 3.97$). Post hoc tests showed that the negative condition endorsed by an expert differed significantly from the two positive conditions.[8] As expected, I did not find any differences in the assessments of prospective personal or national economic developments.

The importance rating task substantiated our expectation that frames endow certain constructs with greater importance (see Table 8.2). I expected that participants in the negatively framed conditions would rate concepts such as costs and risks higher than participants in the positively framed conditions. Conversely, I expected participants in the positively framed conditions to rate economic growth and stability higher. The results in Table 8.2 support these expectations (H2). Participants in the negatively framed conditions rated costs as a consideration higher ($M = 5.58$ and $M = 5.35$) than participants in the control condition ($M = 4.97$) and the positively framed conditions ($M = 4.68$ and $M = 4.67$), $F(4, 176)$

Table 8.1  Economic Expectations by Experimental Condition

| | Positive economic framing | | Negative economic framing | | Control group |
|---|---|---|---|---|---|
| | By journalist | By expert | By journalist | By expert | No EU news |
| Personal economic expectations | 4.46 (.99) | 4.21 (1.15) | 3.97 (1.00) | 4.18 (1.16) | 4.32 (1.24) |
| National economic expectations | 4.43 (1.01) | 4.38 (1.29) | 4.22 (1.17) | 4.65 (.85) | 4.58 (.92) |
| EU economic expectations | 3.97a (1.14) | 3.79a (1.32) | 4.47 (1.00) | 4.79b (.88) | 4.32 (.83) |

Note: Data entries are means and standard deviations. Means with different subscripts differ at p < .05. Higher numbers denote negative economic expectations.

*Table 8.2*    Importance Ranking by Experimental Condition

| | Positive economic framing | | Negative economic framing | | Control group |
|---|---|---|---|---|---|
| | By journalist | By expert | By journalist | By expert | No EU news |
| Stability | 6.03ₐ | 5.72 | 5.33_b | 5.82 | 5.87 |
| Economic growth | 6.00 | 5.72 | 5.50 | 5.56 | 5.74 |
| Unity | 5.11 | 4.79 | 4.64 | 4.56 | 4.58 |
| Costs | 4.68ₐ | 4.67ₐ | 5.58_b | 5.35_b | 4.97 |
| Risks | 4.70ₐ | 4.82 | 5.50_b | 5.59_b | 5.00 |
| Corruption | 4.68ₐ | 5.21 | 5.78_b | 5.65_b | 5.58_b |

Note: Entries are mean ratings of importance, ranging from one to seven. Means with different subscripts differ at p < .05.

= 4.65, $p < .001$. Similarly the idea of risks was rated higher in the negative conditions ($M = 5.50$ and $M = 5.59$) than in the positively conditions ($M = 4.70$ and $M = 4.82$), $F(4, 176) = 5.73$, $p = .001$. Corruption was also rated higher in the negative conditions ($M = 5.78$ and $M = 5.65$) than in the positive conditions ($M = 4.68$ and $M = 5.21$), $F(4, 176) = 6.02$, $p < .001$. Conversely, the notion of stability was rated higher by the positive condition participants ($M = 6.03$ and $M = 5.72$) than participants in the negative conditions ($M = 5.33$ and $M = 5.82$), $F(4, 176) = 2.36$, $p < .05$. Along these lines, participants in the positive conditions rated economic growth and unity higher than participants in the negative conditions, but these differences did not attain significance.

### Effects of News Frames on Support for EU Enlargement

Both our measures of support for the EU enlargement corroborate our expectation that news framed in terms of economic consequences affects support. As Table 8.3 shows, participants in the positively framed conditions listed, on average, more positive responses in our open ended measure while participants in the negatively framed conditions listed, on average, negative responses. Participants in the control condition listed, on average, more positive responses. A one-way ANOVA showed a main effect of condition on the valence of the responses, $F(4, 176) = 3.19$, $p < .05$. Post-hoc tests showed that the negative framing condition, endorsed by a journalist, differed significantly from the mean of the positive condition endorsed by a journalist.

Table 8.4 shows the level of support for EU enlargement assessed by using our multiple-item index. Table 8.4 also provides evidence supportive of Hypothesis 3, with participants in the negatively framed condi-

Table 8.3    Positive, Negative, Neutral, and Mixed Arguments by Condition

| | Positive economic framing | | Negative economic framing | | Control group |
|---|---|---|---|---|---|
| | By journalist (n=37) | By expert (n=39) | By journalist (n=36) | By expert (n=34) | No EU news (n=31) |
| Positive arguments | 17 | 17 | 7 | 9 | 15 |
| Negative arguments | 7 | 12 | 18 | 13 | 8 |
| Neutral and mixed arguments | 13 | 10 | 11 | 12 | 8 |
| Mean valence | +.29$_a$ | +.13 | −.31$_b$ | −.12 | .23 |

Note: Means are calculated as the sum of positive arguments minus the sum of negative arguments divided by the n. Means with different subscripts differ at p < .05.

tions being less supportive of the EU enlargement ($M$ = 3.57 and $M$ = 3.50) compared to participants in the positive conditions ($M$ = 4.46 and $M$ = 4.19), $F(4, 176)$ = 7.18, $p$ < .001. Post hoc tests showed that the two negative framing conditions differed significantly from the positive framing condition endorsed by a journalist.[9]

## Mediation Analysis

Following Asher (1983), Nelson et al. (1997), and later Druckman (2001a), a mediation analysis was performed to test whether framing effects are mediated by belief importance such that considerations endowed with salience drive policy support. In the present case, this would imply that concepts rated important by participants should drive support for EU enlargement. As demonstrated in Table 8.2 participants rated considerations higher that were consonant with the news frame they had been exposed to. Next, these considerations should be driving policy support—see Baron and Kenny (1986) for a standard reference on mediators and moderators and Preacher and Hayes (2008) for a more recent discussion of issues of multiple moderation.

Table 8.4    Support for EU Enlargement by Experimental Condition

| | Positive economic framing | | Negative economic framing | | Control group |
|---|---|---|---|---|---|
| | By journalist | By expert | By journalist | By expert | No EU news |
| EU enlargement support | 4.46$_a$ (.80) | 4.19$_{ax}$ (1.04) | 3.57$_{by}$ (1.03) | 3.50$_b$ (.96) | 4.20 (.89) |

Note: Data entries are means and standard deviations. Means with different subscripts differ at p < .05.

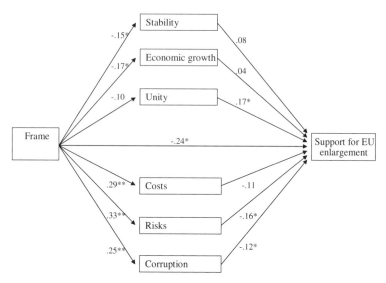

*Figure 8.1*   Mediation model of framing effects.

Figure 8.1 shows results that partially support these expectations. The framing condition, which is represented in the Figure as a dummy variable expressing exposure to negatively framed news, affected participants' perception of relevant concepts. Negatively framed news endowed costs, risks, and corruption with greater importance, while it depressed the importance of stability, growth and unity (i.e., positively framed news fueled the salience of these). In turn the endowed considerations affected the level of policy support in the expected direction. Considerations about costs, risk, and corruption depressed support for EU enlargement, while considerations such as stability, growth, and unity encouraged support. This pattern was consistent, but not significant, in all cases.

I also found a significant direct effect of framing condition on the dependent variable, which suggested that the effect is both direct and mediated through construct importance (RQ1). I conducted an additional stepwise regression analysis to estimate the variance explained by the *direct* route of influence and by the *indirect* route. The direct effect accounts for 13% of the variance while the addition of the mediating variables significantly increases the explained variance with 9% to a total of 21% ($R^2 \Delta p < .001$).

As mentioned, the study included a second factor focusing on the sources in the news. The results regarding this moderating role of news sources are not systematic and therefore not addressed in greater detail.

## Conclusion and Outlook for Doing Framing Effects Research

The chapter discusses my research agenda on journalistic framing and includes an experiment that pulls together its various facets by investigating the differential effects of positive and negative economic consequences news framing of a political issue. Specifically, the empirical part of the chapter is a demonstration of the impact of the economic consequences journalistic news frame. This is a frequently used journalistic news frame—and one of great interest to me—because it is part of journalists' news schemata to highlight the relevance of political and economic events and issues. Results showed that the valence of news frames affected participants' economic expectations and support for the enlargement of the EU. This study found differential effects of this news frame contingent upon its valence so that negative interpretations of economic consequences depressed economic expectations and support for the enlargement of the EU while positive interpretations led to more positive economic assessments and greater support for enlargement.

As I stated earlier, my research has examined the valence of news frames (e.g., de Vreese & Boomgaarden, 2003; Schuck & de Vreese, 2006). The differential effects of framing an issue positively, for example in terms of gains, or negatively, for example in terms of losses, are well known from psychology (Kahneman & Tversky 1984) and health communication (Schneider et al., 2001). However, these have not translated extensively to a political communication context. Public debate over political issues is often framed in ways that carry inherent evaluation. When studying the effects of news frames, it is essential to distinguish the valence of such "contestable categories" (Edelman, 1983).

A mediation analysis demonstrated that framing effects occur through a dual process and take place both directly and indirectly by endowing certain considerations with more importance. This in part supports the conclusions of Nelson (2004), Nelson et al. (1997), and Druckman (2001a) that framing effects are not conditioned by construct accessibility as previous framing effects research suggested (e.g., Iyengar, 1991).[10] However, the findings also extend Nelson et al. (1997), who reported *only* a mediated effect. Our study suggests that this is only part of the story. Although news frames affect individuals by making certain considerations more important for subsequent evaluations, an additional and significant portion of the variance in our dependent variable was explained by mere exposure to a frame, a finding which suggests a partial direct path of influence. Supporting evidence for this dual route of influence is provided by Slothuus (2008) and by Lecheler, de Vreese, and Slothuus (2009). This evidence corroborates Price et al. (1997, p. 504), who concluded that "frames can directly influence what enters the minds of audience members." However, contrary to their study, in which they found significant, but only negligible direct influence of the frames, I, in this study, find it to be a substantial part of the explanation. I propose that the notion of *valence* of the news frame gives insights to understand this. Valenced news frames have inherent persuasive power (see Druckman, 2001b). As I see it, valence gives relative weight to direct framing effects and may suppress some of the explanatory power of frames to endow some considerations with more salience for subsequent application.

This study supports that political judgment can be affected through a direct, online form of information processing which can happen "independently" of memory-based activities (Lodge, McGraw, & Stroh, 1989; Lodge, Steenbergen, & Brau, 1995). Future research must address the cumulative effects of repeated exposure to consonant news framing. If frames affect immediate judgments—which, by virtue of the experimental design, are the only results that this study can demonstrate—we are still left with the challenge to demonstrate whether news frames are stored in memory. If that is the case, it is important to empirically assess whether, upon subsequent exposure to a similar issue frame, framing effects are mediated by memory accessibility.

This study has a number of caveats. A focus on the issue of European integration is an asset given the political importance of the topic and the absence of research assessing how the media affect public perceptions of the EU (for an exception, see e.g., De Vreese & Boomgaarden, 2006). However, it raises the question whether the effects and underlying processes demonstrated here travel across issues. Nelson (2004) found somewhat inconsistent results in his study of framing effects across a variety of issues. Future research should test these findings across a range of issues. Moreover, I investigated the effects of news framing for print media only. Some research has found similar evidence for print media and television news (Nelson et al., 1997) while other research found differential effects with stronger effects for frames in television news (Rhee, 1997).

These shortcomings notwithstanding, what does this study tell us about framing and framing effects? First of all, the notion of journalistic news frames is important because it stresses how journalistic conventions and production processes in fact translate into templates for news stories and that these templates make a real difference for the audience. While journalists and news organizations may follow or divert from a political elites' agenda, it is obvious that there is considerable leeway and autonomy on the side of journalism when deciding how to frame issues. This is something that current and future journalists and editors should be aware of. Their framing power is not negligible and has implications for public opinion. Frames in the news are the outcomes of how (elite) sources frame issues and how journalists and news organizations adapt these frames, renegotiate them, or reframe them into a frame following the logic of the news genre.

As discussed in this chapter, my reasoning and research on framing effects has gone through several phases and iterations. New important paths in defining and measuring journalistic frames in my research, in particular the economic consequences frame, have led advances in specifying the conditions under which these frames are most likely to have an impact. These conditions have included contextual matters, such as issue importance (e.g., Lecheler et al., 2009), and individual matters, such as the resonance or distance between a frame and an individual's opinion, which can spark processes of counterframing (Baden & de Vreese 2008).

Other scholars have extended the largely cognitively focused framing research with new and exciting research on emotions and framing (e.g., Gross & Brewer, 2007). This promises to be an important path of research and we recently found that positive news framing (in this case of the 2005 Dutch EU Constitutional Treaty referendum) engaged and mobilized skeptical voters to participate in the elections by raising emotional excitement (Schuck & de Vreese, 2009).

Looking into the glass ball of the future of framing research it is evident, when looking at framing *effects*, that the qualities of the news frame (the nature, valence, strength, and complexity) matter as well as the qualities of the audience. There is no doubt that pushing framing effects research to the next level involves designs that do justice to the presence of multiple and often contradictory news frames in the news flow that is created by elites and journalists, as well as the news audience. This is by no means an easy task. The best thing that can happen for framing effects research is that it is cumulative in nature and incorporates findings and theorizing from previous work so that we can all move toward an attempt to disentangle how framing effects occur, for whom, and under what conditions.

## Notes

1. In fact, Kinder (2007) later advised that research investigating mediation processes within framing should encompass experimental and nonexperimental studies such as panel-based surveys that can address both how frames affect individuals as well as which individuals are affected and through which mechanisms.
2. An ANOVA was conducted for a number of individual characteristics (gender, age, education level, political knowledge, and political interest). No significant between group differences were found, suggesting a successful randomization.

3. All articles are approximately the same length. They are topically unrelated to the EU, one dealing with the winning film of the Dutch academy, and one with a fine for a bar owner for fraudulent accounting. Participants in the control condition additionally read a story about drug traffic at the Rotterdam airport.
4. Manipulating the headline and the lead-out (the final paragraph) is concurrent with other framing effects studies (Tankard, 2001).
5. A manipulation check (with a different sample) confirmed a successful manipulation of the negative and positive valence of the economic news frames. Also, the study included a second factor, namely variation in the source. However as this is not a key focus for this chapter this is only mentioned in passing when relevant.
6. This procedure has successfully been employed in previous experimental research on the effects of frames in the news (e.g., Iyengar, 1991; Price et al., 1997; Tewksbury, Jones, Peske, Raymond, & Vig, 2000; Valentino, Beckmann & Buhr, 2001; Valentino, Buhr, & Beckmann, 2001; Valkenburg et al., 1999).
7. These items are as follows: (a) The enlargement of the EU is a good thing. (b) The enlargement is important for the future of the EU. (c) The Netherlands will have more advantages than disadvantages from the enlargement. (d) The enlargement has more advantages than disadvantages for me personally. (e) The enlargement will affect the Netherlands economy negatively. (f) The long-term gains of the enlargement outweigh the short-term costs.
8. When considering the two framing conditions separately (without the source factor) the two conditions are significantly different from each other and the control group is placed in between.
9. Our control measure of diffuse support for the EU showed no significant between condition differences.
10. The lack of evidence in support of the accessibility model for understanding framing effects is particularly interesting in light of recent work that questions the mediating function of accessibility for priming effects (for priming effects, see Miller & Krosnick, 2000; Valentino, Hutchings, & White, 2002).

## References

Asher, H. B. (1983). *Causal modeling.* Beverly Hills, CA: Sage.

Baden, C., & de Vreese, C. H. (2008). Making sense: A reconstruction of people's understandings of the European constitutional referendum in the Netherlands. *Communications: The European Journal of Communication, 33,* 117–146.

Baron, R. M., & Kenny, D. A. (1986). The moderator–mediator variable distinction in social psychological research: Conceptual, strategic, and statistical considerations. *Journal of Personality and Social Psychology, 51,* 1173–1182.

Bennett, W. L. (1996). *News: The politics of illusion.* New York: Longman.

Cappella, J. N., & Jamieson, K. H. (1997). *Spiral of cynicism: The press and the public good.* New York: Oxford University Press.

Chong, D., & Druckman, J. N. (2007a). A theory of framing and opinion formation in competitive elite environments. *Journal of Communication, 57*(1), 99–118.

Chong, D., & Druckman, J. N. (2007b). Framing theory. *Annual Review of Political Science, 10*, 103–126.

D'Angelo, P. (2002). News framing as a multiparadigmatic research program: A response to Entman. *Journal of Communication, 52*(4), 870–888.

Delli Carpini, M. X. (2005). News from somewhere: Journalistic frames and the debate over "public journalism." In K. Callaghan & F. Schnell (Eds.), *Framing American politics* (pp. 21–53). Pittsburgh, PA: University of Pittsburgh Press.

De Vreese, C. H. (2002). *Framing Europe: Television news and European integration.* Amsterdam: Aksant Academic/Transaction.

De Vreese, C. H. (2004). The effects of frames in political television news on audience perceptions of routine political news. *Journalism & Mass Communication Quarterly, 81*, 36–52.

De Vreese, C. H. (2005). The spiral of cynicism reconsidered: The mobilizing function of news. *European Journal of Communication, 20*(3), 283–301.

De Vreese, C. H., & Boomgaarden, H. (2003). Valenced news frames and public support for the EU. *Communications, 28*(4), 361–381.

De Vreese, C. H., & Boomgaarden, H. (2005). Projecting EU referendums: Fear of immigration and support for European integration. *European Union Politics, 6*(1), 59–82.

De Vreese, C.H., & Boomgaarden, H. (2006). Media effects on public opinion about the enlargement of the European Union. *JCMS: Journal of Common Market Studies, 44*(2), 419–439.

De Vreese, C. H., Boomgaarden, H. G., & Semetko, H. A. (2006). *Effects of issue news framing on public support for Turkish membership in the EU.* Paper presented at the annual meetings of the International Communication Association, Dresden, Germany.

De Vreese, C. H., Boomgaarden, H. G., & Semetko, H. A. (2008). Hard and soft: Public support for Turkish membership in the EU. *European Union Politics, 9*, 511–530.

De Vreese, C. H., Peter, J., & Semetko, H. A. (2001). Framing politics at the launch of the euro: A cross-national comparative study of frames in the news. *Political Communication, 18*, 107–122.

Druckman, J. N. (2001a). The implication of framing effects for citizen competence. *Political Behavior, 23*, 225–256.

Druckman, J. N. (2001b). On the limits of framing effects: Who can frame? *Journal of Politics, 63*, 1041–1066.

Druckman, J. N., & Nelson, T. E. (2003). Framing and deliberation: How citizens' conversations limit elite influence. *American Journal of Political Science, 47*(4), 729–745.

Edelman, M. (1983). Contestable categories and public opinion. *Political Communication, 10*, 231–242.

Edwards, G. C., & Swenson, T. (1997). Who rallies? The anatomy of a rally event. *Journal of Politics 59*, 200–212.

Entman, R. M. (1991). Framing U.S. coverage of international news: Contrasts in narratives of the KAL and Iran Air incidents. *Journal of Communication, 41*(4), 6–27.

European Commission. (2004). *Eurobarometer: Public opinion in the European union.* (Reps. No. 59-70). Brussels, Belgium: Directorate-General X.

Gabel, M. (1998). Public support for European integration: An empirical test of five theories. *Journal of Politics, 60,* 333–354.

Gabel, M., & Palmer, H. (1995). Understanding variation in public support for European integration. *European Journal of Political Research, 27,* 3–19.

Gamson, W. A. (1992). *Talking politics.* Cambridge, England: Cambridge University Press.

Gamson, W. A., & Modigliani, A. (1989). Media discourse and public opinion on nuclear power: A constructionist approach. *American Journal of Sociology, 95*(1), 1–37.

Graber, D. A. (1997). *Mass media in American politics.* Washington, DC: CQ Press.

Gross, K., & Brewer, P. R. (2007). Sore losers: News frames, policy debates and emotions. *Harvard International Journal of Press/Politics, 12,* 122–133.

Hetherington, M. J. (1996). The media's role in forming voters' national economic evaluations in 1992. *American Journal of Political Science 40,* 372–395.

Huckfeldt, R., Johnson, P. E., & Sprague, J. (2004). *Political disagreement: The survival of diverse opinions within communication networks.* Cambridge, England: Cambridge University Press.

Iyengar, S. (1991). *Is anyone responsible? How television frames political issues.* Chicago: University of Chicago Press.

Iyengar, S. (1996). Framing responsibility for political issues. *Annals of the American Academy,* 59–70.

Iyengar, S., & Kinder, D. R. (1987). *News that matters.* Chicago: The University of Chicago Press.

Jasperson, A. E., Shah, D. V., Watts, M., Faber, R. J., & Fan, D. P. (1998). Framing the public agenda: Media effects on the importance of the federal budget deficit. *Political Communication, 15,* 205–224.

Kahneman, D., & Tversky, A. (1984). Choice, values, and frames. *American Psychologist, 39,* 341–350.

Kevin, D. (2001). Coverage of the European Parliament elections of 1999: National public spheres and European debates. *Javnost/The Public, 8*(1), 21–38.

Kinder, D. R. (2003). Communication and politics in the age of information. In D. O. Sears, L. Huddy, & R. Jervis (Eds.), *Oxford handbook of political psychology* (pp. 357–393). New York: Oxford University Press.

Kinder, D. R. (2007). Curmudgeonly advice. *Journal of Communication, 57*(1), 155–162.

Kinder, D. R., & Palfrey, T. (Eds.). (1993). *Experimental foundations of political science.* Ann Arbor: University of Michigan Press.

Kinder, D. R., & Sanders, L. M. (1990). Mimicking political debate with survey questions: The case of white opinion on affirmative action for blacks. *Social Cognition, 8*(1), 73–103.

Krosnick, J. A., & Brannon, L. A. (1993). The impact of the Gulf War on the ingredients of presidential evaluations: Multidimensional effects of political involvement. *American Political Science Review, 87*(4), 963–997.

Lecheler, S., de Vreese, C. H., & Slothuus, R. (2009). Issue importance as a moderator of framing effects. *Communication Research, 36*(3), 400–425.

Lodge, M., McGraw, K., & Stroh, P. (1989). Inside the mental voting booth: An impression-driven model of candidate evaluation. *American Political Science Review, 87*, 399–419.

Lodge, M., Steenbergen, M. R., & Brau, S. (1995). The responsive voter: Campaign information and the dynamics of candidate evaluation. *American Political Science Review, 89*, 309–326.

Matthes, J., Wirth, W., & Schemer, C. (2007). Measuring the unmeasurable? Toward operationalizing on-line and memory-based political judgments in surveys. *International Journal of Public Opinion Research, 19*(2), 247–257.

McManus, J. H. (1994). *Market-driven journalism: Let the citizen beware.* Thousand Oaks, CA: Sage.

Miller, J. M., & Krosnick, J. A. (2000). News media impact on the ingredients of presidential evaluations: Politically knowledgeable citizens are guided by a trusted source. *American Journal of Political Science, 44*, 301–315.

Mutz, D. C., & Reeves, B. (2005). The new video malaise: Effects of televised incivility on political trust. *American Political Science Review 99*(1), 1–15.

Nelson, T. E. (2004). Policy goals, public rhetoric, and political attitudes. *Journal of Politics, 66*, 581–605.

Nelson, T. E., Clawson, R. A., & Oxley, Z. M (1997). Media framing of a civil liberties conflict and its effect on tolerance. *American Political Science Review, 91*, 567–584.

Nelson, T. E., & Kinder, D. R. (1996). Issue frames and group-centrism in American public opinion. *Journal of Politics, 58*, 1055–1078.

Nelson, T. E., & Oxley, Z. M. (1999). Issue framing effects on belief importance and opinion. *Journal of Politics, 61*, 1040–1061.

Neuman, W. R., Just, M. R., & Crigler, A. N. (1992). *Common knowledge: News and the construction of political meaning.* Chicago: University of Chicago Press.

Norris, P. (2000). *A virtuous circle. Political communications in postindustrial societies.* Cambridge, England: Cambridge University Press.

Patterson, T. E. (1993). *Out of order.* New York: Knopf.

Peter, J. (2003). Country characteristics as contingent conditions of agenda-setting. *Communication Research, 30*(6), 683–712.

Preacher, K. J., & Hayes, A. F. (2008). Asymptotic and resampling strategies for assessing and comparing indirect effects in multiple mediator models. *Behavior Research Methods, 40*, 879–891.

Price, V., & Tewksbury, D. (1997). News values and public opinion: A theoretical account of media priming and framing. In G. Barnett & F. J. Boster (Eds.), *Progress in communication science* (pp. 173–212). Greenwich, CT: Ablex.

Price, V., Tewksbury, D., & Powers, E. (1997). Switching trains of thought: The impact of news frames on readers' cognitive responses. *Communication Research, 24*, 481–506.

Rhee, J. (1997). Strategy and issue frames in election campaign coverage: A social cognitive account of framing effects. *Journal of Communication, 47*(3), 26–48.

Scheufele, D. A. (1999). Framing as a theory of media effects. *Journal of Communication, 49*(1), 103–122.

Scheufele, D. A. (2000). Agenda-setting, priming, and framing revisited: Another look at cognitive effects of political communication. *Mass Communication & Society, 3*, 297–316.

Schneider, T. R., Salovey, P., Apanovitch, A. M., Pizarro, J., McCarthy, D., Zullo, J., et al. (2001). The effects of message framing and ethnic targeting on mammography use among low-income women. *Health Psychology, 20*, 256–266.

Schuck, A. R. T., & de Vreese, C. H. (2006). Between risk and opportunity: News framing and its effects on public support for EU enlargement. *European Journal of Communication, 21*(1), 5–32.

Schuck, A. R. T., & de Vreese, C. H. (2009). Reversed mobilization in referendum campaigns: How positive news framing can mobilize the skeptics. *International Journal of Press/Politics, 14*(1), 40–66.

Semetko, H. A., & Valkenburg, P. M. (2000). Framing European politics: A content analysis of press and television news. *Journal of Communication, 50*(2), 93–109.

Shah, D. V., Kwak, N., Schmierbach, M., & Zubric, J. (2004). The interplay of news frames on cognitive complexity. *Human Communication Research, 30*, 102–120.

Shah, D., Watts, M. D., Domke, D., & Fan, D. (2002). News framing and cueing of issue regimes: Explaining Clinton's public approval in spite of scandal. *Public Opinion Quarterly, 66*, 339–370.

Shen, F., & Edwards, H. H. (2005). Economic individualism, humanitarianism and welfare reform: A value-based account of framing effects. *Journal of Communication, 55*(4), 795–809.

Slothuus, R. (2007). Framing deservingness to win support for welfare state retrenchment. *Scandinavian Political Studies, 30*(3), 323–344.

Slothuus, R. (2008). More than weighting cognitive importance: A dual-process model of issue framing effects. *Political Psychology, 29*(1), 1–28.

Sniderman, P. M., & Theriault, S. M. (2004). The dynamics of political argument and the logic of issue framing. In W. E. Saris & P. Sniderman (Eds.), *Attitudes, nonattitudes, measurement error, and change* (pp. 133–165). Princeton, NJ: Princeton University Press.

Tankard, J. W. (2001). The empirical approach to the study of media framing. In S. D. Reese, O. H. Gandy, & A. E. Grant (Eds.), *Framing public life: Perspectives on media and our understanding of the social world* (pp. 95–106). Mahwah, NJ: Erlbaum.

Tewksbury, D., Jones, J., Peske, M. W., Raymond, A., & Vig, W. (2000). The interaction of news and advocate frames: Manipulating audience perceptions of a local policy issue. *Journalism and Mass Communication Quarterly, 77*, 804–830.

Valentino, N. A., Beckmann, M. N., & Buhr, T. A. (2001). A spiral for of cynicism for some: The contingent effects of campaign news frames on participation and confidence in government. *Political Communication, 18*, 347–367.

Valentino, N. A., Buhr, T. A., & Beckmann, M. N. (2001). When the frame is the game: Revisiting the impact of "strategic" campaign coverage on citizen's information retention. *Journalism and Mass Communication Quarterly, 78*, 93–112.

Valentino, N. A., Hutchings, V. L., & White, I. K. (2002). Cues that matter: How political ads prime racial attitudes during campaigns. *American Political Science Review, 96*, 75–90.

Valkenburg, P. M., Semetko, H. A., & de Vreese, C. H. (1999). The effects of news frames on readers' thoughts and recall. *Communication Research, 26*, 550–568.

van Dijk, T. A. (1988). *News as discourse.* Hillsdale, NJ: Erlbaum.

Zaller, J. (1992). *The nature and origins of mass opinion.* New York: Cambridge University Press.

## Appendix: Stimulus Material

### de Volkskrant

Enlargement Leads to Economic Instability
From our correspondent

BRUSSELS—The European Council of Ministers will decide at the end of October if all ten countries that have been recommended by the European Commission are ready to finalize the negotiations about entry into the European Union. The final negotiations are primarily about agriculture and finances. The intention is to close all deals at the Euro Summit in Copenhagen in December.

The European Commission concludes that the enlargement is best implemented in a "big bang." If the current member states and the European Parliament agree, ten new countries will join the union in 2004. In addition to Poland and Slovakia, these are the Czech Republic, Hungary, Slovenia, Estonia, Latvia, Lithuania, Malta and Cyprus.

At this point not all countries comply fully with requirements, but the Commission expects that they can all meet these within two years. A final progress report is scheduled six months ahead of the possible entry date. If problems remain after joining, the Commission can impose special sanctions, such as import or export limits or border control.

Rumania and Bulgaria are not yet ready to commence the negotiations according to the Commission. These countries are scheduled for membership of the EU in 2007. Turkey will not be given a date yet for the pre-negotiations.

Most governments in the ten applicant countries reacted positively to the report. The report specifies a number of areas of progress. Each country has successfully implemented a democratic system of governance. But in some countries crime and corruption is still insufficiently addressed. And also human rights standards are not fully meeting the expectations of the Commission.

The high unemployment (18 percent) and the declining economic growth mean extra worries and raise the question whether the candidate countries meet the political and economic criteria of the EU. More than one billion euro is reserved to strengthen the judicial system in the countries. Only if this succeeds will the enlargement lead to more unity in the European continent and contribute to stability and peace.

European governments are faced with the challenge of explaining the risks of a 'big bang' to citizens in Europe and also account for the political and economic consequences of enlargement for the current member states.

Note: Above is "negative journalist" condition. Other conditions differed as follows:

| Condition | Differences |
| --- | --- |
| Negative expert condition | As above, with headline and second paragraph from the bottom stated by an expert as a quotation |
| Positive journalist condition | headline reads **stability** (rather than instability), second paragraph from the bottom reads: |
| | The unemployment (18 percent) and the declining economic growth mean that the candidate countries almost meet the political and economic criteria of the EU. Extra funding is reserved to strengthen the judicial system in the countries. The expectation is that the enlargement leads to more unity in the European continent and contribute to stability and peace. |
| Positive expert condition | As positive journalist condition, with headline and second paragraph from the bottom stated by an expert as a quotation |

# Chapter 9

# Specificity, Complexity, and Validity

## Rescuing Experimental Research on Framing Effects

*Dhavan V. Shah, Michael P. Boyle, Mike Schmierbach, Heejo Keum, and Cory L. Armstrong*

The framing of news has rapidly gained attention in mass communication as a means to describe how subtle changes in press reports influence audience understanding. By exploring the potential power of the press to shape *how people think about policy issues and public figures*, a framing perspective counters the axiomatic view that the press is not successful in telling the public what to think, just what to think about (Cohen, 1963). News frames—the organizing devices used to thematically structure press accounts—are thought to influence individuals' mental activation and issue interpretations, thereby shaping social judgments and decisions. The literature exploring framing has ballooned, with many times as many studies focused on the topic as on such central communication theories as agenda setting and priming (Weaver, 2007). Yet with this growth have come numerous critiques and correctives, with some scholars attempting to give structure to the fragmented conceptions of framing effects (Shah, McLeod, Gotlieb, & Lee, 2009), others calling for an expansion of the paradigms used to explore framing itself (D'Angelo, 2002), and yet others lamenting the apparent methodological stagnation of research on the topic (Kinder, 2007). In short, not only can scholars not agree on the meaning of a frame, they can't even agree on what's wrong with the scholarship on framing.

While we concur with many of the critiques of the framing literature, we take particular issue with the concern of Kinder (2007) that too much framing research is driven by experimental methods. By contrast, we propose that further experimentation can resolve some of the most notable shortcomings in current research. In particular, we address several common flaws. First, most demonstrations of framing effects purport to manipulate a particular organizing dimension, such as episodic versus thematic, ethical versus material, strategy versus policy, loss versus gain, and then assess consequences on a range of higher order attitudinal or behavioral variables (see also Iyengar, 1991; Quattrone & Tversky, 1988). We contend that extant research often confounds differences in several aspects of a news story into a single "frame." This approach to framing, in which each story is seen as possessing just one overarching frame, is flawed in several respects. In practice, few news stories can easily be categorized as presenting a single view of an issue. Instead, journalists often combine frames of various types, assembling a complete story by drawing upon several potential frames. Thus, an approach to framing that tries to assign a single label to each story likely misses important, ecologically valid variations both between stories and within a given story.

Second, by assuming that all aspects of a story work together to produce an overall frame, scholars ignore the potential for different components that comprise a frame within which to interact. Even in studies that assume multiple elements can be present within a story—for example, the attribute agenda-setting literature (e.g., Kim, Scheufele, & Shanahan, 2002)—the effects of these elements are treated as cumulative. Whether representing frames, attributes, or some other aspect of a story, components are tallied and their effect is assumed to vary monotonically with their frequency. The more an attribute or "frame" appears in a story, the greater its influence. To that end, our previous work on this issue shows this may not be the case (Shah, Kwak, Schmierbach, & Zubric, 2004). In fact, we contend that a frame that has an effect in one story may have a different effect when paired with a different frame in another story. Chong and Druckman (2007) have made this point most forcefully by conceiving of frames as at times being in competition with one another. This is a critically important insight.

Third, in addition to addressing this notable shortcoming with the independent variable in framing research, we also explore a potentially important dependent variable. Most examinations of framing effects treat basic cognitive network variables, such as mental elaboration and conceptual integration, as latent mediating factors to instead focus on "higher order" attitudes and behaviors. As such, these cognitive variables are often ignored as criterion measures in framing studies. Given that the primary influence of news framing and cueing is on the cognitive responses of audience members, greater attention should be paid to the nature and structure of their thoughts (Price & Tewksbury, 1996). Unfortunately, little work has done this, and thus left the actual mechanism of framing effects underexplored. We argue media effects research must ground itself in an understanding of human mental systems and cognitive activation, which is most possible in experimental research settings with microlevel measurement strategies.

Finally, and perhaps most important, this chapter considers how farreaching or complex a frame needs to be in order to provoke cognitive changes. In contrast to studies in which the entirety of a news story must be altered to generate an effect, we consider quite limited differences between stories. Indeed, we attempt to replicate one of our earlier studies (Shah et al. 2004)[1] showing an interaction between two specific frames: individual/societal and gain/loss. However, we reduce the gain/loss frame to a simple linguistic cue for this chapter, using differences in labels to show the effect of even minor aspects of a story on cognition. Such a nuanced approach, we argue, more closely mimics the reality of news consumption, where an inattentive audience may overlook subtle shifts in content.

All of this leads us to counter Kinder's (2007) "curmudgeonly advice" to move away from experiments in framing effects research. In contrast, our goal here is to rescue experimental research from the very critiques Kinder (a great advocate and practitioner of the method) offers. Although we share Kinder's view that other methods should be applied to the study of framing effects, we believe his three central critiques of experimental framing research are somewhat misplaced if study designs are modified in the ways we advocate. His first critique, that "experiments are normally carried out in such a way that virtually everyone receives the message" (p. 157), can be addressed by employing more subtle manipulations embedded in contexts that mimic the complexity of real world media content. We respond to his second critique, that "experiments do not speak very convincingly to the presentation of frames in everyday life," by creating cross-cutting designs in which frame components are combined or put in competition, so that subjects are no longer "assigned to one of two conditions" (p. 158). Finally, his critique—that "in all the studies of frames and framing, understanding itself is almost never directly addressed or measured" (p. 159)—also leads us back to experimentation and the potential to measure basic cognitive network variables using this method.

To illustrate our approach to experimental framing research, we highlight a study in which we simultaneously manipulated two dimensions of news content about the issue of urban growth: (1) discussion of the problem at the individual versus the societal level, and (2) labeling of the issue as "urban sprawl" or "suburban development." We then assess individuals' verbatim responses for the structure and detail of their lay theories on this topic, providing a detailed look at their understanding of the topic. Notably, this experiment involved playing a radio news report that featured the frame manipulations to participants, all of which was embedded within an RDD survey, providing a more convincing presentation of frames in everyday life.

## Situating Framing Effects Research

### Associative Networks and Cognitive Complexity

The conceptualization of the human mind as a network of interlinked or *associated* concepts has frequently been used as a basis for sociocognitive research (Acton, Johnson, & Goldsmith, 1994; Carley, 1986; Carley & Palmquist, 1992; Lazo, Kinnel, Bussa, Fisher, & Collamer, 1999). Scholars who study mental networks have theorized that intercognitive propositions are the beams and girders of cognitive organization, and as such play a critical role in construct activation and information processing. To explain these processes, Anderson (1983) proposed the *spread of activation* concept, following the priming paradigm of Meyer and Schvanneveldt (1971). *Spreading activation* is a mechanism by which the arousal of one aspect of the mental system can spread throughout the network of interconnected cognitive units, leading to the activation of related constructs and a strengthening of the ties among these mental units.[2] Accordingly, Anderson (1983) proposes that spreading activation plays a critical role in *elaborative processing*, whereby individuals bring fine-grained details of a concept to mind.

Spreading activation may also influence the complexity of cognitive responses. Neuman (1981) proposed cognitive complexity is comprised of two elements: differentiation and integration. Differentiation refers to the number of evaluatively distinct dimensions or elements of a problem that are taken into account in interpreting events. Integration is defined as the spontaneous and explicit organization of ideas and information in terms of abstract or ideological constructs. These two dimensions are complementary in the sense that an individual must differentiate between elements in order to integrate new ones into cognition.

Beyond Neuman's conceptualization, investigations into cognitive complexity may be informed by research on social attribution. Attribution theory asserts that the social context influences individuals' inferences about the causes and consequences of certain behaviors (Fiske & Taylor, 1991). From this perspective, the cognitive complexity of individuals' thoughts may be context dependent and defined by two concepts: cause and consequence. Fletcher, Danilovics, Fernandez, Peterson, and Reeder (1986) suggest that people differ in the complexity of the attributional schemata they use in explaining social issues. In general, people high in attributional complexity are able to consider many possible causes for issues and can engage in complex causal reasoning about potential outcomes of actions.

Drawing upon this past examination of cognitive and attributional complexity, social scientists have become interested in extracting individuals' *mental models* from their cognitive structures to empirically examine the relationships between individual cognition and social behavior (Carley, 1986; Carley & Palmquist, 1992; Roberts, 1989). Many methods for representing mental models use some form of textual content analysis to extract a sense of the connections among cognitions from written text and then use mapping techniques to visualize these models (Langston & Kramer, 1998; Lazo et al., 1999; Novak & Gowin, 1984; Rye & Rubba, 1998; Wallace & Mintzes, 1990).

Common to many studies is an interest in the overall dimensions of mental models, and ultimately the cognitive structures that individual mapping represents. For example, Lazo et al. (1999) proposed that the number of discrete propositional strands and the depth of these strands could serve as a measure of the complexity of mental models (Carley & Palmquist, 1992; Novak & Gowin, 1984). This view assumes that an assessment of the number of discrete categories that serve as the starting points for causal connections is the first step to understanding the causal ordering of concepts or events. That is, tracking individual mental models may be particularly useful in studying framing and cueing effects because of their correspondence to processes of individual internal categorization, allowing a glimpse at the basic nature of the effects.

### The Interplay of Frames and Cues

The framing of a communication text or the presence of a particular cue may encourage the activation of certain cognitions, which may, in turn, trigger other aspects of long-term memory as activation spreads. Indeed, researchers who have explored the relationship between the information environment and individual cognitions have concluded that the attitudes people form are significantly affected by the context in which they are asked to form them (Krosnick, 1991; Tourangeau & Rasinski, 1988). Zaller (1992; see also Zaller & Feldman, 1992) offers a compelling model of how contextual features interact with individual cognitions. He assumes people hold multiple, sometimes opposing "considerations" on many issues. As a result, media frames and cues interact with individuals' predispositions to activate some subset of their available considerations, resulting in the construction of an attitude "on the fly" (Sniderman, Brody, & Tetlock, 1991; Tesser, 1978).

As this suggests, media content may influence cognitive responses as well as the complexity and coherence of expressed thought. Certain frames and cues may encourage richer, more complete information processing, whereas others may foster more simplified processing. For example, Shah, Domke, and Wackman (1996) found that framing an issue in ethical or material terms affected the thoroughness of information processing. Research on voter decision-making processes lends some support to this view. Similarly, Iyengar (1991) explored the impact of media framing on the assignment of responsibility for solving social problems. He found marginal differences between episodic frames (focusing on concrete situations and specific individuals) and thematic ones (focusing on societal trends at an abstract level). The latter appeared to encourage people to see responsibility for problems as collective, while the former fostered an attribution of responsibility for the problem on the individual featured in the story.

Most relevant to this study, our previous work in this area (Shah et al. 2004) established that specific frames could interact in prompting cognitively complex responses, suggesting new avenues for experimental framing effects research. The combination of individual and loss frames or societal and gain frames worked to increase cognitive complexity. Based on this initial finding, we argue that such an interaction illustrates the shortcomings of current framing research and provides direct evidence that more work is needed to clarify the nature of these interactive findings. For example, in the literature on episodic and thematic framing, an episodic frame may vary in terms of the focus on an individual (versus society), the time frame represented (short or long), and the kinds of issue attributes discussed. By providing a narrow focus on single frames, our initial study was able to more precisely identify the components of a news text that affect users than extent research to that point.

In this study, we extend this result further. The gain or loss frame provided in the initial Shah et al. (2004) study is still fairly broad, with different information and implications presented across story versions. For the current study, we explore how an even smaller difference in a story can still produce an interactive effect by looking at story cues. This directly addresses Kinder's critique about frame reception; when such subtle changes are made, they can often go overlooked. Scholars interested in political information processing and persuasion have considered the role of cues; that is, smaller, more discrete attempts to encourage particular understandings through the labeling of events and issues. Edelman (1993) argues that the public's beliefs about the causes and consequences of political issues are often swayed by transparent "categories" offered up by political elites.

We distinguish a cue from a frame in that the former is restricted entirely to differences in labeling, but this distinction is not necessarily maintained in the overall framing literature. Indeed, cueing as presented here may well be seen as a particular type of framing. These cueing categories constrain a range of potential realities, shaping political "enthusiasms, fears and antagonisms" when presented as natural, self-evident or simple descriptions rather than carefully constructed rhetorical devices (Edelman, 1993, p. 232). That is, the labels used as shorthand for discussing complex social issues are most effective at encouraging certain modes of thought when at first blush they appear to be simple factual portrayals (Kuklinski & Hurley, 1994). In addition, cues are most effective when they are quite simple, encouraging the adoption of the heuristic and discouraging careful reflection or skepticism.

*Validating Framing Effects*

In replicating and extending our initial study (Shah et al., 2004), this time with a gain/loss cue rather than the corresponding frame, we nonetheless offer a similar prediction. Specifically, we assert that gain versus loss cues, reflected in the labels "suburban development" and "urban sprawl," respectively, are ideologically contested ways of categorizing the issue of urban growth (community expansion). The term *suburban development* focuses on the positive effects or gains associated with urban growth. In contrast, the term *urban sprawl* brings the focus to the negative effects or losses incurred as a result of growth. Building upon the insights offered by Tversky and Kahneman (1981; also Kahneman & Tversky, 1984) and others (see Hale & Dillard, 1995), we contend that *losses will loom larger than gains* in the minds of individuals.

Further, we maintain that this will only be the case when problems are framed at the *individual level*, where people can make a connection between the problem and their own life situation. This is consistent with research that finds feelings of personal threat foster more thorough information processing than feelings of personal mastery (Marcus, 1988; Marcus, Sullivan, Theiss-Morse, & Wood, 1995). Thus, the combination of an individual frame and a loss cue should encourage people to connect the potential threat and their personal situation, generating more cognitively complex models, specifying the nature of framing effects.

In contrast, when the issue is framed in societal terms alongside a loss cue, threat perceptions may dissipate due to expectations of impersonal effects (Gunther & Mundy, 1993). Yet problems framed at the societal level may encourage the generation of complex mental models when they are presented alongside a gain cue (Shah et al, 2004). This is because of the basic tendency to perceive oneself as the beneficiary of general gains (Jones, 1990; Ross, 1977). Research on economic voting supports this view; it indicates that citizens apply sociotropic criteria when deciding between candidates (Feldman, 1982; Kinder & Kiewiet, 1981; Niemi & Weisberg, 1993), but they reduce the use of such criteria when they are doubtful of the capacity of a politician to make positive changes (Krause, 1997).[3] Thus, we predict that subjects who encounter a news story containing the combination of an individual frame with a loss cue or a societal frame with a gain cue will express more complex mental models than subjects who encounter the same news story containing the opposing frame and cue combinations.

## Testing Our Approach

To examine the relationship between individuals' cognitive models and particular media content, it was necessary to develop a study that centered on a particular issue. For this study, we dealt with the issue of urban growth. The data were collected through telephone interviews with a probability sample of 357 respondents from Madison, WI and its surrounding areas. A combination of systematic sampling and a variant of random digit dialing was used to ensure the inclusion of unlisted phone numbers in our sample. Respondents were randomly selected from within each household to produce a representative sample of the locality.

### Design

To test the effects of media frames and cues on cognitive structure, we needed to provide respondents with frames and cues regarding urban growth. For this purpose, a 2×2 experimental design was developed using simulated radio broadcasts as the manipulation. The broadcasts were recorded and reproduced using professional equipment and trained readers. The broadcasts were framed as dealing with the issue at the individual or societal level and different cues were added for each condition. Respondents receiving the societal condition heard about growth in terms of its effects on their entire region without mention of individuals. Those receiving the individual condition heard about the same effects of growth through the lens of two individuals' experiences. Within each story, the term *urban growth* was replaced with a positive or negative cue. The term *suburban development* was used as the positive cue, connoting the benefits that urban growth can bring to a community. The term *urban sprawl* was used as a cue for the negative consequences of growth.

Across all conditions, the factual information remained the same and the language was kept as constant as possible. Respondents were presented with contrasting perspectives that discussed how growth both generates an influx of new businesses and an increasing tax base at the same time that it increases traffic and creates pollution and safety issues.

To make the manipulations as "real" as possible, the recording closely simulated a radio news item. As stated above, professional equipment and trained announcers were used to record the experimental manipulations, and the time length was kept under 30 seconds. Different voices were used to inject "sound bites" into the piece for the individual condition. The survey experiment has the added advantage of exposing listeners to the news item in the comfort of their own home surrounded by the many usual distractions that accompany radio listening.

### Cognitive Mapping

After hearing the news story, the respondents were asked, "If you were talking with someone who was not from Madison and they asked you to explain the issue of urban growth and its impact on the quality of life in the Madison area, what would you tell them?" Interviewers were trained to use neutral probes to encourage respondents to provide as much information as possible. Responses were tape recorded and transcribed.

Using the transcriptions, a small group of trained coders worked to map the structure of the responses. Initially, distinguishable unique ideas were identified. Care was taken to separate unique ideas, or facets, from elaboration of a single idea as well as from ideas that were mere recapitulations of the taped news story. The identified facets were then classified as being causally or noncausally connected to the issue of urban growth. A causal connection was coded only if the connection was explicit. Using this coding approach, a measure of total *number of causal connections* ($M = 2.53$; $SD = 1.93$) was computed.

Next, to identify distinct strands of thought, each response was diagramed into strands of causally connected facets. Each strand of thought represented separate lay theories of how urban growth works or is manifested in the community. Using this information, a measure of *unique strands* ($M = 1.37$; $SD = 1.30$) was coded. The facets in each strand were then placed in the order in which the respondent connected them. Each facet was identified as either a unique antecedent to or a unique consequence of urban growth. There were very few antecedents found in the responses, so for the purpose of this analysis, the more substantive measure of *unique consequences* ($M = 1.61$; $SD = 1.63$) was coded. If respondents mentioned a solution to the problems of urban growth, it was placed as a link in their causal strand. With this, a measure of the *length of each strand with solutions* was computed. The length of longest causal strand was then used to compute *maximal depth with solutions* ($M = 1.22$; $SD = 1.13$).

### Blocking Variables

Previous studies have found that people's cognitive complexity is influenced by preexperimental factors such as formal education, knowledge, and communicative behaviors. Several of these factors are included in this study to help control extraneous variance and to increase the precision of the analyses. Essentially, we want to be able to consider the particular influence of the experimental manipulations above and beyond any influence demographic characteristics and communicative behaviors might play. As such, we statistically "block off" their influence so each category of variable can be considered separately. This analytic approach allows us to safeguard against the possibility that preexisting differences that may be consequential were not randomly distributed across the experimental conditions.

*Demographic Variables* Four demographic variables were used as controls. Gender (56.1% female) was coded by the interviewer. Age (*M* = 42.55; *SD* = 15.65; range=18-83) was measured by asking the respondent's age on his or her last birthday. Education (*M* =15.18; *SD* = 3.20, range = 4-26) was measured by asking the respondent the highest year of school completed. Income (*Mdn.* = $50–60,000) assessed the respondent's estimate of their total household income for the previous year.

*Communication and Knowledge Variables* Newspaper hard news use consists of six measures of attention and exposure to international, national and local content (α = .95; *M* = 5.51; *SD* = 2.81). Television hard news use was constructed from three measures of attention to content about international, national, and local news (α = .89; *M* = 5.90; *SD* = 2.55). Discussion frequency was assessed by asking the respondents how often they talked about local political or community issues with the following groups of people: neighbors, people in the Madison area, coworkers, and family. Each item was measured on a 10-point scale from seldom to often. The items were combined into a single measure of discussion frequency (α = .66; *M* = 5.13; *SD* = 1.91). Finally, a measure of factual knowledge was computed from six questions concerning local political knowledge. Responses were coded as incorrect if either the answer given was not right or if there was not an answer given. The six items were combined into a single measure of factual knowledge (α = .73; *M* = .62; *SD* = .34)

## The Illustrative Case

To test the effects of the illustrative case presented in this chapter, we conducted a series of hierarchical regressions that blocked the effects of the demographic items, the communication measures, and the public affairs knowledge measure as controls. In these analyses, the blocking variables were entered first, the main effects of the frame and cue manipulations were entered in the second block, and the transverse interaction term was entered in the third block (see Table 9.1).

We first analyzed *unique consequences*. Controlling for people's pre-experimental conditions such as education, knowledge, media use, and interpersonal discussion accounted for 7.7% of the variance, a significant contribution (*p* < .01). The second block, the frame (Beta = .02, *n.s.*) and cue (Beta = .01, *n.s.*) manipulations, failed to account for any change in the variance. When entered in the third block, the interaction effect (Beta = .09, *p* < .05) accounted for an additional .8% of variance, which was statistically significant.

A similar pattern was found when examining *causal connections*.

Table 9.1   Hierarchical Regression Predicting Four Measures of Cognitive Complexity for Frame and Cue Manipulations Controlling for Demographic Measures and Media Use

|  | Unique Consequences | Causal Connections | Unique Strands | Maximal Depth |
|---|---|---|---|---|
| Control Block[a] | | | | |
| Control incremental $R^2$ | 7.7%*** | 10.2%*** | 8.4%*** | 8.6%*** |
| Main manipulations | | | | |
| Frame: Individual/societal | .02 | .06 | .03 | -.01 |
| Cue: Sprawl/Development | .01 | .03 | -.02 | -.01 |
| Main effect incremental R2 | .0% | .5% | .1% | .0% |
| Transverse interaction[b] | | | | |
| Frame x Cue | .09* | .08# | .16** | .09# |
| Interaction incremental $R^2$ | .8%* | .6%# | 2.5%** | .7%# |
| Model info | | | | |
| Total R | 8.6%*** | 11.2%*** | 11.0%*** | 11.2%*** |

Note: Entries refer to standardized regression coefficients obtained after controlling for control block and main manipulation measures
# p < 10. *p < .05. **p < .01. ***p < .001.
[a] Control blocks include demographics, newspaper hard news use, television hard news use, political discussion, and public affairs knowledge
[b] Frame interaction coded as individual/sprawl and societal/development = high

After the control block, which accounted for a significant 10.2% of the variance, the frame (Beta = .06, $n.s.$) and cue (Beta = .03, $n.s.$) manipulations failed to account for a significant increase in model performance. The interaction effect (Beta = .08, $p$ = .08) accounted for .6% of the incremental variance, a marginally significant change.

When effects on number of *unique strands* were examined, the same basic pattern emerged. The control block accounted for 8.4% of the variance ($p$ < .001), whereas the frame (Beta = .03, $n.s.$) and cue (Beta = -.02, $n.s.$) manipulations accounted for 0.1% of additional variance. In contrast, the interaction (Beta = .16, $p$ < .01) accounted for 2.5% of the variance above and beyond the effects of the control variables and the experimental main effects.

Finally, effects on *maximal causal depth* were examined. The control block accounted for a sizable 8.6% of the variance ($p$ < .001), while the frame (Beta = -.01, $n.s.$) and cue (Beta = -.01, $n.s.$) manipulation block accounted for no additional variance. However, the interaction (Beta = .09, p = .06) block explained an additional .7% of the variance, which was marginally significant. The findings demonstrate that the frame and cue manipulations interacted to encourage individuals' to express more complex mental models about urban growth when presented with an individual frame with a loss cue or a societal frame with a gain cue, as we hypothesized. The fact that this relationship remains largely robust after blocking other explanatory variables provides greater confidence in the observed results.

To more closely observe the patterns of interactions between frames and cues on cognitive complexity, the estimated marginal mean values (generated from ANCOVA) for the experimental conditions are plotted in Figure 9.1. Each plot consistently displays a transverse interaction between the frame manipulation and the cue manipulation, where the two lines indicating urban sprawl/suburban development cues cross over with opposite slopes across frame conditions. These interactions appear in the expected direction.

As these plots make clear, individual frames tended to generate more complex cognitive responses among subjects who encountered the sprawl cue, as compared with other respondents who received the same individual frame but heard the development cue. In contrast, the effect of the

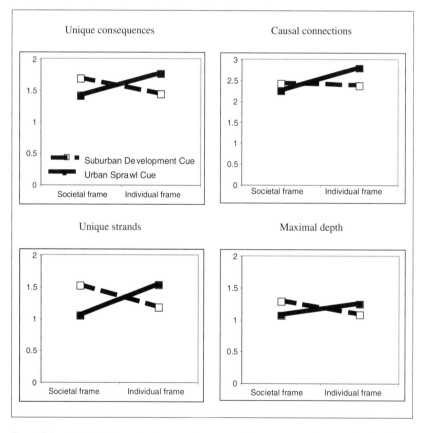

*Figure 9.1* Estimated marginal means demonstrating transverse interaction for frame and cue manipulation on four measures of cognitive complexity: Unique consequences, causal connections, unique strands, and maximal depth.

societal frame on cognitive measures was greater when presented with the development cue as compared with the sprawl cue. In short, Figure 9.1 shows a consistent pattern across the four criterion variables examined. Respondents expressed more complex mental models about urban growth when consequences were framed at the individual level with a sprawl cue and at the societal level with a development cue as compared with the other frame and cue combinations.

## Implications for Framing Effects Research

The results of the illustrative case presented above highlight a number of important issues for framing effects research that we laid out at the beginning of this chapter. At the most basic level, these results provide general support for the central hypothesis that frames and cues interact to affect cognitive processing. Subjects receiving the societal news frame with the gain cue of "suburban development" and the individual news frame with the loss cue of "urban sprawl" mentioned more consequences of urban growth, made causal connections among discrete aspects of the issue, activated multiple lay theories about how urban growth occurs, and extend these theories to greater lengths than those receiving opposing frame/cue combinations.

More generally, the data presented in this chapter have clear implications for understanding media effects research. The integration by reporters of certain types of language cues (loss or gain) and certain perspectives derived from journalist norms (individual or societal) have effects on the complexity of individuals' thoughts. This is an important implication; the results here show a specific cognitive reaction to news content, a critical early step that may influence not only differences in opinions but also a number of other responses. Too few framing studies have looked at how mental models regarding an issue are shaped by news content. Although the effects observed were not strong, frames do have distinct effects when used in conjunction with certain cues. It is important to remember, however, that these modest but compelling effects were observed after only a single manipulation delivered over the telephone and after significant statistical controls were employed. If the media were to consistently present certain frames and cues in conjunction, the long-term effects may be far stronger.

There are two possible reasons why respondents who simultaneously received the loss cue and the individual frame or gain cue and the societal frame generally expressed more complex mental models: (1) the combination caused individuals to consciously feel more motivated to think about and respond to the open-ended question regarding urban growth, and (2) the combination triggered increased associations with existing mental structures, thus activating a greater number of constructs when responding. Future research interested in exploring the underpinning of framing effects should explore these possibilities.

If individuals consciously felt more motivated to contemplate and discuss growth under the conditions described above, we might expect them to talk in greater detail and to draw more connections among attributes, rather than simply recalling more concepts. This was in fact the case. The gain cue/society frame and the loss cue/individual frame both led to an apparent increase in total causal connections and maximal causal depth, albeit a marginally significant result in both cases. However, these results do not clearly indicate that respondents deliberately thought harder about the issue at hand. The combination of certain frames and cues may simply be triggering cognitive associations formed from prior thinking about the issue (see Barguley & Payne, 1999). The individual/loss and the societal/gain combination may simply encourage greater spreading activation due to the fact that these frames and cues co-occur with greater frequency in the media, producing certain heuristic reactions. Ultimately, given that the results mirror the findings from Shah et al. (2004), the underlying process may also be similar.

Apart from the general findings presented here, these data have specific implications for clarifying our understanding of what framing is and how to best approach studying it. First, this work underscores the idea that framing effects represents an accumulation of small elements within a story, each of which may have a contribution, and some of which may offset one another. As such, research must continue to move away from the notion that news coverage of issues are dominated by single frames or cues and continue to develop the notion that meaning comes from the intersection of these frames and cues.

Second, the complex interplay of discrete elements of a news story reinforces the value of experimental research on news framing effects. Only in an experimental context can we pick these apart, allowing us to make sense of often contradictory findings from survey research and guide reasonable, theoretically coherent content analysis. Experimental work represents an integral component of helping us to develop a coherent theory of framing that clarifies the effects of specific types of framing elements. It is through the specificity of experimental framing studies that we can examine how the complex interplay of textual features produces the kinds of primary effects illustrated in the case presented above.

Third, in that same vein, the integration of research methods is essential to a more fully developed understanding not only of how frames work but how frames and other story elements are structured within a news story. As such, subsequent content analysis of framing must be matched more closely with experimental work. At present, too much framing research involves content analysis in which a unique set of frames are proposed for a specific segment of media content; after these "frames" are tallied, the work is left as an isolated description with little to offer to the development of a larger theory. In this regard, we argue Kinder (2007) was off the mark, despite the value of many of his critiques. Curtailing experimental research will only further the atheoretical nature of framing and make it harder to draw valid conclusions about the nature of framing effects that stretch beyond a single instance or issue.

That said, the fourth key point is that we must present framing experiments in an ecologically valid fashion, to the extent possible. In this study, several steps were taken to ensure the content mirrored a realistic news story and was delivered to the participant in their own home. While people may not normally listen to news over the phone, it is not inconsistent with how someone might receive a radio broadcast. Framing experiments in which the entire story varies between versions may lack this ecological validity; few real news stories are entirely one-sided or contain only one interpretation of an issue. Once again, this highlights the importance of seeing frames and cues as varied, cross-cutting elements within a story, rather than a dominating element that shapes the entire text.

Fifth, the use of cues in this study further illustrates that large changes in stories are not necessary to produce differences in cognitive responses. Simply changing a single label was enough to sharply moderate how individuals responded to the individual/societal frame. It may be that the individual/societal frame was in fact broader than necessary, and a more specific element of that "frame"—perhaps even a single cue—would be adequate to produce the same effect. Only careful experimental research can test this possibility.

In conclusion, the theory advanced and tested here suggests that frames and cues can interact to produce cognitive differences. The results mirror prior research showing that two frames can interact in a similar fashion, bolstering the overall findings. Of course, further research with broader populations and considering different issues would still be necessary to fully explore how these specific frames and cues work together and how universal that effect might be. But the findings here clearly demonstrate the potential for such an interaction and the importance of careful experimental research capable of detecting such an effect.

## Notes

1. Both of these studies are part of a long-running program of research on framing effects conducted by Dhavan Shah and Doug McLeod with an evolving group of student scholars. This work has been done within the Mass Communication Research Center (MCRC) at the University of Wisconsin-Madison's School of Journalism & Mass Communication. The MCRC brings together graduate students and faculty who collaborate to design and conduct political communication research. This work-

ing group has a long history in the school, where it has been a center of research activity focusing on media and politics for over 35 years. Dozens of students have moved through the MCRC over the last decade, with many continuing their explorations of media influence as assistant professors throughout the world. This piece is a testament to that process and reflects the organizing principles of Maier-Bascom Professor Emeritus and longtime chair of the MCRC, Jack McLeod.

2. For familiar items, when a concept is presented to an individual, its mental "representation" can easily be activated and can then spread to closely linked constructs. For less familiar items, linkages may be created to existing cognitive structures that then become sources of activation at a later time.

3. Further, Mutz and Mondak (1997) found that such sociotropic decisions may be made at group, rather than national levels. Presumably, such groups could be extended to include most any "imagined community"; Mutz (1992) finds support for such an effect at the state level.

## References

Acton, W. H., Johnson, P. J., & Goldsmith, T. E. (1994). Structural knowledge assessment: Comparison to referent structures. *Journal of Educational Psychology, 86,* 303–311.

Anderson, J. R. (1983). *The architecture of cognition.* Cambridge, MA: Harvard University Press.

Barguley, T., & Payne, S. J. (1999). Recognition memory for sentences from spatial descriptions: A test of the episodic construction trace hypothesis. *Memory & Cognition, 27,* 962–973.

Carley, K. A. (1986). An approach for relating social structure to cognitive structure. *Journal of Mathematical Sociology, 12,* 137–189.

Carley, K., & Palmquist, M. (1992). Extracting, representing, and analyzing mental models. *Social Forces, 70,* 601–636.

Chong, D., & Druckman, J. N. (2007). Framing public opinion in competitive democracies. *American Political Science Review, 101,* 637–655.

Cohen, A. R. (1963). *Attitude change and social influence.* New York: Basic Books.

D'Angelo, P. (2002). News framing as a multiparadigmatic research program: A response to Entman. *Journal of Communication, 52,* 870–888.

Edelman, M. (1993). Contestable categories and public opinion. *Political Communication, 10,* 231–242.

Feldman, S. (1982). Economic self-interest and political behavior. *American Journal of Political Science, 26,* 446–466.

Fiske, S., & Taylor, S. E. (1991). *Social cognition.* New York: McGraw-Hill.

Fletcher, G. J. O., Danilovics, P., Fernandez, G., Peterson, D., & Reeder, G. D. (1986). Attributional complexity: An individual difference measure. *Journal of Personality and Social Psychology, 51,* 875–884.

Gunther, A. C., & Mundy, P. (1993). Biased optimism and the third-person effect. *Journalism Quarterly, 70,* 58–67.

Hale, J. L., & Dillard, J. P. (1995). Fear appeals in health promotion campaigns:

Too much, too little, or just right? In E. Maibach & R. L. Parrott (Eds.), *Designing health messages: Approaches from communication theory and public health practice* (pp. 65–80). Thousand Oaks, CA: Sage.

Iyengar, S. (1991). *Is anyone responsible? How television frames political issues.* Chicago: University of Chicago Press.

Jones, E. (1990). *Interpersonal perception.* New York: Freeman.

Kahneman, D., & Tversky, A. (1984). Choice, values, and frames. *American Psychologist, 39*, 341–350.

Kim, S., Scheufele, D. A., & Shanahan, J. (2002). Think about it this way: Attribute agenda-setting function of the press and the public's evaluation of a local issue. *Journalism & Mass Communication Quarterly, 79*, 7–25.

Kinder, D. R. (2007). Curmudgeonly advice. *Journal of Communication, 57*, 155–162.

Kinder, D. R., & Kiewiet, D. R. (1981). Sociotropic politics. *British Journal of Political Science, 11*, 129–161.

Krause, G. A. (1997). Voters, information heterogeneity, and the dynamics of aggregate economic expectations. *American Journal of Political Science, 41*, 1170–1200.

Krosnick, J. (1991). Response strategies for coping with the cognitive demands of attitude measures in surveys. *Applied Cognitive Psychology, 5*, 231–236.

Kuklinski, J. H., & Hurley, N. L. (1994). On hearing and interpreting political messages: A cautionary tale of citizen cue-taking. *Journal of Politics, 56*, 729–751.

Langston, W., & Kramer, D. C. (1998). The representation of space in mental models derived from text. *Memory & Cognition, 26*, 247–262.

Lazo, J. K., Kinnel, J., Bussa, T., Fisher, A., & Collamer, N. (1999). Expert and lay mental models of ecosystems: Inferences for risk communication. *Risk: Health, Safety, and the Environment, 10*, 45–64.

Marcus, G. E. (1988). The structure of emotional response: 1984 presidential candidates. *American Political Science Review, 82*, 735–761.

Marcus, G. E., Sullivan, J. L., Theiss-Morse, E., & Wood, S. L. (1995). *With malice toward some: How people make civil liberties judgments.* New York: Cambridge University Press.

McLeod, J. M., Zubric, J., Kwak, N., Powell, M., Zhang, W., & Deshpande, S. (2000). *Cognitive structure as a mediator of the influence of communication.* Paper presented to the Association for Education in Journalism and Mass Communication, Phoenix, AZ.

Meyer, D. E., & Schanneveldt, R. W. (1971). Facilitation in recognizing pairs of words: Evidence of a dependence between retrieval operations. *Journal of Experimental Psychology, 90*, 227–234.

Mutz, D. C. (1992). Mass media and the depoliticization of personal experience. *American Journal of Political Science, 36*, 483–508.

Mutz, D. C., & Mondak, J. J. (1997). Dimensions of sociotropic behavior: Group-based judgments of fairness and well-being. *American Journal of Political Science, 41*, 284–308.

Niemi, R. G., & Weisberg, H. J. (1993). *Controversies in voting behavior* (3rd ed.). Washington, DC: Congressional Quarterly.

Neuman, W. R. (1981). Differentiation and integration: Two dimensions of political thinking. *American Journal of Sociology, 86,* 1236–1267.

Novak, J. D., & Gowin, D. B. (1984). *Learning how to learn.* Cambridge, England: Cambridge University Press.

Price, V., & Tewksbury, D. (1996). News values and public opinion: A theoretical account of media priming and framing. In G. Barnett & F. Boster (Eds.), *Progress in communication sciences* (pp. 173–212). Norwood, NJ: Ablex.

Quattrone, G. A., & Tversky, A. (1988). Contrasting rational and psychological analyses of political choice. *American Political Science Review, 82,* 719–737.

Roberts, C. W. (1989). Other than counting words: A linguistic approach to content analysis. *Social Forces, 68,* 147–177.

Ross, L. (1977). The intuitive psychologist and his shortcomings: Distortions in the attribution process. In L. Berkowitz (Ed.), *Advances in experimental social psychology* (Vol. 10, pp. 177–221). New York: Academic Press.

Rye, J. A., & Rubba, P. A. (1998). An exploration of the concept map as an interview tool to facilitate the externalization of students' understandings about global atmospheric change. *Journal of Research in Science Teaching, 35,* 521–546.

Shah, D. V., Domke, D., & Wackman, D. B. (1996). "To thine own self be true": Values, framing and voter decision-making strategies. *Communication Research, 23,* 509–560.

Shah, D. V., Kwak, N., Schmierbach, M., & Zubric, J. (2004). The interplay of news frames on cognitive complexity. *Human Communication Research, 30,* 102–120.

Shah, D. V., McLeod, D. M., Gotlieb, M., Lee, N-J. (2009). Framing and agenda setting. In M. B. Oliver & R. L. Nabi (Eds.), *The Sage handbook of media processes and effects* (pp. 83–98). Thousand Oaks, CA: Sage.

Sniderman, P. M., Brody, R. A., & Tetlock, P. E. (1991). *Reasoning and choice: Explorations in political psychology.* New York: Cambridge University Press.

Tesser, A. (1978). Self-generated attitude change. In L. Berkowitz (Ed.), *Advances in experimental social psychology* (Vol. 11, pp. 290–338). New York: Academic Press.

Tourangeau, R., & Rasinski, K. (1988). Cognitive processes underlying context effects in attitude measurement. *Psychological Bulletin, 103,* 299–314.

Tversky, A., & Kahneman, D. (1981). The framing of decisions and the psychology of choice. *Science, 211,* 453–458.

Wallace, J. D., & Mintzes, J. (1990). The concept map as a research tool: Exploring conceptual change in biology. *Journal of Research in Science Teaching, 27,* 1033–1052.

Weaver, D. H. (2007). Thoughts on agenda setting, framing, and priming. *Journal of Communication, 57,* 142–147.

Zaller, J. (1992). *The nature and origins of mass opinion.* Cambridge, England: Cambridge University Press.

Zaller, J., & Feldman, S. (1992). A simple theory of the survey response: Answering questions versus revealing preferences. *American Journal of Political Science, 36,* 579–616.

# Chapter 10

# Framing the Pictures in Our Heads

## Exploring the Framing and Agenda-Setting Effects of Visual Images

*Renita Coleman*

Walter Lippmann coined the famous phrase "the pictures in our heads" in 1922 (Lippmann, 1922), yet the importance of images for social scientific study has remained undervalued even as late as 1990, when Doris Graber (1990) issued her call for more research on television visuals. As Graber noted, the study of visual information in news stories is stymied by a lack of appropriate theories and methodological hurdles. Today, framing theory has emerged as one of the life lines for visual research. As Messaris and Abraham (2001) spelled out in the bible of framing theory, *Framing Public Life* (Reese, Gandy, & Grant, 2001), "the special qualities of visuals...makes them very effective tools for framing" (p. 220). Even Erving Goffman, the sociologist who was the earliest to describe frame analysis theory, recognized the potential of photographs when he conducted his study of gender frames in advertising images (Goffman, 1979).

Until communication scholars began to embrace framing theory, many researchers of news visuals largely cast about in atheoretical waters, especially the lonely few using quantitative methods. Most scholarly visual work relied on semiotics or structuralism for intellectual ballast. But those theories could only be developed so far by studies of news visuals, and they were not as well suited for the counting and measuring of visual units of analysis required by quantitative methods. Now, numerous visual studies rely on framing theory as their intellectual guide. And, importantly, framing theory is as appropriate for quantitative research as for critical–cultural work, allowing us greater confidence in our conclusions by virtue of triangulation.

Of course, other theories can and do undergird visual studies, but framing theory has been one of the notable new favorites, with researchers gravitating toward it not only for its ability to explain and predict visual content and its effects, but also for the opportunity to build on this valuable theory in ways that word-based studies cannot. In sum, visual framing provides an important new direction for theory building and future research.

This chapter will examine some of the noteworthy visual studies that use framing theory as a foundation, noting, too, that framing theory is sometimes an unacknowledged perspective within studies of visuals in news texts. In addition, it will discuss a program of research undertaken by myself and colleagues that develops the visual side of a theory, agenda-setting, often linked to framing analysis (Coleman & Banning, 2006; Coleman & Wu, 2006a). In all, this chapter explores not only how visual images contribute to framing in the news, but also takes a look at the evolution of work on visual images within the realm of agenda setting, in particular, into what is known as second-level agenda setting research.

## The Importance of Visual Framing Research

Few scholars today argue that examining visuals is not worthwhile, as they did before Graber (1990) laid out her case. My own work, as does that of most scholars working in visuals today, draws heavily from the works of Doris Graber and is deeply indebted to her pioneering efforts in this area. Still, one can't help but wonder if the continuing paucity of visual studies is connected to latent beliefs within academia that words are more important than pictures, over and above the daunting obstacles engendered by coding visual images. Nowadays, even when the primarily visual medium of television is studied, frames tend to be examined in the verbal content only. This comes despite scholars' declarations that "all too often, the visual information is so powerful that it overwhelms the verbal" (Baran & Davis, 1995, p. 271), or that "the visual impact of (a candidate) on television and in newspaper photos may have left a very different impression" from the one conveyed in words (Domke et al., 1997, p. 733). Early on, Gitlin (1980) argued for visual as well as verbal framing, and scholars routinely include images (D'Angelo, 2002) or "visual items" (Esser & D'Angelo, 2003) in their definitions of framing devices. Yet visuals remain understudied compared with text in terms of their ability to frame media messages.

Scholars arguing the case for inclusion of images in framing studies generally acknowledge that pictures *are* different from words as a medium of communication. As Messaris and Abraham (2001) noted, visual images "constitute a largely analogical system of communication" (p. 216), adding that "the relationship between most words and their meanings is purely a matter of social convention, whereas the relationships between images and their meanings are based on similarity or analogy" (p. 216). In addition, Messaris and Abraham (2001) held that images, unlike words, are indexical—they are "treated as direct pointers, as opposed to constructed representations of reality" (p. 217). Finally, images, in contrast to verbal or written language, "lack an explicit propositional syntax" (Messaris & Abraham, p. 217). In other words, visual images do not allow a communicator to make explicit claims, such as causal statements or comparisons.

The special qualities of visual images underscore the point that, in some cases, visual framing may actually matter more than verbal framing. For example, everyone knows anecdotal evidence about the impact of images from September 11, or the chilling impression of mental illness conveyed in the video diary of the Virginia Tech shooter. More ordinary news events include the stereotypical visuals laced with racial and gender stereotypes that would never pass newsroom muster if communicated in words. In these cases, it is more than a saying that pictures show what words could never convey. Later in this chapter, visual framing studies that underscore these points will be reviewed.

Turning again to the goals of this chapter, I intend to illustrate the importance of conducting framing studies on visual as well as verbal content. Also, I intend to help framing scholars feel less lost in the visual forest by providing a methodological trail of breadcrumbs. It is important to understand how frames become embedded in news visuals and how that framing influences audiences' thinking. Visual and verbal messages occur together in media, and audiences process them simultaneously. It is artificial for research to view one channel of communication in isolation as this can result in an incomplete understanding of any media event. Because media audiences process visual and verbal information together, none of the studies of verbal-only content conducted to date can say definitively that any effects found were due solely to verbal information. It is possible that visual and verbal information worked together, given the overwhelming evidence of visual images' effects. This one-sided approach overlooks a great deal of complexity and subtlety about the way news is constructed and how humans process information.

That being said, it is important to acknowledge the daunting task of conducting essentially two studies in one—both of visual and verbal information—not to mention the difficulty of containing such a study within the usual 30-page limit of journal articles. The practical compromise entails splitting the two, with the hope that academic readers make the connection, or synthesizing them later in a monograph or book. Yet, when this happens, there is a bias toward publishing the verbal half of the study, with the visual half receiving skeptical responses from reviewers. I often receive comments on visual studies that say "the author should have examined the words." I have never yet received a comment on a word-based study that said "the author should have examined the visuals." The academy must get past its discomfort with the more unfamiliar visual studies and begin to see it as equally valid as verbal research. The fact remains that there needs to be more integrative work on framing visual and spoken or written texts, and a first step toward that goal is to accord visual-only research the same standing as verbal-only studies.

### Defining Visual Framing

I define "visual" to mean media content that is processed by the eye alone. For print and television journalism, that includes still photographs and moving images, drawings, and color. Facial expressions, as well as the body posture and gestures of journalists, sources, and subjects are added visual components of television news. In contrast, verbal content includes written and spoken words, that is, what the anchors, reporters, sources and subjects say, as well as written components, which include the crawl at the bottom of the television screen. The main source of visual components in news is, of course, the printed photograph or drawing, or video footage of the person, place, or event being covered by the journalist reporting the story.

Other visual elements in news stories include maps and graphics commonly displayed over the shoulder of an anchor—for example, red-white-and-blue flaglike graphics in election coverage. More complicated are the hybrid forms that encompass both words and pictures such as infographics made popular by *USA Today*. As I will discuss later in this chapter, readers use all their processing faculties to decode a graphic that contains both words and images. Therefore, separating the framing effects is difficult to do in empirical terms. To my knowledge, few scholars have focused on the framing of these hybrid forms.

One hybrid form that has received scholarly attention is the meaning conveyed by visual cues such as placement on a page, above or below the fold, or the size of a headline or picture (Ghanem, 1997; Stempel & Culbertson, 1984; Wanta, 1988). These elements, as well as story hierarchy in TV news and length of the story, typically are studied as aspects of framing. My own studies and those of other scholars routinely include these prominence and dominance features (Banning & Coleman, 2009; Grabe, 1996; Lacy & Fico, 1991; Moriarty & Popovich, 1991).

The topic of hybrid forms begs the question of whether visual framing can be conceptualized and studied independently of framing that occurs within the verbal and spoken parts of news stories. The answer, in my mind, is "yes and no." Written and spoken elements sometimes work together with visual elements to frame topics, and sometimes, visual elements frame stories independently of the verbal elements. Messaris and Abraham (2001) point out the synergy and symbiosis between these elements in the conclusion of short case study: "Thus the news media use visuals to subtly frame racial subtexts to their narratives on racial pathology" (p. 224). But other research has shown that visual frames are not always congruent with verbal frames, and when that is the case, visual framing predominates (Gibson & Zillmann, 2000; Grimes & Drechsel, 1996). This phenomenon will be discussed in greater detail later. Suffice it to say that it is never enough to study framing in one mode of communication and not the other.

Returning to the definition of visual framing, one weakness of any definition that dichotomizes visual and verbal is that it ignores sounds, such as music or birds chirping, and voice intonation and inflection, which interpersonal communication scholars study as a form of nonverbal communication that normally encompasses the visual medium. This type of auditory information may very likely carry frames of its own, but to my knowledge has not yet been studied in news messages. It would certainly be a fruitful frontier for news framing research to include the auditory channel, but at this point, I have limited my studies to this definition of visual information, as have most other scholars working in media visuals, in order to make the studies manageable.

Entman's (1993) famous phrase has become mandatory for inclusion in most framing studies of text, and that is no different for visual framing. Visual framing in the media also "selects some aspects of a perceived reality and makes them more salient in a communicating text, in such a way as to promote a particular problem definition, causal interpretation, moral evaluation, and/or treatment recommendation" (Entman, 1993, p. 52). In visual studies, *framing* refers to the selection of one view, scene, or angle when making the image, cropping, editing or selecting it. When a journalist chooses which photograph or piece of video to use, it is an act of framing. Schwalbe (2006) provides another excellent definition: "Visual framing is a continuous winnowing process. It begins with the choice of events to cover, followed by the selection of what pictures to take, how to take them (angle, perspective, assumptions and biases, cropping, and so forth), and which ones to submit" (p. 269). She adds that, "the process continues in the newsroom with decisions about which images to publish, what size to make them, and where to position them on the page" (p. 269).

### News Visuals and Ideology

One of the first studies of visual framing, although the authors did not refer to it as such, was an examination of how television editing can shape perceptions of an event (see Messaris & Abraham, 2001, p. 218, for a related discussion). In Lang and Lang's (1952) seminal piece, coding of crowd reaction at parades and of the broadcast images of the parades showed that journalists chose video of enthusiastic crowds over the more common subdued parade watchers. Those who only saw the mediated versions of the parades got the impression that people supported the cause of the event more strongly than those who were at the actual event. *That* is visual framing.

The Lang and Lang study introduced the notion that news conventions dictate decisions about visual framing made by individual journalists and editors. For example, showing an action photo is considered better news judgment than showing a passive photo. Consider the case of protest coverage, a frequent topic of visual framing studies (e.g., Arpan et al., 2006; Detenber, Gotlieb, McLeod, & Malinkina, 2007; Gitlin, 1980; McLeod & Detenber, 1999). A photo of protesters being arrested would more likely be chosen over those protesting peacefully: even though most of the protest was peaceful, a few minutes of *conflict* would likely result in journalists' choosing dramatic arrest photographs for a news story. Even granted that journalists intended to dispassionately cover the protest—that is, they had no vested interest in its outcome— framing decisions arising from largely unstated news conventions render the event potent with meanings that stoke viewers' passions and shape their attitudes (cf. McLeod & Detenber, 1999). Thus, once we emphasize that news conventions guide decisions about framing, we rather quickly encounter the point that visual framing is a prime site of ideological constructions expressed within news stories. As Messaris and Abraham noted, "The special qualities of visuals—their iconicity, their indexicality, and especially their syntactic explicitness—makes them very effective tools for framing and articulating ideological messages" (p. 220). In this vein, Huxford argued that journalists have created codes and conventions for photographs to create "visual illusions that can frame and mislead" (Huxford, 2001, p. 45).

Later in this chapter, I take up this theme again, focusing on news conventions, visual framing, and social stereotypes. But for now, suffice it to say that just as viewers may be unaware of the framing process when it occurs visually, so, too, may journalists. Becoming aware of this can encourage journalists to scrutinize their decisions about images as much or more than their choice of words.

## Supporting Theories of Visual Framing

The notion that journalists may not always be aware of the meaning of their visual choices is supported by evidence from various theories in social psychology, especially the dual processing theories such as the Elaboration Likelihood Model and schema theory. Whereas these theories typically pertain to how (news) information is processed, they can also be used to gain insight into the production of frames by journalists—to frame building, in Scheufele's (1999) terminology. In my own 15-year career as a newspaper journalist, I found that one of the most common reasons for selecting one photograph over others was that it was "powerful" or conveyed emotion. Another reason was that the photograph told the story in a way that words could not. These and other reasons that journalists might use to select an image that helps frame a story find theoretical explanations in cognitive processing theories, and empirical evidence shows the effect these choices can have, intended or not.

### Elaboration Likelihood Model

One of the most useful theories for understanding how people process visual images is the elaboration likelihood model (ELM; Petty & Cacioppo, 1986). The term *elaboration* refers to the inner dialogue that occurs when people think about the claims made in an argument, either one in which they are directly involved or one that they are witnessing (Iguarta, Cheng, & Lopes, 2003). According to the ELM, people process messages in two ways: a high-effort "central route" that requires conscious and rational thinking, or the low-effort, or "peripheral" route, which is an automatic and instinctive type of processing that focuses on superfluous message cues, such as the appearance or perceived credibility of an interactant, rather than the logic, relevance, or information quality of a claim. Critical to this theory is the idea that any type of claim may be processed either centrally or peripherally (Petty & Cacioppo, 1986).

Generally, but not in all cases, it is expected that people will think about the information contained in a textual message that they are paying attention to, but not about the information contained in visual messages. Even though a visual message does not possess a propositional syntax (Messaris & Abraham, 2001), it may nonetheless be subject to elaboration. To "think about" a visual within a news story—a still photograph in a print story, for example—requires an effort to sort out its relevance to the story itself. Such thoughts, it would seem, routinely occur, as when a reader lingers over the photograph(s) (or graphs, charts, or other visual matter) that accompany a story she or he is reading. But ELM also suggests that this same photograph—or any visual message in a news story, for that matter—engenders peripheral thinking by virtue of activating emotional responses to the story. All of us can recall photographs in print news stories that have affected us emotionally. A recent example (as of this writing) is the photograph by Steven Day (Associated Press) of passengers standing on the wings of the Airbus A320 that landed in the Hudson River on January 15, 2009. ELM suggests that photographs, particularly highly evocative ones such as the AP photo just mentioned, will become part of a reader's memory of this story, leaving an emotional trace that in time will supplant most of the written or spoken details (who, what, when, where) of the story. "Processing" this story, then, involves an emotional lamination that occurs mainly through visual cues that are processed peripherally. Such visual cues engender emotions—happy, sad, perplexed, and so on—which are not integral to processing factual material and argumentative claims within the story but are nonetheless integral to what the reader knows, or can recall, about the story.

Moving over to frame building, ELM suggests that journalists who *take* visuals, as well as those who edit moving visuals into video packages (re: broadcast news) or those who decide which still shots will accompany a print story, make decisions to create and use visual material owing at least as much to peripheral processing of the visual's relationship to the story as to rational decision making (or "central" processing). Thus, important framing decisions are made on the basis of a mixture of the news value of the visual material (a central route), the emotions activated within the journalist(s), and the emotions the journalist(s) hope to activate within audience members. Placing ELM at the heart of the frame-building, therefore, suggests that studying framing effects, such as thoughts and opinions about the topic of the story, cannot be fully understood without examining the role of both verbal/written *and* visual components of the story.

### Schema Theory

Schemas work in tandem with peripheral information processing. A schema is defined as a knowledge structure that organizes people's memories (Fiske & Taylor, 1984). Schema theory basically says that people filter new information though their preexisting knowledge and beliefs (Azjen & Fishbein, 1975; Brewer & Nakamura, 1984; Petty & Cacioppo, 1981). While people routinely incorporate new information within their previously formed schemas, these knowledge structures are the default mode of information processing when a person uses low-effort processing (Harris, 1994).

It stands to reason that journalists have schemas, too. Journalists might rely on their schemas for selecting photographs of people accused of crimes, for example, by choosing images that show jail jumpsuits and handcuffs. Photographs of the accused in a suit and tie might be passed over because they don't instantly convey the stereotypical idea of a criminal. How people's schemas can be activated by the messages they receive is the subject of frame analysis. Framing essentially involves selection and salience. The frames that the media use help define problems and call attention to some things while obscuring others (Entman, 1993). What is left out also contributes to the power of frames. At the most general level, framing refers to subtle alterations in statement or presentation, such as the presentation provided by a visual image. Visual framing also expresses Entman's four functions: defining problems, assigning blame, declaring right or wrong, and fixing them (Entman, 1993). In the example above of accused criminals in jumpsuits, the visuals reinforce the problem as one of crime by individuals who are morally corrupt and should be punished. It leaves out the possibility that people may not have wanted to break the law but felt they had no choice because of social conditions such as poverty, and that aid, job training, or other programs could be used to fix the problem.

## Building Framing Theory with Visuals

Visual scholars have ample opportunity to build theory by considering framing theory's largely word-based theoretical foundations and ask how visual framing is similar or different. In addition to the inherent connections between Entman's framing functions and visual framing that I have already discussed, we need to ask if visuals can be observed within the parameters of other known frames, such as those identified by Iyengar (1991) and Semetko and Valkenburg (2000). That is, do *news values* such as "conflict" or "consequences," which are identified in the literature as "generic" frames (cf. de Vreese, 2005), find expression within visual frames, thereby lending themselves to an analysis of visual framing as easily as they do to more typical analyses of verbal or written news text (cf. Price, Tewksbury, & Powers, 1997)? Indeed, notions of conflict and human interest can be inferred from the content of photographs, but what does a morality *frame* look like in pictures—doctors tending to patients and aid workers distributing food and water? How about economic consequences—foreclosure signs and welfare lines? These questions have only been rarely explored (see Arpan et al., 2006). Therefore, much more work needs to be done to determine if the generic frames suitable for textual analysis are also suitable for visual analysis.

If visuals express unique frames, what might they be? In addition to asking whether visuals can be observed within frames typically relegated to framing of verbal or written text, visual framing scholars need to ask how technical aspects of visual production work to create frames independently. For example, does power, as operationalized in camera angles (looking up at someone = power, looking down on someone = weakness) operate as a visual frame? How about the paraproxemic variables (close-ups versus long-shots) that convey social distance and thus empathy and relationship? What about nonverbal expressions of emotion, posture, and gesturing? These questions and others have been included in visual framing studies, but have not been adequately theorized (Coleman & Banning, 2006). My own studies with my colleagues have proceeded as if these variables do serve as visual frames, but, in the beginning, even we shortchanged in-depth theoretical explanations for why they operate as such.

Additionally, scholars should ask what role culture plays in visual framing. For example, there is much research on visual framing of war

(Griffin, 2004; Schwalbe, Silcock, & Keith, 2008) that has resulted in the identification of a "master war narrative," including a visual one, but other types of events lack a cumulative body of knowledge.

While theory building regarding visual framing is sorely needed, there are some studies that do just that. One example is demonstrated in a study that synthesized framing and gate keeping theories and found that the dominant frames in wire service offerings of photographs were not the ones ultimately chosen by photo editors (Fahmy, Kelly, & Kim, 2007). This study considered visual framing in broader perspective, offered generalizable contributions, and synthesized visual framing with another theory. Still, too often visual framing research neglects theory building. In addition to complementing textual studies, visual framing studies can add unique theoretical statements to framing analysis.

## Effects of News Visuals

Much evidence exists about the power of news visuals on viewers. In one of the earliest studies, Graber (1990) showed that viewers' remembered TV news stories better when they contained visuals. Moreover, unusual images and close-ups of people were even better at helping people remember and learn the verbal information. For instance, Hurricane Katrina proved to be a visual learning experience about New Orleans because the images of the abject poverty in the Ninth Ward were unusual compared to the normal visual fare of Bourbon Street and upscale tourist areas. Not only do visuals enhance learning, but the combination of visual and verbal messages can merge together and change audiences' perceptions of issues. If the visual message is different from the verbal message, people's impressions tend to go with the information conveyed by the visual rather than the one conveyed by text. For example, Grimes and Dreschel (1996) found this interaction between video and text, with viewers misremembering information along the lines conveyed by the images.

Earlier and in separate studies, Grimes (1990) and Pezdek (1977) found that information presented in pictures and in words tended to fuse over time in people's minds, with words being remembered as pictures and vice versa. These studies show that text and word information that merges can result in distorted perceptions of issues. When that happens, if the words and pictures are not congruent, people remember the information or perceive the viewpoint of the picture over the words. This is known as the *picture superiority effect* (Gibson & Zillmann, 2000), and is vividly illustrated by Leslie Stahl's story about her coverage of Ronald Reagan. Her voice-overs were critical of his use of manipulated images in "photo ops," but the images themselves were positive. Even after the manipulation was pointed out, viewers made positive associations about Reagan from the story; they did not really hear her words but reacted to the images (see Lichter & Noyes, 1995, pp. 36–37; Paletz & Guthrie, 1987). Researchers think that the unique, vivid features of pictures make them more readily available in memory; thus, images exert a more powerful influence on memory and perceptions than text. Gibson and Zillmann (2000) investigated the influence of pictures alone and found that even when the information in pictures was not also mentioned in text, audiences' perceptions were in line with the pictures. The authors stated, "The use of images amounts to additional storytelling that journalists may not be aware of" (Gibson & Zillmann, 2000, p. 365).

Another line of research is concerned with the emotions elicited by images and their effects on viewers. It is well known that negative messages are more powerful than positive ones in a number of ways; negative visual images also have been shown to have greater effects (Newhagen & Reeves, 1990). For example, Arpan et al. (2006) found that negative photographs of social protests caused viewers to feel more negatively about the cause. Other work found that people read more of the story and remembered it better when it was accompanied by a negative photo showing victimization (Zillmann, Knobloch, & Yu, 2001). Negative images had an agenda-setting effect on people's affective impressions of candidates but positive images did not (Coleman & Wu, 2006a).

This evidence of the power of images, combined with viewers' lack of awareness of that power, makes the framing of images even more important to understand. It is especially important to make visual journalists—which includes just about everyone in this age of convergence and multimedia—aware of the possible unintended consequences of their choices. New journalism graduates are increasingly expected to shoot pictures and video as well as write stories. Failure to understand the nuances and power of images is not an option. Choosing something based on journalistic values or because the image grabs attention, or even simply because the page needs a photo, can have consequences beyond what the journalist envisioned.

Research on visual framing is more far-reaching that might be expected—it even has been done with political cartoons (Greenberg, 2002). Some evidence shows visual framing is more balanced than verbal framing. In one study of an environmental topic, researchers found that visual frames showed both the sides of the issue of whether to cut or save old-growth forests (Liebler & Bendix, 1996). Examinations that include both visual and verbal framing of the same content in a single study are rare; however, such work is the best way to understand the holistic message that viewers receive. One such study was an analysis of press coverage of itself (Esser & D'Angelo, 2003) that found the largest percentage (24%) of frames about the press were visuals of journalists at a campaign site, meant to show viewers the media's presence at staged events. A controlled experiment, which is rare in visual framing research—manipulated the valence of visual framing and found that negative photographs of social protests caused viewers to feel more negatively about the cause (Arpan et al., 2006). Because the verbal framing remained the same in all the stories, this study concluded that visuals *alone* can affect how people process news and their perception of issues. This is one of the few studies that isolated the impact of visual frames (but see Kamhawi & Grabe, 2008). It is noteworthy also because it used one of the standard news frames (cf. Semetko & Valkenburg, 2000), conflict, to study visual framing effects. The result was that when more conflict was shown in photos, viewers' evaluations of the protest and protesters were more negative, too. This vividly illustrates that the news value of showing action, such as protesters screaming and waving signs vs. people signing petitions around a table, is an act of framing that has consequences far beyond the intention of news values and journalistic conventions.

When news topics are not part of a reader's or viewer's personal experience—for example, international news (Groshek, 2008)—the frames of the stories are a source of information and orientation about the topic. The literature points out that people learn about foreign people, places, and events primarily through visual media (Perlmutter, 1998). One of the most frequent topics of visual framing research is war (Aday, 2005; Dimitrova & Stromback, 2005; Griffin, 2004; Hatley Major & Perlmutter, 2005; Schwalbe, 2006). One study (Schwalbe, Silcock, & Keith, 2008) traced the rapid evolution of visual frames from conflict to human interest in televised images of the Iraqi war. It also identified microframes of war visuals and discovered frames which the authors labeled "shock and awe," "conquering troops," "hero," "victory," and "control." Aday and colleagues (2005) found that this victory frame crowded out other frames, including coverage of battles. This does much more to advance framing theory from a visual perspective than studies that merely document visual content. These microframes are congruent with the "master war narrative" identified in text, indicating that visual framing echoed verbal framing in this case.

Another frequent topic of visual framing research is the portrayal of race and gender stereotyping. Because of the likelihood that visuals will be processed without much conscious thought, and because the information in them is processed through people's preexisting schemas, visual framing makes stereotyping less obvious than verbal framing (Messaris & Abraham, 2001). Because the brain initially processes visual images in an automatic, unconscious way, viewers are less likely to notice implicit meaning. One of the effects of framing is that it is taken for granted or not questioned. That gives visual frames the ability to convey meaning that would be protested as inappropriate if it were conveyed in words

(Messaris & Abraham, 2001). As a consequence, "racial appeals now often take place through visual imagery, without any explicit or overt reference to race" (Messaris & Abraham, 2001, p. 221). This also goes for gender stereotyping, leading to another prolific line of research, especially in political communication. Research shows that women politicians receive significantly more coverage of their sex, marital status, and children than their male colleagues (Bystrom, Robertson, & Banwart, 2001; Witt, Paget, & Matthews, 1994), and more attention is given to their personal lives, personalities, and appearances (Devitt, 1999).

These two lines of research provide especially convincing evidence that framing research should include visual as well as verbal content. News stories may well contain no verbal references to stereotypes about women or minorities, yet the visuals could be rife with images of African Americans and violent crime, drugs, and poverty, or women as mothers, homemakers, and sex objects. If the visual and verbal information is indeed incongruent with visual messages perpetuating stereotypes not in the verbal text, then that is discouraging news given the tendency for viewers to believe and remember the visual message over the verbal message(s).

## Methodological Questions

One of the most frequent questions I hear from scholars contemplating a study of visuals is concerned with how to identify and measure the aspects, or variables, in still pictures and in moving (e.g., videotaped) images. I began studying visuals as a master's student, unfamiliar with academic research, and was basically, too naïve to know better. Nobody had yet told me I couldn't do that, or that it would be too hard. Ignorance worked to my advantage. Unable to find much guidance in the journalism literature, I turned to sociology, interpersonal communication, political communication, and social psychology. Scholars in these fields had indeed figured out ways to measure images, and also people's expressions, which made up a lot of media images. I used my 17 years of experience as a working journalist to adapt these measures to news visuals. As I tell my students taking their first visual communication course, the grading of visual work is no more subjective than the grading of written stories; it only seems that way if you are unfamiliar with the criteria. The same goes for *coding* of visual messages compared with coding verbal ones. Some helpful guidebooks have come out over the past few years. I particularly like Philip Bell's chapter on content analysis of visual images in the *Handbook of Visual Analysis* (Bell, 2001). I also rely on *The Sourcebook of Nonverbal Measures: Going Beyond Words* (Manusov, 2005), and the *Handbook of Visual Communication* (Smith,

Moriarty, Barbatsis, & Kenney, 2005). Many chapters in those texts should inspire confidence and initiate ideas.

## Multiple Methods

The qualitative and quantitative counterparts of textual analysis and content analysis still are the most predominant methods used to study visual frames. This does not, however, preclude other methods from getting at the important questions of framing. Experiments are a valuable yet underused tool for studying the effects of visual framing. By manipulating specific frame elements in a photograph, which is easily done with PhotoShop, scholars can make statements of cause and effect that are unreachable with content analysis. When considering methodology, we again find inspiration in Graber's work (1990). One of her main points in this article is that previous studies showing that audiences didn't learn from visuals did not measure information gain or images appropriately. She pointed out that scholars adapted measures used in verbal studies to visual ones and fell into the trap of measuring visuals by what they contribute to the words rather than by what they contribute independently.

## Units of Analysis

The most obvious and easiest visual unit for coding is the still photograph in a newspaper or magazine. Doing only that, however, ignores the fact that most people get their news from television and that a growing contingent of young people get their news online. Television presents a more daunting number of visuals—30 video frames per second (Schwalbe et al., 2008)—and Web visuals present a completely different challenge with pages updated as often as necessary and frequently on no particular schedule. The unit of analysis for visuals is typically the photograph, map, or graphic. For the Internet, it has been those same items on the home page or a few main section pages (Schwalbe et al., 2008). Moving images such as television or video on the Web also have primary units of analysis: the scene and the shot. The defining feature of a scene, which can consist of a single shot or more than one shot, is that the theme, concept, or idea is the same (Choi & Lee, 2006). A new scene occurs when a different subject is presented. Motion can occur within a scene such as a pan, zoom, or angle change, without changing the scene (Graber, 1990). A shot is the smallest unit of a visual message, defined as a fragment of visual material that has no break in continuity of action; that is, video that does not contain editing cuts (Gianetti, 1982). In a shot, the camera's position may change due to zoom or pans, but not cuts. This is different from a scene in that a scene may contain cuts as long as the subject of the visual remains the same; a new shot occurs when there is a cut, even if the subject stays the same.

### Coding Categories

Different units of analysis are called for depending on the subject of study. In my own work on facial expressions, for example, the smaller unit of a shot is appropriate because different meanings are conveyed by different facial muscle movements, many of which could occur in the longer unit of a scene (Coleman & Banning, 2006; Miller, Coleman, & Granberg, 2007). The total number of shots might seem daunting, but the advantages include no dearth of content and, random sampling or constructed weeks can be used to make it manageable. For instance, in a quasi-experiment I did with colleagues, 50 to 60 shots were used per election year for 3 years (Miller, Coleman, & Granberg, 2007). In another study of 23 randomly sampled days, my colleague and I ended up with 1,315 shots (Coleman & Banning, 2006). Both studies had acceptable reliabilities. Coders (the usual suspects from undergraduate and graduate school) had experience with verbal coding projects and found the training and extra time it took to code visuals to be only moderately more difficult than with text. As with textual coding, it is important to train coders well and to determine objective measures; the measurement scale also matters. For example, in two studies (Coleman & Banning, 2006; Coleman & Wu, 2006b), my colleagues and I measured facial expressions by coding muscle movement—if eyebrows were raised, lowered or in neutral position, for example—not coders' subjective interpretation of emotions. We later recoded the facial expressions into positive, negative, or neutral according to findings from previous studies designed to determine that.

After reading deeper in the relational communication literature, another colleague and I discovered how to measure nonverbal communication on a 1 to 7 point scale (Coleman & Wu, 2006a) instead of the 3 points of positive, negative, and neutral. For this, it was necessary to make finer distinctions. Much to our surprise, intercoder reliability was still high, as it had been in interpersonal studies (Burgoon, Birk, & Pfau, 1990). However, we also found that some of the indexes applicable to interpersonal communication didn't work so well for studies of broadcast journalists. For instance, news journalists doing "stand-ups" tend to, well, stand up rather than sit down, which would also have allowed for measurement of leaning. We eliminated that variable and also the one of gesturing because broadcasters tend to stand still and hold a microphone and notepad rather than waving their arms about.

## Structural Features

Another important aspect of visual framing includes the structural features of visuals such as camera angles and distance (Grabe, 1996; Moriarty & Popovich, 1991). A number of studies have found that manipulations in these characteristics can produce changes in viewers' evaluations, and the perceptions they create are not neutral (see Waldman & Devitt, 1998, for a summary). Berger (1981) offers definitions and explanations of the connotations of each. For example, of the three basic camera angles, eye level or straight on is considered neutral, shot from above is negative, and from below is positive. Camera distance includes close-up or the head and shoulders (positive), a long shot with the full figure (negative), and a medium shot from the waist up (neutral). These structural features and the impressions they convey are not conventions that viewers must learn, but are derived from studies of paraproxemics, or social distance. Standing closer to someone, as re-created in close-up shots, usually means that person is more liked than someone kept at arm's length. Likewise, an image of a person "looking you straight in the eye" conveys honesty, whereas someone looking away would be considered suspect. Shooting up at someone or down on them conveys the sense of power we learned as children—those we look down on are less powerful than those we look up to. Camera movement includes action shots where people are shown in motion, which is generally considered more positive than nonaction shots. Structural features are frequently indexed by summing all the positive positions into one, the negative positions into another, and the neutral positions into a third variable. In one study, my colleague Denis Wu (Coleman & Wu, 2006b), discovered the Janis Fadner coefficient of imbalance, which we used to form one variable that measured valence while eliminating the problem of positive and negative values canceling each other out (Janis & Fadner, 1965).

These coding categories represent latent meaning and are offered in addition to the manifest content such as whether the images show happy crowds or angry protesters, women in burquas, or ethnic and racial minorities in jail jumpsuits and handcuffs. These microframes arise out of the subjects being studied and the images themselves. It is also important to continue to study the framing of photographs and their design elements such as color, typography, juxtaposition, size, and spatial arrangements for the latent meaning they convey. As Huxford (2001) pointed out in an example of a story that verbally portrays a rape victim as having "moved on" and being in a position of power, the photograph of a woman looking vacantly out to sea, washed in blue, and cropped into a passive, round shape, shows a continuing victim instead.

### Emotional Frames and Nonverbal Behavior

My own work in visual framing includes close-ups of people and their facial expressions and nonverbal behavior. These images are not something typically included as a type of visual "frame." However, I include this feature of images of people within the rubric of framing for reasons grounded in theory and past evidence. Early on, Graber (1990) found that close-ups of people are by far the most frequent type of visual on TV. Not to include these images would ignore a vast amount of what Americans see on their most popular news source. This makes sense from a learning perspective also; visuals of places and objects that illustrate stories about social and political problems tend to be highly routine, stereotypical, and familiar (Graber, 1990). For example, pictures of factories belching smoke to illustrate a story about pollution or images of tractors plowing fields to illustrate farm failures give viewers little new information. They become important information sources only when they are novel; that is, when people have not previously seen them and have not established a mental image. Not surprisingly, these were the kinds of images that researchers coded in studies that found visuals didn't matter. Far more valuable than these images of places and things are pictures of people; the most frequently recalled types of visuals involved close-ups of people. Even when the people were highly familiar, such as the president, the images were still memorable (Graber, 1990). The emphasis on people, both public and private figures, initially serves to draw in the viewer emotionally but then goes on to provide rich sources of information of all types. In addition to the people who are the subject and sources of the news image, the frequent occurrence of close-ups of reporters and anchors helps enhance the trust and credibility of the news outlet. Thus, visual studies should include journalists' as well as sources and news subjects.

What accounts for this greater learning from close-up images of people? Other research indicates that about 40% of the information we get about others comes from nonverbal sources such as body movements rather than words (Lamb & Watson, 1979). Merely counting and categorizing people by roles misses the major messages that this type of visual conveys, namely, that facial expressions provide information about people's affective states (Burgoon, Birk, & Pfau, 1990), which leads viewers to infer character traits about people. Nonverbal behaviors are important in viewers' formation of impressions; positive expressions have been linked to judgments of higher credibility (Burgoon, Birk, & Pfau, 1990) and have been shown to convey that the sender is trustworthy, or reliable, having integrity and good character, whereas negative expressions convey the opposite (Boone & Buck, 2003). Much subtle and implicit information is conveyed through nonverbal channels in a few seconds or even a fraction of a second (Rosenthal, Hall, DiMatteo, Rogers, & Archer, 1979), and people are quite accurate in decoding these brief instances of nonverbal communication (Burns & Beier, 1973; Izard, 1977). For example, President Bush's nonverbal communication in his first TV address on September 11, 2001, affected the emotions and feelings of self-control of viewers in one experiment (Bucy, 2003). Of all the nonverbal cues, facial expressions carry the most information (Mehrabian, 1968). They are rich sources of direct and inferred information because they readily reveal mental states (Ekman, 1983). It is well established that specific nonverbal behaviors accompany certain feelings and that nonverbal cues are especially adept at communicating information about emotion and mood (Ekman, 1983). In studies that included nonverbal behaviors outside the face, a person's credibility increased as they were shown closer to the people observing, when they had a more relaxed body orientation, made more eye contact, nodded more, smiled, and gestured moderately (Coker & Burgoon, 1987; Helmsley & Doob, 1978). In fact, positive nonverbal behaviors fostered favorable credibility assessments on all but one dimension studied (Burgoon, Birk, & Pfau, 1990). Another study showed similar results for different traits; positive expressions convey higher dominance and affiliation, negative expressions lower dominance and affiliation, and these were independent of facial attractiveness (Montepare & Dobish, 2003).

Most importantly for work with political candidates, bias studies have found that emotional expressions by political leaders had a direct emotional effect on television viewers (Lanzetta, Sullivan, Masters, & McHugo, 1985; McHugo, Lanzetta, Sullivan, Masters, & Englis, 1985). Even a single photograph conveyed a distinct image of a candidate's competence, integrity, and fitness for office, and altering that image produced significant differences in people's assessments of the candidate, even when political party and issue position were unchanged (Rosenberg, Bohan, McCafferty, & Harris, 1986; Rosenberg & McCafferty, 1987). Other studies made the same link between candidates' appearance and voters' perceptions (Abelson, Kinder, Peters, & Fiske, 1982). A number of studies have found that manipulations of various photo characteristics, including facial expressions, can produce changes in evaluations of candidates (see Waldman & Devitt, 1998, for a summary). Although not the traditional definition of framing, these effects of nonverbal behaviors on voters' perceptions of politicians surely qualify as framing consequences. By choosing certain images—politicians smiling, waving, or looking tired—rather than other images, journalists, whether intending to or not, impart powerful framing effects to viewers. Therefore, it seems prudent to include facial expressions and nonverbal behaviors under the visual framing rubric.

## Visual Framing and Second-Level Agenda Setting

All this evidence of the power of news media visuals and their framing abilities has led to another line of thought—how visual framing connects to agenda-setting, specifically the second-level agenda, which, among other things, examines the effects of exposure to frames on affective impressions such as emotions, or to an individual's assessment of personality and character traits. First, let's be clear about the definitions of a "frame" from framing theory and an "attribute" from second-level agenda-setting theory: all frames have attributes, but not all attributes are frames. More specifically, a frame is a "more encompassing concept" (Aday, 2006, p. 768) than an attribute. A frame is the overarching master narrative, under which there can be several attributes. Although frames and attributes are somewhat different, frames can be viewed as connected with agenda setting, which is quintessentially described as the idea that the media do not tell people what to think, but what to think about (Cohen, 1963). Second-level agenda setting deals with how the media transfer the attributes of issues and people in the news to the public, focusing on how the issue is defined (Yioutas & Segvic, 2003). Although definitional lines are not always clearly drawn between these two concepts, it is fruitful to look at second-level agenda-setting as one of the potential effects of framing, which will be discussed later.

The first study to examine visuals for their agenda-setting effects did so from a first-level analysis. Wanta (1988) found that the size of a photograph had the ability to influence people's assessment of an issue's importance, with larger photographs leading to perceptions of more importance. Size, as well as placement of images, is certainly a framing issue, well within the power of journalists to control. But it is the second level of agenda setting that is more fruitful from a framing perspective. On that count, the concept of affective framing in agenda setting also was intriguing from a visual perspective because it was described by various agenda-setting authorities as including production issues such as presentation, size and placement, editing—all structural features of video and photographs. Beyond structural features, the affective level of agenda-setting also deals with emotion and tone, which greatly opens up the possibilities for visual framing. As shown previously, visual images, and especially the most prevalent kind in news visuals—those of people—are uniquely qualified to convey emotion and tone. While other scholars had studied photographs and video from a framing perspective, it appeared there were many questions still to be answered about visuals and their potential agenda-setting effect at the second-level. It seemed a rather large gap and an excellent way to expand the theory of agenda-setting to include an understanding of visual images' role.

More fodder was added as I worked with a colleague on a visual bias study of the 2000 election. While reading the literature for ways to measure visual bias, I was struck by similarities to the concepts of affective attributes in second-level agenda-setting. In many of these studies, bias is defined as a systematic slant (Waldman & Devitt, 1998), differential amounts of negative, positive, and neutral content (Moriarty & Popovich, 1991), the relative amount of positive and negative quotes or comments (Lowry & Shidler, 1995; Robinson & Sheehan, 1983), or the positivity and negativity of facial expressions (Friedman, Mertz & DiMatteo, 1980; Mullen, et al., 1986). The way bias is operationally defined bears remarkable similarity to the operational definition of affective attributes as positive vs. negative information in second-level agenda-setting research using verbal or written content (Wanta, Golan, & Lee, 2003). Bias studies frequently code for valence, that is, the number of stories or visuals with a positive, negative, or neutral tone toward each candidate or party (Waldman & Devitt, 1998). This use of valence to operationally define bias is comparable to the way the affective dimension is measured in agenda-setting research, where the distinction is between neutral and valenced content; that is, positive and negative tone content combined (Kiousis et al., 1999).

Of course, none of the agenda-setting work discussed affective attributes in terms of visual images, but previous work I had done on affect and emotion conveyed by visual images led me to think about how that might relate to agenda setting. Affective framing also was described as including affect or emotional tone, and agenda-setting authors said the second-level agenda-setting effect sought to capture the impact of attributes such as candidate appearance and personal style (McCombs, Shaw, & Weaver, 1997). The intersection of these areas converged to become this question: if written and spoken words in the media describing attributes of people and issues could set the public's agenda, could visual images do the same? There was a mountain of evidence that visual images could affect people in other important ways—memory, attitude, learning, voting, etc.—but no link had yet been made between the media's and the public's affective impressions.

The first visual agenda-setting study by my colleague and me (Coleman & Banning, 2006) set out to expand the theory of second-level agenda setting to include affective framing of the candidates as conveyed through visual information. A basic assumption of agenda setting is that the media have an "agenda" to convey; that is, that news images convey gestures, facial expressions, and other visual information about the candidates that is positive and flattering, or negative and unflattering, and there are differences between the images of the two candidates. Therefore, the first task was to determine if an affective agenda existed in visual images in the media. Using the 2000 presidential election, we sought to discover what affective attributes the television news media conveyed to audiences through the visuals, and if an "agenda" existed in terms of portraying the candidates differently. That is, does visual and nonverbal information in the media convey an affective attribute agenda just as verbal information does? If this necessary condition existed, then there was the possibility that a second-level agenda-setting effect could have occurred through visual framing.

In that first study, there was a significant difference between the media's visual framing of the two candidates: there were more positive visual images of Al Gore than of George Bush. In addition, there were more negative visual images of Bush than Gore. As explained above, we analyzed the content using nonverbal behaviors such as facial expressions, gesturing, and body language to determine the valence of visual images.

The second necessary condition to establish second-level agenda setting was to determine the public's affective impressions of the candidates. Using survey data from the National Election Studies (NES), we also found significant differences between the candidates on their affective attributes by indexing a host of questions about character traits of the candidates and emotional reactions that people had to each candidate. Interestingly, the public's impressions of the candidates mirrored the media's visual portrayals: people felt more positive about Gore and ascribed more positive character traits to him than to Bush, and also felt more negative emotions about Bush and rated him higher on the negative character traits than they did Gore. In both the content analysis and the survey questions, negative and positive dimensions were measured separately as much research has shown they are separate dimensions, not opposite ends of a single continuum.

The final task was to connect the media's visual portrayals of the candidates' affective attributes to the public's affective impressions of them. In verbal agenda-setting studies, a list of five to nine attributes would be rank ordered for their prevalence in the media and also for their prominence in public opinion. Here we faced a unique methodological issue: in order to have an apples-to-apples comparison, we collapsed all our measures of nonverbal behavior in the content. In addition, we constructed feelings about the candidates and their character traits in public opinion into two measures of valence (positive and negative). Rank ordering two categories—positive attributes and negative attributes—would be absurd, not to mention that it would introduce glaring confounds. We needed to find another way to compare the media agenda with the public agenda. We had chosen to collapse our content and public opinion measures this way for good reason. While verbal content analyses in second-level agenda-setting studies frequently identified specific aspects of affective framing such as intellectual ability, moral quality, or leadership and counted the references to each in text, it was difficult to differentiate between such specific characteristics in pictures or video.

For example, does looking directly at someone indicate honesty or leadership? What does "moral" or "intelligent" gesturing look like? No studies have linked specific personality traits, such as intelligence and honesty, to objective operational definitions of nonverbal behaviors such as waving hands or furrowed brows. However, research has shown that *valence* is an essential, defining feature of affect (Dillard & Wilson, 1993), and a person who exhibits positive nonverbal behavior leads perceivers to infer positive personality traits about that person. Because it would be impossible to achieve intercoder reliability by trying to link specific behaviors such as a bowed head or raised arms with character traits such as morality and leadership, we collapsed the affect and trait variables from the public opinion survey into categories representing valence. This gave us a more direct comparison with our positive and negative categories of nonverbal behavior, and is congruent with bivariate models of positive and negative affect as separate but interacting systems (Dillard & Meijnders, 2002). This approach is compatible with every theory of affect, which accords valence a central role and shows that it accounts for twice as much variance as any specific emotion, and also corresponds to the second-level agenda-setting studies that identify positive and negative valence. To construct a variable that measured each survey respondent's exposure to the negative and positive visual portrayals of Bush and Gore, we weighted those measures by the amount of TV news that each person watched. Because we now had interval measures, we used Pearson's correlation instead of the more standard Spearman's rank correlations to calculate the valence of the public's affective impressions of the candidates with the portrayals of those same affective dimensions in the media. There were significant direct correlations on three of the four comparisons: exposure to positive nonverbal imagery of both Gore and Bush significantly correlated with positive affective impressions, and exposure to negative nonverbal imagery of Bush significantly correlated with negative affective impressions of Bush. We found no significant correlations for Bush on the negative dimension, and could come up with no good explanations for it.

This first study was encouraging for its findings that affective framing through visual images does have a second-level agenda-setting effect. My colleague and I did not measure the verbal affective agenda in this study, but conversely, none of the studies of second-level agenda-setting that measure words includes visuals, either. Therefore, none of these studies, ours included, can definitively say that effects are due to either the words or the visuals. We believe that the two work together to create agenda-setting effects. Our purpose here was to show that visuals can indeed contribute to that process. We found merit in pursuing explanations for affective framing in the visual aspects of news coverage as well as in the verbal content. It is likely that the valence of visual and verbal frames is congruent; that is, that if the verbal frames are positive, the visuals also will be positive. However, because no research has determined this, it is an important question for future studies. A second visual agenda-setting study conducted in two parts, visual and verbal (Wu & Coleman, 2007), sought to do just that (in addition to answering other questions). If, indeed, the media are consistent in framing both visual and verbal content with the same valence, it makes it difficult to distinguish whether differences are due to one mode of communication or the combination of the two. Therefore, yet another study is underway to tease out those questions, a controlled experiment that will allow us to see whether the visual framing or verbal framing has the stronger effect.

The first visual agenda-setting study was conducted on the 2000 election; so when the 2004 campaign came around, my colleagues and I decided to replicate and extend the study. For this study, our main focus was on the explication of affect. In previous verbal studies of the second level, and also our own visual study, affect was operationalized by two very different concepts that were lumped together: the candidates' character traits, as measured by people's assessment of their integrity, leadership, intelligence (among other traits), and people's own emotional reactions to the candidates; that is, if the candidates made people feel sad, proud, afraid, and so on. Evaluations of character traits seem to be a more cognitive conceptualization of affect than the more visceral emotions. In this study (Coleman & Wu, 2006a), we proposed that communication scholars define "affect" too narrowly; that psychology's construct of emotions and feelings also should be explored as part of affective agenda-setting, and should be explored separately from character traits. The 2004 study tests this theoretical addition by finding that visual media portrayals of the candidates can set the agenda for viewers' emotional responses as well. Another theory expansion in this study proposes and then shows that negative visuals are more powerful than positive ones.

As with any new line of research, there are some inconsistencies between the two: the 2000 study showed agenda-setting effects for positive visuals; the 2004 study did not. Of course, the campaigns, candidates, and situations were different. Also, the measures of nonverbal behavior were changed from the 2000 to the 2004 study. In 2008, my colleagues and I plan to address these issues and also to code the content along both sets of nonverbal measures to help us understand measurement issues. I view these questions as opportunities for new directions in our research and understand that single studies cannot explain everything. The future of visual agenda-setting and visual framing is ripe for research and we hope others will join us on this interesting journey.

## References

Abelson, R. P., Kinder, D. R., Peters, M. D., & Fiske, S. T. (1982). Affective and semantic components in political person perception. *Journal of Personality and Social Psychology, 42*(4), 619–630.

Aday, S. (2005). The real war will never get on television: An analysis of casualty imagery in American television coverage of the Iraq War. In P. Seib (Ed.), *Media and conflict in the twenty-first century* (pp. 141–156). New York: Palgrave Macmillan.

Aday, S. (2006). The framesetting effects of news: An experimental test of advocacy versus objectivist frames. *Journalism & Mass Communication Quarterly, 83*(4), 767–784.

Aday, S., Cluverius, J., & Livingston, S. (2005). As goes the statue, so goes the war: The emergence of the victory frame in television coverage of the Iraq war. *Journal of Broadcasting & Electronic Media, 49*(3), 314–331.

Arpan, L. M., Baker, K., Lee, Y., Jung, T., Lorusso, L., & Smith, J. (2006). News coverage of social protests and the effects of photographs and prior attitudes. *Mass Communication & Society, 9*(1), 1–20.

Azjen, L., & Fishbein, M. (1975). *Belief, attitude, intention, and behaviour: An introduction to theory and research*. Reading, MA: Addison-Wesley.

Banning, S., & Coleman, R. (2009). Louder than words: A content analysis of presidential candidates' televised nonverbal communication. *Visual Communication Quarterly, 16*(1), 4–17.

Baran, S. J., & Davis, D. K. (1995). *Mass communication theory: Foundations, ferment and future*. Belmont, CA: Wadsworth.

Bell, P. (2001). Content analysis of visual images. In T. van Leeuwen & C. Jewitt (Eds.), *Handbook of visual analysis* (pp. 10–34). London: Sage.

Berger, A. A. (1981). Semiotics and TV. In R. R. Adler (Ed.), *Understanding television: Essays on television as a social and cultural force* (pp. 91–114). New York: Praeger.

Boone, R. T., & Buck, R. (2003). Emotional expressivity and trustworthiness: The role of nonverbal behavior in the evolution of cooperation. *Journal of Nonverbal Behavior, 27*(3), 163–182.

Brewer, W. F., & Nakamura, G. V. (1984). The nature and functions of schemas. In R. S. Wyer & T. K. Srull (Eds.), *Handbook of social cognition* (pp. 119–160). Hillsdale, NJ: Erlbaum.

Bucy, E. (2003). Emotion, presidential communication, and traumatic news: Processing the World Trade Center attacks. *Harvard International Journal of Press/Politics, 8*(4), 76–96.

Burgoon, J. K., Birk, T., & Pfau, M. (1990). Nonverbal behaviors, persuasion, and credibility. *Human Communication Research, 17*(1), 140–169.

Burns, K. L., & Beier, E. G. (1973). Significance of vocal and visual channels in the decoding of emotional meaning. *Journal of Communication, 23*(1), 118–130.

Bystrom, D. G., Robertson, T. A., & Banwart, M. A. (2001). Framing the fight: An analysis of media coverage of female and male candidates in primary races for governor and U.S. Senate in 2000. *American Behavioral Scientist, 44*(12), 1999–2013.

Choi, Y-J., & Lee, J-H. (2006). The role of a scene in framing a story: An analysis of a scene's position, length, and proportion. *Journal of Broadcasting and Electronic Media, 50*(4), 703–722.

Cohen, B. (1963). *The press and foreign policy.* Princeton, NJ: Princeton University Press.

Coker, D. A., & Burgoon, J. K. (1987). The nature of conversational involvement and nonverbal encoding patterns. *Human Communication Research, 13*(4), 463–494.

Coleman, R., & Banning, S. (2006). Network TV news' affective framing of the presidential candidates: Evidence for a second-level agenda-setting effect through visual framing. *Journalism & Mass Communication Quarterly, 83*(2), 313–328.

Coleman, R., & Wu, H. D. (2006a). *Affective priming of the 2004 presidential candidates: Exploring the second-level agenda-setting effect through visual information.* Paper presented at the annual conference of the Association for Education in Journalism and Mass Communication, San Francisco, CA.

Coleman, R., & Wu, H. D. (2006b). More than words alone: Incorporating broadcasters' nonverbal communication into the stages of crisis coverage theory—Evidence from September 11. *Journal of Broadcasting & Electronic Media, 50*(1), 1–17.

D'Angelo, P. (2002). News framing as a multiparadigmatic research program: A response to Entman. *Journal of Communication, 52*(4), 870–888.

de Vreese, C. H. (2004). The effects of frames in political television news on issue interpretation and frame salience. *Journalism & Mass Communication Quarterly, 81*(1), 36–52.

Detenber, B.H., Gotlieb, M. R., McLeod, D. M., & Malinkina, O. (2007). Framing intensity effects of television news stories about a high-visibility protest issue. *Mass Communication & Society, 10*(4), 439–460.

Devitt, J. (1999). *Framing gender on the campaign trail: Women's executive leadership and the press.* Washington, DC: The Women's Leadership Fund.

Dillard, J. P., & Meijnders, A. (2002). Persuasion and the structure of affect. In J. P. Dillard & M. Pfau (Eds.), *The persuasion handbook: Developments in theory and practice* (pp. 309–327). Beverly Hills, CA: Sage.

Dillard, J. P., & Wilson, B. J. (1993). Communication and affect: Thoughts, feelings, and issues for the future. *Communication Research, 2*(5), 637–646.

Dimitrova, D. V., & Stromback, J. (2005). Mission accomplished? *Gazette: The International Journal for Communication Studies, 67,* 399–417.

Domke, D., Fan, D., Fibison, M., Shah, M. V., Smith, S. S., & Watts, M. D. (1997). News media, candidates and issues, and public opinion in the 1996 presidential campaign. *Journalism and Mass Communication Quarterly, 74,* 718–737.

Ekman, P. (Ed.). (1983). *Emotion in the human face* (2nd ed.). New York: Cambridge University Press.

Entman, R. M. (1993). Framing: Toward clarification of a fractured paradigm. *Journal of Communication, 43*(4), 51–58.

Esser, F., & D'Angelo, P. (2003). Framing the press and the publicity process: A content analysis of meta-coverage in campaign 2000 network news. *American Behavioral Scientist, 46*(5), 617–641.

Fahmy, S., Kelly, J. D., & Kim, Y. S. (2007). What Katrina revealed: A visual analysis of the hurricane coverage by news wires and U.S. newspapers. *Journalism & Mass Communication Quarterly, 84*(3), 546–561.

Fiske, S. T., & Taylor, S. E. (1984). *Social cognition*. Reading, MA: Addison-Wesley.

Friedman, H. S., Mertz, T. I., & DiMatteo, M.R. (1980). Perceived bias in the facial expressions of television news broadcasters. *Journal of Communication, 30*(4), 103–111.

Ghanem, S. (1997). Filling in the tapestry: The second level of agenda setting. In M. McCombs, D. Shaw & D. Weaver (Eds.), *Communication and democracy* (pp. 3–14). Mahwah, NJ: Erlbaum.

Gianetti, L. D. (1982). *Understanding movies*. Englewood Cliffs, NJ: Prentice-Hall.

Gibson, R., & Zillmann, D. (2000). Reading between the photographs: The influence of incidental pictorial information on issue perception. *Journalism & Mass Communication Quarterly, 77*(2), 355–366.

Gitlin, T. (1980). *The whole world is watching*. Berkeley: University of California Press.

Goffman, E. (1979). *Gender advertisements*. London: Macmillan.

Grabe, M. E. (1996). The South African Broadcasting Corporation's coverage of the 1987 and 1989 elections: The matter of visual bias. *Journal of Broadcasting and Electronic Media, 40*(2), 153–179.

Graber, D. (1990). Seeing in remembering: How visuals contribute to learning from television news. *Journal of Communication, 40*(3), 134–155.

Greenberg, J. (2002). Framing and temporality in political cartoons: A critical analysis of visual news discourse. *Canadian Review of Sociology and Anthropology, 39*(2), 182–198.

Griffin, M. (2004). Picturing America's "War on Terrorism" in Afghanistan and Iraq: Photographic motifs as news frames. *Journalism, 5*(4), 381–402.

Grimes, T. (1990). Encoding TV news messages into memory. *Journalism Quarterly, 67*, 757–766.

Grimes, T., & Drechsel, R. (1996). Word-picture juxtaposition, schemata, and defamation in television news. *Journalism & Mass Communication Quarterly, 73*(1), 169–180.

Groshek, J. (2008). Homogenous agendas, disparate frames: CNN and CNN International coverage online. *Journal of Broadcasting and Electronic Media, 52*(1), 52–68.

Harris, R. J. (1994). *A cognitive psychology of mass communication* (2nd ed.). Hillsdale, NJ: Erlbaum.

Hatley Major, L., & Perlmutter, D. (2005). The fall of a pseudo-icon: The toppling of Saddam Hussein's statue as image management. *Visual Communication Quarterly, 12*(1 & 2), 38–45.

Helmsley, G. D., & Doob, A. T. (1978). The effect of looking behavior on perceptions of a communicator's credibility. *Journal of Applied Social Psychology, 8*, 136–144.

Huxford, J. (2001). Beyond the referential: Uses of visual symbolism in the press. *Journalism, 2*(1), 45–71.

Iguarta, J. J., Cheng, L., & Lopes, O. (2003). To think or not to think: Two pathways towards persuasion by short films on Aids prevention. *Journal of Health Communication, 8*(6), 513–528.

Iyengar, S. (1991). *Is anyone responsible? How television frames political issues.* Chicago: University of Chicago.

Izard, C. E. (1977). *Human emotions.* New York: Plenum Press.

Janis, I. L., & Fadner, R. (1965). Coefficients of imbalance. In H. Laswell, N. Leites, & Associates (Eds.), *Language of politics* (pp. 153–169). South Norwalk, CT: George W. Stewart.

Kamhawi, R., & Grabe, E. (2008). Engaging the female audience: An evolutionary psychology perspective on gendered responses to news valence frames. *Journal of Broadcasting and Electronic Media, 52*(1), 33–51.

Kiousis, S., Bantimaroudis, P., & Ban, H. (1999). Candidate image attributes: Experiments on the substantive dimension of second-level agenda setting. *Communication Research, 26*(4), 414–428.

Lacy, S., & Fico, F. (1991). Fairness and balance in the prestige press. *Journalism Quarterly, 68*(3), 363–370.

Lamb, W., & Watson, E. (1979). *Body code: The meaning in movement.* London: Routledge & Kegan Paul.

Lang, K., & Lang, G. E. (1952). The unique perspective of television and its effect: A pilot study. In W. Schramm & D. F. Roberts (Eds.), *The process and effects of mass communication* (pp. 169–188). Urbana, IL: University of Illinois Press.

Lanzetta, J. T., Sullivan, D. G., Masters, R. D., & McHugo, G. J. (1985). Viewers' emotional and cognitive responses to televised images of political leaders. In S. Kraus & R. M. Perloff (Eds.), *Mass media and political thought: An information processing approach* (pp. 85–116). Beverly Hills, CA: Sage.

Lichter, R. S., & Noyes, R. E. (1995). *Good intentions make bad news: Why Americans hate campaign journalism.* Lanham, MD: Rowman & Littlefield.

Liebler, C. M., & Bendix, J. (1996). Old-growth forests on network news: News sources and the framing of an environmental controversy. *Journalism & Mass Communication Quarterly, 73*(1), 53–65.

Lippmann, W. (1922). *Public opinion.* New York: Macmillan.

Lowry, D., & Shidler, J. (1995). The sound bites, the biters, and the bitten: An analysis of network TV new bias in campaign '92. *Journalism & Mass Communication Quarterly, 72*(1), 33–44.

Manusov, V. (Ed.). (2005). *The sourcebook of nonverbal measures: Going beyond words.* Mahwah, NJ: Erlbaum.

McCombs, M., Shaw, D. L., & Weaver, D. (1997). *Communication and democracy: Exploring the intellectual frontiers in agenda-setting theory.* Mahwah, NJ: Erlbaum.

McHugo, G. J., Lanzetta, J. T., Sullivan, D. G., Masters, R. D., & Englis, B. G. (1985). Emotional reactions to a political leader's expressive displays. *Journal of Personality and Social Psychology, 49*(6), 1513–1529.

McLeod, D. M., & Detenber, B. H. (1999). Framing effects of television news coverage of social protest. *Journal of Communication, 49*(3), 3–23.

Mehrabian, A. (1968). Inference of attitudes from the posture, orientation, and distance of a communicator. *Journal of Consulting and Clinical Psychology, 32*(3), 296–308.

Messaris, P., & Abraham, L. (2001). The role of images in framing news stories. In S. D. Reese, O. H. Gandy, & A. E. Grant (Eds.), *Framing public life: Perspectives on media and our understanding of the social world* (pp. 215–226). Mahwah, NJ: Erlbaum.

Miller, A., Coleman, R., & Granberg, D. (2007). TV anchors, elections, and bias: A longitudinal study of the facial expressions of Brokaw, Rather, Jennings. *Visual Communication Quarterly, 14*(4), 244–257.

Montepare, J. M., & Dobish, H. (2003). The contribution of emotion perceptions and their overgeneralizations to trait impressions. *Journal of Nonverbal Behavior, 27*(4), 237–254.

Moriarty, S. E., & Popovich, M. N. (1991). Newsmagazine visuals and the 1988 presidential election. *Journalism Quarterly, 68*(3), 371–380.

Mullen, B., Futrell, D., Stairs, D., Tice, D. M., Baumeister, R. F., Dawson, K. E. et al. (1986). Newscasters' facial expressions and voting behavior of viewers: Can a smile elect a president? *Journal of Personality and Social Psychology, 51*(2), 291–295.

Newhagen, J., & Reeves, B. E. (1990). Emotion and memory responses for negative political advertising: A study of television commercials used in the 1988 presidential election. In F. Biocca (Ed.), *Television and political advertising* (Vol. 1, pp. 197–220). Hillsdale, NJ: Erlbaum.

Paletz, D., & Guthrie, K. K. (1987). The three faces of Ronald Reagan. *Journal of Communication, 37*(4), 7–23.

Perlmutter, D. (1998). *Photojournalism and foreign policy: Framing icons of outrage in international crisis.* Westport, CT: Greenwood Press.

Petty, R. E., & Cacioppo, J. T. (1981). *Attitudes and persuasion: Classic and contemporary approaches.* Dubuque, IA: Brown.

Petty, R. E., & Cacioppo, J. T. (1986). *Communication and persuasion: Central and peripheral routes to attitude change.* New York: Springer-Verlag.

Pezdek, K. (1977). Cross-modality semantic integration of sentence and picture memory. *Journal of Experimental Psychology 3,* 515–524.

Price, V., Tewksbury, D., & Powers, E. (1997). Switching trains of thought: The impact of news frames on readers' cognitive responses. *Communication Research, 24*(5), 481–506.

Reese, S. D., Gandy, O. H., & Grant, A. E. (Eds.). (2001). *Framing public life: Perspectives on media and our understanding of the social world.* Mahwah, NJ: Erlbaum.

Robinson, M., & Sheehan, M. (1982). *Over the wire and on TV.* New York: Russell Sage Foundation.

Rosenberg, S. W., Bohan, P., McCafferty, P., & Harris, K. (1986). The image and the vote: The effect of candidate presentation on voter preference. *American Journal of Political Science, 30*(1), 108–127.

Rosenberg, S. W., & McCafferty, P. (1987). The image and the vote: Manipulating voters' preferences. *Public Opinion Quarterly, 51*(1), 31–47.

Rosenthal, R., Hall, J., DiMatteo, M. R., Rogers, P., & Archer, D. (1979).

*Sensitivity to non-verbal communication: The PONS test.* Baltimore, MD: Johns Hopkins University Press.

Scheufele, D. A. (1999). Framing as a theory of media effects. *Journal of Communication, 49*(1), 103–122.

Schwalbe, C. B. (2006). Remembering our shared past: Visually framing the Iraq war on U.S. news websites. *Journal of Computer-Mediated Communication, 12,* 264–289.

Schwalbe, C. B., Silcock, B. W., & Keith, S. (2008). Visual framing of the early weeks of the U.S.-led invasion of Iraq: Applying the master war narrative to electronic and print images. *Journal of Broadcasting & Electronic Media, 52*(3), 448–465.

Semetko, H. A., & Valkenburg, P. M. (2000). Framing European politics: A content analysis of press and television news. *Journal of Communication, 50*(2), 93–108.

Severin, W. J., & Tankard, J. W. (1992). *Communication theories: Origins, methods, and uses in the mass media.* New York: Longman.

Smith, K., Moriarty, S. E., Barbatsis, G., & Kenney, K. (Eds.). (2005). *Handbook of visual communication: Theory, methods, and media.* Mahwah, NJ: Erlbaum.

Stempel, G., & Culbertson, H. (1984). The prominence and dominance of news sources in newspaper media coverage. *Journalism Quarterly, 61*(3), 671–676.

Waldman, P., & Devitt, J. (1998). Newspaper photographs and the 1996 presidential election: The question of bias. *Journalism & Mass Communication Quarterly, 75*(2), 302–311.

Wanta, W. (1988). The effects of dominant photographs: An agenda-setting experiment. *Journalism Quarterly, 65*(1), 107–111.

Wanta, W., Golan, G., & Lee, C. (2004). Agenda-setting and international news: Media influence on public perceptions of foreign nations. *Journalism & Mass Communication Quarterly, 81*(2), 364–377.

Witt, L., Paget, K. M., & Matthews, G. (1994). *Running as a woman: Gender and power in American politics.* New York: The Free Press.

Wu, H. D., & Coleman, R. (2007). *Advancing agenda-setting theory: A comparison of the relative strength of the two levels of agenda setting, and proposing new contingent conditions.* Paper presented at the annual conference of the Association for Education in Journalism and Mass Communication, Washington, DC.

Yioutas, J., & Segvic, I. (2003). Revisiting the Clinton/Lewinsky scandal: The convergence of agenda setting and framing. *Journalism & Mass Communication Quarterly, 80*(3), 567–582.

Zillmann, D., Knobloch, S., & Yu, H. (2001). Effects of photographs on the selective reading of news reports. *Media Psychology, 3*(4), 301–324.

# Part III

# Theoretical Integration in News Framing Analysis

# Chapter 11

# Researching Political News Framing

## Established Ground and New Horizons

*Regina G. Lawrence*

A key question in much of the literature on media framing of politics and public affairs is, How independently do the media frame issues and events, versus simply passing along to the public the frames originated by powerful political actors?

The empirical dimension to this question is straightforward and can be linked to the two foundational articles by Scheufele (1999) and D'Angelo (2002) referenced throughout this volume. Many issues and events that citizens encounter in the news have been framed by political actors, particularly government officials, but sometimes also other political actors such as interest group leaders (Callaghan & Schnell, 2001), academic experts (Brewer & Sigelman, 2002) and grassroots movement spokespersons (Pride, 1995). Quite often these frames have political purposes—they are intended to influence public perceptions and guide public discourse. Not surprisingly, political actors typically target the news media to convey intact their preferred frames to the public. Yet a prevalent theme within the news framing literature is that issues and events are framed as much by the decisions of journalists and editors as by the intentions of political actors. As Gamson and Modigliani (1989, p. 3) observed, journalists "may draw their ideas and language" from a variety of sources, but they also "contribute their own frames" to the news. From the perspective of journalists, these frames are not normally conceived as ways to influence public opinion so much as they are part of the norms and routines of the news business. Reporters seeking an interesting angle on a story, for example, may choose not to lead with a government official's or a candidate's preferred frame. In fact, journalists dedicated to the "watchdog" role may not readily accept a political actor's framing of an issue or event at face value; rather, they may see it as their job to *reframe* the actor's point of view. Editors, too, will often demand that reporters obtain additional quotes for a story from across the political aisle in order to observe "objectivity," a news norm that Tuchman (1978), in her seminal work, convincingly showed to be implicated in news framing, and which, to this day, continues to occupy framing scholars interested in understanding the complex information environments of politics (Chong & Druckman, 2007a, 2007b).

So, the big question addressed by much of the literature on political news framing is this: To what degree does the news reflect and emphasize the intended frames of political actors, and to what degree does the news introduce other possible ways of framing issues and events—particularly frames that those in government oppose? Another way of asking this question is simply: *Where do political news frames come from?*

In this chapter I wish to accomplish three main goals. First, I offer a "political context" framework to organize the various answers researchers have given to answer these big questions, adding observations from my own research as it has evolved to address these questions. Second, I wish to direct attention to the normative dimensions of these questions about political news framing. Historically, political communication research has with grappled normative concerns (Bucy & D'Angelo, 1999). Underlying much of the formative framing literature discussed here are implicit—and sometimes explicit—normative assumptions about what constitutes good quality news. These assumptions have powerfully shaped the course of framing research. Finally, I examine the emerging debate among scholars about the normative expectations underlying news framing research. While many scholars of political news framing have implicitly or explicitly criticized the mainstream media for lacking thoughtful independence from the political actors who try to shape the news, some scholars are now wondering if these calls for greater media independence are unrealistic. This debate, I believe, will shape the future of research on news frames because so many scholarly studies of news frames at heart are concerned about the quality of the information provided to the public by the media.

## A Political Context Framework: An Overview

As outlined in several chapters in this volume, research on framing has proliferated. So have studies of how the news frames politics and public affairs. This proliferation has created some fairly firm established ground—a set of concepts and propositions about political news that, if not entirely agreed upon by all scholars, does form a core of knowledge to guide further exploration and testing. However, less attention has been paid to incorporating the array of studies and their somewhat contradictory findings into a coherent framework. In this section, I offer a "political context" framework that helps make sense of the burgeoning political news framing literature.

My argument hinges on the point that the media's independence in crafting news frames varies across political contexts. This expands upon

Sparrow's argument that "whether journalists are adversarial or cooperative in their relationship with public officials" depends upon context: "They are attack dogs when covering political contests, but they are lapdogs, a 'handout press,' when covering a policy monopoly" (1999, p. 26). The political context framework sketched here acknowledges this dynamic, but also points to institutional and cultural features that distinguish some policy contexts from others.

There are three contexts across which the findings of news framing research differ: (1) news about foreign policy and national security, particularly in high-stakes contexts of war and international conflict; (2) news about domestic policy, particularly pertaining to social issues; and (3) news about electoral campaigns. In the foreign policy and national security context, research indicates that the mainstream media typically show less independence in framing issues and events, instead tending to rely heavily on high government officials to frame the news. In the domestic policy context, the playing field is more open to a wider variety of would-be news framers, and journalists themselves may exhibit more independence in introducing and sustaining particular news frames. In the electoral campaign context, journalists may exhibit considerable independence from their main sources, the candidates and their campaign staff, often offering some alternative perspective in a way that reporters are often hesitant to do when reporting in the national security context. In sum, the implicit norms of journalistic independence appear to shift depending upon the context in which reporters are working.

Focusing for a moment on high-stakes foreign policy news, particularly at elite, well-placed news organizations like the *New York Times* and the *Washington Post*, reporters and editors may see it as unprofessional and irresponsible to introduce perspectives not authorized, so to speak, by high officials; that is, ideas that currently lie outside what Hallin (1986) described as the "sphere of legitimate controversy." This reluctance to amplify voices and views from outside the Washington consensus was vividly on display in the run-up to the U.S.-led war in Iraq. As numerous observers and studies have documented, in the face of a determined campaign by the Bush administration to make its case for going to war, including ominous talk about "WMDs" and "mushroom clouds" and hints that Saddam Hussein had conspired in the September 11 attacks on the United States, the nation's most elite news organizations marginalized questions that lower-level government experts and others were raising about the administration's case (see Bennett, Lawrence, & Livingston, 2007; Frontline, 2007; Massing, 2004; Kurtz, 2004; Rich, 2007). Indeed, reluctance to challenge high officials often remains in wartime (e.g., Aday, 2005). In fact, in an unusual admission that this norm had led them astray, both the *New York Times* and the *Washington Post* issued public mea culpas after the war began. According to

Leonard Downie, Executive Editor of the *Post*, "We were not giving the same play to people who said it wouldn't be a good idea to go to war and were questioning the administration's rationale. Not enough of those stories were put on the front page" (quoted in Kurtz, 2004).

In campaign news, in contrast, journalists often see it as a mark of unprofessionalism *not* to introduce alternative perspectives on what the candidates are saying and doing. Patterson (1993) has documented, for example, the increasingly prominent role of reporters as interpreters in campaign news. In contrast to earlier eras, the news audience is now more likely to hear or read journalists' interpretations of what candidates have said than the original words of the candidates themselves. Other studies document a "campaign disconnect" wherein the news focuses on issues other than those emphasized by the candidates; for example, in presidential campaigns, the national media may highlight issues from state-level primary contests without providing the national audience with adequate context for understanding the positions that candidates take (Vinson & Moore, 2007). And as reviewed further below, a high percentage of campaign news is filtered through a "game frame" that highlights strategic and tactical aspects of the campaign over the substantive policy issues candidates try to address. All of these patterns in campaign coverage point to a press that routinely reframes candidates' messages.

As stated, this chapter aims to develop theoretical propositions related to a context-specific perspective on news framing and to address the normative question of how much press independence is "enough" to satisfy democratic norms. Before I proceed, however, I must make the reader aware that the literature and theories discussed below are focused primarily on the so-called MSM, the mainstream media. These include elite and popular newspapers ranging from the *New York Times* and the *Wall Street Journal* to *USA Today* and your own city's newspaper. On the broadcast side, the theories discussed here are most applicable to the traditional evening news programs like the *NBC Evening News* that reach an audience of tens of millions. To be sure, an interesting question in the development of theories of news framing and press independence is how well they can describe the workings of the burgeoning new forms of "news," including the explicitly politicized harangues of cable news talk shows and political bloggers, the entertainment-oriented "news" on shows ranging from *Oprah* to *The View*, and the politically savvy satire of *The Daily Show with Jon Stewart*. Research on those forms of news and how they frame politics is burgeoning as well (e.g., Baum, 2002; Jones, 2005). Though the rise of these alternative venues has challenged the mainstream media's predominance in setting the public agenda, mainstream news remains at the core of the political communications apparatus in the United States.

## From Indexing to the Game Frame

If there is one thing on which scholars of political news framing agree, it is that government officials are generally the most prevalent voices in the news (see Bennett, 2007 for an overview of this research; see also Entman, 2004; Wolfsfeld, 1997). This starting proposition guides much news framing research. It immediately raises the question of how thoroughly the news is dominated by official government perspectives. While it is crucial to democracy that citizens be informed about what government is saying and doing, news that reflects only the voices and perspectives of those within government might not satisfy other democratic norms of diverse and robust public debate (more on that point later).

An important insight into the question of media independence in the framing process is provided by the "indexing hypothesis" (Bennett, 1990), which has become a leading theory of government–press relations in the United States. The core idea is that journalists "index," that is, calibrate news stories to the power balance they perceive amongst those in government (Bennett, 1990). In other words, "the mainstream news generally stays within the sphere of official consensus and conflict displayed in the public statements of the key government officials who manage the policy areas and decision-making processes that make the news" (Bennett et al., 2007, p. 49). Indexing attempts a more nuanced account of media gate keeping of public discourse: "The press gatekeepers open the gates wider or close them more tightly as they perceive potentially decisive challenges or a lack of challenges to the most powerful institutional players and their agendas" (p. 49). The news thus tends to reflect the perspectives promulgated by those whom journalists perceive to have the most power to influence the situation, and who have the greatest institutional capacity and communications apparatus to put across their point of view. This core dynamic, albeit with some variation across contexts, has been uncovered in a variety of studies (Althaus, 2003; Entman, 2004; Mermin, 1999; Zaller & Chiu, 1996), though it has also been challenged (e.g., Althaus, 2003; Entman, 2004).

The indexing process is, analytically speaking, distinct from the framing process in the sense that indexing attempts to explain and predict the types of stories and voices that will receive greatest news play. But the indexing hypothesis speaks directly to the question of news framing in two ways: (1) The main *voices* in the news are likely to be those with the greatest power over the issue at hand, and (2) the *views* presented in the news are likely to roughly reflect the current range of political debate in Washington and other power centers. Indexing theory also suggests that news frames on any particular issue are not static, but will shift in conjunction with shifts in power. Elections may bring new political players into key institutional arenas; evolving real-world events may change the political calculations of those players; and different players will be important and powerful in different context. So, we should expect news frames to shift over time and across contexts.

The literature on press–government relations identifies several enabling factors that buttress the indexing routine, and one of the most consistent factors is policy context. Indexing is most readily apparent in news coverage of foreign affairs, particularly in reporting on U.S. national security and military conflict. For example, Bennett and Klockner (1996) compared news coverage of a foreign policy controversy from the 1980s—the U.S. funding of the insurgent *contra* war against the socialist government of Nicaragua—with coverage of a perennial social policy issue in the U.S., abortion rights. They found much closer indexing of the news to congressional and White House positions in the coverage of the contra war, and a comparatively wider range of perspectives in news about abortion. While some research has also found indexing-like patterns in domestic policy news (see Jacobs & Shapiro, 2000; Lawrence, 2000a; Lawrence & Birkland, 2004; Sparrow, 1999), the pattern seems particularly clear in foreign policy news. Indeed, though he moves theoretically beyond the core indexing dynamic, Entman's important book *Projections of Power* (2004) shows that foreign affairs reporting is closely tied to policy views expressed by officials.

There are several possible reasons why indexing may be most pronounced in reporting on foreign policy. The executive branch has strong constitutional powers in that realm and legislators often show more deference to the president as commander-in-chief, particularly in times of perceived international crisis. Foreign affairs, particularly issues touching on national security, raise questions of patriotism for officials and journalists that are not usually present in domestic affairs. Of course, these constraints do not rule out all debate. In fact, as Entman (2004) argues, the dissolution of the Cold Ward created more leeway for Congress to criticize presidential policies because it rendered irrelevant the underlying paradigm of anticommunism and ushered in new rationales for military campaigns, ranging from humanitarian intervention to toppling dictators. In the changed cultural climate of the post-Cold War world, Congress has been less reticent to challenge a president, even when U.S. troops are on the ground, thus widening the range of legitimate debate for journalists to cover (Entman 2004). In sum, the institutional and cultural context of foreign policy reinforces journalists' instinct to bind their reporting to perspectives that are validated by key policymakers, particularly in the White House, Congress, the military, and the national security establishment.

In my own research, which has encompassed both foreign and domestic policy issues, I have often noticed a tighter connection between the frames that high officials promulgate and the framing of the news in foreign policy than in domestic policy contexts. Interestingly, the closest parallel I have seen between foreign and domestic issue coverage involved the issue of police brutality. Looking closely at the coverage of all reported police use of force incidents in two newspapers, the *New York Times* and the *Los Angeles Times* (Lawrence 2000a), I found that in the vast majority of cases the official frame—in this case, the view from the police department—prevailed. The news nearly always framed such incidents in terms that normalized police officers' use of violence (for example, by emphasizing the threatening or deviant behavior of those subjected to it). The media maelstrom that followed the widely publicized footage of LAPD officers beating black motorist Rodney King was unusual precisely because that reporting did not hew to the official line, and ultimately led to the ouster of LAPD Chief Daryl Gates, who had publicly defended the officers involved. There are obvious differences between the policy realms of domestic policing and international relations, but it is noteworthy that each realm raises fundamental questions about the legitimacy of force employed by the state—an area fraught with difficulty for democratic societies. This comparison leads me to suspect that the cultural constraints on reporting are correlated not simply with foreign versus domestic policy, but also with fundamental questions about the uses of government power. Whenever government uses force against its own citizens or nations abroad, urgent questions of legitimacy may surface, but journalists may feel constrained from raising those questions directly. The range of "acceptable" debate on U.S. foreign policy is therefore often narrower than for most domestic issues, creating more constraints on the perspectives reporters hear from their sources.

The predominance of indexing in foreign affairs reporting may also reflect the greater institutional complexity of many domestic policy issues. Unlike most questions of foreign policy, political struggles over domestic policy questions ranging from taxation to the death penalty play out in state and local as well as national government arenas, and in the courts as well as legislatures, and are often subject to intense domestic interest group pressure.

The finding that indexing is predominant in foreign affairs reporting may also be, to some extent, an artifact of the comparatively greater ease of studying news coverage of foreign policy. The same institutional complexity that marks domestic policy struggles also can make it more challenging for the researcher to study domestic policy news frames. This may be one reason that some studies have found more complexity and a wider range of voices in news framing of issues like gun control, school violence, and police brutality (Callaghan & Schnell, 2001; Lawrence, 2000b; Lawrence & Birkland, 2004).

But the relatively greater independence of media from elites seen in studies of domestic policy news is not merely artifactual. As indicated in Callaghan and Schnell's (2001) research on news framing of gun control, journalists framed that issue rather independently, relying on a "culture of violence" theme more than their sources did. Jerit (2006) also found significant media independence in reporting on Social Security. She noted: "Contrary to theories of indexing, reporters and journalists exhibited considerable independence in how they described Social Security's financial problems." Ironically, this meant that "media accounts had more misleading rhetoric than the actual statements of government officials" (p. 9).

Indexing patterns may also be less clear-cut in domestic settings because of the prevalence in domestic political news of a different kind of frame: the "game" frame. This way of framing the news makes the issue positions of political players secondary to their strategic positioning. Game-framed news treats politics much like a sports event, with journalists playing the role of commentators and interpreters of various players' strategic moves (Lawrence, 2000a; Patterson, 1993). Varieties of the game frame include the "procedural" frame noted by Cappella and Jamieson (1997) and by Entman (2004), in which the main story is the political process by which a piece of legislation is passed or defeated. Here, in keeping with the game analogy, the focus is on the plays, the strategies, the victory or defeat for the "teams" in politics as they vie to "score" policy wins. Even a causal glance at the day's newspaper will likely reveal that domestic policy making is often portrayed by journalists in this strategic framework. Political players' issue frames can still be found in this kind of news, but those frames are filtered through a meta-frame of political strategy. That added layer of news framing—layering the strategic interpretation on top of the issue frames promulgated by political players—is less prevalent in reporting on U.S. foreign policy, particularly in times of war and crisis.

If game-framing is prevalent in domestic policy news, it is positively dominant in coverage of U.S. elections, our third context. In campaign news, the ties that bind reporters to the preferred frames of their sources are at their loosest. In fact, in stark contrast to most reporting on U.S. foreign policy, the evident professional expectation amongst journalists is that they will bring an explicitly critical eye to what candidates say and do on the campaign trail.

That "critical" eye is rarely informed by policy substance, however. Rather, reporters focus elections through the lens of the game frame, analyzing politicians' strategies for getting elected rather than their proposals for what to do once they are elected. Journalists organize the potentially numbing tide of campaign events and developments with an organizing schema focusing on how each event helps one candidate to win or threatens others with losing. What matters, what is "newsworthy" every day, are those events that contribute to electoral wins and losses. From this perspective, policy issues are not unimportant, but they matter only insofar as they may help one candidate prevail. Patterson's research shows a dramatic increase in this "game" oriented coverage; since 1976, front-page election coverage has been heavily skewed toward the game of electoral politics (Patterson, 1993).

Indeed, perhaps the best-documented pattern in media coverage of elections over the past three decades has been the prevalence of what is often called "horse race" coverage that focuses on who is winning and who is losing—the "process" of the campaign—rather than focusing on policy issues. A significant portion of news coverage of presidential elections—one-third or more, depending upon the medium and the phase of the election—is focused on horse race stories more than issues (Center for Media and Public Affairs 2004; Just, Crigler, Alger, & Cook, 1996; Kovach & Rosenstiel, 2001; Vinson & Moore, 2007).

The upshot of this research, for our purposes here, is that while an indexing pattern of tying the predominant news frames to those proffered by powerful officials is the dominant pattern in foreign policy news, it may be somewhat less dominant in domestic policy news, where issue frames may originate from a greater number of institutional players and arenas and be filtered through journalists' "game" frame. Indeed, two seminal works on game-framing (Cappella & Jamieson, 1997; Patterson, 1993) find that even when the news focuses on domestic policy issues, the issues are focused through the same kind of game frame employed in election coverage. And in electoral news, where game-framing is predominant, the candidates' preferred frames are often layered underneath the reporters' game frame.

It was this observation that lead me to explore the framing of welfare reform during the 1996 presidential election season, for in that year, welfare reform was both a prominent campaign issue and a policy issue that Congress was actively working on as the candidates campaigned. In that study (Lawrence, 2000b), I found that in news from the campaign trail, welfare reform was almost exclusively portrayed as a talking point designed to win over voters and as a symbolic weapon deployed by candidates against each other. Specifically, Republican candidate Bob Dole essentially portrayed Democratic president Bill Clinton as soft on welfare, to which Clinton responded by signing a Republican-sponsored bill that, Clinton claimed, would "end welfare as we know it." But in news from Capitol Hill, welfare reform was also primarily framed in terms of how it helped or hurt players in the political game (for example, how signing the legislation "inoculated" Clinton against Dole's charges). The actual content of the legislation, which would fundamentally transform a government program affecting millions of American men, women, and children and their communities, was rarely reported on in any detail until *after* the legislation had been signed into law.

In short, it appears that journalists take care to deflect charges of irresponsibility when reporting on critical matters of national security by hewing relatively closely to the official line. When reporting on campaigns and on many domestic issues, in contrast, reporters bring a more "independent" perspective to their topic, although that perspective may also distort the issues at hand. Explaining the persistence of the game frame in campaign reporting, journalism professor and critic Jay Rosen argues,

> Who's-gonna-win is portable, reusable from cycle to cycle, and easily learned by newcomers to the press pack. Journalists believe it brings readers to the page and eyeballs to the screen. It "works" regardless of who the candidates are, or where the nation is in historical time. No expertise is actually needed to operate it. In that sense, it is economical. (And when everyone gets the winner wrong the "surprise" becomes a good story for a few days.) (Rosen, 2008)

Thus, reporters seem to take greater liberties in reporting on election campaigns than on foreign policy issues. Arguing that the modern centrality of the press to elections disrupts the process and creates confusion rather than clarity among voters, Patterson argues that, "Journalists... not the candidates are reeds in the wind. The candidates' speeches are filled with pledges of what they will do if elected. [But] since the outcome of these promises is in the future, journalists are free to say nearly anything they want" (Patterson, 1993, p. 33).

## New Empirical and Normative Horizons in News Framing Research

One area of needed empirical research is to clarify and improve upon the basic insight of the indexing hypothesis. Like all propositions in the social sciences, the indexing hypothesis is probabilistic: News frames are *likely* to be driven and bounded by the preferred frames of powerful political players, particularly in the context of reporting on U.S. foreign policy. And like all such propositions, this one immediately invites the question, under what conditions does the proposition *not* hold?

Recent developments in empirical research have added nuance to, and challenged, the basic indexing proposition. Bennett et al. (2007) propose that the indexing dynamic can be limited, even undercut, by three factors. First, "event-driven news" (Lawrence, 2000b) may create dynamics that encourage journalists to move beyond official pronouncements and bring marginalized perspectives to the forefront of the news (at least temporarily). Of course, virtually all news is centered in events of one kind or another. But sometimes events occur that are so dramatic and unexpected that they set off a scramble for sense-making perspectives. When Los Angeles police officers were caught on videotape beating a Black motorist in 1991 (Lawrence, 2000b), or when two White suburban high school students at Columbine shot a number of their classmates and teachers and then themselves (Lawrence, 2001), the news didn't just gather facts, it gathered perspectives on these events from a variety of sources. These perspectives became (sometimes competing) frames on the issues of both police brutality—is it a problem of a few "bad apple" officers, poor police management, or society-wide racism?—and school violence—is it a problem of poor parenting, too-available guns, or a violent media culture?

Even in the foreign policy realm, unexpected events can sometimes knock the news off its well-worn indexing tracks—at least to some degree. The troubling events at Abu Ghraib prison, brought to the American public in photographs that were aired by CBS in April 2004, challenged the Bush administration to frame acts by American soldiers that could have been (and were to a limited degree) labeled as "torture"—even though virtually no U.S. officials would use that term (Bennett et al., 2007; Entman, 2006). Especially important to the continuation of independent news framing around these events appears to be how skillfully officials respond to them. Openings for critical reporting can be created by fumbled official responses to unexpected events (Lawrence, 2000). However, as Livingston and Bennett found in the context of foreign news, officials are often able to regain their predominant position in the news and thus regain control of unexpected world events soon after they occur (Livingston & Bennett, 2003).

One mark of a fruitful proposition is that it can accommodate and even incorporate challenges. My research on event-driven news came about precisely because I was curious about the limits of the indexing dynamic. As I watched public discourse explode in the aftermath of the Rodney King beating with heated debate about the racial and institutional roots of police brutality, and again as the Columbine shooting set off a kind of national soul searching about the social environment that breeds young rampage killers, it seemed that something fundamentally different was going on than the kind of top-down news framing described in Bennett's original work on indexing: news frames were to some degree bubbling up from activists, experts, local communities—and perhaps from journalists themselves. Yet what began as an effort to test the limits of indexing became, in the end, an extension of a larger model of news dynamics that incorporates both the routine indexing of news to officials and the occasional event-driven moments of greater media independence—a model of a "semi-independent press" (Bennett & Livingston, 2003; Bennett et al., 2007).

Bennett et al. (2007) also suggest that indexing may occasionally be undercut by the skillful deployment by political activists of techniques to influence the news; for example, as antiwar activist Cindy Sheehan did when she staged a showdown with a no-show President Bush at his Crawford, Texas ranch during the summer of 2006. And of course, the most time-honored paths out of the indexing dynamic are through some combination of insider leaks to the press and hard-nosed investigative journalism. In these circumstances as well, news can become more independent from the official consensus, opening windows of opportunity for more prominent critical reporting on governmental policies and policy debates.

Entman (2004), too, has both challenged and built upon the indexing hypothesis by suggesting a more nuanced "cascading activation" model. Rather than posing a simple dichotomy of news sources—official and unofficial—and measuring the dominance of one over the other, Entman's model proposes a hierarchy of news sources in foreign policy news, including the White House and national security establishment on top and less-influential sources like congressional staffers and foreign policy experts in the middle levels. A key question in Entman's model is how news frames can sometimes "cascade upward" from these midlevel sources to become predominant in the news.

Althaus (2003) and Entman (2004) have also argued that indexing theory portrays the press as too reactive and passive. While making his case that journalists were actually the source of much of the critical coverage that appeared on the Persian Gulf crisis, Althaus argues that, because they interview many sources both on and off the record, Washington beat reporters are sometimes aware of greater levels of official debate than those officials are willing to reveal for the record. In those circumstances, "journalists may be emboldened to index according to the real [versus the public] level of latent criticism" (2003, p. 384). Entman argues that under some circumstances, journalists themselves can be the catalysts of frame-changing public discourse—that challenging frames sometimes enter the news because enterprising reporters put them there. Entman (2006) offers the example of Seymour Hersh's reporting for the New Yorker on the Abu Ghraib scandal in 2004, which traced the connections between the torture of detainees in U.S. detention centers in Iraq and Afghanistan and the policy decisions of Donald Rumsfeld's Department of Defense. Though Hersh's willingness to talk about the possibility of U.S. torture may have had limited impact on U.S. news coverage (Bennett et al., 2007), his reporting became a flashpoint of conversation within Washington that arguably shaped the contours of elite debate about U.S. policies in prosecuting the war on terror. These debates among scholars form one fruitful area for further research into the particular mechanisms that trigger news frames and the degree to which lower-level and nongovernmental news sources can influence predominant frames in new or developing news stories.

In fact, it is a live question whether frames found in the media are too readily attributed to politicians rather than to reporters themselves, because the researcher may find it difficult to trace the original provenance of particular frames. For example, in a study of how the infamous Columbine high school shooting was framed in the news (Lawrence & Birkland, 2004), my coauthor and I found it difficult to be sure where the predominant frames originated: that Columbine reflected a national problem of widely available guns, and that it reflected a popular media environment saturated with violence. These two frames were promulgated by Democratic and Republican politicians, respectively, in speeches and on TV news programs within a day of the shooting. But in looking closely at transcripts of news articles and press conferences, it became clear that these frames were also introduced almost instantaneously by reporters themselves. It was therefore difficult to know to what degree these were politician-driven frames that the media dutifully amplified versus media-generated frames to which politicians were responding.

A final observation on the empirical horizons of political news framing research involves the problem of "naming" the paradigms that guide our research. The most basic insight of the indexing hypothesis—that in many circumstances the news reflects the views put forth by those in power—had been noted by media scholars for many years (e.g., Gans, 1979; Sigal, 1973; Tuchman, 1978). What the indexing notion adds is the fluctuating dynamic implicit in that early observation: that as political power changes hands the predominant news stories are likely to shift as well. Thus, the range of voices and views most prominent in the news is not necessarily static. Whereas earlier models tried to identify constant patterns in the news, or to identify broad areas of discourse in which the news would be most closely tied to power (see Hallin, 1986), indexing identified a pattern within change, or change within a pattern, that could apply across areas of discourse. Yet the somewhat subtle process by which scholars build upon each others' work to arrive at new models can raise "turf" issues. Because different scholars see similar patterns in the news and they need a common language for talking about it, naming the basic dynamics becomes important. "Indexing" is such a simple and powerful idea that it quickly caught on in scholarly circles. (Entman's "cascading activation" model, in contrast, is marvelously nuanced and has many moving parts that may be daunting to the uninitiated.) But with that parsimony also runs the danger of oversimplification (i.e., everything is indexing), or of deadening dogmatism (i.e., indexing is everything). My ongoing research with Bennett and others has been an effort to build broader theory and a commonly shared language for talking about political news dynamics, and also an effort to push against dogmatism by pushing against the limits of the basic indexing hypothesis.

## Normative Debates

Meanwhile, a significant debate has developed over the standards that scholars apply to normatively evaluate news quality. Most framing analyses are not explicitly normative; that is, they focus on exploring the realm of what is rather than what ought to be in the news. Yet many framing studies rest upon unstated normative expectations; for example, that news frames in political campaign coverage should be more substantive than procedural or "game" oriented; that so-called issue frames in news should accurately reflect the range of available perspectives on an issue; or that greater diversity of frames is better than a narrow range of perspectives in the news. In fact, these normative assumptions are stated rather explicitly in some of the seminal works cited in this chapter, and these assumptions have powerfully shaped the course of framing research. Indeed, such expectations are often part of the very reason for conducting news framing research, because to study framing (as Robert Entman argues in this volume) is to study *power*: the power to shape— and distort—public perceptions; the power to promote—or marginalize—competing perspectives on public problems; and the power, therefore, to promote or inhibit the political goals of various societal groups. Many framing studies, explicitly or implicitly, are grounded in normative concerns about how the power to frame is used.

John Zaller (2003) has argued that many studies of the news implicitly rest on an untenable assumption that the news should allow citizens "to develop opinions about the full range of important issues" and provide "a basis for these opinions independent of what government officials recommend" (p. 116). He labels this the "full news" standard. Zaller argues, in contrast, that scholars should not expect the news to provide more information than studies show the public, particularly the less-informed members of the public, can really monitor and digest. In place of the full news standard, Zaller suggests that scholars should apply a more realistic "burglar alarm" standard, one which stipulates that the news media will kick into high gear with full coverage and a diverse array of information only when some crisis or serious political problem warrants it. Outside of those situations, Zaller contends, informationally limited news is to be expected, and is normatively acceptable, given that most people most of the time do not actively study a wide range of political issues in the news. On this point, Zaller draws on Michael Schudson's (1998) notion of the "monitorial citizen," which states that most people give political matters limited attention unless and until a serious problem arises.

While Zaller is critiquing more than just framing studies per se, his argument generates an important question for scholars who study news framing: What standards should guide our normative evaluation of how political news is framed? While it is unlikely that all scholars will come to agree on a single normative standard of news quality, the debate over what constitutes "good news" can enrich our studies and make them more accessible and useful to the practitioners of journalism and politics that our studies so often end up criticizing.

Zaller's "burglar alarm" standard provides a good starting place for any such discussion about expectations of the public in a democratic society. According to Zaller, normative standards of news are often implicitly grounded in an expectation that an information-hungry citizenry looks to the news for its civic education—an expectation easily refuted by decades of research in cognitive psychology and news consumption patterns. Instead of an information-hungry public, research shows a public glutted with information, or at least with potential information sources, muddling through and "satisficing," making suboptimal use of the wealth of information already available in today's media environment—and only tuning in en masse whenever a sex scandal or a celebrity death dominates the airwaves (Graber, 1988, 2001; Popkin, 1994). In the face of these news habits and the economic incentives they create, he asks, why should we expect news to be like a college classroom, full of vigorous debate among a variety of perspectives? Zaller is correct that too often, framing studies seem strangely out of step with the actual news habits of the public. But does that render groundless the many framing studies that (usually implicitly) critique the news for inadequate or distorted news framing?

Not necessarily. Normative expectations of news have historically been grounded not in empirical insights about the actual news habits of the public, but rather in the theoretical needs of citizens in a democracy (as Zaller also recognizes; see also Porto, 2007). While these arguments about the need for more realistic news standards deserve careful attention, the fact is that normative news standards have developed and survived within American journalism and political culture in spite of the habitual behaviors of citizens—or of journalists, for that matter. In fact, strong normative ideals for journalism persist, in imagination if not always in practice, precisely because of the conviction in Western democratic theory that while the public may not always measure up to the demands of self-governance, they would certainly be unable to do so without a well-functioning independent press.

Fortunately, a useful starting place for the debate over news standards does not need to be constructed from scratch. Several ideals that still reign in journalism textbooks (if not always in the actual practice of daily journalism) offer useful standards for evaluating news framing.

Particularly noteworthy are the "watchdog" ideal, in which journalism serves as the eyes and ears of the public in defense of the public against manipulation and abuse by the powerful, and the "marketplace of ideas" ideal, in which the media serve as an arena for robust public debate (Bennett et al., 2007; Bennett & Serrin, 2005; Lawrence, 2005). Key to these ideals is the *independence* of the news media from any one power center. In theory, independent news media, which are committed to questioning and countering the persuasive efforts of government and other powers that be, serve these ideals by providing members of the public information and ideas from a variety of sources.

These ideals inform some recent efforts to develop normative news framing standards. Most noteworthy is Entman's effort to articulate a standard against which to judge how well the media have performed their inevitable task of framing foreign affairs. Entman argues:

> The media should provide enough information independent of the executive branch that citizens can construct their own counter-frames of issues and events. It is not enough for the media to present information in ill-digested and scattered morsels. Rather, what citizens need is a counterframe constructed of culturally resonant words and images, one that attains sufficient magnitude to gain wide understanding as a sensible alternative to the White House's interpretation. (2004, p. 17)

Bennett et al. (2007) applied Entman's standard to critique the one-sided framing of the Iraq invasion story, in which the Bush administration skillfully dominated the airwaves and the front pages of elite newspapers while questions about the necessity and wisdom of invading Iraq were marginalized. Arguably, such a standard is most needed when it is most difficult to achieve: when political actors and institutions are not performing the checking and balancing roles for which they were designed, and groupthink, conformity, and political calculation create a narrow elite consensus.

Noting that "we are still a long way from a coherent normative theory of journalism," Porto (2007) offers a more exacting "News Diversity" standard that "judges the performance of the news media in terms of the presentation of diverse interpretive frames" (p. 304). Porto's proposed standard is built upon the recognition that "privileged groups might shape citizens' environment in a way that prevents them from identifying issues that deserve their reaction" and that "in politics citizens are presented with an organized menu of choices, and that therefore their preferences depend on the organization of this menu" (p. 311). Therefore, he argues, "democratic theory's expectations must be understood in terms of citizens' ability to *interpret* political reality, as opposed to the demand of being well informed" (p. 312, emphasis added)—a goal that can only be met when the news regularly provides a range of perspectives on public issues, particularly marginalized perspectives from subordinate groups. This standard echoes the call by Herbert Gans (1979), one of the pioneers of news analysis, for "multi-perspectival" news that reflects a range of viewpoints rather than settling for a comfortable, narrow consensus.

Overall, these normative news standards envision political news that routinely offers a full range of competing frames, equally well-developed and prominently reported, in order to allow a variety of public voices to be heard, and to allow the public to weigh different perspectives and form independent conclusions. Such standards are certainly open to critique. Most importantly, it is not clear whether such expectations are in keeping with the nature of the U.S. media system, particularly in its commitment to "objectivity." The goal of producing "objective" news may (ironically) not be compatible with producing news that routinely constructs an alternative frame—or many alternative frames—on every political issue. With only limited time and resources, news organizations routinize objectivity by getting their stories and sound bites from the most powerful and available sources first, "balancing" the views of the leaders of one political party against those of the other (and thus "indexing" the news to those sources). Actively constructing a complete counterframe—or several—in the absence of powerful leaders pushing those frames would likely strike many American journalists as unprofessional, even as "crusading" journalism that the profession strongly discourages. Framing studies that measure the completeness and diversity of news frames against this kind of standard thus risk running head-long into a wall of resistance rooted in decades of journalistic training and practice.

So while these news standards (which I have articulated in my own research) may seem perfectly appropriate from the perspective of democratic theory, they are also problematic. Arguably, to produce this kind of ongoing frame battle in the news would be to ask mainstream journalists to adopt a new model of news altogether. That is one front on which further thought and debate amongst scholars is needed.

Whether standards proposed by Entman, Bennett, and Porto make sense will depend upon one's view of the state of representative democracy in the United States today. In a rather overlooked passage from Bennett's original work on the indexing hypothesis, he suggested that the indexing norm is not necessarily "bad" from a democratic perspective:

> Journalists may be conscious of indexing in another vocabulary entirely—the language of democracy. Government definitions of reality are supposed to be, after all, the best approximation of that

bedrock of political reality, responsible public opinion. If for some reason the voices of government are unrepresentative or irresponsible, does the responsibility to correct the problem lie with journalists or with people who elect governments in the first place? (Bennett, 1990, p. 109)

Bennett's question is in part rhetorical and is posed in order to illustrate a likely journalistic objection to critiques of their working norms. But the question is at the same time an important theoretical one that works on news framing have not always grappled with adequately. Indeed, it seems plausible that when political institutions are working to debate important policy issues and to check and balance one another as intended, then the news that results from the indexing dynamic may be "enough," democratically speaking, because it will faithfully reflect major viewpoints that presumably have significant electoral support. (As Jerit's [2006] study of news coverage of Social Security suggests, news closely indexed to official statements might actually be preferable in terms of the accuracy of information highlighted in the news.) In other words, while the daily news may not reach Porto's standard of frame diversity, it might at least satisfy a less exacting standard of quality *if* democratic institutions are functioning well. If one's view of those institutions is less than sanguine, one will more likely see the need for the media to proactively play the watchdog and marketplace of ideas roles—not simply to reflect what is already being said in the halls of Congress and the White House, but to host, even provoke, a wider-ranging public debate.

Meanwhile, a normative complication arises with regard to news framing of elections, the context in which news frames are likely to be, in a sense, the most "independent." The reigning assumption in much of the research in this area, buttressed by the findings of Cappella and Jamieson (1997), is that the game frame is not particularly informative and may evoke more cynicism than enlightenment. Indeed, Patterson and others have argued that while journalists focus on political strategy, most voters simply want to understand the issues (Fallows, 1997; Patterson, 1993; Rosen, 2008). Perhaps a starting point for this area of debate is to acknowledge that sometimes the game frame is entirely appropriate. After all, electoral politics *is* largely about strategy and attack, winning and losing, and news that did not inform the public about the candidates' political calculations would be guilty of some misrepresentation. In fact, it is interesting that the very skepticism that campaign reporters are often criticized for is lacking in the policy reporting that also comes in for scholarly criticism. Nevertheless, the game frame hardly seems to offer a principled independent stance on par with the "watchdog" ideal.

In covering elections as in covering foreign policy debates, journalists and scholars alike seem in need of clearer standards of performance. The intersection of empirical work on news framing and normative debates over the requirements of media in democracy constitutes an important new horizon for framing research.

## References

Aday, S. (2005). The real war will never get televised: An analysis of casualty imagery in American television coverage of the Iraq War. In P. Seib (Ed.), *Media and conflict in the 21st century* (pp. 141–156). Houndmills, England: Palgrave.

Althaus, S. L. (2003). When news norms collide, follow the lede: New evidence for press independence. *Political Communication, 20,* 381–414.

Baum, M. A. (2002). Sex, lies and war: How soft news brings foreign policy to the inattentive public. *American Political Science Review, 96,* 91–109.

Bennett, W. L. (1990). Toward a theory of press-state relations. *Journal of Communication, 40,* 103–125.

Bennett, W. L. (2007). *News: The politics of illusion* (7th ed.). New York: Longman.

Bennett, W. L., & Klockner, J. D. (1996). The psychology of mass-mediated publics. In A. N. Crigler (Ed.), *The psychology of political communication* (pp. 89–109). Ann Arbor: University of Michigan Press.

Bennett, W. L., Lawrence, R. G., & Livingston, S. (2007). *When the press fails: Political power and the news media from Iraq to Katrina.* Chicago: University of Chicago Press.

Bennett, W. L., & Livingston, S. (2003). A semi-independent press: Government control and journalistic autonomy in the political construction of news. *Political Communication, 20,* 359–362.

Bennett, W. L., & Serrin, W. (2005). The watchdog role. In G. Overholser & K. H. Jamieson (Eds.), *The press* (pp.169–188). New York: Oxford University Press.

Brewer, P., & Sigelman, L. (2002). Political scientists as color commentators: Framing and expert commentary in media campaign coverage. *Harvard International Journal of Press/Politics, 7,* 23–35.

Bucy, E. P., & D'Angelo, P. (1999). The crisis of political communication. In M. E. Roloff (Ed.), *Communication yearbook* (Vol. 22, pp. 301–339). Thousand Oaks, CA: Sage.

Callaghan, K., & Schnell, F. (2001). Assessing the democratic debate: How the news media frame elite policy discourse. *Political Communication, 18,* 183–213.

Cappella, J. N., & Jamieson, K. H. (1997). *Spiral of cynicism: The press and the public good.* Chicago: University of Chicago Press.

Center for Media and Public Affairs. (2004, November/December). Campaign 2004 Final. *Media Monitor,18.* Retrieved June 20, 2008 from http://www.cmpa.com/files/media_monitor/04novdec.pdf

Chong, D., & Druckman, J. N. (2007a). A theory of framing and opinion formation in competitive elite environments. *Journal of Communication, 57,* 99–118.

Chong, D., & Druckman, J. N. (2007b). Framing public opinion in competitive democracies. *American Political Science Review, 101,* 637–655.

D'Angelo, P. (2002). News framing as a multi-paradigmatic research program: A response to Entman. *Journal of Communication, 52*(4), 870–888.

Entman, R. M. (2004). *Projections of power: Framing news, public opinion, and U.S. foreign policy.* Chicago: University of Chicago Press.

Entman, R. M. (2006). Punctuating the homogeneity of institutionalized news: Abusing prisoners at Abu Ghraib versus killing civilians at Fallujah. *Political Communication, 23,* 215–224.

Fallows, J. (1997). *Breaking the news: How the media undermine American democracy.* New York: Vintage.

Frontline. 2007. *News War, Parts 1 & 2: Secrets, Sources and Spin.* Retrieved June 20, 2008, from http://www.pbs.org/wgbh/pages/frontline/newswar/part1/

Gamson, W. A., & Modigliani, A. (1989). Media discourse and public opinion on nuclear power: A constructionist approach. *American Journal of Sociology, 95,* 1–37.

Gans, H. (1979). *Deciding what's news.* New York: Pantheon.

Graber, D. (1988). *Processing the news: How people tame the information tide.* New York: Longman.

Graber, D. (2001). *Processing politics: Learning from television in the Internet age.* Chicago: University of Chicago Press.

Hallin, D. C. (1986). *The uncensored war: The media and Vietnam.* Berkeley: University of California Press.

Jacobs, L., & Shapiro, R. (2000). *Politicians don't pander.* Chicago: University of Chicago Press.

Jerit, J. (2006). Reform, rescue, or run out of money? Problem definition in the Social Security reform debate. *Harvard International Journal of Press/Politics, 11,* 9–28.

Jones, J. (2005). *Entertaining politics: New political television and civic culture.* Lanham, MD: Rowman & Littlefield.

Just, M. R., Crigler, A. N., Alger, D. E., & Cook, T. (1996). *Crosstalk: Citizens, candidates, and the media in a presidential campaign.* Chicago: University of Chicago Press.

Kovach, B., & Rosenstiel, T. (2001, January/February). Campaign lite: Why reporters won't tell us what we need to know. *Washington Monthly.* Retrieved March 15, 2008, from http://www.washingtonmonthly.com/features/2001/0101.kovach.rosenstiel.html

Kurtz, H. (2004, August 12). The Post on WMDs: An inside story; prewar articles questioning threat often didn't make front. *Washington Post,* A1.

Lawrence, R. G. (2000a.) Game-framing the issues: Tracking the strategy frame in public policy news. *Political Communication, 17,* 93–114.

Lawrence, R. G. (2000b.) *The politics of force: Media and the construction of police brutality.* Berkeley: University of California Press.

Lawrence, R. G. (2001). Defining events: Problem definition in the media arena.

In R. P. Hart & B. H. Sparrow (Eds.), *Politics, discourse, and American society* (pp. 91–110). Lanham, MD: Rowman & Littlefield.

Lawrence, R. G. (2005). Daily news and first amendment ideals. In T. Cook (Ed.), *Freeing the presses: The First Amendment in action* (pp. 87–108). Baton Rouge: Louisiana State University Press.

Lawrence, R. G., & Birkland, T. A. (2004). Guns, Hollywood, and criminal justice: Defining the school shootings problem across public arenas. *Social Science Quarterly, 85,* 1193–1207.

Livingston, S., & Bennett, W. L. (2003). Gatekeeping, indexing, and live-event news: Is technology altering the construction of news? *Political Communication 20,* 363–380.

Massing, M. (2004). *Now they tell us.* New York: New York Review of Books.

Mermin, J. (1999). Debating war and peace: Media coverage of U.S. intervention in the post-Vietnam era. Princeton, NJ: Princeton University Press.

Patterson, T. (1993). Out of order. New York: Vintage.

Popkin, S. (1994). *The reasoning voter: Communication and persuasion in presidential campaigns.* Chicago: University of Chicago Press.

Porto, M. (2007). Frame diversity and citizen competence: Towards a critical approach to news quality. *Critical Studies in Mass Communication, 24,* 303–321.

Pride, R. (1995). How activists and media frame social problems: Critical events versus performance trends for schools. *Political Communication, 12,* 5–26.

Rich, F. (2007). *The greatest story ever sold: The decline and fall of truth in Bush's America.* New York: Penguin.

Rosen, J. (2008). The beast without a brain: Why horserace journalism works for journalists and fails us. Retrieved March 17, 2008, from http://tomdispatch.com/post/174883/

Scheufele, D. A. (1999). Framing as a theory of media effects. *Journal of Communication, 49*(1), 103–122.

Schudson, M. (1998). *The good citizen.* New York: Free Press.

Sigal, L. V. (1973). *Reporters and officials: The organization and politics of newsmaking.* Lexington, MA: D.C. Heath.

Sparrow, B. H. (1999). *Uncertain guardians: The news media as a political institution.* Baltimore: Johns Hopkins University Press.

Tuchman, G. (1978). *Making news: A study in the construction of reality.* New York: Free Press.

Vinson, C. D., & Moore, W. V. (2007). The campaign disconnect: Media coverage of the 2000 South Carolina presidential primary. *Political Communication, 24,* 393–413.

Wolfsfeld, G. (1997). *Media and political conflict: News from the Middle East.* Cambridge, England: Cambridge University Press.

Zaller, J. (2003). A new standard of news quality: Burglar alarms for the monitorial citizen. *Political Communication, 20,* 109–130.

Zaller, J., & Chiu, D. (1996). Government's little helper: U.S. press coverage of foreign policy crises, 1945–1991. *Political Communication, 13,* 385–405.

Chapter 12

# Framing Analysis
# from a Rhetorical Perspective

*Jim A. Kuypers*

I was recently talking with one of my graduate students about framing analysis. When I mentioned *rhetorical* framing analysis, the student expressed surprise: she was unaware of such studies. I was not surprised by her response, but it did spark the desire to find out in more detail what was out there in our communication and political science journals. Armed with our library's Communication & Mass Communication Complete database in EBSCOhost, I did some informal investigating. I went away with the impression that since the mid-1990s the majority of framing research has derived from a social scientific orientation, with an especially noticeable surge of such work since 2003 (see also, Bryant & Miron, 2004). I see, however, something new brewing in conferences I've attended over the past few years. I have noticed an upswing in framing work derived from a quite different orientation. Increasingly I see qualitative, most notably rhetorical, framing work at conferences and, more slowly still, in print (e.g., Edwards, 2009; Kuypers & Cooper, 2005; Kuypers, Cooper, & Althouse, 2008; Ott & Aoki, 2002; Valenzano, 2009). If my observations have some degree of viability, and there is a domination of the social scientific orientation in framing research, how should those unfamiliar with more qualitative, and in particular, with rhetorical uses of framing research make sense of this rise in the popularity of framing in homes outside of the social sciences?[1] Additionally, I noted that one sees rhetoricians use framing studies generated from within the social sciences, but one finds a dearth of rhetorical studies cited in social scientific work. My own experiences (personal and second hand) of trying to get rhetorically based framing research published in journals dominated by a social scientific orientation suggests that rhetorical work in framing is dismissed out of hand by social scientists, even in journals clearly stating that they are open to all research methods.

So just how are social scientifically oriented reviewers to make sense of those rhetorically based studies as they wend their way from office computer, to conference presentation, to journal submission? I am inclined to believe one reason rhetorical work in framing is so easily ignored is because researchers trained in the social sciences are unfamiliar with what constitutes validity in a rhetorical study. I do not imply that one orientation is more worthwhile than the other, but that central questions and goals lead to the construction of different knowledge. Each orientation must be judged by the standards inherent to it. Just what are some of the main differences, and how does this lead to differences between social scientific and rhetorical framing analysis?

The bulk of framing analysis research is derived from a social scientific orientation; it is grounded in quantitative assumptions. Although often drawing upon social scientifically generated theoretical insights, framing analysis from a rhetorical orientation is firmly grounded in qualitative assumptions. These distinctions between quantitative and qualitative research are important to understand if we are to better use the framing research generated by both orientations.

If we push to extremes for the sake of discussion, we can make numerous generalizations concerning the nature of research from quantitative and qualitative orientations:

- Qualitative often focuses on the interpretation of something; quantitative often counts something, then statistically explains what was counted.
- Qualitative work often begins with vague questions, or even a hunch, guiding the inquiry; quantitative work usually begins with clearly articulated hypotheses subjected to testing.
- Qualitative work emphasizes the researcher or critic as the research tool; quantitative work places the researcher in the background, and uses equipment or surveys/questionnaires to collect data.
- Qualitative work incorporates the subjectivity of the researcher into the final product; quantitative work seeks to minimize this subjectivity.[2]

There are, of course, numerous exceptions to these distinctions. My purpose in highlighting the differences is twofold. First, I aim to suggest that tensions exist between the assumptions flowing from more hardcore quantitative and hardcore qualitative studies; and second, I aim to place rhetorical studies firmly into the qualitative side of these assumptions. How research projects are constructed, the type of knowledge generated, and even the very purpose of studies will differ greatly depending upon the orientation embraced. The purpose of this chapter is to highlight how a qualitative (i.e., a rhetorical) version of framing analysis works. Specifically, I will discuss the nature of rhetorical criticism, discuss framing analysis as a rhetorical perspective, and provide an overview of a rhetorically based framing study.

## Nature of Rhetorical Criticism

Framing theory and research, regardless of quantitative or qualitative origin, can be used fruitfully to guide rhetorical criticism. As I argue later in this chapter, framing research from a rhetorical perspective yields different knowledge than does framing research from a social scientific orientation. To better appreciate this difference, in this section I provide a brief overview of rhetoric and of criticism.

### Definition of Rhetoric

There are numerous definitions of rhetoric. Traditionally, much research focuses upon the pragmatic uses of rhetoric, and thus my definition reflects this aspect: *The strategic use of communication, oral or written, to achieve specifiable goals.* Two main ideas are highlighted here: the strategic, or intentional, nature of the language we use, and knowledge of the goals we wish to reach through the language we use.

Rhetoric may be viewed as strategic since it is intentional; that is, it is employed only when words can make a difference. Persons who are interested in influencing how their messages are received will plan ahead; they think ahead to the potential impact of their words. In this manner, they act to provide good reasons for their audiences to agree with them. In this sense, then, rhetoric is persuasive. It seeks to influence our personal and collective behaviors by having us voluntarily agree with the communicator that a certain value, action, or policy is better than another. As Bitzer (1968) wrote,

> Rhetoric is a mode of altering reality, not by the direct applica-
> tion of energy to objects, but by the creation of discourse which
> changes reality through the mediation of thought and action. The
> rhetor alters reality by bringing into existence a discourse of such
> a character that the audience, in thought and action, is so engaged
> that it becomes mediator of change. In this sense rhetoric is always
> persuasive. (p. 4)

This perspective leads us to a consideration of goals. On this point Kuypers and King (2005) stated,

> Since there is no scientific certainty to human affairs, that is, we do
> not know for certain which policy will produce the absolute best
> results, rhetoric attempts to persuade listeners that one policy will
> *probably* be better than another. It is in this sense, then, that rheto-
> ric is based upon probability—communicators try to convince us
> not that their proposed course of action is the only correct one, or

that it will work with guaranteed certainty, but rather that it *prob-ably* has a good chance of success. The trick for the person trying to persuade is to make certain that the level of probability is high enough to convince the particular audience being addressed. This is to say, that the audience will believe that a certain course of action will *probably* be better than another course of action. (p. 7)

In short, those using rhetoric think ahead about their goals so that they can better plan what they say to achieve the desired effect. Hauser (2002) put all of this in a slightly different manner when he stated that,

> Rhetoric, as an area of study, is concerned with how humans use symbols, especially language, to reach agreement that permits coor-dinated effort of some sort. In its most basic form, rhetorical commu-nication occurs whenever one person engages another in an exchange of symbols to accomplish some goal. It is not communication for communication's sake; rhetorical communication, at least implicitly and often explicitly, attempts to coordinate social action. (pp. 2–3)

Rhetoric therefore works at both the personal level and the public level. It involves the sharing of information, and both active and passive attempts at persuasion. Friends deciding on dinner use rhetoric, politi-cians giving stump speeches use rhetoric, and news writers use rhetoric. All are rhetorical acts. For Bazerman (1988), rhetoric is the study

> of how people use language and other symbols to realize human goals and carry out human activities. Rhetoric is ultimately a practi-cal study offering people greater control over their symbolic activ-ity. Rhetoric has at times been associated with limited techniques appropriate to specific tasks of political and forensic persuasion.... Consequently, people concerned with other tasks have considered rhetoric to offer inappropriate analyses and techniques. These peo-ple have then tended to believe mistakenly that their rejection of political and forensic rhetoric has removed their own activity from the larger realm of situated, purposeful, strategic symbolic activity. I make no such narrowing and use rhetoric...to refer to the study of all areas of symbolic activity. (p. 6)

We can enrich our understanding of rhetoric further if we pause to consider that it does not always have to be intentional for it to have a persuasive effect. As Burke (1951) noted, traditionally "the key term for...rhetoric was 'persuasion' and its stress was upon deliberate design. The key term for the 'new' rhetoric would be 'identification,' which can include a partially 'unconscious' factor in appeal" (p. 203). For example, a person might use symbols associated with wealth or class when writing news stories. Upon exposure to these symbols, a reader might identify with the nuances of wealth or class without being fully aware of doing so (Burke, 1950/1969). Quigley (1998) explained that,

> The need to identify arises out of division; humans are born and exist as biologically separate beings and therefore seek to identify, through communication, in order to overcome separateness. We are aware of this biological separation, and we recognize additional types of separation based on social class or position. We experience the ambiguity of being separate yet being identified with others at the same time.

Burke (1969) wrote that humans are "both joined and separate, at once a distinct substance and consubstantial with another" (p. 21). Burke was interested in the "processes by which we build social cohesion through our use of language. His goal [was] that we learn to perceive at what points we are using and abusing language to cloud our vision, create confusion, or justify various and ever present inclinations toward conflict, war and destruction—or our equally-present inclinations toward cooperation, peace and survival" (Quigley, 1998).

### Definition and Purpose of Criticism[3]

When critics analyze and interpret instances of rhetoric, we are allowing ourselves to take a closer, critical, look at these efforts—intentional or not—to persuade and influence. Criticism has many broad applications, but in general it is a humanistic activity. That is to say, it explores those qualities that make us human, and does so in a manner that involves self-expression. It falls center circle into the realm of qualitative work. As Andrews, Leff, and Terrill (1998) stated, criticism is "the systematic process of illuminating and evaluating products of human activity. [C]riticism presents and supports one possible interpretation and judgment. This interpretation, in turn, may become the basis for other interpretations and judgments" (p. 6).

There exist various reasons for performing criticism, but in general we perform criticism for two broad reasons: to promote greater appreciation and understanding. Simply put, we wish to enhance both our own and others' understanding of a rhetorical act; we wish to share our insights with others, which we hope will lead to an enhanced appreciation of the rhetorical act. Through understanding we also produce knowledge about human communication; in theory this could help us to better govern our interactions with others. On this point Brockriede (1974) wrote, "By 'criticism' I mean the act of evaluating or analyzing experience. A person can function as critic either by passing judgment on the experience or by analyzing it for the sake of a better understanding of that experience or of some more general concept of theory about such experiences" (p. 165).

### Criticism as Method

In its most basic form, a method may be understood as a particular manner or process for accomplishing a task. The researcher's task, both humanist and scientist, is to generate knowledge. How they go about this task—the methods they use—is quite different. The use of rhetoric is an art; as such, rhetoric does not lend itself well to scientific methods of analysis. Criticism is an art as well; as such, it is well suited for examining rhetorical creations. Nichols (1963) wrote that "humane" studies, of which the study of rhetoric fits prominently, are "concerned with the formation of judgment and choice" (p. 7). They teach us that "technical efficiency is not enough, that somewhere beyond that lies an area in which answers are not formulary and methods not routine" (p. 7). Beyond "the area of the formula," she continued, "lies an area where understanding, imagination, knowledge of alternatives, and a sense of purpose operate" (p. 7). That area is criticism.

Of course, various methods exist for studying phenomena that surround us, and these methods differ greatly in the amount of personality allowed to influence the results of the study. For example, in both the hard sciences and social sciences researchers purposefully adhere to a strict method (the scientific method). All researchers are to use this same basic method, and successful experiments are intended to be replicable by others. Generally speaking, the researcher's personality, likes and dislikes, religious and political preferences are supposed to be as far removed as possible from the actual study. Even the language employed to describe the results of their studies distance the researchers from the results of their studies. In scientific essays one normally finds a detached language use, with researchers forcing themselves into the background by highlighting the working of the study itself: "This study found...."

In sharp contrast, criticism (one of many humanistic methods of generating knowledge) actively involves the personality of the researcher. The personal qualities of the researcher heavily influence the very choices of what to study, how to study, and why to study a particular instance of rhetoric. In the sciences, the application of the scientific method may take numerous forms, but the overall method remains the same—and the personality of the researcher is excised from the study. In the humanities, methods of research may also take many forms—criticism and ethnography, for example—but the personality of the researcher is an integral component of the study.

Further personalizing criticism, we find that rhetorical critics use a variety of perspectives when examining a particular instance of rhetoric, with some critics even developing their own unique perspective.[4] Even the manner in which many critics express themselves in their writing brings the personal to the fore: critics write, "I found" instead of "This study found." "I argue" instead of "This study argues." This distinction was not lost on Black (1978), who wrote:

> Methods, then, admit of varying degrees of personality. And criticism, on the whole, is near the indeterminate, contingent, personal end of the methodological scale. In consequence of this placement, it is neither possible nor desirable for criticism to be fixed into a system, for critical techniques to be objectified, for critics to be interchangeable for purposes of [scientific] replication, or for rhetorical criticism to serve as the handmaiden of quasi-scientific theory. [The] idea is that critical method is too personally expressive to be systematized. (p. xi)

In short, criticism is not a science, but an art. It uses subjective methods of argument; it exists on its own, not in conjunction with other methods of generating knowledge (i.e., social scientific or scientific).

### Argumentative Nature of Criticism

When critics share their criticism with others, they do more than simply provide a detailed picture of their opinions. They instead share propositions with those who will be reading their work. Propositions are simply unsupported assertions, however, until critics provide a very basic step: giving supporting evidence with which to back up those assertions. In short, criticism is an argument. Smith (2000) argued that critics must hold themselves to "standards of argumentation" when writing criticism. Specifically, he believes that when we produce "criticism…we ought to confine ourselves to solid argumentation inclusive of valid arguments built on sufficient and high quality evidence produced from close textual readings and masterings of context" (n.p.). In short, critics must invite their audiences to agree with them. This is accomplished through stating their case and then providing evidence for the audience to accept or reject.

The main point to be remembered from this is that critics are trying to argue for a certain understanding of the rhetorical artifact. As Brockriede (1974) wrote,

> When a critic only appreciates the rhetoric or objects to it, without reporting any reason for his like or dislike, he puts his criticism near the nonargument end of the continuum. On the other hand, when an

evaluating critic states clearly the criteria he has used in arriving at his judgment, together with the philosophic or theoretic foundations on which they rest, and when he has offered some data to show that the rhetorical experience meets or fails to meet those criteria, then he has argued. (p. 167)

In this sense critics are actually using rhetoric to try to gain acceptance of their ideas. The best critics simply do not make a judgment without supplying good reasons for others to agree with them. On this point Brock, Scott, and Chesebro (1989) wrote,

[S]tatements of tastes and preference do not qualify as criticism. [Criticism is] an art of evaluating with knowledge and propriety. Criticism is a reason-giving activity; it not only posits a judgment, the judgment is explained, reasons are given for the judgment, and known information is marshaled to support the reasons for the judgment. (p. 13)

### Validity of Criticism

As one would expect, validity in criticism is different than validity in scientific work. According to Drislane and Parkinson (2002), scientific validity is one "of two criteria (the other being reliability) by which researchers judge their results or measurement tools. A valid result is one that accurately measures what it claims to be measuring" (p.1). Reliability, on the other hand, is associated with consistency of results over time. One could think of validity as linked with accuracy and reliability linked with consistency. This fits in well with science's twin goals of replication and prediction. However, the goals of criticism are appreciation and understanding; thus, what constitutes validity in criticism is different from what constitutes validity in the sciences. Critics look for how certain standards or criteria have been met. Criticism is an art, it is interpretive, it is creative, it is an argument. The best criticism allows for flexible application of a perspective, allowing for personal insight and interests to guide the criticism. The personality of the critic begins to blend with the perspective used. According to Leff (1980), "Interpretation is not a scientific endeavor. Systematic principles are useful in attempting to validate interpretations, but the actual process of interpretation depends on conjectures and insights particular to the [rhetorical act being analyzed]" (pp. 343–344).

Since it is both an artistic and argumentative enterprise, one that necessitates the interpretive powers of the critics to make it work, measures of successful criticism rely on different standards from those used in the sciences. Since its ruling metaphor is art, scientific standards of validity and reliability simply do not obtain. Instead, one looks to different criteria for judging the results of criticism. Foss (1983) suggested three presuppositions that can guide constructive criticism. First, and in sharp contrast to prevailing thought in the sciences, critics recognize that due to its symbolic nature, "data" cannot be verified objectively: "If knowledge of data is symbolic, the terminology the critic uses will yield various interpretations" (p. 284). Second, human beings have freedom of choice. Simply put, "Not only is there choice in rhetorical criticism of the framework used to describe the subjects of the study, but they are seen as having the freedom to choose their actions. Implicit in [this] is the assumption that humans are self-defining, initiating, flexible, capable of choosing alternative vocabularies with which to view the world, and thus diverse in interpretations and motive" (p. 287). Third, for some critics rhetorical criticism has a theory-building dimension: "When we approach our data, we bring to them our particular [perspective], a form that allows us to apprehend content of those data. Our knowledge of the content has the potential to cause us to revise the theory or form in light of our experience with the content" (p. 287).

Each of these presuppositions suggest criteria for adequate criticism, according to Foss (1983). First, if data cannot be objectively verified, then one must *justify* the choices made in the criticism: "The critic must be able to justify what he or she says, provide warranted assertibility [sic], offer reasons, or argue in support of his or her claims" (p. 289). This is, simply put, movement from "correspondence between the explanation and the data to a criterion that deals with the symbolic level at which we approach reality—choosing among alternative standards of justification" (p. 289). Second, freedom of choice in our symbol using activities suggests that the critic need acknowledge in some way the effects of this choice. Different choices available to a rhetor could be pointed out, for instance. Or, the critic could "allow the rhetors being studied to express themselves in their own terminology and context as fully as possible" (p. 291). Another way of looking at this is to suggest that if the "critic truly sees the individual as having choice, then he or she will not present his or her claims as being the truth about reality, but rather as one way of describing the data. Third, when looking at the theoretical aspects of criticism, one must look for a coherent presentation of the theoretical framework or perspective used. This includes both internal aspects (how the rhetorical artifact is described) and external aspects (the form or theory itself). Fourth, and also related to theory, criticism should be able to incorporate other perspectives. By this I mean that the rhetoric that the critic examines should "be presented as more than raw data; the critic should see them as generalizable to a theory of some sort or meaningful within another metaphor or perspective" (p. 294). In short, how can examination of the rhetorical artifact help to enlarge our understanding of the perspective/theory being used?

Although Foss (1983) offers a starting point for evaluating the products of criticism, there still exist numerous critical touchstones used by critics in evaluating their work. As both art and argument, judgment of criticism's validity must draw upon standards for assessing both aesthetic and argumentative dimensions. In the end, criticism is about passing judgment on the rhetorical artifact, and in doing so critics touch three areas that interanimate the aesthetic and the argumentative: objectivity, discernment, and logical integrity.

In 2001 I offered what I considered a reasoned definition of objectivity in the realm of rhetorical criticism. Quoting at length:

> When I use the term "objective," I do not mean that critics ought to possess or are capable of possessing a scientific detachment from the object of criticism. This would surely produce a sterile criticism devoid of its lifeblood: the critic's intermingled intuition, insight, and personality. What I am suggesting is that the critic may approach the artifact under consideration with a fair and open mind. In this sense the critic sets aside personal politics or ideological "truths" and approaches the artifact with a sense of curiosity. The artifact under consideration ought not to be altered to fit the prejudgments of the critic, but be allowed to voice its inner workings to the world. The work of the critic is to make certain that this voice is intelligible to and approachable by the public.
>
> This in no way detracts from the critic bringing to bear an individual stamp upon the criticism produced. Nor is it the antiseptic application of a method upon an unsuspecting rhetorical artifact. What it does suggest is that the critic must learn how to appreciate the inner workings of a text, even if personally the critic finds that text to be repugnant, or wishes it to be other than it is. In this sense, the critic is being "objective," or disinterested, when approaching and describing a text.

Discernment is usually taken to mean judging well the workings of the rhetorical artifact under consideration. On this point I also wrote that,

> Judgments may certainly be made, and appreciation or disdain expressed, but they must be made *after* two conditions are met: one, the fair minded description of the inner workings of the artifact have been presented for the world to see; and two, the *standards* of judgments used by the critic are provided for all to see. In this way readers may themselves judge whether or not the critic imposed his ideology upon the artifact. (2001).

In addition to judgments, discernment also includes how well the critic is able to provide insights about the rhetorical artifact under consideration. Consumers of criticism should ask, What has been learned? What is new here? Perceptive critics are the engines that drive a rhetorical study, which is a far cry from social scientific orientations in which the method itself drives the study. From a critical point of view, it is the critic's intermingled intuition and insight that produces the interesting study.

Logical integrity involves the principles of sound argumentation. In its simplest form one could say a sound argument takes the structure of stating one's case and then proving it. In short, an assertion followed with evidence. Deceptively simple, there are numerous questions that need to be asked in judging the integrity: Does the case laid out make sense? Is it sufficiently grounded in previous research? Does it lay out an objective context (when necessary) to make the argument? Does the evidence connect with the claims of the author? Logical integrity involves clearly laying out the links between evidence and claims. With a logical essay, another scholar should be able to look at the same rhetorical text and see exactly how the author made the claims he or she did based on the textual evidence. They do not necessarily have to agree with the claims, or the conclusions, but they should see them as reasonable. I think the best criticism proves itself as the most useful in understanding the nature and value of the rhetorical artifact it seeks to consider. Insightful criticism generally allows us to see an instance of rhetoric from more than one open-minded perspective.

### Construction of Critical Lens or Perspective

The main method for obtaining data in science is the scientific method. Humanistic studies have numerous methods for obtaining "data," criticism being one well suited to the study of rhetoric. I put the word *data* in quotation marks since critics rarely use the term. Criticism produces insight and new ways of seeing and understanding our world; it is, at its best, an artistic expression. An artist painting a picture does not produce data; neither does a critic. Just as an artist may paint in numerous styles, a critic has numerous options on how to proceed. One common avenue for performing criticism involves the use of different *perspectives* on criticism. Because a rhetorical act is a multidimensional, complex, and nuanced event, there exists no one best way of viewing it. Moreover, no one effort to describe or evaluate it will yield all the knowledge that there is to know about that artifact. With this in mind, criticism usually takes its structure from a particular perspective. Simply put, a critical perspective serves as a frame of reference for the critic; it guides the apprehension of and interaction with the rhetorical act being analyzed.

Different perspectives allow critics to see different aspects of the rhetorical act. For instance, a perspective grounded in the theory of narrative will orient the critic to narrative elements; a perspective grounded in the theory of framing will orient the critic to framing elements. When a perspective is adopted, it allows critics to see an artifact differently than if no perspective was adopted. In a sense, the critic is allowed to see the world in a particular way.

The best criticism does not use perspectives as formulas. Although they do suggest a particular way of viewing the world, it is the critic who directs the criticism. As Black (1965) wrote:

> It is inevitable that any expositor will approach a work from a certain point of view. His frame of reference may be subconscious and unsystematized, but it will assuredly be present, shaping the bias of his interpretation by influencing the direction of his attention, selectively sharpening some and sullying others of his sensibilities, and molding the nuances of his judgment in a thousand imperceptible ways. (p. 68)

Regardless of the perspective chosen, a critic must be cautious in its application. Perspectives are to help a critic, not direct the criticism; a successful critic's ideas blend in with those of the perspective. Black (1978) put this idea and its consequences in proper perspective:

> Because only the critic is the instrument of criticism, the critic's relationship to other instruments will profoundly affect the value of critical inquiry. And in criticism, every instrument has to be assimilated to the critic, to have become an integral part of the critic's mode of perception. A critic who is influenced by, for example, [Burkean Dramatism] and who, in consequence of that influence, comes to see some things in a characteristically dramatistic way—that critic is still able to function in his own person as the critical instrument, and so the possibility of significant disclosure remains open to him. But the would-be critic who has not internalized [Dramatism], who undertakes to "use" it as a mathematician would use a formula— such a critic is certain (yes, certain!) to produce work that is sterile. An act of criticism conducted on mechanistic assumptions will, not surprisingly, yield mechanistic criticism. (p. 21)

Another area of difference with criticism and social science research is how the data and analysis are summed up. Criticism involves evaluation, and the evaluation of the rhetorical act boils down to the judgments the critic makes about it. The types of judgments made will differ depending upon the type of perspective used and also upon the critic's personality.

## Framing Analysis as a Rhetorical Perspective

A rhetorical version of framing analysis falls within what D'Angelo (2002) described as the critical paradigm. Entman (2007) suggested that framing research in the critical paradigm can also look into "news media interventions in the day-to-day contests to control government power *within* the snug ideological confines of mainstream American politics." He added, "These set the boundaries for public discourse on most government policies" (p. 170). This follows the case I have made since 1997, that framing analysis can fruitfully be used to detect bias in news media reports that induce an audience to interpret political news in a media supported direction (Kuypers, 1997, 2002, 2006). Many researchers operating within the critical paradigm suggest that news frames are actually the "outcome of newsgathering routines by which journalists convey information about issues and events from the perspective of values held by political and economic elites" and that these frames act to "dominate news coverage" (D'Angelo, 2002, p. 876). Denton and Kuypers (2008) wrote that some "researchers have even found that the press inserts its own political perspective into its framing process. Ultimately, though, those operating from within this paradigm look for how news frames act to affect the political consciousness of news audiences" (pp. 117–118). This is so, according to D' Angelo, because frames "that paradigmatically dominate news are also believed to dominate audiences" (p. 876). A critic operating from this perspective would be asking: How do language choices invite us to understand an issue or event?

So, what might framing look like from a rhetorical perspective? Critics using this perspective need not use the same elements as others, or use the same exactly constructed perspective each time. The critic must, however, in academic criticism, share with others how the perspective will guide the criticism. It is not so much about constructing a perspective with which everyone will agree as it is constructing a perspective so that others will understand how the criticism was guided. A rhetorical perspective on framing analysis could take several forms. The one I share below is constructed to emphasize the meaning shaping nature of frames, and to suggest ways in which frames can be detected. A rhetorical version of framing analysis can operate in many different ways. In my own work (1997, 2002, 2006; Cooper & Kuypers, 2005; Kuypers, Cooper, & Althouse, 2008), I have developed an approach that begins inductively by looking for themes that reside within news narratives across time and then determining how those themes are framed.

### Agenda-Extension

It is well known that news media provide contextual cues "by which to evaluate the subject matter" under consideration (Trent & Friedenburg,

2008, p. 142). Although the news media must provide a proper context in which to understand the news, reporting the news so a *press-supported context* is produced moves beyond agenda-setting and involves the influencing of public opinion. This extra dimension of press reporting is called *agenda-extension* by some researchers; it is the process whereby news stories and editorials act to shape our awareness, understanding, and evaluations of issues and events in a particular direction (Denton & Kuypers; Kuypers, 1997, 2002, 2006; Kuypers & Cooper, 2005; Valenzano, 2009). As D'Angelo (2002) noted, "Framing shapes public dialogues about political processes" (p. 874). Thus, looking for frames in news media narrative may help us to better understand these dialogues.

This is not the same as studies that posit that the media can focus public attention on particular attributes within an event or issue—second level agenda-setting. An understanding of second level effects allows us to see how the news media can elevate one attribute over another in the mind of the public. Since a particular attribute on an issue would be in the forefront, it seems likely that the public would use that particular attribute to evaluate a politician's actions. The public becomes primed to evaluate political actors by how well they handle the particular attributes of an issue covered by the news media. The more the news media cover that particular issue, the more the public will evaluate the political actors' actions in relation to the content of media coverage.

Agenda-extension begins when media gatekeepers—station managers, producers, or editors—decide to publish a particular story, decide how much attention to give the story, and then decide how to *tell* a particular story. As Graber (2005) pointed out, it is at this "point where ordinary agenda-setting activities can most readily turn into deliberate agenda-building [agenda-extension]" (p. 288). On this matter Callaghan and Schnell (2001) stated: "Beyond agenda setting...the media have the power to actively shape public discourse by selecting from many available frames offered by interest groups and politicians. Further... media professionals are free to create and emphasize their own [framing] on issues..." (p. 203). Furthering this observation, D'Angelo (2002) noted that, "Critical scholars argue that news organizations select some information and intentionally omit other information such that different frames of a topic either will not exist or will still foster a single viewpoint supportive of the status quo [or the ideological assumptions of the news organization]" (p. 876).

The news media can so focus on an issue that it takes center stage on the nation's attention stage. A classic example of this is explained by G. E. Lang and K. Lang (1984), who found that the national news coverage of Watergate was first framed as part of the 1972 election campaign. After a few weeks of coverage, however, the news media switched to a new frame, that of a never-ending stream of Washington corruption. It is at this point that the notion of agenda-extension moves beyond second level agenda-setting in that it posits that the media not only focuses attention on particular attributes of an issue, making some portions more salient than others, it does so in such a manner that a particular point of view is advanced. More to the point, second level agenda-setting examines *what* attributes are stressed, whereas agenda-extension asks *how* those attributes are stressed to influence audience reaction. A rhetorical version of framing analysis can be used to explore how agenda-extension works. Framing involves how the press organizes the context through which the public will view news. At its heart, this is a rhetorical process, and to this aspect of framing I now turn.

### Defining Frames

The power of frames subtly induces us to filter our perceptions of the world in particular ways; they make some aspects of our reality more noticeable than other aspects. In a sense, the *saliency* of some information is increased over others; frames "highlight some features of reality while omitting others" (Entman, 1993, p. 53). Because our attention is highly selective, we do not often notice this process. Instead, we rely upon information that, in whatever form, is most easily accessible to us. Gamson (1989) asserted that a "frame is a central organizing idea for making sense of relevant events and suggesting what is at issue" (p. 157). He stressed that facts "take on their meaning by being embedded in a frame or story line that organizes them and gives them coherence, selecting certain ones to emphasize while ignoring others" (p. 157). Framing, then, is the process whereby communicators act—consciously or not—to construct a particular point of view that encourages the facts of a given situation to be viewed in a particular manner, with some facts made more noticeable than others.

Similar to much of the social scientific literature, a rhetorical version of framing analysis begins with the assumption that frames induce us to view issues and situations in a particular way. There are numerous studies that demonstrate this. For example, Sniderman, Brody, and Tetlock (1991) used mandatory testing for HIV as the controlled frame for one of their studies. They found that the effect "of framing is to prime values differentially, establishing the salience of the one or the other. [A] majority of the public supports the rights of persons with AIDS when the issue is framed to accentuate civil liberties considerations—and supports... mandatory testing when the issue is framed to accentuate public health considerations" (p. 52). Nelson, Clawson, and Oxley (1997) used a local news story about a Ku Klux Klan march as their controlled frame. The researchers presented audiences with either one of two videotaped stories. The first story stressed a free speech frame—Klan members and protesters wanting to share their respective messages. The second story stressed a disruption of public order frame—Klan marches were shown as disorderly and potentially violent. The researchers concluded that, "Participants who viewed the free speech story expressed more tolerance for the Klan than those participants who watched the public order story" (p. 567). Ott and Aoki (2002) enlarged our understanding of framing analysis by incorporating the work on "terministic screens" birthed by Kenneth Burke. These researchers looked at print media coverage of the Matthew Shepard murder. They found that the news media imposed a "tragic" frame on the event, which emphasized a scapegoating process. This "functioned rhetorically," they believed, "to alleviate the public's guilt concerning anti-gay hate crimes and to excuse the public of any social responsibility" (p. 483). Callaghan and Schnell (2001) suggested: "[T]he media are not simply intermediaries between political actors and the mass public. Journalists can actively limit the public's right to access and evaluate different policy platforms and thus diminish the quality of political dialogue. Such actions have the potential to inhibit pluralism by blocking out the preferred themes of interest groups and politicians" (p. 203).

When highlighting some aspect of reality over other aspects, frames act to define problems, diagnose causes, make moral judgments, and suggest remedies. They are located in the communicator, the text, the receiver, and the culture at large. It is important to note that they are a natural and normal part of the communication process. We need ways to make sense of the enormous amounts of information that comes to us everyday. Frames thus act as central organizing ideas within a narrative account of issues or events; they provide the interpretive cues for otherwise neutral facts. When considering news narratives, "frames reside in the specific properties of the news narrative that encourage those perceiving and thinking about events to develop particular understandings of them" (Entman, 1991, p. 7). Frames can be detected by looking for specific properties within news narratives: key words, metaphors, concepts, symbols, visual images, and names given to persons, ideas, and actions. These will consistently appear within a narrative and "convey thematically consonant meanings across...time" (Entman, 1991, p. 7). Especially when comparatively examining the news accounts of different events, it is apparent that framing makes some ideas in news stories more salient than others, while making some ideas virtually invisible to an audience. Framing begins when editors decide to publish a particular story, and through time, frames develop that guide the creation of each successive story. Frames impose a specific interpretation onto events; they also often obscure contrary information that may be presented in a particular case: "for those stories in which a single frame thoroughly pervades the text," wrote Entman (1991), "stray contrary opinions...are likely to possess such low salience as to be of little practical use to most audience members" (p. 21).

## A Rhetorical Example

What does a rhetorical framing study look like? To answer this question I review a recent large scale framing study I authored: *Bush's War: Media Bias and Justifications for War in a Terrorist Age*. In this study I investigated how the mainstream news media relayed to the public what President Bush said about the War on Terror. It is a comparative analysis in that it compares the content of the president's speeches to the content of the reporting about those speeches. My central questions were, What did Bush say, and what did the press say he said? I examined important speeches given by President Bush between September 11, 2001 and November 2005. For comparative purposes, I looked at all reports concerning each of the President's speeches found in *The New York Times, The Washington Post, USA Today, ABC News, CBS News,* and *NBC News*. The general flow of the analysis was to first look for any themes that the president stressed in his speeches, and then to see how he framed those themes. A theme is the subject of discussion, or that which is the subject of the thought expressed. The frame, of course, is suggesting a particular interpretation of the theme. I then repeated this same process with the news reports and articles, looking for what themes the press highlighted and how they framed those themes. Since the press reports usually spread out over several weeks, this analysis also allowed for discovery of how themes and frames develop over time. There were no preestablished themes or frames. Instead, I engaged in a close textual reading to determine what the Bush and news texts *offered* as themes and frames.

So, for instance, reading one of Bush's speeches might yield several different themes: "good versus evil," "patience," "the economy." After determining these, I returned to the texts and looked for key words, phrases, concepts, and labels that shed light on how these themes were framed; that is, how did the president wish for the themes to be understood? This process was then repeated for each news article and broadcast. I looked for themes repeated over time, and then for evidence of how those themes were framed over time as well. As Levin (2005) wrote, "The reason themes [are] taken as a measure of the presence of frames [is] the difficulty of finding a completely developed frame in a single press release. [Frames] are built across a series of news media articles, and not all elements are present in any single article" (p. 89).[5]

What I found was that the news media echoed the president's themes and the framing of those themes *immediately* following 9/11.[6] Themes such as the "nature of the enemy" and "safety" were reported, and the way the president framed these themes was relayed as well. Echoing does not mean that alternative points of views were not presented—they were. The press was not uncritical during this period; both critics and oppositional points of view were presented. However, the press did not interject its *own point of view* into the hard news coverage; instead it reported what the president said (both the themes and the framing of those themes) and what others said about the president's speeches (compliments, criticisms, and alternate interpretations). Just 8 weeks later, however, the president spoke to the United Nations. By this time the press had changed its manner of reporting, and was actually framing Bush as an enemy of civil liberties. Important to this time period, the press was also ignoring several major themes relayed by President Bush: themes such as "good versus evil" and "civilization versus barbarism," important elements of the president's speech and reasoning, were not relayed by the press. Those themes that were relayed, "nature of the war" and the "economy" were framed in such a way that the president's original meaning was lost. As each year passed, this oppositional framing continued and increased. Additionally, much research in framing suggests a single, pervasive frame that dominates a news story. My work here contraindicates this, in part because the response of the news media was examined over a period of time, thereby allowing for a more nuanced look at the total response. Although the strength of frames have been examined in other studies, the idea of a frame being composed of themes—each of which is individually framed—has yet to be examined fully.

The results of this study demonstrate the insight-producing power of a rhetorical version of framing analysis. Numerous studies of the period following 9/11 argue that the news media relayed uncritically the assertions of the president, and that this uncritical passing of information on to the American public facilitated our war with Iraq; for example, Bennett, Lawrence, and Livingston (2007), Jamieson and Waldman (2004), Waldman (2004). As a specific example, Coe, Domke, Graham, John, and Pickard (2004) looked at 15 speeches by President Bush delivered between January 2001 and March 2003 (start of Iraq war). They looked for predetermined binary opposites: good/evil and security/peril. They next looked at editorials published in 20 U.S. newspapers within 2 days from each address. They found that both the speeches and the editorials contained references to these binaries. Because of this, they reasoned, the news media "echoed" the words of the president. This "echoing," they suggested, acted to provide him with unprecedented public support: "it seems highly likely that the press, through consistent amplification of the president's communications, contributed to the president's remarkable successes with Congress between September 11 and the Iraq War and to the Republican Party's 2002 election triumph..." (pp. 248–249).

From a rhetorical point of view, however, Coe et al. found only *content*. They did not analyze or interpret the *context* in which the binaries were found; indeed, the scientific method does not allow for such interpretive judgments. They mistook the presence of *themes* as evidence of a particular *frame*. What is left out of many of the studies suggesting a permissive press is information on *how* the discovered themes are framed. The news media may well relay what the president says, but it does not necessarily follow that the president's framing of those themes is accurately conveyed prior to the press offering commentary or criticism from themselves or others. Thus we often find the echo of the *theme*, but not of the *frame*.[7]

Thus a rhetorical version of framing analysis found that the press actively contested the framing of the War on Terror as early as 8 weeks following 9/11. This complicates other literature that suggests a news media that supported the president in his efforts after 9/11. How is this reconciled? I found that the press framed its response in such a way that it could be seen supporting the *idea* of the War on Terror, but actively opposing the initiatives of the president. For example, Jamieson and Waldman (2004) suggested the news media echoed the Bush administration following 9/11. These researchers argued that prior to 9/11, the news media framed President Bush as "unqualified," inexperienced," and "not too bright"; following 9/11, they argued, the news media switched to framing him as a "strong leader" and as a "unifier." Although these researchers hint that the press slowly became more circumspect, their analysis focuses on the immediate time after 9/11. The point remains regardless—they focused on *what* was said, not on *how* it was said. In a separate work, Waldman (2004) asserted that President Bush "lies," and stated that the mainstream media were unquestioning in their treatment of Bush following 9/11, essentially failing to criticize his policies at all. Entman (2003) suggested that a sense of "general cooperation… characterize[d] media responses to the Bush administration after 9/11" (p. 424). Additionally, Entman suggested that the news media only challenged the president in "limited ways," and that "news organizations' resistance to the Bush frame" showed "weakness" (p. 424).

Complicating the findings of the studies above is the evidence I found that suggests news framing which supports the *idea* of the War on Terror, but actively opposes the initiatives of the president. What is left out of such studies as that above is information on *how* themes are framed, and an awareness of how the presentation of both themes and the framing of those themes subtly shifted following the invasion of Afghanistan. So, for the first 4 to 5 weeks, we did see a news media that relayed what the president said. However, by 8 weeks, it did not necessarily follow that it was framed in the same manner; thus, an echo of the *theme*, but not of the *frame*.

The rhetorical study, focusing on individual texts for the generation of themes and frames, was able to detect how some themes were used by both president and press, and then how the press stopped using particular themes. It was also able to determine how those themes were framed, thus producing strikingly different conclusions about the nature of press coverage during the years following 9/11. My study, *Bush's War*, demonstrated that shortly after 9/11 the news media were beginning to actively counter the Bush administration and beginning to leave out information important to understanding the Bush administration's conception of the War on Terror.

## Summary

By way of summary I will share how various receptions of my book suggest judgments from either a social scientific or rhetorical orientation and how these differences in approach can limit scholarly understanding. Since most of the responses to the book are directly linked with the standards of judgments used by the reviewers, we can look for moments of judgment in reviews to backtrack to the standards used. Of great interest to me is that those looking at the study using social scientific standards have offered negative assessments, whereas those using rhetorical standards have offered positive assessments.

For example, Niven (2008) offered several hints that he is operating from a social scientific orientation when he assessed my book. One such hint is derived from his charge that I never operationalized the term *media bias* (p. 223). Yes, from a social scientific orientation I never "operationalized" the term (something critics do not do). Instead, I specifically discuss the concept of fair, objective reporting (Kuypers, 2006, pp. 10–12), and I use the news media's own words to describe their ideals for reportorial practice (Kuypers, 2006, pp. 136–139). The concluding chapter compares the actual reportorial practices of the news agencies covered in the study with the reportorial ideals established by these same news agencies. The entire book project is a discussion aimed at understanding bias based on norms provided by the news media itself. I brought with me no a priori assumptions on what would constitute a particular example of bias. Thus, I never set out to look for a particular type of bias; rather, through a comparative analysis, I used the news media's self-reported norms for objective reporting and then compared that to the actual coverage. The nature of the bias could not be predetermined and defined, since the nature of the study was to determine the nature of any bias if bias was actually operating: "Through this comparative analysis, we can detect differences in the frames presented to the American people and determine the nature of any press bias" (Kuypers, 2006, p. 15). The entire conclusion is a discussion of how this works and what was found. To have "operationalized" bias would have been to establish an a priori category for bias, thus artificially narrowing the scope of what might actually have been perceived as operating as bias.

Another hint at the social scientific orientation of the reviewer is the use of the term "data." The reviewer makes the claim that in "all but a few cases there are no data whatsoever in his chapters. Without data, or an underlying coding scheme, he nevertheless is able to make declarations…" (Niven, 2008, p. 223). Yes, from a social science orientation I offered no statistical "data." Instead, each chapter is a case study, filled with quotations from both the president and the press. Each chapter consists of perhaps hundreds of these quotes that are offered as direct evidence to support later claims: Thus the repeated format—assertion-evidence—found throughout the book. There are no numbers, no "data"; from a social scientific orientation this is surely a deathblow. But from a rhetorical perspective, viewed as an argument, the form of assertion-evidence is valid scholarship.

The use of the term *coding scheme* in the above example is another hint at the social scientific orientation of the reviewer. A coding scheme suggests that the reviewer was looking at the study as a content analysis, and as such it would need preestablished and well defined codes for the listing of content units. These schemata would then be used to code the various speeches and press reports. To engage in a content analysis without this would be, again, a deathblow to the study. However, the book is a critical, rhetorical work, not a social scientific essay. There was no "coding scheme" but, rather, an act of criticism guided by a rhetorical perspective. There is no "data" and no "coding scheme" because the type of study involved, criticism, does not use them. Themes were discovered, not a priori, but through close textual analysis; frames were discovered in the same manner.

As a final hint at the reviewer's social scientific orientation, consider the charge made that because articles were not randomly selected that "Kuypers selected for analysis articles that supported the conclusion he, apparently, had already made. Kuypers has rigged the game with a textbook case of selection bias" (Niven, 2008, p. 223). The selection process is explained in the book, and reflects a rhetorical effort:

> In the weeks leading up to the military action against Afghanistan, over one thousand articles were published in the above papers and over 600 news broadcasts were aired; I did not read them all. Instead the focus was upon articles and broadcasts following speeches given by President Bush, and also upon articles that reflected best what I saw as the general thrust of press reporting. These reports are the ones whose purpose was to relay the words of the President. (Kuypers, 2006, p. 171)

That last sentence contextualizes the entire procedure. The reviewer makes it seem as if I cherry-picked articles, yet in the example mentioned above, I actually used all available articles that focused on President Bush's speeches. So, positive or negative, if the press reported Bush's words, they were included. In the other chapters I also used all available articles/broadcasts containing references to the speech being analyzed.

When reviewers looked at the study as a rhetorical effort, the comments were quite different. For example, S. Farnsworth (2007) recognized that the study was a "close textual analysis" that allowed "for the richness of detail found via the case study method" (p. 783). Moreover, recognizing the discussion oriented nature of a qualitative study, Farnsworth wrote that the book is "written in a lively, accessible style that can generate thoughtful undergraduate discussion in classes on rhetoric, the presidency, and the news media" (p. 782). Another important hint that Farnsworth views the study as a rhetorical effort: he noted that I could have linked my

> findings more extensively to content analysis studies that examined...news coverage of the White House. Although academic studies based on content analysis sometimes lack the fascinating detail found in case studies, a discussion that combines the richness of the qualitative and the comprehensiveness of the quantitative can produce an even more convincing examination of the differences between what the president actually said and what the media report the president said. (p. 783)

Braden (2007) also implied a rhetorical understanding of my study, in particular focusing on the argumentative nature of such rhetorical studies:

> Kuypers' analysis offers conclusions different from what much of the work surrounding news coverage of 9/11 suggests: that the news media aided President Bush to the point of war by echoing his every word. What Kuypers argues is that as one moves chronologically further from 9/11, the news media became more opinionated and more contentious: one even might argue they became irresponsible. Although one may disagree with the assessment, all the evidence is provided. Kuypers offers a well-developed argument worthy of debate. (p. 426)

Braden also picks up on the invitation to discussion: having used my book in a communication course, he wrote that students "discuss[ed] the excerpts in detail." He added that, "I [Braden] was delighted to discover that my students not only understood Kuypers' arguments, but that they argued for the importance of this research" (p. 423). Later he wrote that while "reading this book I felt the scholarly obligation to refute Kuypers' research.... H[is] arguments are clear and cogent" (p. 424).

I am of the opinion that framing analysis is a rich area of research, one particularly suited to both rhetorical and social scientific inquiry. I have argued in this chapter that qualitative and quantitative oriented research can be quite different, but there exist also areas of overlap. Whereas the hard sciences and statistically grounded studies most readily fall into the quantitative area, there are some quantitative studies that approach or even spill into qualitative areas. Certain mainly quantitative content analyses that employ an inductive approach come readily to mind. However, interpretive commentary and contextualization further move content analysis into the realm of the qualitative. At the far end of this qualitative realm we find rhetorical criticism, so even those social scientific studies with qualitative influences will be remarkably different from rhetorical studies. That has been one of the points of this chapter.

I have pointed out that studies that come from a rhetorical orientation have quite different methodological assumptions than social scientific studies. This does not mean knowledge produced from one orientation is better than the other, only that different knowledge will be produced. The epistemological dimensions should be further explored, definitely, but with an aim toward better understanding how each adds to our fund of knowledge about communication. Additionally, judgments about these different types of studies should be made based not on the methodological preference of the judge, but rather upon the standards of validity inherent to each type of study. Just as it is absurd to judge a social scientific study based on rhetorical norms, it is equally absurd to judge rhetorical work based on social scientific standards. The real strength of rhetorical framing studies is that they allow the researcher to move from a more descriptive notion of framing research to a fully critical and interpretive endeavor. Thus, questions can easily move beyond what was said or what frame exists to how something was said or how something was framed. It is my hope that this chapter lends a greater understanding of rhetorical work and how it fits into framing research. Looked at from a broad perspective, framing analysis can provide a safe place for the interaction of rhetorical and social scientific work. And that is an encouraging thought.

## Notes

1. This is not to say that some research deriving from a social scientific orientation does not incorporate qualitative assumptions. As my coeditor and I discussed privately, qualitative work encompasses more than just rhetorical work. It can also include (a) measures that use words rather than

numbers to gather and analyze data; (b) methods that rely more on field work (e.g., ethnography, interviews, or focus groups) rather than those that mainly, but not exclusively, employ quantitative techniques to measure concepts and create samples; and (c) paradigmatic approaches that tell researchers to think about doing (a) and (b) in humanistic rather than scientific terms. Regardless, all three qualitative aspects rely more on scientific assumptions than with humanistic interpretive assumptions, which is something with which the remainder of this chapter is concerned.

2.  For additional sources for information about these distinctions see: http://www.gifted.uconn.edu/siegle/research/Qualitative/qualquan.htm
3.  This section on criticism is in part derived from my chapter, entitled "The Art of Criticism," in Kuypers (2005, see pp. 13–26). Used with permission.
4.  For examples, see Kuypers (2009).
5.  This argument is also made by Kuypers in *Bush's War.*
6.  Some social scientific based studies of the period find commensurate results—see, e.g., Ryan (2004).
7.  This summary of *Bush's War* is found in part in my chapter, "Framing Analysis," in J. A. Kuypers (2009) (Ed.), *Rhetorical criticism: Perspectives in action.* Used with permission.

## References

Andrews, J., Leff, M. C., & Terrill, R. (1998). *Reading rhetorical texts: An introduction to criticism.* Boston: Houghton Mifflin.

Bazerman, C. (1988). *Shaping written knowledge: The genre and activity of the experimental article in science.* Madison: University of Wisconsin Press.

Bennett, W. L., Lawrence, R. G., & Livingston, S. (2007). *When the press fails: Political power and the news media from Iraq to Katrina.* Chicago: University of Chicago Press.

Bitzer, L. F. (1968). The rhetorical situation. *Philosophy and Rhetoric, 1,* 1–14.

Black, E. (1965). Plato's view of rhetoric. In L. Crocker & P. A. Carmack (Eds.), *Readings in rhetoric* (pp. 68–88). Springfield, IL: Thomas.

Black, E. (1978). *Rhetorical criticism: A study in method.* Madison: University of Wisconsin Press.

Braden, S. W. (2007). Bush and the justification for war. *The Review of Communication, 7,* 423–426.

Brock, B. L., Scott, R. L., & Chesebro, J. W. (Eds.). (1989). *Methods of rhetorical criticism: A twentieth-century perspective* (3rd ed.). Detroit: Wayne State University Press.

Brockriede, W. (1974). Rhetorical criticism as argument. *Quarterly Journal of Speech, 60,* 165–174.

Bryant, J., & Miron, D. (2004). Theory and research in mass communication. *The Journal of Communication, 54,* 662–704.

Burke, K. (1951) Rhetoric—old and new. *Journal of General Education, 5,* 203–205.

Burke, K. (1969). *A rhetoric of motives.* Berkeley: University of California Press. (Original work published 1950)

Callaghan, K., & Schnell, F. (2001). Assessing the democratic debate: How the news media frame elite policy discourse. *Political Communication, 18,* 183–212.

Coe, K., Domke, D., Graham, E. S., John, S. L., & Pickard, V. W. (2004). No shades of gray: The binary discourse of George W. Bush and an echoing press. *Journal of Communication, 54,* 234–252.

D'Angelo, P. (2002). News framing as a multiparadigmatic research program: A response to Entman. *Journal of Communication, 52,* 870–888.

Denton, R. E., & Kuypers, J. A. (2008). *Politics and communication in America: Campaigns, media, and governing in the 21st century.* Carbondale, IL: Waveland Press.

Drislane, R., & Parkinson, G. (2002). Validity. *Online dictionary of the social sciences.* Athabasca University and The International Consortium for the Advancement of Academic Publications. Retrieved January 8, 2008 from http://bitbucket.icaap.org/dict.pl?term=VALIDITY

Edwards, J. A. (2009). *Navigating the post-cold war world: President Clinton's foreign policy rhetoric.* Lanham, MD: Lexington Books.

Entman, R. M. (1991). Framing U.S. coverage of international news: Contrasts in narratives of the KAL and Iran air incidents. *Journal of Communication, 41,* 6–27.

Entman, R. M. (1993). Framing: Toward clarification of a fractured paradigm. *Journal of Communication, 43,* 51–58.

Entman, R. M. (2003). Cascading activation: Contesting the White House's frame after 9/11. *Political Communication, 20,* 415–432.

Entman, R. M. (2007). Framing bias: Media in the distribution of power. *Journal of Communication, 57,* 163–173.

Farnsworth, S. J. (2007). Bush's war: Media bias and justifications for war in a terrorist age, by J. A. Kuypers. *Presidential Studies Quarterly, 37,* 782–783.

Foss, S. K. (1983). Criteria for adequacy in rhetorical criticism. *The Southern Communication Journal, 48,* 283–295.

Gamson, W. A. (1989). News as framing: Comments on Graber. *American Behavioral Scientist, 33,* 157–161.

Graber, D. A. (2005). *Mass media and American politics* (7th ed.). Washington, DC: Congressional Quarterly Press.

Hauser, G. A. (2002). *Introduction to rhetorical theory* (2nd ed.). Prospect Heights, IL: Waveland Press.

Jamieson, K. H., & Waldman, P. (2004). *The press effect: Politicians, journalists, and the stories that shape the political world.* New York: Oxford University Press.

Kuypers, J. A. (1997). *Presidential crisis rhetoric and the press in the post-cold war world.* Westport, CT: Praeger.

Kuypers, J. A. (2001). Must we all be political activists? *The American Communication Journal 4.* Retrieved July 8, 2008, from http://acjournal.org/holdings/vol4/iss1/special/kuypers.htm

Kuypers, J. A. (2002). *Press bias and politics: How the media frame controversial issues.* Westport, CT: Praeger.

Kuypers, J. A. (2005). Framing analysis. In J. A. Kuypers (Ed.), *The art of rhetorical criticism* (pp. 186–211). Boston: Pearson, Allyn & Bacon.

Kuypers, J. A. (2006). *Bush's war: Media bias and justifications for war in a terrorist age*. Lanham, MD: Rowman & Littlefield.

Kuypers, J. A. (Ed.) (2009). *Rhetorical criticism: Perspectives in action*. Lanham, MD: Lexington Press.

Kuypers, J. A., & Cooper, S. (2005). A comparative framing analysis of embedded and behind-the-lines reporting on the 2003 Iraq War. *Qualitative Research Reports in Communication, 6*, 1–10.

Kuypers, J. A., Cooper, S., & Althouse, M. (2008). The president and the press: The framing of George W. Bush's speech to the United Nations on November 10, 2001. *The American Communication Journal, 10*, n.p.

Kuypers, J. A., & King, A. (2005). What is rhetoric? In J. A. Kuypers (Ed.), *The art of rhetorical criticism* (pp. 1–12). Boston: Pearson Education.

Lang, G. E., & Lang, K. (1984). The media and Watergate. In D. A. Graber (Ed.), *Media power in politics* (pp. 202–209). Washington, DC: Congressional Quarterly Press.

Leff, M. (1980). Interpretation and the art of rhetorical criticism. *Western Journal of Speech Communication, 44*, 337–349

Levin, D., (2005). Framing peace policies: The competition for resonate themes. *Political Communication, 22*, 83–108.

Nelson, T. E., Clawson, R. A., & Oxley, Z. M. (1997). Media framing of civil liberties conflict and its effects on tolerance. *American Political Science Review, 91*, 567–583.

Nichols, M. H. (1963). *Rhetoric and criticism*. Baton Rouge: Louisiana State University Press.

Niven, D. (2008). *Bush's war: Media bias and justifications for war in a terrorist age*, by J. A. Kuypers [Review]. *Political Communication, 25*, 222–223.

Ott, B. L., & Aoki, E. (2002). The politics of negotiating public tragedy: Media framing of the Matthew Shepard murder. *Rhetoric & Public Affairs, 5*, 483–505.

Quigley, B. L. (1998). "Identification" as a key term in Kenneth Burke's rhetorical theory. *The American Communication Journal, 1*. Retrieved January 8, 2008 from http://acjournal.org/holdings/vol1/iss3/burke/quigley.html

Ryan, M. (2004). Framing the war against terrorism: US newspaper editorials and military action in Afghanistan. *Gazette: The International Journal for Communication Studies, 66*, 363–382.

Smith, C. R. (2000). Criticism of political rhetoric and disciplinary integrity. *The American Communication Journal, 4*. Retrieved January 10, 2008 from http://www.acjournal.org/holdings/vol4/iss1/special/smith.htm

Sniderman, P. M., Brody, R. A., & Tetlock, P. E. (1991). *Reasoning and choice: Explorations in political psychology*. Cambridge, England: Cambridge University Press.

Trent, J. S., & Friedenberg, R. V. (2008). *Political campaign communication: Principles and practices* (6th ed.). New York: Praeger.

Valenzano, J. M., III. (2009). Framing the war on terror in Canadian newspapers: Cascading activation, Canadian leaders and newspapers. *Southern Communication Journal, 74*, 174–190.

Waldman, P. (2004). *Fraud: The strategy behind the Bush lies and why the media didn't tell you*. Naperville, IL: Sourcebooks.

# Chapter 13

# Framing Through a Feminist Lens

## A Tool in Support of an Activist Research Agenda

*Marie Hardin and Erin Whiteside*

For more than 50 years, news accounts about the movement of mothers into and out of the U.S. workforce have generally relied on similar explanatory themes: motherhood as a natural, primary identity for women, and the departure of women from the workforce as an answer to an internal, biological call toward full-time childrearing (Williams, Manvell, & Bornstein, 2006). In a 2007 *Columbia Journalism Review* essay, E. J. Graff (2007) discussed how these underlying assumptions influence the way facts are interpreted and presented by reporters and, consequently, how the workplace, motherhood, and working women are likely to be understood by readers. In particular, Graff outlined the results of an exhaustive content analysis of a quarter century of newspaper stories conducted by Williams and colleagues (2006). Those stories, Williams et al. found, tended to depict mothers as "opting out" of employment in order to pursue the joys of childrearing. Other equally viable reasons for leaving the workplace, such as frustration with workplace demands or discrimination, tended to be excluded from news stories. After summarizing these findings, Graff described why the results of such research should concern U.S. workers:

> The stories' statistics are selective, their anecdotes about upperechelon white women are misleading, and their "counterintuitive" narrative line parrots conventional ideas about gender roles. Thus they erase most American families' real experiences…. If journalism repeatedly frames the wrong problem, then the folks who make public policy may very well deliver the wrong solution. (p. 54)

Journalists' use of *frames* that reinforce gender-related myths in their reporting of events and issues greatly concern feminist media researchers, who argue that such frames impact social policy decisions and reinforce commonsense assumptions that privilege men in the social hierarchy (Barnett, 2005; Hardin, Simpson, Whiteside, & Garris, 2007; Vavrus, 2007; Williams et al., 2006). Framing, understood as the use of an organizing schema to construct social reality, has guided the media research of feminists since the publication three decades ago of Tuchman's (1978a, 1978b) seminal work on depictions of women. Tuchman's work remains central to meeting feminist goals for social justice in news coverage, as illustrated in recent studies (cf. Akhavan-Majid & Ramaprasad, 1998; Byerly, 1999; Lemish, 2000; McGregor, 2000). In this chapter we explicate the role of framing in the pursuit of feminist ideals, discuss its use within the feminist research tradition, and propose ways for its continued integration in feminist research. In doing so, we discuss the values and concepts we have integrated into our own research agenda from the wide expanse of framing literature. We also argue that a *constructionist* paradigm for framing research, which allows us to consider issues of power and ideology but also feminism as a social movement with strategic opportunities, might be the most fruitful direction for feminist research.

## Framing Within Feminist Media Studies

Framing is a broad concept that is often cited in media research but applied in a variety of ways. The term *framing* can generally be understood as the process in which a "point of view" on a given issue or event is used to interpret and present "reality"—magnifying or shrinking aspects of that issue or event to make it more or less salient (Entman, 1991; Kuypers, 2002). As Entman (1993) explains, frames can be found in the communicator, text, the receiver, and the culture. Framing scholars suggest that in news, frames are manifest in the choice of topics covered and the use of sources, language, and photographs; they persist over time, defining and structuring social relationships (Gardner, 2007; Nacos, 2005; Rohlinger, 2002). These schemas for situating and communicating versions of reality are powerful because they are the basis for the meaning assigned to events, identity, and other culturally significant topics. As Kuypers (2002) state, "Frames actually define our understanding of any given situation" (p. 7).

Frames are not, as Carragee and Roefs (2004) point out, simply "story topics" or definitions of an event with "little or no reference to [framing's] theoretical and substantive implications" (p. 217). Such characterizations of framing ultimately dilute its power as a lens for understanding the interaction between media producers, content, individual media consumers, and the culture.

Framing in media-related research has been associated with so many different operationalizations and methods that Entman (1993) and others have argued that it is a "scattered conceptualization" (p. 51) in need of a "commonly shared theoretical model" (Scheufele, 1999, p. 103). The ability of framing to encompass many approaches can also be seen as one of its strengths, however. That is how we embrace it—as a multiparadigmatic research program that can facilitate various agendas and theoretical frameworks (D'Angelo, 2002). The "hard core" (D'Angelo, p. 873) of framing research involves the identification of frames and the investigation of their antecedent conditions (e.g., the political economy of news organizations), interaction with receivers (e.g., "media effects"), and impact on social-level processes (e.g., public policy).

D'Angelo's (2002) suggestion that framing research can be understood as reflecting three general paradigms is useful in thinking about feminist approaches to framing. These paradigms are *cognitive, constructionist,* and *critical.* D'Angelo characterizes the cognitive paradigm as one in which researchers incorporate the image of *negotiation.* Cognitivists are interested in the interaction between news frames and the experiences, beliefs, and knowledge of individual media receivers; they do not assume that if frames dominate news coverage, they necessarily dominate audiences. Much of their research explores individual effects of news frames. Carragee and Roefs (2004) caution that framing scholars often focus too intently on media effects and "divorce media frames from the context in which they are produced" (p. 217). A cognitivist approach can take media content as a given, ignore the meaning-making process and sites of resistance, and ultimately undermine the potential of such studies to understand the implication of frames on a cultural level.

We believe that feminist research, which is inherently concerned with the relationship between (gendered) power, discourse, and society, concentrates more easily in the two other paradigms explained by D'Angelo (2002): the critical and constructionist. Both involve assumptions about *power* and its relationship with content and audience reception, a consideration Carragee and Roefs (2004) suggest is underdeveloped and often ignored in framing literature. As feminists integrate these paradigms into their research, they contribute to understandings of the role of power in the framing process.

The critical paradigm is characterized by the image of *domination.* Researchers in the critical paradigm draw clear connections between ideology and news frames, arguing that journalists reinforce dominant ideology as natural and universal (Akhavan-Majid & Ramaprasad, 2000). Critical researchers argue that frames reflect political, economic, and cultural power relations, and audience effects are generally assumed in the constriction of political consciousness by way of the normalizing function of frames. In other words, frames can naturalize the arbitrary, a process often explained as hegemony, so that it becomes taken for granted even at the expense of large social groups such as women and racial minorities. Carragee and Roefs (2004) suggest drawing from media hegemony theory to understand frames not just as guides in the meaning-making process, but as "imprints of power" (p. 222).

This notion, which ties the framing process to the reification of power, is key for feminist media researchers because it furthers our goal to inter-rogate manifestations of patriarchy. A critical approach that draws on media hegemony theory considers frames within the context in which they are produced. For instance, D'Angelo (2002) suggests that Tuch-man's *Making News* (1978a), because of its emphasis on the ideologi-cal functions of newswork, supports the critical paradigm. Tuchman's work in *Hearth and Home* (1978b), including her concept of "symbolic annihilation," which focuses on the exclusion of women in news and is routinely used in feminist framing studies, also supports the critical para-digm. The concept of symbolic annihilation, although arguably outdated as a theoretical lens in regard to media treatment of women, has salience for the understanding of diversity within the category of "woman"; for example, women with visible impairments or lesbian female athletes.

D'Angelo (2002) describes the third paradigm, *constructionist*, as one supported by the image of *co-optation*. Constructionist researchers are also interested in media producers, conceptualizing them not as part of an elitist mechanism in support of the status quo (critical) but as infor-mation processors who rely on sources they deem "credible" to make substantive contributions to the 'issue culture' on a given topic (p. 877). In other words, because journalists work as part of the same cultural system as the public, they rely on frames that resonate with themselves and with the media consumers; and "this view is very different from one that pictures the media as an outside entity acting on a malleable pub-lic" (Baylor, 1996, p. 242). This view also allows for a less institutional, more agentic, discourse-centered conceptualization of power, one that may allow for a more realistic, sophisticated understanding of relation-ships between producers, content, and audiences/citizens.

When certain frames are underpinned by widely held cultural assump-tions (ideology), scholars suggest that such frames can dominate in news coverage over a long period of time and potentially thwart social activ-ism and constrict political awareness among individuals. Yet, construc-tionists also understand framing as a dynamic process, one in which frames can evolve and be restructured by journalists to match changing social and political conditions (Bronstein, 2005). Constructionists also see news frames as potentially useful and even tied to the visibility of social movements; they are likely to look for media effects not at the individual level (cognitive paradigm) but in the success of movements or in articulations of progressive public opinion or political socialization (D'Angelo, 2002).

In our work, this paradigm has ultimately been most appealing for several reasons. Unlike the cognitive paradigm, it allows us to interrogate the role of ideology and gendered power relations in the framing process, thus integrating *feminist theory*. Unlike the critical paradigm, it allows us to advocate pragmatic change at the individual and institutional levels, taking advantage of evolving political and social conditions. In one area of our research, centering on media framing of the U.S. civil rights law Title IX, which is about women and sports, this approach has allowed us the freedom to recognize the changing athletic climate for girls and women in the U.S. *and* acknowledge the resiliency of traditional gender ideology. This paradigm is thus suitable for doing framing analysis such that we can advocate pragmatic ways that social movement organizations can advance more progressive framing of women and sports (Hardin et al., 2007).

## Feminism as a Social Movement

Broadly speaking, feminism can be understood as a movement that focuses on social justice issues in regard to gendered power relations. It is overly simplistic, however, to situate feminism only on a global level because feminists often differ on theories of male dominance and power relations. Further, thinking in such "universalist" terms obscures power relations *within* the movement itself (Ramazanoglu & Holland, 2002, p. 6). For instance, attempts to break the so-called glass ceiling, are really rooted in Western, middle and upper-class concerns. Access to birth control in developing countries presents another type of struggle that benefits a different group of women. Thus, the movement should also be considered on a local level, where its goals and effects can more clearly be defined.

Feminism encompasses a set of core principles that involve claims to a loosely shared identity among women and a case for emancipation. But even today, feminism is articulated within multiple and disparate theories, including liberal, radical/cultural, socialist/Marxist, and post-modern perspectives, among others.[1] Feminism as a social movement has been countered by postfeminist iterations, which claim some goals of feminism but generally reject its call for the rejection of patriarchy.[2] Ramazanoglu and Holland (2002, p. 6) write that feminism has developed, like other late 20th century social movements, as

> an unstable intellectual, political and practical activity grounded in a sense of women having some common political interests across their social divisions, and so having some potential interest in acting to transform unjust gender relations.

Activism and social change are also integral, to varying degrees, to the goals of feminist scholarship (Gallagher, 2001). In other words, feminist research is *openly politically committed* and generally rejects the positioning of "objectivity" and "rationality" as neutral; instead, it positions these scientific values as serving patriarchal goals (Ramazanoglu & Holland, 2002; van Zoonen, 1994). We agree with contemporary feminist scholars who argue that quantitative, social science research and its association with (masculinist) empiricism are inherently biased in their definitions and depictions of social reality (Brayton, 1997). As Stanley and Wise (1993) argue, the crux of the feminist critique of empirical work in the social sciences is that, under the guise of objectivity, it has historically ignored or distorted the experiences of women, thus furthering the interests of the powerful (White, middle- and upper-class men). The uncontested value of objectivity has been particularly problematic for feminist epistemologists. Harding (1993, 2005), for instance, has argued that transparent, politically guided research can produce more valuable knowledge than scholarship positioned as "objective" in the terms of traditional social science. She holds that researchers can achieve what she calls "strong objectivity" when they put the subject and object of research on the same plane in order to expose, then reject, "culturewide beliefs" from functioning as evidence in various stages of the research process (1993, p. 69).

Along these lines, feminist research relies heavily on the concept of reflexivity, which is an approach that demands the researcher critically think about her role in the research process and the subsequent assumptions made within it (Ramazanoglu & Holland, 2002). The process should reveal the cultural beliefs that function as taken-for-granted evidence in various stages of the research process, including the selection of research questions, topics and problems, data collection, interpretations, decisions on when to stop the research, and choices in reporting results (Harding, 1993, p. 69; see also Tickner, 2005).

Although considered a "feminist" viewpoint on research, it seems to us that this understanding of social science might seem intuitive to many framing scholars, especially those in the critical or constructionist paradigms who base their work on the reality that "journalistic framing of issues and events does not develop in a political vacuum [but] is shaped by the frames sponsored by multiple social actors" (Carragee & Roefs, 2004, p. 216). Along these lines, Tuchman (1978a) famously argued that in the pursuit of objectivity, professional journalistic standards validate statements by "official" sources, such as government officials, over comments from individuals in nonofficial social locations. The overreliance on "official" sources, and the subsequent claims of neutrality, allow journalists to excuse themselves from accusations of bias by hiding under the cloak of official sources; those in power, meanwhile, continue to shape the news agenda (Tuchman, 1978a). Dolan (2005) applied these ideas to his news coverage analysis of a controversial art exhibit in Santa Fe. Using textual analysis, he argued that the overreliance on official sources advanced only one narrative in the controversy and obscured alternative stories, including the implications of men holding the power to control images of women. From this perspective, it could be argued that to study framing requires the rejection of the idea of "objectivity" in news. Agendas (latent and manifest) exist in texts, and, furthermore, they have material consequences. Perhaps the allure of feminist research for us, then, is that it acknowledges the obvious: that we are not so different from journalists, and that our work is also shaped by multiple sources—including our own identities that stem from our gender, race, class, and sexuality.

This is not to say that we as feminists fully reject the empirical research process; we use reason, logic, and systematic rigor in our research but do not see reason as a "neutralizing" force (Ramazanoglu & Holland, 2002, p. 49). We bring a "female" viewpoint to research where the masculine one has been presented as the objective norm (van Zoonen, 1994). Myriad examples of a female perspective abound, but the common thread tying feminist research together is the female viewpoint and research questions driven by the acknowledgment of a patriarchal system and advocacy for change. A "female" perspective on house and family care work, for instance, has helped change dominant (male) cultural understandings of domestic work *from* a labor of love *to* one of actual, tiring labor; the (ongoing) shift in our shared understandings of domestic labor has been critical in liberating women from feeling guilty if they do not internalize the labor-of-love ideology, a notion famously called "the problem with no name" by feminist writer Betty Friedan (1963/1997).

Another example is in contemporary work on sports by feminists, which has widely critiqued the partnership of athletics and masculinity and the idea that only boys and men are naturally suited for sports (Griffin, 1998; Lenskyj, 1994; Messner, 2002). In our related work (which will be discussed later in more detail), we designed our research to be systematically rigorous through careful attention to issues of validity and reliability, and to incorporate an explicitly defined female/feminist viewpoint, one that rejected the taken-for-granted assumption that sports are naturally masculine activities and, thus, belong to boys and men. We acknowledge that even our choice of topic (framing of a civil-rights law protecting girls and women) is a product of our standpoint, influenced by a number of factors, including our identification as feminist. Thus, if nonfeminists studied the framing of Title IX, for example, and created research questions based on differing assumptions about sports and gender, it is reasonable to assume their subsequent findings and conclusions would differ from a similar study conducted by feminists.

### The Framing of Social Movements

As van Zoonen (1992) has noted, the media have always been at the center of feminist critique and activism—thus the concentration on *media content* in much feminist research. van Zoonen (1992) has characterized the relationship between the women's movement and the media as one fraught with tension: "To judge by the considerable feminist anger directed towards the news media, the media have done much to dismiss the women's movement" (p. 453). To realize the "feminist anger" to which van Zoonen refers, it is important to understand the relationship between *social movements* and *framing*, and how the women's movement and women historically have been framed in news coverage.

Social movements and the media are interdependent: journalists need stories and movements need the publicity and legitimacy that media coverage often provides (Baylor, 1996; Bronstein, 2005). However, the balance of power has been unequal, as journalists can shape how a social movement is presented to the public (Gamson & Wolfsfeld, 1993).[3] Ashley and Olson (1998) outlined the ways that the framing of social movements can be manifested in amount of news coverage, descriptions by journalists of associated groups, use of event-focused or movement-focused stories, emphasis on peripherals (e.g., appearance or age of protesters) or on movement goals, and presentation of protesters as inside or outside the mainstream. These framing elements can be seen as being embedded in three broader framing processes: diagnostic framing, which presents the cause of an injustice; prognostic framing, which recommends a solution; and motivational framing, which calls for change and action (Barnett, 2005). At bottom, framing of a particular movement can have material consequences, including whether citizens will choose to support the movement or even to join it (Baylor, 1996; Bronstein, 2005).

Researchers in the critical paradigm generally position framing of social movements as preserving ideology that serves socioeconomic elites, thus reinforcing the status quo and ultimately making it impossible for any social movement to initiate meaningful change (Barnett, 2005). In his key book on the news media and framing that has often been seen as a companion to Tuchman's (1978a) work, Gitlin (1980) indicts the culture industry that values spectacle and flamboyance over substance in news coverage. He argues that innovation and consolidation in media over the middle part of the 20th century have made it nearly impossible for opposition movements to define themselves on their own terms. In order to matter on a cultural level, says Gitlin, they must submit themselves to the rules of news making and common archetypes, which deform and undermine the movement's original message. Ultimately, Gitlin suggests that the media's routines, norms, and capitalistic interests combine to privilege versions of reality over others, at the detriment of alternative voices and politics. The themes outlined by Gitlin in relation to media framing, power, and dominant ideology have since been pursued by a number of scholars (e.g., Entman, 1991; Hallin, 1987; Nisbet & Lewenstein, 2002; Perlmutter & Wagner, 2004).

Those with a more constructionist approach view framing as reflective of the "intricate interaction between movement and media: a meeting of ideas and ideologies, organizational forms and routines and individual characteristics and preferences of journalists and activists" (van Zoonen, 1992, p. 456). A great deal of literature, focusing on the interaction of media and social movements, has been generated in the constructionist paradigm (e.g., Benford & Snow, 2000; Ferree, 2003; Gamson & Modigliani, 1989; Rohlinger, 2002). This literature explores the "struggle over framing" in the transactional relationship among social movements, dominant institutional interests, and journalists (Gamson & Wolfsfeld, 1993, p. 118). Constructionists generally possess a more hopeful view of the potential for social movements because of their view that frames employed by social movement organizations can lead to desired outcomes, and, perhaps, social change (Benford & Snow, 2000). Rohlinger (2002), for example, examines the ways the organizational structure, identity, and goals of the feminist organization the National Organization for Women (NOW) helped lead it to framing strategies in tune with media norms and values, leading to increased resonance in mainstream media. Such research helps fill a void, that of study of the production of frames by social movements, in the scholarly literature (Carragee & Roefs, 2004).

### Framing and Feminist Media Research

Since the 1970s, feminist researchers have produced volumes of studies analyzing media coverage of women and the women's movement. Much of it, influenced by Tuchman (1978a, 1978b), has focused on stereotypical framing of feminists and women and the reinforcement of male-privileged gender socialization in news (van Zoonen, 1994). As Luebke (1992) pointed out in her review of the research during the 1970s and 1980s, women were, as Tuchman (1978b) proposed, "symbolically annihilated" through routine exclusion and trivialization in news frames— even to the degree that *Editor & Publisher* concluded that women were framed by *The New York Times* in 1990 much the way they had been 100 years earlier, when they still did not have the right to vote. Studies of the modern feminist movement, associated with the launch of the NOW in 1966, also suggest articles included frames that delegitimized feminists and legitimized antifeminists (Ashley & Olson, 1998).

Many studies, stemming from Tuchman's "symbolic annihilation" thesis, have used different labels for the same basic frames regarding marginalization and trivialization found in news coverage of women and the women's movement (Bronstein, 2005). Lind and Salo (2002), in their research on the framing of women, feminists, and feminism in television news, synthesized the frames they found in key studies since 1990.[4] The six frames they observed to be overlapping in previous studies were *demonization*, in which feminists/feminism are framed as deviant; *personalization and trivialization,* in which the appearance, style, or personal qualities of feminists are emphasized; *goals,* in which civil rights, reproductive rights, workplace rights and equality goals receive attention; *victimization,* in which feminists are presented as weak and vulnerable; *agency,* in which feminists are presented as strong and capable; and *site of struggle,* in which the emphasis was on location (e.g., home, work, school, religion). Lind and Salo's (2002) synthesis gives coherence to a large, sometimes disparate, body of feminist work that has focused on media framing. It provides a set of basic frames feminist scholars can use to benchmark progress in specific areas of the wider movement (such as sports). For instance, sports feminists can use their work to examine the struggle over framing of heterosexual and lesbian female athletes and advocates of Title IX and women's sports.

The fact that so many studies have found little change in framing over time (even when employing a term other than *framing*), has given some feminist scholars reason to object to framing-oriented research. Luebke (1992), for instance, argued that it was time for feminists to abandon content analyses of news coverage, arguing that because they have not resulted in dramatic change in the ways women are depicted, "such analyses are essentially academic exercises" (p. 2). Other feminists have objected to quantitative framing studies as theoretically underdeveloped (Jolliffe, 1993). Steeves (1987) criticized content analyses of news coverage as not adequately grounded in feminist theory and only vaguely focused on communication theory. She also took researchers to task, many of whom were working in the critical paradigm, for assumptions that audience members would adopt frames found in coverage. Although we share her concern regarding many feminists' assumptions about the encoding–decoding process, we reject the idea that such assumptions render their work irrelevant. Feminists can rightly argue that the presence of frames that reinforce patriarchal ideology in media accounts are cause for activism in their own right. Furthermore, we argue that feminist consideration of the text–audience relationship has developed considerably in the past 2 decades (e.g., Lindlof, 1991; Lotz, 2006; Radway, 2007; van Zoonen, 1994) and can enrich critical media analysis by feminists.

## The Strength of Framing in Feminist Work

We encourage the continued incorporation of framing, then, as a way for media scholars to participate in the feminist movement through research that is empirically and theoretically grounded but also advocates political goals. We understand programmatic approaches to framing and to feminism to be compatible: the strength of both is a "hard core" agenda combined with multiparadigmatic flexibility to accommodate varying theoretical frameworks and research approaches. We also advocate framing as a research program that has and will continue to facilitate feminist advocacy for nonstereotypical, socially just news coverage of women and men (Byerly, 1999; Jolliffe, 1993). As Gallagher (2001) explains, the data from such research allows feminists a starting point to move "beyond 'complaining' to engagement in constructive dialogue with media professionals" (p. 13).

### Framing and Methodological Flexibility in the Feminist Tradition

Feminist researchers have studied framing using both quantitative (content analyses) and qualitative (various forms of textual analysis) methods of analysis, demonstrating its flexibility as a program of research. Qualitative analyses, such as those by van Zoonen (1992), Meyers (1997), Knight (1999), Barnett (2005), and Vavrus (2007), often more explicitly integrate communication theory and feminist theory than do many quantitative framing studies. The reasons for this have been at least partially explored earlier in this chapter, in our discussion of feminist questioning of assumptions grounded in much empirical (quantitative) research. Qualitative analysis more readily allows for integration of the researcher's standpoint and for the exploration of latent content in texts, both of which are more amenable to the integration of feminist theory because of feminists' acceptance that taken-for-granted understandings of reality reinforce patriarchy. For instance, in our work, we seek to make visible the ways that assumptions of sports as *naturally, essentially belonging to boys and men* are embedded in media content, thus shaping the ways coverage of issues such as Title IX are framed. Although we have incorporated both quantitative (Hardin, et al., 2007) and qualitative (Whiteside & Hardin, 2008) analyses, we find that our qualitative analysis more easily allows us to go beyond the (simplistic) limits of liberal feminism, to radical or socialist points of view.

We do not challenge the role of quantitative framing analyses in feminist scholarship; we have already mentioned several key quantitative studies, including that of Lind and Salo (2002). Furthermore, four recent quantitative studies (content analyses) provide examples of explicit, rigorous application of feminist terms and ideals: Akhavan-Majid and Ramaprasad (1998); Bronstein (2005); Hardin et al. (2007); and Houge (2008). These studies examine the framing of feminists (Akhavan-Majid & Ramaprasad, 1998; Bronstein, 2005), the framing of male victims of sexual war crimes (Houge, 2008), and the framing of women in the sports context (Hardin et al., 2007). In our research examining news frames around Title IX (Hardin et al., 2007), we explicitly rejected what has become transparent, conventional wisdom about the law: that it penalizes boys and men by allowing girls and women to play, as this point of view relies on patriarchal assumptions about gender. We positioned our study as coming from the standpoint that the law and its rules for compliance have resulted in civil rights, equal opportunity, and a better social climate for everyone. Preceding our definitions of variables, we clearly stated that Title IX is not in need of "reform" and is not responsible for losses to men's sports. Thus, as we put it, "the law needs to be protected and preserved and the public needs to be educated about the law, its impact, and its relationship with college athletics" (p. 219).

This position, then, guided our choices about the frames we sought to make visible and how we *evaluated* those frames; those choices differentiated our framing exercises as feminist. Feminist researchers must be explicit in their definitions and interpretations (for instance, *how* do they operationalize frames?) and set up clear, logical, and rigorous analyses that can withstand methodological scrutiny and provide clear evidence.

Our content analysis was driven by a particular research agenda, although we could have, and did, further that same agenda using a different method (Whiteside & Hardin, 2008). We can point to two other, recent studies on the same news coverage as further exemplars of the core strength and paradigmatic flexibility of framing and the consistency of feminism in interpretation of news frames. Vavrus (2007) and Williams et al. (2006) both examined newspaper and magazine stories about the *opt-out revolution*, the term coined for high-wage working mothers who leave the workforce.

Vavrus (2007) used theories of neoliberalism (which articulate the idea that individuals have an equal opportunity to make rational decisions), and postfeminism (a position that argues patriarchy is essentially nonexistent) to make several points in her textual analysis. First she suggested that news frames situated female domesticity as natural. She also argued that frames eschewed second-wave feminism and rationalized antifamily employment policies. Vavrus (2007) made her grounding in the *critical paradigm* clear in her conclusion: "[N]eoliberal perspectives are so firmly entrenched in corporate media culture that they prevent the pursuit in news stories of solutions associated with social democracy," adding, "Neoliberalism is incompatible with social movements that include economic justice as a goal" (p. 59).

In their critique of the opt-out storyline, Williams et al. (2006) adopted more liberal feminist values but still found frames similar to those in the Vavrus (2007) study. They also present their work in a *constructionist paradigm*, positioning reporters as information processors who, through their choices of facts and sources, are misguiding the "issue culture" surrounding women and employment. For instance, the researchers situate the opt-out storyline as "the interpretation of choice" (p. 5) by journalists for decades, but then propose that:

> Simply telling reporters that they are telling the wrong story does not give them new stories to tell; reporters need ready access to accurate data to paint a complete picture…. If critics want to replace the Opt

Out story, they need to provide a new explanation for why so many women do not follow the accepted paths to workplace success.

Similarities in the findings (e.g., identical frames, differently labeled) of Vavrus (2007) and Williams et al. (2006), combined with differences in the way they got to those findings and then situated them, demonstrates the power, flexibility, and resiliency of framing research for feminists. Vavrus and Williams et al. both come at their research with transparent, core feminist values and an advocacy agenda but successfully integrate differing theoretical frameworks and paradigmatic approaches to their analyses. Both advance feminist scholarship and, thus, the movement's overall agenda.

### Moving Toward Feminist Goals

Although some feminists (Barnett, 2005; Gallagher, 2001; Luebke, 1992) contend that the study of media content has made little impact on the framing of women over the past several decades, such is not the case. Feminist research has been able to both play a role and trace the ways the movement has made a difference (Baird, 2004; Byerly, 1999; Jolliffe, 1993; Lind & Salo, 2002). Research indicates that coverage of feminists, for instance, has improved over time, and that positive media portrayals of feminist organizations and their members outnumber negative ones (Abbott, 2006). For instance, Lind and Salo, after conducting a content analysis of 35,000 hours of television news, argued that feminists were more positively framed than they had been in earlier studies and were more likely to be presented as independent and powerful.

Byerly (1999) has outlined specific ways feminist advocacy has significantly impacted news coverage, arguing that feminism has successfully guided news agendas and, perhaps more significantly, news frames. Notably, stories about violence against women, such as those about rape, incest, or sexual harassment, have improved as reporters have become better educated about the realities of such violence. An example is coverage of athletes' off-the-field violence against women; Byerly suggests that high-profile stories during the 1990s incorporated a "feminist frame by foregrounding the players' responsibility for the violence and the harm to victims" (p. 393). Worthington (2005), in a framing analysis of investigative news stories about sexual assault and subsequent student protests of administration response on a college campus, also found the use of frames she saw as harmonious with feminist goals.

Byerly (1999) does not suggest that feminist ideas have universally been adopted into news frames; she concedes that news coverage remains a site of struggle, where blame-the-victim framing also persists. Nevertheless, she concludes that the changes feminist advocacy has prompted in news coverage clearly point to an understanding that "news media are neither monolithic nor static, but widely variable in their ability to incorporate feminism" (p. 391). We contend that this realization has implications for paradigmatic approaches to framing studies.

## Paradigmatic Refinement of Framing Research

Byerly's characterization of the media, supported by framing research spanning more than a decade, is a view best supported by the *constructionist* paradigm. This view, also called "constructivist," accepts media producers as subject to cultural ideologies but also as agentic—responsive to and capable of "alternative storylines" (Williams et al., 2006, p. 5). Houge (2008) presents this paradigm as emphasizing

> the possibilities we have to change the world. It understands the social world as one we construct and comprise as individuals through our intersubjective understanding of the social world, of its norms and its rules—hence, all social knowledge and social reality are socially constructed, and thus, amenable to change. (p. 66)

Framing analyses in the spirit of Tuchman's (1978a, 1978b) *critical* paradigm have contributed tremendously to feminist scholarship by expanding macrolevel understanding of the link between ideology, institutions, and journalistic practice and texts. Vavrus's (2007) article, discussed earlier, is an example of such contributions.

We contend, however, that purely critical media analyses run the risk of falling into two traps. The first is a failure to acknowledge the complexity of media depictions of women, men, and gender relations. Baird (2004), in her analysis of the relationship between female politicians and the mainstream press in Australia, offered a scathing critique of critical feminist scholars, arguing that they had failed to acknowledge the positive impact the women's movement has had on journalism. Too many, in a paradigm she dated to the 1970s, assume the media are "a monolithic block of anti-woman propaganda" that are "hostile and impenetrable" (p. 5). We suggest that as feminist scholars better integrate the constructionist paradigm, they will find ways to incorporate the complexity of the media–movement relationship into their work and move away from being subject to such critiques.

The second risk run by critical scholars is in failing to provide impetus for *social action*, a key feature of feminism. Feminist scholarship is not meant to sit on the sidelines, but is instead part of the movement (Gallagher, 2001; Jolliffe, 1993). We suggest that in key ways, the critical paradigm for framing research may discourage individual activism, as power is conceptualized as centered in social institutions. The constructionist paradigm, conversely, is more inviting to advocacy by social movements and seems to reflect Gallagher's (2001, p. 14) observation that feminist research has moved away from "generalized criticism of media systems and organizations towards a focus on identifiable media production practices." We have sought to further our framing work on Title IX by exploring the attitudes and values of individual journalists in relationship to the law, and we have shared this work with the Women's Sports Foundation, a social movement organization that advocates for more socially just framing of the law (Hardin & Whiteside, 2009a). We have also, through focus-group conversations with media consumers, been able to suggest counterframes and alternative storylines that may be of use to women's sports advocates (Hardin & Whiteside, 2009b). Both of these steps, we believe, reflect our grounding in a constructionist paradigm, which recognizes the power of ideology but also understands the role of discourse and of changing social conditions.

We point to two other examples of feminist constructionist research, Rohlinger (2002) and Barnett (2005), both which use framing as a lens on NOW news releases. In her study, Barnett observed that NOW has used *corrective* frames over the years to counter those that could negatively impact support for it and suggested that the feminist movement incorporate such frames to communicate with various publics, including the media. In doing so, Barnett elevated framing as an essential skill for feminist communicators. Rohlinger's (2002) study is perhaps more illuminating, as it also provides an organizational analysis of NOW, linking it to its framing strategies. Even more instructive for feminist activism, her study also analyzes NOW in contrast to an antifeminist counterorganization, Concerned Women for America. We hope that future research will continue to explore the use of framing by other women's organizations and will examine how such framing is received by journalists and the public.

In conclusion, we urge feminist scholars to continue to integrate framing into the new directions they seek in media-related research (Baird, 1994; Byerly, 1999; Jolliffe, 1993; Luebke, 1992, Steeves, 1987; van Zoonen, 1994). As Carragee and Roefs (2004) contend, the framing process needs to be examined in the context of the "distribution of political and social power," and, as we hope we have demonstrated, this mission is in alignment with feminist goals.

We suggest that feminists engage in more focused work in the constructionist paradigm, incorporating the realities of a technologically changing media environment and offering the "alternative storylines" that promote social justice. We also suggest incorporation of more sophisticated factors in framing analysis, ones that will allow us to draw conclusions about the institutional (e.g., media ownership or newsroom diversity) and individual (e.g., gender or ethnicity of journalists) factors that contribute to the framing of men, women, and gender roles. Finally, we suggest that feminists pay more serious attention to the admonition by Jolliffe (1993) more than 10 years ago that we more thoroughly examine the framing of men and issues related to masculinity, as doing so is in the interest of feminism and ultimately, of our mission toward universal gender justice.

## Notes

1. For a full discussion of the range of feminist thought and how it has evolved since the early Second Wave, see Tong, R. (1998). *Feminist thought: A more comprehensive introduction.* Boulder, CO: Westview Press.
2. For an explanation of the differences between postfeminism and feminism, see Projansky, S. (2001). The postfeminist context: Popular redefinitions of feminism, 1980–Present. *Watching rape: Film and television in postfeminist culture* .New York: New York University Press.
3. We suggest that the rise of the Internet in recent years lessens the imbalance, however, as organizations dedicated to social movements can directly communicate with individuals through discussion boards, mailing lists, and Web sites. Thus, their dependence on traditional journalists to reach the public has subsided although not disappeared.
4. Those studies were Howell (1990); van Zoonen (1992); Terkildsen and Schnell (1997); Costain, Braunstein, and Berggren (1998); Rhode (1997); and Ashley & Olson (1998).

## References

Abbott, J. Y. (2006). Religion and gender in the news: The case of promise keepers, feminists, and the "Stand in the Gap" rally. *Journal of Communication and Religion, 29,* 224–261.

Akhavan-Majid, R., & Ramaprasad, J. (1998). Framing and ideology: A comparative analysis of U.S. and Chinese newspaper coverage of the fourth United Nations Conference on Women and the NGO Forum. *Mass Communication & Society, 1*(3–4), 131–152.

Akhavan-Majid, R., & Ramaprasad, J. (2000). Framing Beijing: Dominant ideological influences on the American press coverage of the fourth U.N. Conference on Women and the NGO Forum. *Gazette, 62*(1), 45–59.

Ashley, L., & Olson, B. (1998). Constructing reality: Print media's framing of the women's movement, 1966 to 1986. *Journalism & Mass Communication Quarterly, 75,* 263–277.

Baird, J. (2004). *Media tarts: How the Australian press frames female politicians.* Melbourne, Australia: Scribe.

Barnett, B. (2005). Feminists shaping news: A framing analysis of news releases from the National Organization for Women. *Journal of Public Relations Research, 17*(4), 341–362.

Baylor, T. (1996). Media framing of movement protest: The case of American Indian protest. *The Social Science Journal, 33,* 241–255.

Benford, R.D., & Snow, D.A. (2000). Framing processes and social movements: An overview and assessment. *Annual Review of Sociology, 26,* 611–639.

Brayton, J. (1997). *What makes feminist research feminist? The structure of feminist research within the social sciences.* Retrieved August 10, 2008, from http://www.unb.ca/PAR-L/win/feminmethod.htm

Bronstein, C. (2005). Representing the third wave: Mainstream print media framing of a new feminist movement. *Journalism & Mass Communication Quarterly, 82*, 783–803.

Byerly, C. (1999). News, feminism, and the dialectics of gender relations. In M. Meyers (Ed.), *Mediated women: Representations in popular culture* (pp. 383–403). Cresskill, NJ: Hampton Press.

Carragee, K. M., & Roefs, W. (2004). The neglect of power in recent framing research. *Journal of Communication, 54*(2), 214–233.

Costain, A. N., Braunstein, R., & Berggren, H. (1997). Framing the women's movements. In P. Norris (Ed.), *Women, media, and politics* (pp. 205–220). Cambridge, England: Cambridge University Press.

D'Angelo, P. (2002). News framing as a multiparadigmatic research program: A response to Entman. *Journal of Communication, 52*, 870–888.

Dolan, K. (2005). Blinded by objectivity: How news conventions caused journalists to miss the real story in the "Our Lady" controversy in Santa Fe. *Journalism, 6*(3), 379–396.

Entman, R. M. (1991). Framing U.S. coverage of international news: Contrasts in narratives of the KAL and Iran air incidents. *Journal of Communication, 41*(4), 6–27.

Entman, R. M. (1993). Framing: Toward clarification of a fractured paradigm. *Journal of Communication, 43*(4), 51–58.

Ferree, M. M. (2003). Resonance and radicalism: Feminist framing in the abortion debates of the United States and Germany. *American Journal of Sociology, 109*(2), 304–344.

Friedan, B. (1997). *The feminine mystique.* New York: Norton. (Original work published 1963)

Gallagher, M. (2001). The push and pull of action and research in feminist media studies. *Feminist Media Studies, 1*(1), 11–15.

Gamson, W., & Modigliani, A. (1989). Media discourse as a symbolic contest: A constructionist approach. *American Journal of Sociology, 95*(1), 1–37.

Gamson, W., & Wolfsfeld, G. (1993). Movements and media as interacting systems. *Annals of the American Academy of Political and Social Science, 528*, 114–125.

Gardner, E. (2007). Is there method to the madness? *Journalism Studies, 8*, 909–929.

Gitlin, T. (1980). *The whole world is watching: The mass media in the making and unmaking of the new left.* Berkeley: University of California Press.

Graff, E. J. (2007). The opt-out myth. *Columbia Journalism Review, 45*(6), 51–54.

Griffin, P. (1998). *Strong women, deep closets: Lesbians and homophobia in sport.* Champaign, IL: Human Kinetics.

Hallin, D.C. (1987). The American news media: A critical theory perspective. In J. Forester (Ed.), *Critical theory and public life* (pp. 121–146). Cambridge, MA: MIT Press.

Hardin, M., Simpson, S. Whiteside, E., & Garris, K. (2007). The gender war in U.S. sport: Winners and losers in news coverage of Title IX. *Mass Communication & Society, 10*(2), 211–233.

Hardin, M., & Whiteside, E. (2009a). Sports journalists satisfied with coverage of women's sports but divided about Title IX and sexuality issues. *Newspaper Research Journal, 30*(1), 58–71.

Hardin, M., & Whiteside, E. (2009b). The power of "small stories:" Narratives and notions of gender equality in conversations about sport. *Sociology of Sport Journal, 26*(2), 255–276.

Harding, S. (1993). Rethinking standpoint epistemology: What is strong objectivity? In L. Alcoff & E. Potter (Eds.), *Feminist epistemologies* (pp. 15–48). London: Routledge.

Harding, S. (2005). *The feminist standpoint theory reader.* London: Routledge.

Houge, A. B. (2008). Subversive victims? The (non)reporting of sexual violence against male victims during the war in Bosnia-Herzegovina. *Nordicom Review, 29*(1), 63–78.

Howell, S. (1990). *Reflections of ourselves: The mass media and the women's movement, 1963 to the present.* New York: Lang.

Jolliffe, L. (1993). Yes! More content analyses. *Newspaper Research Journal, 14*(3), 93–98.

Knight, M. G. (1999). Getting past the impasse: Framing as a tool for public relations. *Public Relations Review, 25,* 381–398.

Kuypers, J. A. (2002). *Press bias and politics: How the media frame controversial issues.* Westport, CT: Praeger.

Lemish, D. (2000). The whore and the other. *Gender & Society, 14*(2), 333–349.

Lenskyj, H. J. (1994). Girl-friendly sport and female values. *Women in Sport & Physical Activity Journal, 3(1),* 35–46.

Lind, R. A., & Salo, C. (2002). The framing of feminists and feminism in news and public affairs programs in U.S. electronic media. *Journal of Communication, 52*(1), 211–228.

Lindlof, T. R. (1991). The qualitative study of media audiences. *Journal of Broadcasting and Electronic Media, 35*(1), 23–42.

Lotz, A. D. (2006). Assessing qualitative television audience research: Incorporating feminist and anthropological theoretical innovation. *Communication Theory, 10*(4), 447–467.

Luebke, B. F. (1992). No more content analyses. *Newspaper Research Journal, 13*(1–2), 2–9.

McGregor, J. (2000). Stereotypes and symbolic annihilation: Press constructions of women at the top. *Women in Management Review, 15*(5/6), 290–295.

Messner, M. A. (2002). *Taking the field: Women, men, and sports.* Minneapolis, MN: University of Minnesota Press.

Meyers, M. (1997). *Engendering blame: News coverage of violence against women.* Thousand Oaks, CA: Sage.

Nacos, B. L. (2005). The portrayal of female terrorists in the media: Similar framing patterns in the news coverage of women in the politics and in terrorism. *Studies in Conflict & Terrorism, 28,* 435–451.

Nisbet, M. C., & Lewenstein, B. V. (2002). Biotechnology and the American media: The policy process and the elite press, 1970 to 1999. *Science Communication, 23*(4), 359–391.

Perlmutter, D. D., & Wagner, G. L. (2004). The anatomy of a photojournalistic icon: Marginalization of dissent in the selection and framing of "a death in Genoa." *Visual Communication, 3*(1), 91–108.

Radway, J. (2007). What's the matter with reception study? Some thoughts on the disciplinary origins, conceptual constraints, and persistent viability of a paradigm. In P. Goldstein & J. L. Machor (Eds.), *New directions in American reception study: Reconsiderations and new directions* (pp. 327–353). New York: Oxford University Press.

Ramazanoglu, C., & Holland, J. (2002). *Feminist methodology: Challenges and choices.* Thousand Oaks, CA: Sage.

Rhode, D. L. (1997). Media images/feminist issues. In M. A. Fineman, & M. T. McCluskey (Eds.), *Feminism, media and the law* (pp. 8–21). New York: Oxford University Press.

Rohlinger, D. A. (2002). Framing the abortion debate: Organizational resources, media strategies, and movement-countermovement dynamics. *The Sociological Quarterly, 43*(4), 479–507.

Scheufele, D. A. (1999). Framing as a theory of media effects. *Journal of Communication, 49*(1), 103–122.

Stanley, L., & Wise, S. (1993). *Breaking out again: Feminist ontology and epistemology.* London: Routledge.

Steeves, H. L. (1987). Feminist theories and media studies. *Critical Studies in Mass Communication, 4*(2), 95–135.

Terkildsen, N., & Schnell, F. (1997). How media frames public opinion: An analysis of the women's movement. *Political Research Quarterly, 50,* 879–900.

Tickner, A. (2005). What is your research program? Some feminist answers to international relations methodological questions. *International Studies Quarterly, 49*(1), 1–22.

Tuchman, G. (1978a). *Making news.* New York: Free Press.

Tuchman, G. (1978b). Introduction: The symbolic annihilation of women by the mass media. In G. Tuchman, A. K. Daniels, & J. Benét (Eds.), *Hearth and home: Images of women in the mass media* (pp. 3–29). New York: Oxford University Press.

van Zoonen, E. A. (1992). The women's movement and the media: Constructing a public identity. *European Journal of Communication, 7,* 453–476.

van Zoonen, L. (1994). *Feminist media studies.* Thousand Oaks, CA: Sage.

Vavrus, M. D. (2007). Opting out moms in the news: Selling new traditionalism in the new millennium. *Feminist Media Studies, 7*(1), 47–59.

Whiteside, E., & Hardin, M. (2008). The rhetoric and ideology behind Title IX: An analysis of U.S. newspapers editorials, 2002–2005. *Women in Sport and Physical Activity Journal, 17*(1), 54–67.

Williams, J., Manvell, J., & Bornstein, S. (2006). *"Opt out" or pushed out? How the press covers work/family conflict.* San Francisco: The Center for Worklife Law, University of California, Hastings College of the Law.

Worthington, N. (2005). Negotiating news representations of rape: Reporting on a college sexual assault scandal. *Media Report to Women, 33*(4), 6–14.

# Chapter 14

# Framing Media Power

*Robert M. Entman*

A significant majority of the public believes the news media are biased and of these, most see the tilt as liberal. This is likely because the dominant discourse in American politics supports the assumption that the news and editorials produced by leading national media—the *New York Times, Washington Post, Time, Newsweek,* AP, UPI, NPR, ABC, CBS, NBC, and CNN—tend systematically to support the left, which suggests that when it comes to the issue of media bias, those same allegedly liberal media support the conservative line.[1] The purportedly liberal media appear to consistently slant in favor of conservatives' preferred framing when the media themselves are on the agenda as a political issue. That seems a strange exception for liberally biased media to make. Yet make it they do.

Entering the phrase "liberal media" into the U.S. Newspaper database of Lexis-Nexis (August 26, 2006 to August 26, 2008) yields 1,544 hits. Some use "liberal media" in the course of challenging the liberal bias claim, but by far its most frequent referent is "the most influential, mainstream national media."[2] The words implicitly assert that the most powerful journalists and news organizations profess objectivity while producing news that usually slants to the left. Enter "conservative media" and the data show 355 mentions, less than a quarter as many as for "liberal media." More important than the numerical disparity is that "conservative media" mostly arises when denoting specific media organizations that *self-identify as conservative* rather than objective. The objects of those organizations dubbed "conservative" thus welcome the label whereas many of those called "liberal" vehemently reject the implicit charge for untruth in labeling.[3]

Entering specifically the terms *liberal bias* or *liberal media bias* and the conservative counterparts yields a similar disparity. Forty-six instances of "conservative bias" and three of "conservative media bias" are found. By comparison, the search yields 52 mentions of "liberal media bias" and 266 of "liberal bias." Adding the two terms in each case yields a liberal bias to conservative bias claim ratio of about 6:1 (318:49).[4]

These figures seem hard to square with the proposition of liberal media bias. The confusion can be traced in major part to the failure of researchers to take liberal or conservative bias sufficiently seriously as objects of study. With all the heat and attention it incites among activists and ordinary citizens, bias has yet to be defined clearly, and despite careful attention from some scholars (see e.g. Kuypers 2002; Niven, 2002; Wasburn & Covert, 2008) remains underdeveloped as a research area. One reason for this, I believe, is the lack of a common conceptual infrastructure for bias studies. The more thoroughly refined concept of framing can provide just such a theoretical foundation for studies of bias that can build new insight into how media affect the distribution and operations of political power.

Before elaborating and illustrating my argument that bias merits a prominent place in studies of political communication and power, I would like to discuss how I arrived at the conclusion that illuminating the media's power in the political process requires a move beyond the standard approach taken in most framing studies.

Most framing effects studies set up artificial conditions that bear little relationship to the real world operations, purposes, and outcomes of framing in politics. Typically researchers vary a few words or occasionally an image in an experimental stimulus. More recently, scholars have begun acknowledging that real world framing usually involves audience exposure to a variety of framing messages that might well compete with each other, offering a potential choice between alternative interpretations. Unfortunately, some of this improved research frames its results misleadingly (and to be clear on this, social scientists engage in framing just as do journalists, natural scientists, film directors, novelists, and the rest of the communicating human race). These writings often assert that exposure to competing frames "reduces" framing effects. It would be more accurate, I believe, to say it "complicates" framing effects (illustrating the complexity is Chong & Druckman, 2007b). Worse, there is a tendency to conflate these purported findings of public resistance to framing effects with the normative conclusion that citizens are more competent than widely believed by social scientists. Yet, as Chong and Druckman (2007a) suggest, resistance to frames that illuminate new or old problems, solutions, or moral dilemmas doesn't necessarily betoken healthy citizenship. Moreover, if the old attitude resistant to the new framing treatment was itself (as is quite likely) influenced by framing effects at earlier times, the resistance provides scant logical basis for empirical or normative generalizations about citizen susceptibility to framing (see Entman, Matthes, & Pellicano, 2008, on the need to study framing diachronically).

More generally, I find much framing research strikingly apolitical. It tends to divorce framing from its use as a tool for exerting power in a system of political relationships. Some scholars (e.g., Riker, 1986) do acknowledge that framing is a mechanism used by strategic actors to induce others to behave as the actor wants, but most empirical framing effects studies neglect this context (cf. Carragee & Roefs, 2004). As a result, the full range of framing's operations and potential effects, especially impacts on political power, receive insufficient scholarly attention. Few framing studies, for instance, acknowledge the role of emotion (though see Gross & D'Ambrosio, 2004) and much of the research into communication effects that incorporate unconscious affective response aren't conceived as "framing" studies at all (e.g., Kang, 2005, for a summary of research on racial attitudes). It seems to me that looking for systematic bias in media framing of issues, actors, and events more thoroughly illuminates the *media's political effects* than the current narrower rubric of *framing effects*.

Although they are generally the least conscious and strategic of the frame choosers in the system, citizens are not passive receptacles for whatever frame dominates the media (if one frame does). My cascading network activation model (Entman, 2004) suggests how perceived public opinion can and does feed back to influence the future framing behavior of elites and journalists. But few citizens ponder which alternative framing of, say, a war or an economic crisis makes the most logical sense or best serves their own personal interests. They are cognitive misers who resist central processing and remain more politically disconnected than engaged (Graber, 2001). And they also tend, at least in America and in politics, not to vote or reason heavily on the basis of self-interest (Hacker & Pierson, 2005; Sears, 1997). Ordinary citizens are therefore quite susceptible to framing effects in the real world, which often involve not one exposure to a slight message variation, but a pattern of repeated exposure to resonant words and images (on the importance of studying framing as a diachronic process see Entman, Matthes, & Pellicano, 2008). An example from the case discussed later, 2008 Republican vice presidential nominee Sarah Palin, was framed by repeating positive, culturally resonant tropes like "hockey mom."

Beyond effects on individual opinions, we need to understand framing effects in terms of power, of who gets their way in politics and policy. For a political actor to win, their frame doesn't have to convince all or even a majority of individual citizens, who may indeed resist the message. What's important to political power is whether a frame has a decisive effect on the swing or undecided voters, or the ideological moderates, those whose opinions are the most malleable. Except for a handful of issues, officials, and candidates, a framing effect on 3 or 4% of the audience—one that might not even reach statistical significance in an experimental setting—can establish which policy garners the decisive imprimatur of majority approval in a survey, or which candidate wins an election.

So even if 90% or more of individuals completely resist manipulative framing, for the purposes of understanding who gets what, when, and how, this individual-level resistance may have limited political relevance. If it further turns out that framing falls into persistent patterns that enhance the power of particular interests to get their way in politics, framing impacts on just a small minority of citizens could have decisive political importance. Seeking enduring patterns of framing is the primary mission of bias research as propounded here.

Although I may sound critical of empirical framing research, I recognize that it is much easier to recommend than to carry out framing studies at elite levels. It makes sense that most empirical studies of framing effects rely on survey experiments or lab experiments using citizens (or students) as subjects; experiments are manageable and often yield compelling results. Nonetheless, as my reasoning suggests, what appear to be null or statistically insignificant results at the individual level might mask important macrolevel effects. If experimental studies often yield marginal results in the lab, those same results translated to the real world might produce outsize political effects. My own conclusion from this point is that carrying out a more ambitious research agenda on framing and political power requires not merely more innovative framing effects studies, but also application of a more sophisticated theoretical/conceptual apparatus to content analysis. Although scholars cannot use content data to definitely prove political effects, my point here is that experimental studies don't prove them either, and content analyses actually might make equally illuminating contributions to understanding the real world of powerful political communication. That at least is why my research remains reliant on nuanced content analyses informed now by my conceptual frameworks of news slant and bias, as well as by my cascading network activation model—which ensures a multilevel focus and diachronic perspective that transcends isolated individual citizens. Another boon to my own work is the availability of powerful computer programs such as QDA Miner, which allow improved efficiency in carrying out more complex content analyses.

## The Concepts of Bias

A review of the literature suggests the term *bias* seems to take on three major meanings. Sometimes it is applied to news that purportedly distorts or falsifies reality (*distortion bias*); sometimes to news that favors one side rather than providing equivalent treatment of both sides in a political conflict (*content bias*); and sometimes to the motivations and mindsets of journalists who allegedly produce the biased content (*decision-making bias*). This essay argues that bias, particularly in the second and third senses, merits closer theoretical and empirical attention.

Furthermore, although agenda setting, framing, and priming have sepa-rately received a great deal of scholarly attention, this chapter contends that they can be integrated under the conceptual umbrella of bias to advance understanding of the media's role in distributing power, reveal-ing new dimensions and processes of critically *political* communication.[5] Such a project would also offer normative guidance for scholars, for journalists striving to construct more "fair and balanced" news—and for the many citizens and activists who feel victimized by biased media (cf. Eveland & Shah, 2003).

Most of the studies that do explicitly explore bias focus on presiden-tial campaigns and administrations, and find little evidence of decisive or consistent ideological or partisan bias (D'Alessio & Allen, 2000; Niven, 2002; Wasburn & Covert, 2008). Yet this conclusion sits uneasily along-side findings, not usually filed under "bias" scholarship, revealing news that consistently favors a side in covering social conflicts and political issues. Some of this is my own work on media's images of minorities (Entman & Rojecki, 2000; see also, Kang, 2005) and their coverage of U.S. foreign policy (Entman, 2004). My research spurred me to think more carefully about the wide applicability of framing as a concept. It also convinced me that despite mainstream journalists' apparently sin-cere conscious commitment to objectivity norms and practices, in certain realms the U.S. media do exhibit lasting patterns of one-sided framing that help to augment the power of some interests while undermining the power of others. Indeed there are few better-supported generalizations in social science than that mainstream media content subtly but consis-tently sustains White anxiety and ignorance about Blacks, directly and indirectly undermining the collective political influence and life condi-tions of African Americans.[6]

Other studies suggest that underneath the apparent quantitative bal-ance in coverage is news that in powerful dimensions, by omission as well as commission, supports Republican talking points. For example, in 2000, the mainstream media did more to promote than undermine unsupported perceptions that Democratic presidential candidate Al Gore was a serial liar (Jamieson & Waldman, 2002), and in 2001 to 2003 that most Americans benefited from tax cuts directly advantaging only the very wealthiest (cf. Bartels, 2008; Entman et al., 2005; Hacker & Pierson, 2005). On the other hand, coverage of such social issues as abortion, homelessness, homosexuality, religion, and gun control might provide examples of news more systematically slanting to the left (see Kuypers, 2002, finding liberal tilt in covering such issues as affirmative action, and writings cited by Wasburn & Covert, 2008, pp. 5–7, 20–21). None of these studies, however, is comprehensive enough to establish the existence of an institutionalized ideological bias as defined here.

This study does not attempt to do so. Instead it advances the more comprehensive conceptualization that would enable such a project. The consolidating question: do the agenda setting and framing content of texts, and their priming effects on audiences, fall into persistent, politically relevant *patterns*? Powerful players devote massive resources to advancing their interests precisely by imposing such patterns on mediated communications. To the extent we reveal and explain them, we illuminate the classic questions of politics: who gets what, when, and how (Lasswell, 1966)?

## Reconsidering Connections

Scholars can shed new light on bias by examining linkages among the three concepts that have received such intense scholarly scrutiny. We can define *framing* as the process of culling a few elements of perceived reality and assembling a narrative that highlights connections among them to promote a particular interpretation. Fully developed frames typically perform four functions: problem definition, causal analysis, moral judgment, and remedy promotion (Entman, 1993, 2004). Framing works to shape and alter audience members' interpretations and preferences through *priming*. That is, frames introduce or raise the salience or apparent importance of certain ideas, activating schemas that encourage target audiences to think, feel, and decide in a particular way (e.g., Chong & Druckman 2007a; Gross & D'Ambrosio, 2004; Iyengar & Simon, 1993; Kim, Scheufele, & Shanahan, 2002; Price, Tewksbury, & Powers, 1997).

The strategic framing contests that occupy the heart of the political process take place in the first instance over the agenda (Riker, 1986). *Agenda setting* can thus be seen as another name for successfully performing the first function of framing: defining those problems worthy of public and government attention. Among other things, agenda problems can spotlight societal conditions, world events, or character traits of a candidate. The second or "attribute" level of agenda setting (McCombs & Ghanem, 2001) centrally involves three types of claims that happen to encompass the core business of strategic framing: to highlight the causes of problems, encourage moral judgments (and associated affective responses), and promote favored policies. Priming then is a name for the goal, the intended effect, of strategic actors' framing activities.[7] The oft-quoted but misleading phrase that inaugurated the modern study of media effects is that: "the media may not be successful much of the time in telling people what to think, but is stunningly successful in telling its readers what to think *about*" (Cohen, 1963, p. 13, emphasis in original). Although the distinction between "what to think" and "what to think *about*," is not entirely clear, the former seems to mean what people decide, favor or accept, whereas the latter refers to the considerations they "think about" in coming to such conclusions. The distinction misleads because, short of physical coercion, all influence over "what people think" derives from telling them "what to think about." If the media really are stunningly successful in telling people what to think about, they must also exert significant influence over what they think. That is, second level agenda setting or telling people what to think about produces framing and priming effects.

Elites presumably care about "what people think" because they want them to behave in certain ways, supporting or at least tolerating elite activities. Given limitations of time, attention, and rationality, getting people to think (and behave) in a certain way requires selecting some things to tell them about, and efficiently cueing them on how these elements mesh with their own schema systems. The best succinct definition of power is the ability to get others to do what one wants (Nagel, 1975). In noncoercive political systems, then, "telling people what to think about"—and thus trying to shape "what they think"—is the way to influence what they do. And it is through framing that political actors shape the texts that influence, or prime, the agendas and considerations that people think about.

Having shown how agenda setting, framing and priming fit together as critical tools in the exercise of political power, we now need to connect them to bias. To help avoid the terminological confusion alluded to earlier, I propose to distinguish bias from *news slant*. Slant characterizes individual news reports and editorials in which the *framing favors one side over the other in a current or potential dispute*. Mainstream news organizations contend that they treat competing frames equivalently, ensuring their reports do not slant. Yet political actors constantly (and strategically) complain that the media favor their opponents. It seems reasonable to hypothesize that these elites might sometimes have it right: they or their opponents do often succeed in imposing slant on mainstream media reports. Slanted news is not, as journalists tend to insist, the rare exception.[8] As suggested by the model explained shortly, rather than being rare, slant is the entirely predictable product of the interactions among forces that only occasionally will combine to yield balance in the short term. And arguably, the short term matters the most in politics and policymaking. To take election coverage, then, if framing of presidential candidates evens out over an entire campaign year, such balance may be politically irrelevant if slant arises during critical times for voter decision making—say, during the introduction of vice presidential candidates (the presidential nominees' "first major executive decision"), coverage of party conventions, and candidate debates.

Scholars need to assess the larger theoretical implications in these demonstrated instances of consistent one-sided framing. These incidences might fall into no consistent pattern, in which case the slant would not support an inference of media bias. However, if the patterns of slant do persist across time, message dimensions, and media outlets, it means the media may be systematically assisting such entities as political parties to induce their preferred behavior in others. That is to say, the media may be helping to distribute political power to groups, causes, or individuals associated with one party. This brings us to the proposed definition of content bias: *consistent patterns in the framing of mediated communication that promote the influence of one side in conflicts over the use of government power.* By this definition, to reveal media content biases, we must show patterns of slant that regularly prime audiences, consciously or unconsciously,[9] to support the interests of particular holders or seekers of political power.

Through the forgoing definitions, this paper seeks to reduce the confusion and imprecision sown by the three most common uses of "bias." One advantage of thinking about slant and bias in this way is that it avoids irresolvable questions about truth and reality. It retires the notion of distortion bias, which serves mainly as an epithet against news that some actors dislike. As political communication research demonstrates, indisputable facts play only a partial role in shaping the framing words and images that flow into an audience's consciousness. Since almost any nontrivial reality will be controversial—susceptible to two or more framings—what we can and should do is determine *whose power over government action is likely enhanced by media framing.* In other words, we should study how the news slants in particular instances, and whether slant falls into recurrent patterns that, in Schattschneider's (1960) classic formulation, "mobilize bias" in the political system by helping some actors regularly prevail over others.[10] Media bias, then, measures any stable textual framing that modifies or reinforces elites' clout through its impact on polyarchy (Dahl, 1989)—on the electorate's choice of office-holders and the political calculations that shape those officials' representation of the public.

Having refined the second common meaning—*content bias*—it remains to consider the third, which refers, usually pejoratively, to the inevitable influence of news workers' belief systems on the texts they produce. It seems pointless either to deny or denounce the existence of these *decision-making biases.* All information-processing persons and organizations employ what might more neutrally be called heuristics. This is the only way they can cope with bounded rationality and information overload. The media's decision biases operate within the minds of individual journalists and within the processes of journalistic institutions, embodied in (generally unstated) rules and norms that guide their processing of information and influence the framing of media texts. In another context (Entman, 1996) I referred to these decision biases as "the real media biases," and it is these that can help us understand why slanted news proliferates despite the mainstream national media's general dedication to fairness, balance, or objectivity.

## Toward More Precise Formulations of Slant and Bias

The equation below serves as a succinct metaphor for the complicated interactions of decision biases with other forces that give rise to news slant. The point of displaying these nonquantifiable forces as an equation is to show that any pattern of news slant has roots that include but are not limited to the decision biases. The formula asserts that the degree to which a single news construction favors one ideology, interest, group, issue stand, or candidate against opponents is a function of the perceived facts, plus the interactions of each side's skill at news management with journalistic decision biases. In this light, it makes little sense to assert, as so many critics do, that journalists' personal ideological views are both the only decision biases of consequence *and* the sole forces shaping slant. The illustrated formula depicts a framing contest between the president's party and the opposition party.

$$NS = F + [S_{WH} \times (B_E + B_M + B_I)] - [S_O \times (B_E + B_M + B_I)] + E$$

Where:
$NS$ = slant of a specific news item
$F$ = perceived facts
$S_{WH}$ = skill of White House/administration news managers
$S_O$ = skill of opposition party news managers
[Skill = charisma, intimidation, flattery, adroit rhetoric, and other strategies to optimize framing given $B_E$, $B_M$, $B_I$]
$B_E$ = Decision biases arising from *evaluation of the political game* (power; popularity; unity; cynicism)
$B_M$ = Decision biases arising from *market* competition (simplification; process (horserace) over substance (policy); fragmentation; personalization)
$B_I$ = Decision biases arising from personal *ideology*
$E$ = event context and other sources of variation

As the equation suggests, any given set of perceived facts can yield news that slants toward one side or the other side or even (as in the journalistic ideal) neither side. Because facts rarely speak for themselves, strategic actors must deploy such assets as charisma, a delicate balance of intimidation and flattery, and rhetorical proficiency to promote favored framing.[11] Journalists' responses to these blandishments emerge most importantly from the evaluative standards they apply to actors playing the political game, and from the production norms encouraged by market competition. The former include a tendency to slant news favorably toward the side journalists regard as most powerful, popular, and unified (Entman 1989; Entman & Page, 1994). The latter include such well-documented qualities of news as simplification and fragmentation (Bennett, 2008). Ideologies held by reporters and editors may also play a role in shaping the news (Patterson & Donsbach, 1996). However, in news stories and even editorials, personal ideology combines with all the other forces in the model, including external spin managers and internal pressures from owners and executives responding to market incentives (Bennett, 2008; Entman, 1989; see also, Bennett, 1990; Gilens & Hertzman, 2000, on editorials). The final term in the equation denotes event context (newsworthy happenings around the same time) and other unpredictable variables that can substantially influence framing. An example would be the way the sudden eruption of war between Hezbollah in Lebanon and Israel displaced coverage of the Iraq war during the summer of 2006, when, arguably, the situation in the latter deteriorated to its all-time low.

If the decision biases persistently converge with stable concentrations of political skill and resources possessed by particular interests, media frames could consistently favor certain policy outcomes and political actors. Such content biases could exist even where journalists and news organizations possess no conscious ideological goals, indeed where they consciously pursue balance (cf. Kuklinski & Sigelman, 1992). Episodes of slanted news are common, because over the short term it seems quite likely that communication skill, facts, and decision biases will mesh in ways that favor one actor over another—and unlikely that these forces will somehow interact to perfectly balance each other out.

## The Party Conventions in 2008: A Case Study of Slant and Decision Biases

Conveniently enough for analysts, the U.S. has two significant political parties, and journalists organize their source networks and news narratives around them. That means we do not have to extend the news slant formula to more than two sides, although that would be possible.

The admittedly preliminary case study presented here covers only a couple of weeks: coverage of the 2008 Democratic and Republican conventions on ABC *World News* (nightly evening newscast) and *This Week* (Sunday morning news talk). Despite this limitation, which means among other things that the empirical data here can only tell us something about slant and nothing about bias, the case does illustrate how the political communication system can work to promote the power of one side over another. Although it will never be definitively provable, we can also find evidence that the slant in covering the conventions did affect swing voters at least for some period.

ABC News was chosen randomly from the three still-dominant news organizations, the news outlets enjoying by far the largest daily audiences (ABC, CBS, and NBC evening newscasts).[12] Each of the networks sponsors a Sunday news talk show aimed at upscale and informed viewers, offering an overview of the week's news and a mix of analysis and opinion that arguably reflects the conventional wisdom of elite Washington. The analysis probed for evaluative assertions about individual nominees or the party's ticket on three dimensions that account for almost all evaluations and for most of the information that goes into voting decisions for those whose choices are not predetermined by partisan loyalty: character and qualifications; campaign skill and horserace standing; and policy stands. The source for each assertion on each dimension was coded as Democratic, Republican, or Journalist. The latter counted as a source where the information was not a quotation or paraphrase of a partisan source but rather was either entirely unattributed or else cited a source without clear partisan affiliation (usually, poll results and "person on the street" interviews) *chosen by the journalist* to illustrate some conclusion on the three evaluative dimensions.

Thus we have a matrix of 36 possible evaluative assertions: Negative for Democrats Sourced to Democrats; Negative for Democrats Sourced to Republicans; Negative for Democrats Sourced to Journalists; Positive for Democrats Sourced to Democrats; and so forth, yielding 12 evaluation objects and sources, with each assertion coded as involving character/personality/ qualifications; campaign skills and standing; or policy.[13]

The research literature suggests the following expectations of campaign news slant given the relationships among facts, communication skill, and media decision biases:

1. Media market biases lead most coverage to focus on candidate character and horserace. This provides an inherent advantage to the party that focuses its campaign on the candidates' qualifications and character as opposed to policy positions.
2. Media evaluation biases favoring power, popularity, and unity benefit the party that successfully cultivates journalists' perceptions of campaign skill and of its candidates' majority or growing popularity.

Put another way, the media's disinclination to cover policy, in my terms their process (over substance) bias, disadvantages a party that focuses its campaign on policy. This is compounded by journalism's tendency to personalize politics, which leads to an emphasis during campaigns on candidates' individual traits and qualifications, perceptions of which are highly susceptible to skillful manipulation. And the media's evaluation biases disadvantage a party that is behind or slipping in the polls, that seems maladroit in handling its power resources, and that appears internally divided. These "real media biases" will in most cases overwhelm any personal ideological biases that reporters and editors might bring to the production of news.

Table 14.1 suggests that these decision biases seemed to combine with superior Republican skill to yield a stark difference in ABC News's treatment of Democrats and Republicans during the 2 weeks spanning the parties' nominating conventions (August 23–September 7).[14] Among the 103 paragraphs on *World News* containing evaluative assertions about the Democrat slate, *nearly four out of five* (79%) offered negative assessments, with just 21% positive. For Republicans, in 114 paragraphs, the split was 61% positive, 39% negative. The net coverage in this perspective was about three times more positive for Republicans: the net for Democrats was deep in negative territory at -58% (-79%+21%) while the net for Republicans was a clearly positive +22% (61%–39%). At this aggregate level, ABC offered neither neutrality for both (which would have yielded net scores around 0% for both parties), nor equally negative or positive treatment. On the two broadcasts of *This Week*, the Sunday news talk show, during the convention weeks, the imbalance is not quite as stark but remains far more negative for Democrats than Republicans.

Now, how might we explain these findings? They certainly do not comport with the notion that mainstream national media such as the ABC News division consistently impose their purported personal ideological liberalism on either the straight news program (*World News*) or the analysis/opinion program (*This Week*). Some might argue that the findings reflect the facts of the matter, that Republicans deserved much more positive treatment because they did a better job of communicating with the media and public, for instance by choosing a fresh, surprising, and attractive vice presidential nominee. But by itself this explanation begs the question by equating "the facts" with the *communicative performance* and dances close to tautology—the media communicated the Republican message more positively because the GOP had a more positive message. Rather than facts, the slant arises from framing; that is, from choice, suppression, emphasis, and connection among (often debatable) facts.

A way to tease this out beyond tautology is to dig further into just what we mean by *skill*. This term in the news slant equation measures the degree to which the communicative performance is orchestrated to emphasize and suppress perceived facts in accordance with the media's decision biases. In the American context, we can assume there will always be potential or actual competition from the other party. A major component of skill is ability to strictly limit the rhetorical options of opponents by constructing a frame so culturally resonant that other interpretations will be incomprehensible or threatening. The skilled elite communicator selects elements of reality to emphasize that will resonate with the

Table 14.1 Negative and Positive Evaluations of Democratic and Republican Candidates During Two Weeks Surrounding 2008 Party Conventions (ABC World News and This Week)

| | Negative on Democrats | | | Positive on Democrats | | | Negative on Republicans | | | Positive on Republicans | | |
|---|---|---|---|---|---|---|---|---|---|---|---|---|
| | Qualify | Horserace | Policy | Qualify | Horserace | Policy | Qualify | Horserace | Policy | Qualify | Horserace | Policy |
| World News | 33 | 42 | 6 | 7 | 11 | 4 | 18 | 10 | 15 | 35 | 20 | 15 |
| This Week | 25 | 17 | 5 | 14 | 12 | 2 | 19 | 5 | 14 | 31 | 10 | 6 |
| Total | 58 | 59 | 11 | 21 | 23 | 6 | 37 | 15 | 29 | 66 | 30 | 21 |

schemas of media communicators, allowing the preferred line to move easily through the news production process and enter repeatedly and coherently into the text, where it will meld with the networks of schemas in the minds of target audiences. Elite actors rarely enjoy 100% success in transferring only the frames they desire and suppressing all signifiers of competing problem agendas. Nor can they freeze out all messages that might prime media to transmit—and audiences to consider—alternative solutions, moral evaluations, and emotional reactions. Rather the goal is to minimize their salience by distracting target audiences through the dazzling correspondence between the communicator's preferred framing messages and the media's decision biases—as well as the audience's own decision biases (i.e., their schema systems as influenced by the dominant culture).

Coverage of Republican vice presidential nominee Sarah Palin, who burst on the political scene during the studied period, would offer a revealing example of constructing a reality selectively by emphasizing some (debatable) facts and using them to fashion a frame compelling enough to distract media and audiences from other readily available framings. In this version "hockey mom" and "maverick" trump "mother who repeatedly violates the 'traditional values' she and her party profess" and "totally inexperienced in the area of McCain's primary strength, foreign policy—and quite likely to replace the elderly, ailing McCain." The trumps can be summarized in a synechdotal word or two immediately triggering familiar, positive associations, whereas the counterframes require more than the two cognitive steps of noticing and understanding.

Call this a *two-step limit*, enforced by journalists' simplification bias, embodying the (generally accurate) assumption that their market consists of cognitive misers uninterested in thinking deeply about politics. Communicators cannot entirely disregard facts, as the news slant equation indicates. But given the simplification and other decision biases, the essence of skill is to select a problem definition, moral stance, or solution (in this case, vice presidential nominee) where the facts can plausibly be routed through the most accessible textual frames and mental schemas, those that dominate the political cultural repertoire.[15]

Inescapably, the interpretation of findings in this chapter also requires framing. How we decipher the findings depends in some part on which slice of the data we want to emphasize. If we look only at the policy evaluations, the coverage seems closer to balanced between positive and negative and between the two parties than on the other dimensions, with a mere 2:1 negative ratio for Democrats and 1.3:1 negative for Republicans. Table 14.2 displays only the other two dimensions, which appear more important for determining election outcomes. It suggests the coverage is slanted in favor of the Republicans by a striking margin—nearly 3:1 negative for Democrats, and about 1.5:1 *positive* for Republicans.

*Table 14.2*   Paragraph Totals for Positive and Negative Treatment of Democrats and Republicans Excluding Policy Dimension

|  | # paragraphs with Negative assertions on qualifications/ character and horserace | # paragraphs with Positive assertions on qualifications/ character and horserace |
|---|---|---|
| Democratic ticket | 123 | 44 |
| Republican ticket | 80 | 117 |

The reason for the slant can be found in the news slant formula, the interaction of facts, media decision biases, and skill of the competing elite factions. During the time studied here, the Democrats' popularity was stagnant or slipping, despite (as reporters often mentioned) 2008 being a year where real world conditions strongly favored their side. In a double whammy promoting negative slant, their campaign's effective use of power was denied by the highly visible discord between Hillary Clinton and Barack Obama supporters—disunity that fed journalists' insatiable bias for stories featuring conflict as it demonstrated the nominee's lack of power to control and discipline the party that he nominally led.

The relative unity of the two parties offers one example of differential in skill (demonstrated by discipline in sticking to a monolithic party line during a time of high media attention) interacting with a media decision bias (favoring unity). This point is supported by the figures on Democratic self-criticism vs. Republican self-criticism displayed in Table 14.3. In the former category we find 28 paragraphs; in the latter, 2. By the same token, whereas Democrats were cited 10 times saying nice things about Republicans, only 4 paragraphs had a Republican complimenting the Democrats. (Only on attacking the other party was there

*Table 14.3*   Sources of Negative and Positive Evaluations During Two Weeks Surrounding 2008 Party Conventions, ABC World News and This Week

|  | Evaluations by Democrats | Evaluations by Republicans | Evaluations by Journalists | Totals |
|---|---|---|---|---|
| Negative Evaluations of Democrats | 28 | 45 | 61 | 134 |
| Negative Evaluations of Republicans | 49 | 2 | 30 | 81 |
| Positive Evaluations of Democrats | 23 | 4 | 23 | 50 |
| Positive Evaluations of Republicans | 10 | 53 | 54 | 117 |
| Totals | 110 | 104 | 168 | 382 |

parity: 49 paragraphs containing a negative evaluation of Republicans by a Democrat, and 45 the reverse.) Given research suggesting that perceived strength of a leader is particularly consequential for swing voters' judgments (Edelman, 1988; Westen, 2007 ), as is a leader's perceived commitment to discipline (Lakoff, 2006 ), it seems reasonable to suspect that the messages conveyed through the negative slant on the horserace dimension in particular were significant for many uncertain citizens. Looking only at the candidate qualification/character dimension, which might seem the more rational basis for voters' decisions, the Democrats also fare poorly: nearly a 3:1 negative ratio, as compared with a close to 2:1 positive ratio for the Republicans.

Table 14.3 also illustrates the contributions of the different sources to the slant, showing that journalists and Democrats together contribute more than half the negative claims about Democrats; Democrats' undermining of themselves compares with self-protective Republicans, a practice that may (given the unity bias) explain the smaller contribution of journalists to the GOP's negative column. Democrats' self-criticism— as the table shows, 14 times more common than Republicans' (bolded figures in Table 14.3: 28 and 2)—stimulated journalists to issue many more negative judgments for the Democrats too (italicized figures in Table 14.3): 61 versus 30. Also important, and further undermining any case for a liberal bias at least in this admittedly small sample from one network, consider not just these negative evaluations uttered or chosen by ABC correspondents, but also the positive: 23 favorable paragraphs for the Democrats, 54 for the Republicans.

One further and more precise way to analyze these data would be to weigh them in accordance with our understanding of how audiences— particularly those not constrained by stable partisan and ideological loyalties—actually process information. If the literature suggests the undecideds in the audience of the two conventions were more likely to be moved by information about candidate qualifications and character than by horserace or policy information, then it would be appropriate to develop a weighted measure of slant that takes the differential impact of the dimensions into account. That task is beyond the scope of this particular chapter, but devising precision gauges of slant and ultimately bias should be possible and beneficial (cf. Entman, 2007).

The idea that the slant during the convention period favored Republicans gains some support from polls. For instance, on August 21, the day before vice presidential nominee Biden was named and 2 days before the Democrats' convention, the "Very Favorable" ratings for Obama were 33% and for McCain 20%; by September 10, these numbers were 36% and 28%—a slight, marginally significant bump of 3 points for Obama and a significant increase of 8 points for McCain. According to two widely circulated state-by-state Electoral College projections, McCain gained significantly after his convention, pulling ahead in projected electoral votes for the first time, a trend that began around August 29, the day Palin was named, and the day after the Democratic convention ended.[16]

In naming Sarah Palin as his running mate, McCain made a pitch for support from undecided females, particularly White women. The likelihood that media (not just ABC) slant favored Republicans during the conventions is suggested by this summary of a Washington Post-ABC News poll:

> The percentage of white women with "strongly favorable" opinions of McCain jumped 12 percentage points from before the parties' national conventions. And nearly six in 10 white women in the new poll said McCain's selection of Palin increased their confidence in the decisions he would make if elected. In the Post-ABC poll, it is white women who helped McCain erase Obama's late-August advantage and seriously cut into the Democratic nominee's lead as the one who would bring more needed change to Washington.[17]

In other words, the polls suggest (without proving, of course) that slanted framing helped distribute more power to the McCain and Palin ticket, at least for a time.

Given the media's decision biases, the indisputable facts (and also the disputed ones) of the Palin selection *could* have been "spun" to create quite a different impression of McCain and his vice presidential nominee, had the Democrats been more skilled, the Republicans less adroit, or both. By the same token, a shift in these forces later in the campaign could have substantially altered slant, possibly providing advantage to the Democrats.[18] This case is the proverbial snapshot in time, chosen to illustrate how a study of slanted framing might work. To further develop into a study of *bias*, at least in covering presidential elections, the research would have to probe coverage across a representative sample of media at critical junctures throughout several campaign cycles.

## Conclusion

The case study is manifestly limited and serves only as a pilot for larger-scaled future research on slant and bias in covering campaigns. It includes but one TV network, albeit arguably their two most influential programs. Although the polling evidence just cited and prior research lends support to the expectation that the other two broadcast networks' coverage (and that of CNN) probably exhibited similar slant (see Cook, 2005; Graber 2005, pp. 252, 272, 304 and passim) this remains conjecture. The study only looks at the brief period covering the party conventions, taking advantage of the unusual timing that had one almost immediately following the other. At most, we can say that coverage apparently slanted against the Democrats for this period. But this phase may be important, as research suggests convention-time offers one of the most important opportunities for the undecided and poorly informed to gather information and make choices (e.g., Jamieson & Birdsell, 1990).

Returning from slant to *bias*, by my definition the present study constitutes only a bare sliver of the necessary research. Some researchers in the critical studies traditions might conclude that whatever the vicissitudes of presidential elections, the media meet the suggested standards for bias at a more fundamental level: consistent framing in favor of capitalism, patriarchy, heterosexism, individualism, consumerism, and White privilege, among other deeply entrenched values that certainly help to allocate power in American society (Budd, Craig, & Steinman, 1999). This seems to me pretty well supported by a wide range of cultural studies.

However, my own research has always been more concerned with media interventions in the day-to-day contests to control government power *within* the snug ideological confines of mainstream American politics. These set the boundaries for public discourse on most government policies. They also set the boundaries for discussions of the media as political actors, which are widely seen as exhibiting a marked liberal bias. Yet as I have argued, the causes, nature, and consequences of slanted framing and perhaps, bias, are far too complicated and underexplored to support such a conclusion.

As an example of the complications, consider the 2008 presidential campaign. Democrats said they wanted the campaign to be about issues, whereas McCain campaign manager Rick Davis said he wanted a campaign about personality (Martin & Vandehei, 2008). All things equal this meant the media's decision bias against policy coverage unintentionally boosted McCain's strategy. The horse race or what I call "process over substance" bias is among the most thoroughly supported findings in political communication research (e.g., Patterson, 1993). The personalization bias is also well established (Hart, 1998). What is not widely recognized is that these sorts of nonideological decision biases can help to distribute political power. They create a tendency to slant in favor of a party that campaigns skillfully on the alleged positive elements of their candidate's character and horserace proficiency while attacking their opponent on these dimensions. Arguably, with swing voters by definition casting the decisive ballots, the elections of 2000, 2004, and 2008 all turned on Republicans understanding and playing to the process and personalization biases—even as they helped their case by crying "liberal bias" as a way of pressuring (i.e., skillfully intimidating) news organizations to remain responsive to the messages they tuned for compatibility with the real media biases (cf. Westen, 2007, on Democrats' tendency to damage their campaigns by neglecting what I call the personalization and horserace biases to emphasize issues). Again, however, we need more conceptual refinement and empirical research before reaching any final conclusions on content bias.

Two of my own normative priorities particularly move me to promote such further study of slanted and perhaps biased framing as a way of illuminating media effects on power over public policy: my support for democratic accountability, and my strong belief that the United States is best served by relying on soft power and diplomacy with war as a last resort. Based on these normative predilections, on my personal observations as a "political junkie" increasingly prone to view news through the prism of framing and slant analysis, *and* on the series of empirical case studies I have been engaged in for three books (on media bias, media scandals, and media and war) the widespread conviction that mainstream media exhibit liberal bias severely misreads journalists' behavior and texts. Entrenched despite the lack of empirical evidence or careful conceptualization of "bias," this misimpression has become a valuable power resource for conservative elites (cf. Watts, Domke, Shah, & Fan 1999). For instance, although there are multiple explanations and forces at work, fearful of being tarred as liberally biased, news organizations seem to pursue potential scandals less energetically when they involve Republicans than Democrats. This can have significant policy consequences while undermining government accountability. Trapped by the "liberal bias" stereotype, news organizations also seem more reluctant to question national security policies chosen by Republicans than Democrats, and, worse, more prone to promote military force over sophisticated multimodal approaches to international relations (e.g., Entman 2004; Entman, Livingston, & Kim, 2009). In my view, the unrecognized, unmeasured, and misperceived natures of news slant and bias demand correction not merely because empirical accuracy should always be valued, but because in some cases, slanted framing can affect politicians' life and death decisions.

## Notes

1. Note that Fox News is omitted because it has been shown to—in practice if not in slogan—consistently slant its coverage to the right (e.g., Aday, 2006). Watts, Domke, Shah, and Fan (1999) find that most coverage of the bias issue asserts that liberal bias permeates, and most of the public as of the 1990s accepted the premise. The perception persisted, according to Rasmussen polls and many others. As of September 2008, for instance, most respondents believed the media were favoring Obama over McCain: 50% said media were helping Obama, 11% helping McCain, 26% helping neither. This broke down along partisan lines with 83% of Republicans,

53% of Independents, and 19% of Democrats feeling the press favored Obama. Retrieved from http://www.rasmussenreports.com/public_content/politics/election_20082/2008_presidentialelection/69_say_reporters_try_to_help_the_candidate_they_want_to_win )

2. This includes all mentions including those in letters to the editor and editorials.

3. Many mainstream journalists do plead guilty to being center-left Democrats and to their views possibly coloring their reporting in some cases; none to my knowledge has ever publicly said their personal views constitute the primary force driving their political coverage—as often charged by conservative critics such as Bernard Goldberg.

4. Some of these mentions in each case attacked the applicability of the term, although most endorsed it. In any case, what's noteworthy for the purposes here is the heavy predominance of concerns with alleged preference for the left in media discussions of media bias.

5. This paper considers only the mainstream power struggles, usually between liberals and conservatives roughly, but increasingly aligned with the two major U.S. parties that structure the electoral system (cf. Hacker & Pierson, 2005). Space limitations preclude exploration of the media's role in reinforcing (or refereeing conflicts over) deeper structures of power (cf. Carragee & Roefs, 2004).

6. There are arguable exceptions, especially at the individual level. Some might argue that such Black politicians as Colin Powell, Condoleeza Rice, and Barack Obama benefited from a positive media slant. The first two are conservatives, the last liberal, so ideological bias appears irrelevant to the exceptions, as predicted by the analysis below. Moreover, discrimination and unfavorable public policies continue to damage the living conditions and opportunities of the average African American in ways that show up clearly in most studies (see Entman & Gross, 2008, for summaries of such findings).

7. Kimberly Gross (personal communication) suggests that scholars seem often to choose among the three terms based less on theoretical distinctions among them than on the dependent variable of interest. They tend to use agenda setting when explaining the "most important problem" survey response; framing, when tracing impacts on policy preferences; and priming, when exploring evaluations of political leaders. See Chong and Druckman (2007a) on the functional equivalence of framing and priming effects.

8. Beyond racial issues and foreign policy, scholars often discover a decided tilt—at least on the dimensions that they (imperfectly) measure. These include coverage of congressional candidates (Druckman & Parkin, 2005; Kahn & Kenney, 2002), protest movements (Rojecki, 1999), and unions (Martin, 2004; but cf. Manheim, 2005).

9. The literature repeatedly demonstrates impacts of unconscious reactions on attitudes and actions (see Kang, 2005).

10. Writing at a time when the minimal media consequences paradigm reigned, Schattschneider himself was not referring to media bias, but his use of the term inspires the one advanced here.

11. As complex as the illustrative formula already is, it omits such complications as the interactions of perceived "facts" with the skill of opposing media manipulators. Elements of reality perceived as relevant facts themselves are malleable constructions in the hands of skilled players.

12. In an average month, according to Nielsen research for the Newspaper Association of America, about 68 million Americans visit a newspaper Web site; the average visitor comes back about 8.3 times a month. This figure includes most newspaper Web sites, so any individual site has a much lower audience. In any case the figure suggests than average audience for all newspaper Web sites for a given day is well under 9 million (68/8.3).Retrieved from http://www.naa.org/PressCenter/SearchPressReleases/2008/NEWS-PAPER-WEB-SITES-ATTRACT-RECORD-AUDIENCES-IN-FIRST-QUARTER.aspx). The evening newscasts on the three venerable networks still attracted nearly 24 million households (and more individuals) per day in 2008. Retrieved from http://www.nytimes.com/2008/08/04/business/media/04ratings.html?_r=1&scp=2&sq=evening%20news%20ratings&st=cse&oref=slogin.

The highest circulation newspaper, *USA Today*, had about 2.5 million daily readers in 2008, followed by the *Wall Street Journal* with 2.05 million and the *New York Times* with 1.7 million. Retrieved from http://www.infoplease.com/ipea/ A0004420.html

13. Policy assertions were coded under slightly less rigorous standards for exhibiting explicit evaluative content, on the assumption that when stating their policy positions, candidates or supporters are uttering approval for them. Of course, when a policy stand was explicitly attacked, it was coded as a negative evaluation of his or her policy position.

14. Transcripts of ABC's daily *World News* program were retrieved from Lexis-Nexis by searching for "Obama or Biden or McCain or Palin." All stories containing at least one evaluative assertion were included. No transcript of *World News* is available for Saturday, September 6, 2008, presumably because the program was not broadcast due to a sports event. Transcripts of *This Week* were coded for the Sunday preceding the Democratic convention and the following Sunday, which preceded the Republican conclave.

15. In the 21st century, where boundaries between entertainment and news are blurring and younger citizens pay less attention to traditional news than their parents (see Entman, 2005; Delli Carpini & Williams, 2001), the importance of skilled framing by communicators to maximize resonance with dominant culture might actually be intensified. Although the common assumption is that the information cornucopia of the Internet, mobile telecommunications connectivity, and the rest empower citizens, these could as easily distract citizens, making it even more difficult to get through with a counterframe requiring more complicated thought processes.

16. As shown by the "SuperTracker" analysis of Fivethirtyeight.com whose data also showed McCain with a 40 electoral vote margin as of mid-September. Retrieved from http://www.fivethirtyeight.com/2008/09/538s-battlegrounds-as-of-mid-september.html. Rassmusen Reports showed five battleground states moving in McCain's direction after the GOP convention and none moving in Obama's. Retrieved from http://www.rasmussenreports.com/public_content/ politics/election_20082/2008_presidential_election/election_2008_electoral_college_update).

17. Kornblut, A. E. (2008, September 10). Palin energizing women from all walks of life. *Washington Post*, p. A4. Also see a Gallup Poll showing an increase from 40 to 52% support for McCain among independents after the convention and an even bigger leap, a doubling from 20 to 39% support

among what Gallup calls "pure" independents who lean toward neither party (with 40% of them undecided at the time of the poll). Retrieved from http://www.gallup.com/poll/110137/McCain-Now-Winning-Majority-Independents.aspx

Such sizable changes are beyond the large margin of error in data on small subgroups.

18. In fact, Palin's ratings and McCain's standing in the polls deteriorated markedly in the second half of September. The economic crisis with its massive failures in the financial sector and major declines in the stock market no doubt contributed heavily, but it is also possible that the news shifted to more negative framing of McCain and Palin, more positive framing of Obama and Biden, or both. ABC/Washington Post polls taken September 4 and September 27–29 showed an increase in the percentage of respondents saying the choice of Palin made them less likely to vote for McCain from 19 to 32% and a sharp drop in her support among the all-important independents (Cohen & Agiesta, 2008).

## References

Aday, S. (2006). *Be careful what you wish for: An analysis of 2005 Iraq War coverage on NBC and Fox News Channel.* Paper presented at the Annual Conference of the International Studies Association, Dresden, Germany.

Bartels, L. (2008). *Unequal democracy: The political economy of the new gilded age.* Princeton, NJ: Princeton University Press.

Bennett, W. L. (1990). Toward a theory of press-state relations in the United States. *Journal of Communication, 40*(2), 103–125.

Bennett, W. L. (2008). *News: The politics of illusion* (8th ed.). New York: Longman.

Budd, M., Craig, S., & Steinman, C. (1999). *Consuming environments: Television and commercial culture.* New Brunswick, NJ: Rutgers University Press.

Carragee, K. M., & Roefs, W. (2004). The neglect of power in recent framing research. *Journal of Communication, 54*(2), 214–233.

Chong, D., & Druckman, J. (2007a). Framing theory. *Annual Review of Political Science, 10*(1), 103–126.

Chong, D., & Druckman, J. (2007b) . A theory of framing and opinion formation in competitive elite environments. *Journal of Communication, 57*(1), 99–118.

Cohen, B. (1963). *The press and foreign policy.* Princeton, NJ: Princeton University Press.

Cohen, J., & Agiesta, J. (2008, October 2). Skepticism of Palin growing, poll finds. *Washington Post*, A-01.

Cook, T. E. (2005). *Governing with the news* (2nd ed.). Chicago: University of Chicago Press.

Dahl, R. A. (1989). *Democracy and its critics.* New Haven, CT: Yale University Press.

D'Alessio, D., & Allen, M. (2000). Media bias in presidential elections: A meta-analysis. *Journal of Communication, 50*(4), 133–156.

Delli Carpini, M., & Williams, B. (2001). Let us infotain you. In W. L. Bennett & R. M. Entman (Eds.), *Mediated politics: Communication in the future of democracy* (pp. 160–181). New York: Cambridge University Press.

Druckman, J. N., & Parkin, M. (2005). The impact of media bias: How editorial slant affects voters. *Journal of Politics, 67*(4), 1030–1049.

Edelman, M. (1988). *Constructing the political spectacle.* Chicago: University of Chicago Press.

Entman, R. M. (1989). *Democracy without citizens: Media and the decay of American politics.* New York: Oxford University Press.

Entman, R. M. (1993). Framing: Toward clarification of a fractured paradigm. *Journal of Communication, 43*(4), 51–58.

Entman, R. M. (1996). Reporting environmental policy debate: The real media biases. *Harvard International Journal of Press/Politics, 1,* 77–92.

Entman, R. M. (2004). *Projections of power: Framing news, public opinion, and U.S. foreign policy.* Chicago: University of Chicago Press.

Entman, R. M. (2005). Media and democracy without party competition. In J. S. Curran & M. Gurevitch (Eds.), *Mass communication and society* (4th ed., pp. 251–270). London: Arnold.

Entman, R. (2007). Framing bias: Media in the distribution of power. *Journal of Communication, 57*(1), 163–173.

Entman, R. M., & Gross, K. (in press). Race to judgment: Stereotyping media and crime in the Duke lacrosse case. *Law and Contemporary Problems.*

Entman, R. M., Livingston, S., & Kim, J. (2009). Doomed to repeat: Media and the Iraq War, 2003–2007. *American Behavioral Scientist, 52,* 689–708.

Entman, R. M., Matthes, J., & Pellicano, L. (2008). The nature, sources and effects of framing. In K. Wahl-Jorgensen & T. Hanitzch (Eds.), *Handbook of journalism studies* (pp. 175–190). New York: Routledge.

Entman, R. M., & Page, B. (1994). The news before the storm: The Iraq War debate and the limits to media independence. In W. L. Bennett & D. Paletz (Eds.), *Taken by storm: The media, public opinion, and U.S. foreign policy in the Gulf War* (pp. 82–103). Chicago: University of Chicago Press.

Entman, R. M., & Rojecki, A. (2000). *The black image in the white mind: Media and race in America.* Chicago: University of Chicago Press.

Eveland, W., & Shah, D. (2003). The impact of individual and interpersonal factors in perceived news media bias. *Political Psychology, 24*(1), 101–117.

Gilens, M., & Hertzman, C. (2000). Corporate ownership and news bias: Newspaper coverage of the 1996 Telecommunications Act. *Journal of Politics, 62*(2), 369–386.

Graber, D. A. (2001). *Processing politics: Learning from television in the internet age.* Chicago: University of Chicago Press.

Graber, D. A. (2005). *Mass media and American politics* (7th ed.). Washington: CQ Press.

Gross, K., & D'Ambrosio, L. (2004). Framing emotional response. *Political Psychology, 25*(1), 1–29.

Hacker, J. S., & Pierson, P. (2005). *Off center: The Republican revolution and the erosion of American democracy.* New Haven, CT: Yale University Press.

Hart, R. (1998). *Seducing America: How television charms the voter* (rev. ed). Newbury Park, CA: Sage.

Iyengar, S., & Simon, A. (1993). News coverage of the Gulf Crisis and public opinion: A study of agenda-setting, priming, and framing. *Communication Research, 20*(3), 365–383.

Jamieson, K., & Birdsell, D. (1990). *Presidential debates.* New York: Oxford University Press.

Jamieson, K., & Waldman, P. (2002). *The press effect: Politicians, journalists, and the stories that shape the political world.* New York: Oxford University Press.

Kahn, K. F., & Kenney, P. J. (2002). The slant of the news: How editorial endorsements influence campaign coverage and citizens' views of candidates. *American Political Science Review, 96*(2), 381–394.

Kang, J. (2005). Trojan horses of race. *Harvard Law Review, 118*(5), 1489–1593.

Kim, S. H., Scheufele, D.A., & Shanahan, J. (2002). Think about it this way: Attribute agenda-setting function of the press and the public's evaluation of a local issue. *Journalism & Mass Communication Quarterly, 79*(1), 7–25.

Kuklinski, J., & Sigelman, L. (1992). When objectivity is not objective. *Journal of Politics, 54*, 810–833.

Kuypers, J. (2002). *Press bias and politics: How the media frame controversial issues.* New York: Praeger.

Lakoff, G. (2002). *Moral politics: How liberals and conservatives think* (2nd ed.). Chicago: University of Chicago Press.

Lasswell, H. D. (1966). *Politics: Who gets what, when and how.* New York: World.

Manheim, J. B. (2005). *Biz-war and the out-of-power elite: The progressive-left attack on the corporation.* Mahwah, NJ: Erlbaum.

Martin, C. R. (2004). *Framed! Labor and the corporate media.* Ithaca, NY: ILR Press/Cornell University Press.

Martin, J., & Vandehei, J. (2008). McCain, Palin push biography, not issues. *Politico* (2008, September 9). Retrieved September 9, 2008, from http://www.politico.com/news/ stories/0908/13275.html

McCombs, M., & Ghanem, S. I. (2001). The convergence of agenda setting and framing. In S. D. Reese, O. H. Gandy, & A. E. Grant (Eds.), *Framing public life: Perspectives on media and our understanding of the social world* (pp. 67–82). Mahwah, NJ: Erlbaum. Associates.

Nagel, J. (1975). *The descriptive analysis of power.* New Haven, CT: Yale University Press.

Niven, D. (2002). *Tilt? The search for media bias.* New York: Praeger.

Patterson, T. (1993). *Out of order.* New York: Knopf.

Patterson, T. E., & Donsbach, W. (1996). News decisions: Journalists as partisan actors. *Political Communication, 13*(4), 455–468.

Price, V., Tewksbury, D., & Powers, E. (1997). Switching trains of thought: The impact of news frames on readers' cognitive responses. *Communication Research, 24*(5), 481–506.

Riker, W. (1986). *The art of political manipulation.* New Haven, CT: Yale University Press.

Rojecki, A. (1999). *Silencing the opposition: Anti-nuclear movements and the media in the Cold War.* Urbana: University of Illinois Press.

Schattschneider, E. E. (1960). *The semi-sovereign people: A realist's view of democracy in America.* Englewood Cliffs, NJ: Prentice-Hall.

Sears, D. O. (1997). The impact of self-interest on attitudes. *Journal of Personality & Social Psychology, 72*(3), 492–496.

Wasburn, P. C., & Covert, T. J. (2008). *Media bias? A comparative study of* Time, Newsweek, *the* National Review, *and the* Progressive. Lanham, MD: Lexington Books.

Watts, M., Domke, D., Shah, D., & Fan, D. (1999). The politics of conservative elites and the liberal media argument. *Journal of Communication, 49,* 35–58.

Westen, D. (2007). *The political brain: The role of emotion in deciding the fate of the nation.* New York: Public Affairs Books.

Chapter 15

# Conclusion

## Arriving At the Horizons of News Framing Analysis

*Paul D'Angelo*

In the epilogue to *Framing Public Life*, Oscar Gandy (2001) opened with a metaphor about the horizon. "Funny thing about the horizon," he wrote. "It never gets any closer. Indeed, as we are often reminded, if we walk toward the horizon long enough, we eventually arrive back at the point from which we began our journey" (p. 355). The horizon is an interesting frame of reference for a volume on framing. As commonly defined, it is the apparent intersection of the earth and sky as seen by an observer. Most relevant, perhaps, to seafaring travel, the horizon always looms far off in the distance no matter how long or far one has traveled. But the funny thing about the horizon is that one traveler can be viewed as being on it from the perspective of another traveler. What's more, the horizon becomes less mesmerizing when the traveler spots land, particularly when the land is the traveler's destination coming ever closer. In both cases, dedicated yet unfulfilled pursuit of a goal that is visible on the horizon can be reframed as an arrival at a new horizon, whether this arrival concerns the sea (the other ship that's on the horizon) or land (we've reached the destination that was once on the horizon).

The idea of an arrival is what led Jim Kuypers and me to undertake this volume on framing. Notwithstanding the obvious interest in framing in our journals and at our conferences, there are numerous indications that framing research has indeed arrived. One of them takes into consideration the orienting role of the seminal volume *Framing Public Life* (Reese, Gandy, & Grant, 2001). Many scholars understandably feel that this volume signaled the arrival of framing research. As its chapters have taught us, communicators are bound to frame topics—bound by strategic considerations that make participating in public life an exercise in framing "both for one's own sensemaking and for contesting the frames of others" (Pan & Kosicki, 2001, p. 39); bound to a process of social influence that entails articulating propositions and catchphrases embedded within culturally resonant themes (Hertog & McLeod, 2001; Reese, 2001); and bound to heeding the time- and context-sensitive nature of frames, and thus, paradoxically, to tracking and advantageously harnessing the shifting meanings of these themes (Miller & Riechert, 2001). Public life is scarcely possible without frames and framing (Callaghan & Schnell, 2005). So, whether you conceive of *Framing Public Life* as the arrival of framing research and this volume a continuing exploration of its important themes, or consider this volume to be on a new horizon, espied by that one's telescopic view, it seems fitting to say that framing research is now grounded by firm theoretical understandings and stable trends of empirical findings.

Put another way, framing research has arrived because the range of experience, knowledge, and interest about this concept—the horizons, so to speak—have grown dramatically since *Framing Public Life* appeared, and certainly since the 1970s, when landmark studies on framing were published. Of course there are many matters that have yet to be resolved. Clarifying how agenda-setting relates to framing seems to be one of these matters (see Maher, 2001). But even on that issue we are surely at the horizon. As Renita Coleman's chapter in this volume attests, it is possible, and necessary, for scholars to continue to debate how, and how well, attribute agenda-setting integrates the theory with framing (e.g., Ghanem, 1997; McCombs, 1992; McCombs & Ghanem, 2001, p. 69) and still open up and explore new horizons of framing research.

Beyond its connection to an important volume in the literature, this volume signals in another way that framing research has reached new horizons. Namely, it acknowledges that a preponderant number of framing studies has settled within four interrelated sites: the minds of journalists, the conventions of newsrooms, the texts of news stories, and the political and cultural contexts in which news stories are made. Even though many studies in the vast framing literature have examined other types of mediated communication, such as political advertising (e.g., Schenck-Hamlin, Procter, & Rumsey, 2000; Shen, 2004), sports broadcasting (e.g., Billings & Eastman, 2003), and prime-time television programs (Holbert et al., 2005), it seems clear that the signature theoretical and empirical horizons of framing analysis have been opened because researchers in the myriad subfields of mass communication and political communication are fascinated with an institution that professes to reflect reality in stories when in practice it does much more than that. To paraphrase the eloquent argument of John Durham Peters (1989), if you could lay the entire framing project down on a psychoanalytic couch, you would find that it is concerned not merely with examining media content and its effects, but with understanding the perils and possibilities of the news media's role as a political actor in the deliberative settings of policy making, political and social activism, and campaigns. True, the term *media framing* is commonly found in the literature. In fact, a few of the chapters in this volume appear to prefer it over *news framing* (e.g., chapter 5 by Bertram and Dietram Scheufele). Yet, framing analysis affords boundless opportunities to understand how instances of an evolving narrative form—"hard" and "soft" stories that "break" or "continue" in formats ranging from packages, side-bars, analyses, editorials, and panel discussions—construct meanings of seemingly isolated incidents and events. These meanings percolate into the definitions and evaluations of the issues and problems of public life, and into proposed solutions to them as well (Entman, 1993).

News framing analysis has thus arrived at a conceptual horizon—news constructs the realities through which public life unfolds—long espied by academic observers of news. "Reality is not given," contended James W. Carey (1988); it is "brought into existence, is produced, by communication..." (p. 25). News is rooted in this epistemic framework. Reporting an event is "inevitably part of a double reality," stated Manoff and Schudon (1986), "both separate from the world it tells stories about and a constituent of that world, an element of the story" (p. 4). So, journalists not only convey what sources have to say about an event—words that, themselves, coax realities into existence—but, as Michael Schudson (1995) holds, they also "add something to every story they run" (p. 19). What journalists add can be determined by observing the difference between what sources wish to directly convey to audience members or known constituents and what news stories *do to* those messages. Some say that journalists *do too much* to sources' issue frames, claiming, for example, that news distorts messages and meanings that are best left intact (e.g., Patterson, 1993). Others point out that journalists *aren't doing enough* to sources' issue frames, asserting, for example, that journalists shirk their responsibility to be skeptical of, or to unpack and expose, the premises and propositions upon which issue frames are built (e.g., Bennett, Lawrence, & Livingston, 2006). In both cases, however, the difference can be boiled down to the notion that a journalist "has the professional obligation to frame the message" (Schudson, 1995, p. 20).

Journalists frame sources' preferred meanings of a public event—a war, a crime, an air disaster—in each stage of its development within a deliberative process. This makes news framing routine and ubiquitous, evident, for instance, in a story about Congressional debate during the build-up to a war; in a story about a mayoral press conference calling for an investigation of a city's parole process following the murder of a police officer; and in a story about federal-level hearings about regulating air traffic safety after a plane crash. Beyond this, journalists frame public life, as Stephen Reese (this volume and elsewhere; see Reese, 2001, 2007) maintains, from an institutional base, one whose routines and values end up adding a veneer of order and interpretation to the "facts"—facts being what sources say during, and about, events that grow into public issues. A strict culturalist thesis recognizes that reality is inherently formless—"the world is entropic," stated Carey (1988, p,

26)—and that reporters impose an artificial organization upon reality. Though debated by scholars, variations of the culturalist thesis give us pause to consider how important news framing is, and how important it is to study news framing.

To most news framing scholars, Gaye Tuchman's *Making News* (1978) is the prototype framing study of the hidden aspects of newswork that create realities through which public life unfolds (see also, Tuchman, 1976). As such, news framing analysis today stands at the horizon upon which she once gazed. Tuchman did field work in the print and television newsrooms of "Seaboard City" (among other sites). Adapting Goffman's (1974) notion of frame, she conceived of a "frame of facticity" (pp. 100–103) that heuristically guided journalists to search for authoritative accounts from within officialdom. Tuchman took a culturalist approach to news framing analysis—that news constructs reality—in order to achieve a critical purpose. The legacy of her work is that news framing is both an interpretive and ideological process, for in the process of framing events, news organizations underwrite status quo positions on important public issues.

News framing analysts are also on the horizon gazed upon by Tuchman because she gently repudiated the Goffmanian concept of "frame." To Tuchman (1978), neither Goffman's sociological conception of framing nor his rigorous yet idiosyncratic method of seeing speech acts as deeply embedded in social events, went far enough in helping observers to understand how and why journalists frame events. "[Goffman] is interested in the moods and gestures that 'key' a phenomenon from one frame to another, not in the institutional mechanisms that accomplish transformation," Tuchman asserted (1978, p. 195).

Regina Lawrence (this volume) provides a fitting testament to where Tuchman's ideas have led us. Her chapter opens as follows: "A key question in much of the literature on media framing of politics and public affairs is, How independently do the media frame issues and events, versus simply passing along to the public the frames originated by powerful political actors?" Hardly academic, this question cuts to the core of current controversies within news framing analysis that run among the chapters of this volume, particularly those that look at the institutional and cultural contexts of frame building (cf. Scheufele, 1999). In earlier times journalists were seen as unreflectively adhering to the frame of facticity, demonstrating, as a result, little autonomy when adding layers of meaning to—that is, framing—sources' preferred meanings of events. At today's horizon stand Marie Hardin and Erin Whiteside, whose chapter redounds to Tuchman's thesis by warning journalists of the perils of unreflectively infusing gender stereotypes into news coverage of events. Paternalistic gender framing in news stories about sports, politics, and other realms of public life, they argue, adversely shapes policy decisions and reinforces commonsense assumptions that privilege men in the social hierarchy. In certain respects, Stephen Reese follows this line of thinking too, only he seems to give journalists more leeway to cruise the cultural firmament for frames that nonetheless end up serving the aims of political elites.

Although it may seem as though the framing research of Hardin and Whiteside, and that of Reese, is in the same boat as Tuchman, their position on her horizon is evidenced by ways that they observe in texts the frames, and framing strategies, of both sources and journalists. Tuchman's qualitative framing analysis of the women's movement (1978, chap. 7) is, of course, evocative and brilliant. But today news framing scholars have at their disposal more sophisticated techniques of textual analysis. Perhaps a better way to say this is that news framing scholars have moved to a point where melding the strengths of quantitative and qualitative textual analysis is seen as the best way to get "at" the complex, latent structures of meaning communicated by news frames. Van Gorp's chapter (this volume) presents a state-of-the art approach that integrates inductive and deductive approaches to content analyzing news stories for frames. He presents a set of procedures designed to be systematic enough to ensure that observed frames are both valid and not so latent as to be undetectable by someone else. This approach usefully guides news framing researchers to conduct propositional-level analysis of framing devices using a larger sample of stories, not one or only a few. Pan and Kosicki (1993) proposed such an approach for framing analysis; so did van Dijk (1983), only he called it "discourse analysis." Both remarked upon the difficulty of doing this sort of news analysis with more than a few news stories.

The chapter by Jim Kuypers (this volume) urges news framing researchers to enlarge this method of framing analysis by taking into consideration newsroom norms and dynamics. This, of course, is good advice, considering the premise that the news media play an active, participatory role in constructing social reality when they frame events in news.

Being at this methodological horizon means that others have already scouted these positions. Indeed, like Van Gorp's approach, Tankard's (2001) "empirical approach to media framing" was meant to "take the subjectivity out of the identification of frames" (p. 104). Owing to the "diffuse nature of frames and their openness to varied interpretation," Hertog and McLeod (2001, p. 153) also recommended a mixture of quantitative and qualitative approaches. Indeed, in the long and rich history of content analysis in mass communication can be read many attempts to reconcile quantitative and qualitative approaches (e.g., Holsti, 1969, pp. 5–12; Krippendorff, 2004, pp. 15–17, 87–90). So, while the rhetorical approach of Kuypers unabashedly wishes to keep subjectivity in news framing analysis, it also recognizes the value of quantitative–qualitative integration, favoring qualitative in order to bring the full force of rhetorical criticism to bear upon (textual) strategies the news media use to exert political power over other social actors. In some respects his approach dovetails with that of Robert Entman (this volume; see also, Entman, 2007), who reorganizes framing research around the hoary concept of bias. Both see the main action in news framing analysis to occur in textual configurations in which the news media act to distribute political power to groups, political parties, and even individuals. Whereas Entman's model may allow for more diffusion of power among constituent actors, both he and Kuypers acknowledge that finding, seeing, and substantiating deep textual structures require sophisticated tools and complex operating manuals.

The question of press autonomy—the one Regina Lawrence begins her chapter with—is a focal point at the horizon of news framing research. Asking this question requires framing analysts to square up to an entrenched conceit of the Westernized journalistic enterprise: the credo of objectivity which holds that story and storyteller stand outside of the flow of events. Asking the autonomy question also leads framing analysts to speculate that journalists are political actors who know *that* they construct reality and who know *how to* construct reality. In this analytical space, "hard" news becomes an act of "strong explanation," which, according to Latour (1988) entails "acting at a distance"—telling stories both to explain something *and* to act on what one is explaining (p. 159). Matthew Nisbet's chapter (this volume) shows that doing news framing analysis within a framework of strong explanation requires the analyst to be sensitive to the mutual responsiveness between journalists and their sources. For Nisbet, doing framing analysis requires playing the roles of "translator" and "go-between." Aiming to educate journalists and issue advocates, and ultimately to play a part in helping build better science-related social policy (e.g., on climate change), he plays these roles in part by relating to each actor the results of empirical analyses of how each one frames science-related topics. In this brew of influence and interaction journalists come to recognize that they are social actors in whose stories unfold the conditions within which public issues are defined, evaluated, and resolved.

If doing framing analysis allows researchers to speculate that journalists know that they construct reality and how to construct reality, then it seems reasonable to think that an awareness of the processes and complexity of framing is woven into journalists' ideas about making news. Theorizing such ideas, which is in large part the goal of the chapter by Bertram and Dietram Scheufele (this volume), who call them journalists' cognitive schemas, tells us that journalists regularly refresh their notions of how to cover events, with which sources, and with what frames. In addition, if journalists are generally aware of their role as framers of events, then it seems reasonable to speculate that they at times find irresistible the urge to write into stories their own involvement in framing public life. Such a scenario is evident in the chapter by Stephen Cooper (this volume). His work illustrates how bloggers "talk back to power" by inveighing against the order and meaning reporters impart to events via framing. It seems logical to think that mainstream journalists hear these criticisms, as blogs are often the topic of news and blogs are said to influence how mainstream journalists cover events. Gamson and Modigliani (1989) espied this position a while ago, stating, "Many journalists straddle the boundary between producers and consumers of meaning" (p. 9).

So, to an important extent, the horizon at which news framing researchers stand today is surveyed by how we address the autonomy question. As noted, asking and answering this question puts us on some rugged terrain. It is traversed, on one hand, by how accurately we measure the degree to which journalists question and deviate in stories from the framing of elites (e.g., Bennett, Lawrence, & Livingston, 2006). On the other hand, it is traversed when framing analysts engage with a peculiar journalistic mindset, namely, if journalists shape reality, and if they know that they do so, then they can reflect on this state of affairs. And the ways journalists reflect upon their autonomy give shape to richly textured news frames. Even this point was espied by Making News, wherein Tuchman contended that news is a "reflexive enterprise" (1978, pp. 188–200). News is reflexive because stories are "embedded in the very reality that they characterize, record, or structure" (p. 189). As I see it, Tuchman felt that the reflexivity of news could engender stories that broke from the ideological commitments dictated by adherence to the frame of facticity. "Despite the reflexive production of news," she stated, "stories are frequently presented indexically—divorced from the context of their production" (1978, p. 192). However, according to a rather large body of research, journalists are uneasy about covering facets of news that bespeak journalism's involvement in creating reality. Such stories are deemed to be defensive and unedifying attempts to "repair the paradigm" of news's objectivity credo (e.g., Bennett, Gressett, & Haltom, 1985; Hindman, 2005; Levy, 1981).

Still, at the horizon of news framing research, answering the autonomy question gives us an opportunity to see framing studies in a new light. For example, we can see the whole of "strategy" framing research in light of the analytical framework of news as a reflexive enterprise. This body of research is based on the notion that the initiative political campaign journalists take in shaping the meanings of campaign events is a kind of renegade meditation upon their own roles in shaping meanings. The ideas journalists have of their involvement—their cognitive schemata in Scheufele and Scheufele's terms (this volume)—develop, among other ways, from an interaction with sources who wish to communicate certain messages to audiences through the pipeline of the news media. The realization that they are involved in shaping meanings is simply too hard for journalists to resist writing into the narrative of campaign stories. This analytical framework is evident in content analyses of strategy framing (e.g., Cappella & Jamieson, 1997; Esser & D'Angelo, 2003; Lawrence, 2000; Patterson, 1993) and in work that discusses the nature of journalism (e.g., Schudson, 1995, chap. 1). It is also evident in studies that examine effects of exposure to strategy framed news (e.g., Cappella & Jamieson, 1997; de Vreese & Elenbass, 2008; Valentino, Beckmann, & Buhr, 2001). Although no chapters in this volume specifically focus on strategy framing, researchers who herein write about doing framing *effects* analysis strike me as being keenly aware of the conceptual horizon on which we stand—that news constructs the realities through which public life unfolds. And while the focus of news framing effects research is to understand how and for whom news frames matter, it provides valuable insights into the role of news as a social actor. It is interested in what happens *once* stories have set the conditions in which realities such as social policy are defined, evaluated, and resolved. As such, framing effects research is indispensable to building normative models of what "good" news is.

The chapters by Claes de Vreese and by Dhavan Shah and colleagues explain news framing effects research and then illustrate it with an experiment. Thirty years ago, Walter Gans (1979) characterized the relationship between sources, journalists, and audiences as being a "tug of war" rather than a "functionally interrelated organism" (p. 81). These two chapters dig into the thoughts of readers and viewers of news frames, theorizing that in the ecology of news framing, individuals' thoughts (the organism) are under certain conditions quite susceptible to changes in textual frames (the environment). Both create ecologically valid stimuli—de Vreese with an economic consequences frame and Shah and colleagues with variations of individual/societal and gain/loss frames—by drawing from content analyses of these frames, in some cases their own (e.g., de Vreese, Peter, & Semetko, 2001). Both are aware of the limitations of their data and their findings. Along these lines, framing effects research generally benefits from a healthy internal dialogue. Witness the chapter (this volume) by Paul Brewer and Kimberly Gross. It takes stock of effects research, arguing that the decisions that researchers make regarding how to study the effects of frames on public opinion about policy issues may shape their conclusions about the nature and extent of such effects.

It is tempting to see as a shortcoming that the effects chapters in this volume indirectly address the autonomy question. These chapters do not fully theorize or examine the extent to which journalistic transformations of the "facts" move out of the orbit of their sources' preferred meanings; they do not fully see the tug of war between journalists and sources as a process of reality-construction. In general, news framing effects research appears to be ambivalent about the autonomy question.

Some experiments parse source elements linguistically, manipulating, for example, journalistic paraphrase, a source quote, or both—see de Vreese and Elenbass (2008) for a manipulation of "mostly journalistic material" (p. 293); see Valentino, Beckmann, and Buhr (2001) for a manipulation of expert commentary rather than journalistic material (pp. 354–355). Both Reese and Entman (this volume) reprove experimental research for being out of touch with the institutional and cultural processes that give rise to definitions and evaluations of, and remedies for, issues in public life. Entman (this volume) even remarked on the strikingly apolitical aspect of framing research (which I take to mean framing *effects* research), evidently agreeing with Carragee and Roefs (2004), who chastise the effects tradition for neglecting to connect news frames to broader issues of social and political power.

Yet, in certain respects, the chapters of de Vreese, Shah and colleagues, and Brewer and Gross illustrate that it is difficult to avoid theorizing power in the course of doing framing effects research. At the individual level, stated Pan and Kosicki (2005), "Framing means adopting...an interpretive framework for thinking about a political object," adding, "Framing is in part driven by the need for cognitive structuring concerning that object in some real participatory process" (p. 177). But, Pan and Kosicki argue, coming to a judgment is not a one-way street. News stories that invoke premises and considerations do not monotonically dictate which judgments individuals will make in a deliberative situation (see also, Neuman, Just, & Crigler, 1992). There is more than enough ambivalence (a necessary condition for framing effects, according to Pan and Kosicki, 2005) to go around. In a 24/7 news cycle and even in news of events and issues gathered via the routines of news beats, news stories regularly relate incompleteness and speculation, indecision and ambiguity. To paraphrase Pan and Kosicki (2005), real-world ambiguities about an event set the stage for ambivalence that journalists necessarily (and, it would seem, frequently) encode into stories. As Scheufele and Scheufele (this volume) imply, journalists come to judgment in much the same way as do audiences for a news story. For all parties concerned, coming to judgment is an act of exercising power.

In the epilogue to *Framing Public Life*, Oscar Gandy wrote, "In this chapter I call to your attention the ways in which our authors come closer to, but still stop short of, our desired goal, that of establishing the place of framing research at the core of communications study" (2001, p. 356). In the short span of time between that important volume and this volume, has framing research reached the core of communications study?

Of course, this question is open to debate, and answering it depends on what we mean by communications study. Defining our discipline has occupied communication scholars since its inception—and even the narrative of the field's inception is open to interpretation (e.g., Bineham, 1988; Chaffee & Hochheimer, 1985). As John Durham Peters (1986) argued, despite outpourings of self-scrutiny, efforts to define the core of communications study (and even there, with the –s, Gandy implies that the core lies in mass communication or political communication) have suffered setbacks owing to the way the field was institutionalized and set apart from the social sciences. As Peters put it, "Debates about communication...have a more specific etiology that has to do, in large part, with the paradoxical attempt to create a particular institutional entity (an academic field) out of a universalistic intellectual entity (communication)" (p. 528). Robert Craig (1999) compellingly shifted the argument about whether or not there exists a field of communication to one which held that we should look at the practical nature of communication from different perspectives. He proposed a "constitutive metamodel" (meta- because we need to communicate to study the practice of communication) consisting of seven intersecting intellectual traditions: rhetorical, semiotic, phenomenological, cybernetic, sociopsychological, sociocultural, and critical. "Disciplinarity," he argued, "does not require that diversity and interdisciplinarity be suppressed" (p. 124).

Individually and collectively, the chapters in this volume show that the field has advanced in no small part because of news framing research. Framing is a powerfully integrative concept that encourages disciplinarity. Doing news framing analysis therefore requires due diligence on the analyst's part in understanding the intellectual traditions that feed communication theory. What news framing is and how news framing works cannot be ascertained otherwise. This is how I understand Reese's point that framing is a "bridging model for media research" (see Reese, 2001; this volume), and this is what I meant in asserting that framing is a multiparadigmatic research program (D'Angelo, 2002).

In *The Sociology of News*, Michael Schudson (2003) remarked that, "Framing is as central a concept there is in the study of news" (p. 35). Opening new horizons of news framing analysis vividly shows us that framing is as central a concept there is to the study of communication. I have no doubt that in doing news framing analysis, researchers will to continue to develop better tools that aid in detecting frames in stories; that furbish the generative roles of individuals' cognitions in the news framing process; and that illuminate shrouded newsroom conventions that shape story and reality alike.

## References

Bennett, W. L., Gressett, L. A., & Haltom, W. (1985). Repairing the news: A case study of the news paradigm. *Journal of Communication, 35*(3), 50–68.

Bennett. W. L., Lawrence, R. G., & Livingston, S. (2006). None dare call it torture: Indexing and the limits of press independence in the Abu Ghraib scandal. *Journal of Communication, 56*, 467–485.

Billings, A. C., & Eastman, S. T. (2003). Framing identities: Gender, ethnic, and national parity in network announcing of the 2002 Winter Olympics. *Journal of Communication, 53*(4), 569–586.

Bineham. J. L. (1988). A historical account of the hypodermic needle model in mass communication. *Communication Monographs, 55*, 231–246.

Callaghan., K., & Schnell, F. (Eds.). (2005). *Framing American politics*. Pittsburgh, PA: University of Pittsburgh Press.

Cappella, J. N., & Jamieson, K. H. (1997). *The spiral of cynicism: The press and the public good*. New York: Oxford University Press.

Carey, J. W. (1988). *Communication as culture: Essays on media and society*. New York: Routledge.

Carragee, K. M., & Roefs, W. (2004). The neglect of power in recent framing research. *Journal of Communication, 54*(2), 214–233

Chaffee, S. H., & Hochheimer, J. L. (1985). The beginnings of political communication research in the United States: Origins of the "limited effects" model. In E. M. Rogers & F. Balle (Eds.), *The media revolution in America and Western Europe* (pp. 267–296). Norwood, NJ: Ablex.

Craig, R. T. (1999). Communication theory as a field. *Communication Theory, 9*(2), 119–161.

D'Angelo, P. (2002). News framing as a multi-paradigmatic research program: A response to Entman. *Journal of Communication, 52*(4), 870–888.

de Vreese, C. H., & Elenbaas, E. (2008). Media in the game of politics: Effects of strategic metacoverage on political cynicism. *International Journal of Press/Politics, 13*(3), 285–309.

de Vreese, C. H., Peter, J., & Semetko, H. (2001). Framing politics at the launch of the Euro: A cross-national comparative study of frames in the news. *Political Communication, 18*, 107–122.

Entman, R. M. (1993). Framing: Toward clarification of a fractured paradigm. *Journal of Communication, 43*(4), 51–58.

Entman, R. M. (2007). Framing bias: Media in the distribution of power. *Journal of Communication, 57*, 163–173.

Esser, F. E., & D'Angelo, P. (2003). Framing the press and the publicity process: A content analysis of meta-coverage in Campaign 2000 network news. *American Behavioral Scientist 46*, 617–641.

Gamson, W. A., & Modigliani, A. (1989). Media discourse and public opinion on nuclear power: A constructionist approach. *American Journal of Sociology, 95*(1), 1–37.

Gandy, O. H., Jr. (2001). Epilogue—Framing at the horizon: A retrospective assessment. In S. D. Reese, O. H. Gandy, Jr., & A. E. Grant (Eds.), *Framing public life: Perspectives on media and our understandings of the social world* (pp. 355–378). Mahwah, NJ: Erlbaum.

Gans, W. (1979). *Deciding what's news*. New York: Pantheon Books.

Ghanem, S. I. (1997). Filling in the tapestry: The second level of agenda setting. In M. McCombs, D. L. Shaw, & D. Weaver (Eds.), *Communication and democracy: Exploring the intellectual frontiers in agenda-setting theory* (pp. 3–14). Mahwah, NJ: Erlbaum.

Goffman, E. (1974). *Frame analysis: An essay in the organization of experience.* Boston: Northeastern University Press.

Hertog, J. K., & McLeod, D. M. (2001). A multiperspectival approach to framing analysis: A field guide. In S. D. Reese, O. H. Gandy, Jr., & A. E. Grant (Eds.), *Framing public life: Perspectives on media and our understandings of the social world* (pp. 139–161). Mahwah, NJ: Erlbaum.

Hindman, E. B. (2005). Jayson Blair, *The New York Times*, and paradigm repair. *Journal of Communication, 55,* 225–241.

Holbert, L. A.., Tschida, D. A., Dixon, M., Cherry, K., Steuber, K., & Airne, D. (2005). *The West Wing* and depictions of the American presidency: Expanding the domains of framing in political communication. *Communication Quarterly, 53*(4), 505–522.

Holsti, O. R. (1969). *Content analysis for the social sciences and humanities.* Reading, MA: Addison-Wesley

Krippendorff, K. (2004). *Content analysis: An introduction to its methodology* (2nd ed.). Thousand Oaks, CA: Sage.

Latour, B. (1988). The politics of explanation: An alternative. In S. Woolgar (Ed.), *Knowledge and reflexivity: New frontiers in the sociology of knowledge* (pp. 155–177). London: Sage.

Lawrence, R. G. (2000). Game-framing the issues: Tracking the strategy frame in public policy news. *Political Communication, 17,* 93–114.

Levy, M. (1981). Disdaining the news. *Journal of Communication, 31*(3), 24–31.

Maher, T. M. (2001). Framing: An emerging paradigm or a phase of agenda-setting? In S. D. Reese, O. H. Gandy, Jr., & A. E. Grant (Eds.), *Framing public life: Perspectives on media and our understandings of the social world* (pp. 83–94). Mahwah, NJ: Erlbaum.

Manoff. R. K., & Schudon, M. (1986). Reading the news. In R. K. Manoff & M. Schudson (Eds.), *Reading the news* (pp. 3–8). New York: Pantheon Books.

McCombs, M. E. (1992). Explorers and surveyors: Expanding strategies for agenda-setting research. *Journalism Quarterly, 69*(4), 813–824.

McCombs, M. E., & Ghanen, S. I. (2001). The convergence of agenda setting and framing. In S. D. Reese, O. H. Gandy, Jr., & A. E. Grant (Eds.), *Framing public life: Perspectives on media and ou runderstandings of the social world* (pp. 67–81). Mahwah, NJ: Erlbaum.

Miller, M. M., & Riechert, B. P. (2001). The spiral of opportunity and frame resonance: Mapping the issue cycle in news and public discourse. In S. D. Reese, O. H. Gandy, Jr., & A. E. Grant (Eds.), *Framing public life: Perspectives on media and our understandings of the social world* (pp. 107–121). Mahwah, NJ: Erlbaum.

Neuman, W. R., Just, M. R., & Crigler, A. N. (1992). *Common knowledge: News and the construction of political meaning.* Chicago: University of Chicago Press.

Pan, Z., & Kosicki, G. M. (1993). Framing analysis: An approach to news discourse. *Political Communication, 10*(1), 55–76.

Pan, Z., & Kosicki, G. M. (2001). Framing as strategic action in public deliberation. In S. D. Reese, O. H. Gandy, Jr., & A. E. Grant (Eds.), *Framing public life: Perspectives on media and our understandings of the social world* (pp. 35–65). Mahwah, NJ: Erlbaum.

Pan, Z., & Kosicki, G. M. (2005). Framing and the understanding of citizenship. In S. Dunwoody, L. B. Becker, D. M. McLeod, & G. M. Kosicki (Eds.), *The evolution of key mass communication concepts: Honoring Jack M. McLeod* (pp. 166–204). Cresskill, NJ: Hampton Press.

Patterson, T. E. (1993). *Out of order.* New York: Knopf.

Peters, J. D. (1986). Institutional sources of intellectual poverty in communication research. *Communication Research, 13*(4), 527–559.

Peters, J. D. (1989). Democracy and American mass communication theory: Dewey, Lippmann, Lazarsfeld. *Communication, 11*, 199–220.

Reese, S. D. (2001). Prologue—Framing public life: A bridging model for media research. In S. D. Reese, O. H. Gandy, Jr., & A. E. Grant (Eds.), *Framing public life: Perspectives on media and our understandings of the social world* (pp. 7–31). Mahwah, NJ: Erlbaum.

Reese, S. D. (2007). The framing project: A bridging model for media research revisited. *Journal of Communication, 57*, 148–154.

Reese, S. D., Gandy, O. H., Jr., & Grant, A. E. (Eds.) (2001). *Framing public life: Perspectives on media and our understandings of the social world.* Mahwah, NJ: Erlbaum.

Schenck-Hamlin, W. J., Procter, D. E., & Rumsey, D. J. (2000). The influence of negative advertising frames on political cynicism and political accountability. *Human Communication Research, 26*(1), 53–74.

Scheufele, D. A. (1999). Framing as a theory of media effects. *Journal of Communication, 49*(1), 103–122.

Schudson, M. (1995). *The power of news.* Cambridge, MA: Harvard University Press.

Schudson, M. (2003). *The sociology of news.* New York: Norton.

Shen, F. (2004). Chronic accessibility and individual cognitions: Examining the effects of message frames in political advertisements. *Journal of Communication, 54*(1), 125–137.

Tankard, J. W., Jr., (2001). The empirical approach to the study of media framing. In S. D. Reese, O. H. Gandy, Jr., & A. E. Grant (Eds.), *Framing public life: Perspectives on media and our understandings of the social world* (pp. 95-106). Mahwah, NJ: Erlbaum.

Tuchman, G. (1976). What is news? Telling stories. *Journal of Communication, 26*(4), 93–98.

Tuchman, G. (1978). *Making news: A study in the construction of reality.* New York: Free Press.

Valentino, N. A., Beckmann, M. N., & Buhr, T. A. (2001). A spiral of cynicism for some: The contingent effects of campaign news frames on participation and confidence in government. *Political Communication, 18*(4), 347–367.

van Dijk, T. A. (1983). Discourse analysis: Its development and application to the structure of news. *Journal of Communication, 33*(2), 20–43.

# Index